Selectivity in State Aid Law and the Methods for the Allocation of the Corporate Tax Base

EUCOTAX Series on European Taxation

VOLUME 60

Series Editors

Prof. Dr Peter H.J. Essers, Fiscal Institute Tilburg/Center for Company Law, Tilburg University

Prof. Dr Eric C.C.M. Kemmeren, Fiscal Institute Tilburg/Center for Company Law, Tilburg University

Prof. Dr Dr h.c. Michael Lang, WU (Vienna University of Economics and Business)

Introduction

EUCOTAX (European Universities Cooperating on Taxes) is a network of tax institutes currently consisting of eleven universities: WU (Vienna University of Economics and Business) in Austria, Katholieke Universiteit Leuven in Belgium, Corvinus University of Budapest, Hungary, Université Paris-I Panthéon-Sorbonne in France, Universität Osnabrück in Germany, Libera, Università Internazionale di Studi Sociali in Rome (and Università degli Studi di Bologna for the research part), in Italy, Fiscaal Instituut Tilburg at Tilburg University in the Netherlands, Universidad de Barcelona in Spain, Uppsala University in Sweden, Queen Mary and Westfield College at the University of London in the United Kingdom, and Georgetown University in Washington DC, United States of America. The network aims at initiating and coordinating both comparative education in taxation, through the organization of activities such as winter courses and guest lectures, and comparative research in the field, by means of joint research projects, international conferences and exchange of researchers between various countries.

Contents/Subjects

The EUCOTAX series covers a wide range of topics in European tax law. For example tax treaties, EC case law, tax planning, exchange of information and VAT. The series is well-known for its high-quality research and practical solutions.

Objective

The series aims to provide insights on new developments in European taxation.

Readership

Practitioners and academics dealing with European tax law.

Frequency of Publication

2-3 new volumes published each year.

The titles published in this series are listed at the end of this volume.

Selectivity in State Aid Law and the Methods for the Allocation of the Corporate Tax Base

Jérôme Monsenego

Published by:
Kluwer Law International B.V.
PO Box 316
2400 AH Alphen aan den Rijn
The Netherlands
E-mail: international-sales@wolterskluwer.com
Website: lrus.wolterskluwer.com

Sold and distributed in North, Central and South America by:
Wolters Kluwer Legal & Regulatory U.S.
7201 McKinney Circle
Frederick, MD 21704
United States of America
Email: customer.service@wolterskluwer.com

Sold and distributed in all other countries by:
Air Business Subscriptions
Rockwood House
Haywards Heath
West Sussex
RH16 3DH
United Kingdom
Email: international-customerservice@wolterskluwer.com

Printed on acid-free paper.

ISBN 978-90-411-9413-8

e-Book: ISBN 978-90-411-9414-5
web-PDF: ISBN 978-90-411-9415-2

© 2018 Jérôme Monsenego

All rights reserved. No part of this publication may be reproduced, stored in a retrieval system, or transmitted in any form or by any means, electronic, mechanical, photocopying, recording, or otherwise, without written permission from the publisher.

Permission to use this content must be obtained from the copyright owner. More information can be found at: lrus.wolterskluwer.com/policies/permissions-reprints-and-licensing

Printed in the United Kingdom.

MIX
FSC® C103993

About the Author

Jérôme Monsenego is an Associate Professor of International Tax Law at Stockholm University. He obtained his PhD *summa cum laude* in 2011, and was awarded an honourable mention by the jury of the IFA Mitchell B. Carroll Prize for his doctoral thesis (*Taxation of Foreign Business Income within the European Internal Market*, IBFD 2012). He has published articles in English, French, and Swedish on various issues of international tax law, and a book on transfer pricing (*Introduction to Transfer Pricing*, Kluwer Law International 2015). He has previously worked at PwC in Paris and in Stockholm.

Table of Contents

About the Author	v
Foreword	xiii
Preface	xvii
List of Abbreviations	xix

CHAPTER 1
Introduction 1
1.1 Background and Problem Statement 1
1.2 Purpose of the Study and Expected Contribution 8
1.3 Limitations 9
1.4 Previous Research 11
1.5 Method of Research 13
1.6 Outline 18

PART I
Elements of the Selectivity Test That Are Common to the Three Allocation Methods 21

CHAPTER 2
Determination of the Reference System 23
2.1 Introduction 23
2.2 The Relevance of Article 107(1) of the TFEU for the Determination of the Reference System 25
    2.2.1 Introductory Remarks and Peculiarities of the Allocation Methods 25
    2.2.2 Does the *Forum 187* Judgment Imply an Obligation to Apply the Arm's Length Principle as an Allocation Method? 30

Table of Contents

	2.2.3	Does Article 107(1) of the TFEU Imply a General Principle of Equal Treatment That Requires the Application of the Arm's Length Principle?	34
		2.2.3.1 Introductory Remarks	34
		2.2.3.2 The Arm's Length Principle and the Principle of Equal Treatment	36
		2.2.3.3 The Principle of Equal Treatment and Alternative Allocation Methods	41
		2.2.3.4 Concluding Remarks	43
2.3	The Determination of the Material Content of the Reference System		44
	2.3.1	Determination of the Scope of the Reference System	45
	2.3.2	Determination of the Sources of Law That Constitute the Reference System	52
2.4	Conclusion		55

CHAPTER 3
Potential Relevance of the Market Economy Operator Test 57
3.1 Introduction 57
3.2 May the Market Economy Operator Test Have a Binding Effect on the Selectivity Assessment of the Allocation Methods? 58
3.3 Interpretation of the Effects of the Market Forces under the Market Economy Operator Test 63
    3.3.1 Introduction 63
    3.3.2 Comparison Between the Market Economy Operator Test and the Arm's Length Principle 64
3.4 The Relevance of the Market Economy Operator Test for the Selectivity Assessment of the Allocation Methods 72
3.5 Conclusion 74

CHAPTER 4
Comparability Analysis 75
4.1 Introduction 75
4.2 Determination of the Objective of the Tax System 75
4.3 The Comparability Between Different Categories of Undertakings 82
    4.3.1 Introduction 82
    4.3.2 Assessment of the Relevance of the Notion of Comparability in Free Movement Law for State Aid Law Purposes 83
    4.3.3 Comparability from a Factual Perspective 85
    4.3.4 Comparability from a Legal Perspective 95
4.4 Conclusion 101

PART II
Selectivity Assessment of the Three Allocation Methods 103

CHAPTER 5
Prima Facie Selectivity of a Generally Formulated Arm's Length Provision — 111

5.1	Introduction		111
5.2	De Jure Selectivity		111
	5.2.1	The Limited Corrective Effect of the Arm's Length Principle	112
	5.2.2	The Assumed Correctness of the Benchmark Provided by the Average Effect of the Market Forces	114
5.3	De Facto Selectivity		116
	5.3.1	The Importance Given to the Parameters Chosen in the OECD Transfer Pricing Guidelines	117
	5.3.2	The Approximation of Results for Intercompany Transactions with No Direct Benchmark Provided by the Open Market	119
5.4	Prima Facie Selectivity That Stems from Certain Aspects of the Application of the Law		124
	5.4.1	The Choice of a Transfer Pricing Method	125
	5.4.2	The Relevance of Sources of Interpretation for the Assessment of Deviations from the Reference System	132
	5.4.3	The Assessment of Deviations from the Reference System in Relation to the Approximation of Values	136
5.5	Conclusion		144

CHAPTER 6
Prima Facie Selectivity of Transfer Pricing Safe Harbours — 147

6.1	Introduction		147
6.2	De Jure Selectivity		148
	6.2.1	Transfer Pricing Safe Harbours That Enforce the Arm's Length Principle	148
	6.2.2	Transfer Pricing Safe Harbours That Deviate from the Arm's Length Principle	150
6.3	De Facto Selectivity		154
6.4	Conclusion		155

CHAPTER 7
Prima Facie Selectivity of a System of Formula Apportionment with Firm-Specific Factors — 157

7.1	Introduction		157
7.2	De Jure Selectivity		159
7.3	De Facto Selectivity		161
	7.3.1	Introduction	161
	7.3.2	Is a System of Formula Apportionment with Firm-Specific Factors a General or a Selective Measure?	163
		7.3.2.1 The Sales Factor	165

Table of Contents

		7.3.2.2	The Assets Factor	167
		7.3.2.3	The Labour Factor	168
		7.3.2.4	Conclusion	169
	7.3.3	The Parameters of a System of Formula Apportionment That May Influence the De Facto Selectivity Test		170
		7.3.3.1	Number and Spread of the Apportionment Factors	170
		7.3.3.2	Connection of the Apportionment Factors to the Concept of Income	172
		7.3.3.3	Connection of the Apportionment Factors to the Market Forces	176
7.4	Conclusion			178

CHAPTER 8
The Justification and Proportionality Tests — 181
8.1 Introduction — 181
8.2 The Justification of an Allocation Method Limited to Members of Multinational Enterprises — 186
8.3 The Justification and Proportionality Tests Applied to the Selective Aspects of a Generally Formulated Arm's Length Provision — 189
  8.3.1 The Limited Corrective Effect of a Generally Formulated Arm's Length Provision — 189
  8.3.2 Prima Facie Selectivity for Situations That Lack a Direct Benchmark Provided by the Open Market — 192
8.4 The Justification and Proportionality Tests Applied to the Selective Features of Transfer Pricing Safe Harbours — 194
8.5 The Justification and Proportionality Tests Applied to the Selective Aspects of a System of Formula Apportionment with Firm-Specific Factors — 196
  8.5.1 De Jure Selectivity — 197
  8.5.2 De Facto Selectivity — 201
8.6 Conclusion — 203

CHAPTER 9
Conclusion — 205
9.1 Introduction — 205
9.2 Main Learnings from the Study — 205
9.3 Classification of the Allocation Methods from the Least to the Most Selective One — 208

Bibliography — 213

Table of Cases — 227

Table of Legislation — 233

European Commission	235
OECD Council Recommendations	239
Index	241

Foreword

This book is an ambitious attempt to provide a general analytical framework to the true meaning of the State aid rules in the EU in their application to tax rules that allocate the corporate tax base among multinational enterprises. The author does so on the basis of an overwhelming abundance of sources, in many different languages, thereby demonstrating that English is not the only language with creative ideas about taxation. The study confronts three types of allocation rules, the arm's length principle, transfer pricing safe harbours and formula apportionment systems with the core concept of any state aid rule, the concept of selectivity. Do not expect to find clear-cut answers that can be used in the pleadings of the recent spectacular state aid cases against multinationals that have aroused public and political opinion on both sides of the Atlantic. The author looks to state aid rules in general and from a distance, acknowledging the fact that EU state aid rules are embedded in the concept of economic market integration that is the basis of the TFEU.

In doing so the author is delving deep into the underground of concepts that prima facie are familiar to students of state aid rules, such as the reference system and the criterion of selectivity. However the outcomes of this intellectual mining exercise are not so familiar and rather surprising. He demonstrates that whether an allocation rule is part of a general corporate income tax system is not a given, but rather a policy choice which has consequences for the type of competitive conditions in a particular market. In the comparability analysis, which is so crucial in analysing the selectivity of a tax measure the author asks the critical question 'whether or not independent and associated enterprises, as well as members of domestic and cross-border groups, are in a comparable situation'. The conviction that multinationals and stand-alone enterprises were comparable was one of the main positions of the Commission in its action against multinationals.

In his reasoning the author moves forward very systematically, very cautiously and with an iron logic. He refuses to take sides in the battle between the legal arguments in state aid that is at present raging between the parties involved. The result is a high wire act of abstract legal reasoning, which has the merit of exposing relentlessly all presuppositions that are hidden in the discourse on state aid. The result requires an intense intellectual effort from the reader because the author manages in keeping so many plates spinning in the air, before coming down safely. At the same time the complexity of the issues, if it is to be dealt with in depth and systematically, is certainly challenging. The author provides a rational and convincing analytical framework to help understand these complex issues.

In the end the conclusions are rather reassuring and formulated in a simple way. But as I already indicated there are some surprises. The first conclusion is that it does not follow from Article 107(1) TFEU that there is an obligation to apply the arm's length principle, or any other allocation method in order to comply with the state aid rule. The article only implies an obligation to provide equal treatment and in that sense is only a different application of the non-discrimination rule flowing from the fundamental freedoms. Both applications are based on the treaty goal of the economic integration of the internal market.

Because of this requirement of equal treatment, the issue of comparability is the central theme of this study. The author emphasises the economic differences between multinational enterprises on the one hand and independent enterprises or members of domestic groups on the other, a difference that has not always been recognised by the European Commission in its state aid actions. Yet, despite the factual and legal differences existing between these categories of enterprises the author concludes that when the comparison is made in the light of the objective of the corporate income tax, i.e., the taxation of the net income of all corporations – the three categories of enterprises are in a comparable situation. This conclusion on comparability is essential for the application of the selectivity test under Article 107(1) TFEU. Without this conclusion of comparability between multinationals and other categories of enterprises it would not be possible to apply the obligation of equal treatment. The author emphasises that if the notion of comparability would be defined in a more narrow manner, the room for manoeuvre for the tax policies of the Member States would be quite large. By accepting the essence of the general corporate income tax system as the reference system for all categories of companies the EU state aid rules restrict substantially the tax policy choices and hence the fiscal sovereignty of the Member States.

In the second part of the book the author analyses the selectivity of each of the three different allocation methods and ranks these methods in accordance with an increasing degree of selectivity. The ranking also contains a surprise, because transfer pricing safe harbour rules are considered less selective than the generally formulated arm's length principle. Not surprisingly formula apportionment is ranked as most selective. However the author concludes that the selectivity of all methods can be justified if certain conditions are fulfilled.

If, after reading the last three paragraphs, you do not understand what the book is all about, but you would like the answer to these issues, you should read the book. The author takes you along a challenging intellectual journey, developing new insights and providing fresh ideas for a debate on a fundamental question of tax policy: to what extent should tax law provide a level playing field in order to guarantee free and fair competition? Above all the book is a launching pad for fundamental debate on tax policy and academic discussion. As the author has been studying and publishing for

Foreword

more than a decade on issues of EU and international taxation, he is well equipped to fulfil his role as a leader in such a debate.

Finally the book leaves me, as a lifelong student of EU tax problems, with a riddle. One of the final conclusions of the author is that a general system of formula apportionment with firm-specific factors is most likely prima facie selective and impossible to justify by the logic of the corporate income tax system. A general system of formula apportionment with firm-specific factors could only be implemented by the Member States if the reference system is made of the sole allocation method or if the comparison is only between associated enterprises. Since the position of the Commission under the state aid rules is that the reference system is the general corporate income tax system, implying a comparison between multinationals and stand alone enterprises, I am left with the question how the juxtaposition of formula apportionment in the CCCTB proposal for multinationals and the taxation of stand-alone companies on net income, can be brought in line with the equal treatment requirement of Article 107(1) TFEU. Without any doubt the author will know the answer to my riddle, but he will have to write a new book or at least a new article on this question. I am already looking forward to such a new publication.

Frans Vanistendael
Prof. em. KU Leuven

Preface

The purpose of this book is to analyse the theoretical issues that arise when applying the selectivity test in State aid law to three methods for the allocation of the corporate tax base between the members of multinational enterprises: the arm's length principle, transfer pricing safe harbours, and systems of formula apportionment. This research project is conducted at a theoretical level, without considering national provisions or tax treaties. In this book, I suggest an analytical framework on the application of the selectivity test to the three allocation methods. It is concluded that these methods are likely to have certain selective features, with varying possibilities to be justified by the inner logic of a corporate income tax system. It is also demonstrated that selectivity occurs for different reasons, due to the different rationales of the three allocation methods.

This book is intended at contributing to the academic literature on the impact of State aid law on the principles for the taxation of the income of multinational enterprises. The outcome of this research project is also relevant for lawmakers who need to reconcile the imperatives of State aid law with the design of rules that match their tax policies, as well as for judges or lawyers who apply the rules on State aid to tax provisions.

Financial support to this project was provided by the Nordic Tax Research Council and the research foundation TOR/Skattenytt. Financial support was also provided by the research foundation Uppsala Center for Tax Law, which enabled stays at the European University Institute, the College of Europe, and the International Bureau of Fiscal Documentation. I am grateful for this generous support, which made it possible to write this book.

I would like to thank colleagues from academia and from the tax community for many fruitful discussions during this research project, as well as for the comments provided on previous drafts of this book. My deepest thanks and thoughts go to my family.

This book takes into account legal developments up to 31 January 2018.

Jérôme Monsenego,
Stockholm, 25 February 2018

List of Abbreviations

AG	Advocate General
Art.	Article
Arts	Articles
BEPS	Base erosion and Profit Shifting
CCCTB	Common Consolidated Corporate Tax Base
CFC	Controlled Foreign Corporation
Ch.	Chapter
CJEU	Court of Justice of the European Union
CUP	Comparable Uncontrolled Price
Ed	Editor
Eds	Editors
Etc.	Et cetera
EU	European Union
GC	General Court
Ibid.	Ibidem
OECD	Organisation for Economic Co-operation and Development
OJ	Official Journal of the European Union
Para.	Paragraph
Paras	Paragraphs
R&D	Research and Development
Sec.	Section
TEU	Treaty on European Union
TFEU	Treaty on the Functioning of the European Union
UK	United Kingdom

List of Abbreviations

UN	United Nations
US	United States
VAT	Value Added Tax

CHAPTER 1
Introduction

1.1 BACKGROUND AND PROBLEM STATEMENT

This book is about the application of the selectivity test in State aid law to tax rules implementing three methods for the allocation of the corporate tax base among multinational enterprises: the arm's length principle, transfer pricing safe harbours, and systems of formula apportionment. These methods, whether they stem from national law or from tax treaties, need to comply with State aid law to be used by the Member States of the European Union (EU) when taxing the income of multinational enterprises. The research conducted in this book does not aim at fully analysing whether the allocation methods are compatible with State aid law; it focuses only on one of the elements of the definition of State aid: the notion of selectivity. Indeed, as is argued throughout the book, the three allocation methods have certain selective features, such as their limited scope of application to multinational enterprises, or the differences that they imply between various categories of undertakings.

It is common ground that the Member States of the EU must exercise their competence in the area of direct taxation consistently with the law of the EU, including the State aid rules.[1] As explained by the European Commission, 'a loss of tax revenue for the State is equivalent to consumption of State resources in the form of fiscal expenditure'.[2] The applicability of State aid law to tax measures is not new, as the rules preventing State aid that were part of the Treaty constituting the European Coal and

---

1. *See* in particular Case 173/73, *Italian Republic v. Commission of the European Communities*, ECLI:EU:C:1974:71, para. 28; Case C-449/14 P, *DTS Distribuidora de Televisión Digital, SA v. European Commission*, ECLI:EU:C:2016:848, para. 65: 'taxes do not fall within the scope of the provisions of the Treaty relating to State aid unless they constitute the method of financing an aid measure'.
2. *See* Commission Decision of 19 December 2017 on State aid SA.33829 (2012/C) Maltese tonnage tax scheme and other State measures in favour of shipping companies and their shareholders, para. 183.

Steel Community were already found applicable to tax measures.[3] The rules on State aid contribute to the broader objective of ensuring that competition is not distorted within the EU, as Article 107 of the Treaty on the Functioning of the European Union (hereafter TFEU) is included in the part of the Treaty related to the 'rules on competition'.[4] This refers mainly to the competition between private undertakings;[5] fiscal aids may indeed alter the competition through relieving certain undertakings of tax burdens. However, the State aid rules have also – as illustrated by the landmark *Gibraltar* case[6] – an impact on the tax competition between the Member States,[7] although these rules are not designed to tackle that issue.[8]

The notion of State aid according to Article 107(1) of the TFEU lies on four criteria,[9] all of which must be fulfilled for an aid to be illegal.[10] One of these criteria is the selectivity test.[11] The notion of selectivity has a large impact on the design and on

---

3. See Case 30/59, *De Gezamenlijke Steenkolenmijnen in Limburg v. High Authority of the European Coal and Steel Community*, ECLI:EU:C:1961:2.
4. In this respect see Case C-225/91, *Matra SA v. Commission of the European Communities*, ECLI:EU:C:1993:239, where at para. 42 the CJEU found that State aid law pursues 'the objective of undistorted competition in the common market'. Moreover, according to Art. 3(1)(b) of the TFEU, the rules on competition – which include the State aid rules – are within the exclusive competence of the European Union.
5. There is a debate on the content of the 'competition' that the State aid rules aim at protecting. It has been argued that State aid law focuses more on preventing the distortion in the competition faced by the economic actors, than on fostering an actual competition that leads to an increase in consumer welfare, which would weaken the link between State aid law and antitrust law: see e.g., Christian Ahlborn and Claudia Berg, 'Can State Aid Control Learn from Antitrust? The Need for a Greater Role for Competition Analysis under the State Aid Rules' in Andrea Biondi, Piet Eeckhout, and James Flynn (eds), *The Law of State Aid in the European Union* (Oxford University Press 2004) 48.
6. See Joined Cases C-106/09 P and C-107/09 P, *European Commission v. Government of Gibraltar*, ECLI:EU:C:2011:732.
7. On the relevance of State aid law for the competition between the Member States, see Leigh Hancher, 'EU State Aid Law – Déjà Vu All Over Again?' in Leigh Hancher, Tom Ottervanger, and Piet Jan Slot (eds), *EU State Aids* (5th edn, Sweet & Maxwell 2016) para. 1-029.
8. See e.g., Emily Forrester, 'Is the State Aid Regime a Suitable Instrument to Be Used in the Fight Against Harmful Tax Competition?' (2018) 27 EC Tax Review 19, 30–35.
9. For a description of the four components of the notion of State aid, see e.g., Case T-1/08, *Buczek Automotive sp. z o.o. v. European Commission*, ECLI:EU:T:2011:216, para. 66: '(c)lassification as aid within the meaning of [Art. 107(1) of the TFEU] requires that all the conditions set out in that provision are fulfilled. First, there must be an intervention by the State or through State resources. Second, the intervention must be likely to affect trade between Member States. Third, it must confer an advantage on the recipient by favouring certain undertakings or the production of certain goods. Fourth, it must distort or threaten to distort competition'. For an overview see Mona Aldestam, 'Skatteåtgärder som statligt stöd enligt artikel 87 i unionsfördraget' (2001) Skattenytt 87.
10. See Case C-74/16, *Congregación de Escuelas Pías Provincia Betania v. Ayuntamiento de Getafe*, ECLI:EU:C:2017:496, para. 38.
11. The selectivity test is often described as the most important and complex element of the definition of State aid, when State aid law applies to tax measures. In this respect, Advocate General Kokott has observed that 'In matters of tax law (…) the decisive criterion is whether a provision is selective, because the other conditions laid down in Article 107(1) TFEU are almost always satisfied' (see Case C-66/14, *Finanzamt Linz v. Bundesfinanzgericht, Außenstelle Linz*, ECLI:EU:C:2015:242, Opinion of AG Kokott, para. 114). For a study of the other elements of the definition of State aid in relation to the allocation of the corporate tax base among multinational enterprises, see e.g., Adrien Giraud and Sylvain Petit, 'Tax Rulings and State Aid Qualification: Should Reality Matter?' (2017) 16 European State Aid Law Quarterly 233.

Chapter 1: Introduction

the application of tax rules, which is partly due to the broad definition of this notion in the case law of the Court of Justice of the European Union (CJEU).[12] The selectivity test in the field of tax law consists in investigating whether a tax measure applies to all undertakings and is thus general, or if it applies only to certain undertakings or certain production, thus being selective. It is indeed settled case law that general measures applicable without distinction to all economic operators do not constitute State aid.[13] In contrast, a measure that introduces a difference in treatment between undertakings that are in a comparable situation is prima facie selective;[14] such a measure may, however, be justified by the nature or the general scheme of the system of which it forms part.[15] Accordingly, the idea of non-discrimination is central to the notion of selectivity,[16] which has been described by Quigley as 'an application of the general principle of equal treatment'.[17] Although there is a debate relating to whether or not the selectivity criterion should be limited to a discrimination test,[18] the CJEU defines the notion of selectivity in a manner that is close to a principle of non-discrimination.[19]

The problem that is investigated in this book concerns the application of the selectivity test to three methods for the allocation of the corporate tax base among multinational enterprises. The three allocation methods are a generally formulated arm's length provision, transfer pricing safe harbours, and systems of formula apportionment with firm-specific factors. Before further discussing the problem analysed in

---

12. As an indication, it was estimated that in 2016, 32% of total State aid expenditure concerned tax exemptions, which is the second highest expenditure: *see* European Commission, 'State Aid Scoreboard 2017: Results, trends, and observations regarding EU28 State Aid expenditure reports for 2016' (European Commission 2017) 11.
13. *See* e.g., Case C-143/99, *Adria-Wien Pipeline GmbH*, ECLI:EU:C:2001:598, para. 36; Case C-417/10, *Ministero dell'Economia e delle Finanze, Agenzia delle Entrate v. 3M Italia SpA*, ECLI:EU:C:2012:184, para. 39.
14. *See* Joined Cases C-20/15 P and C-21/15 P, *European Commission v. World Duty Free Group*, ECLI:EU:C:2016:981, para. 57.
15. *See* Joined Cases C-20/15 P and C-21/15 P, *European Commission v. World Duty Free Group*, ECLI:EU:C:2016:981, para. 58.
16. *See* Case C-524/14 P, *European Commission v. Hansestadt Lübeck*, ECLI:EU:C:2016:971, para. 53; Case C-70/16 P, *Comunidad Autónoma de Galicia and Redes de Telecomunicación Galegas Retegal, SA (Retegal) v. European Commission*, ECLI:EU:C:2017:1002, para. 58; Claire Micheau, *Droit des Aides d'État et des Subventions en Fiscalité – Droit de l'Union Européenne et de l'OMC* (Larcier 2013) para. 708; Peter J. Wattel, 'Some Fringe Areas of EU State Aid Law in Direct Tax Matters' in Dennis Weber (ed), *EU Income Tax Law – Issues for the Years Ahead* (IBFD 2013), where the author at 146 finds that selectivity and discrimination are 'conceptually identical'; Richard Lyal, 'Transfer Pricing Rules and State Aid' (2015) 38 Fordham International Law Journal 1017, 1032. *See also* Commission Notice on the notion of State aid as referred to in Art. 107(1) of the Treaty on the Functioning of the European Union [2016] OJ C 262/1, para. 125.
17. *See* Conor Quigley, *European State Aid Law and Policy* (3rd edn, Hart Publishing 2015) 64.
18. *See* particularly Wolfgang Schön, 'Tax Legislation and the Notion of Fiscal Aid: A Review of 5 Years of European Jurisprudence' in Isabelle Richelle, Wolfgang Schön, and Edoardo Traversa (eds), *State Aid Law and Business Taxation* (Springer 2016) 8–14, with further references.
19. *See* Case C-524/14 P, *European Commission v. Hansestadt Lübeck*, ECLI:EU:C:2016:971, para. 53; Joined Cases C-20/15 P and C-21/15 P, *European Commission v. World Duty Free Group*, ECLI:EU:C:2016:981, paras 54 and 75. This position was recommended by Advocate General Wathelet, who considered selectivity and discrimination as close, if not synonymous concepts (*see* Joined Cases C-20/15 P and C-21/15 P, *European Commission v. World Duty Free Group*, ECLI:EU:C:2016:624, Opinion of AG Wathelet, paras 7 and 80).

this book, I will describe the rationale of the three allocation methods. I will then return to the problem statement of this research project.

First, the allocation method that is mostly relied on by the Member States, at the time of writing this book, is a generally formulated provision implementing the so-called arm's length principle, or 'arm's length standard'. In a nutshell, the arm's length principle implies that the terms and conditions of cross-border intercompany transactions be determined as if no legal or economic relations existed between the parties to a transaction, something that is achieved through setting the transfer prices assuming that the market forces apply to a particular intercompany transaction.[20] The arm's length principle supposes often an approximation of a market value through different statistical methods.[21] One would compile the best available observations on the open market in a range of values and choose, among that panel of observations, a value or a range thereof that is deemed to be the best estimate of an arm's length value.[22] The arm's length principle is a principle of taxation that may be relied on as part of several types of tax rules. It is mainly used for the purpose of the allocation of the corporate tax base between the different countries where associated enterprises that transact with each other are resident, i.e., transfer pricing. It is in this respect that the arm's length principle is studied in this book. The arm's length principle may also be used as part of rules achieving other purposes, such as rules relating to the attribution of profits to permanent establishments,[23] the determination of a certain limit for the deduction of interest expenses,[24] or the determination of a maximum relief of source taxation for royalty income.[25] The notion of market value is also found in other areas, such as value added taxes (hereafter VAT),[26] or certain domestic corporate taxation rules.[27] The analyses contained in this book apply to the arm's length principle when it is relied on for the allocation of the corporate tax base between associated enterprises resident of different Member States. However, this study may also, incidentally, be useful for the analysis of the consequences of State aid law on other tax rules that rely on the arm's length principle or on the notion of market value.

---

20. See OECD, *Model Tax Convention on Income and on Capital* (OECD 2017), Art. 9 (hereafter the 2017 OECD Model Tax Convention).
21. See OECD, *Transfer Pricing Guidelines for Multinational Enterprises and Tax Administrations* (OECD 2017), para. 3.38 (hereafter the 2017 OECD transfer pricing guidelines).
22. See para. 1.13 of the 2017 OECD transfer pricing guidelines. For a deeper presentation of the arm's length principle *see* Jérôme Monsenego, *Introduction to Transfer Pricing* (Kluwer Law International 2015) 3–35.
23. See e.g., OECD, *2010 Report on the Attribution of Profits to Permanent Establishments* (OECD 2010), part I, 12, para. 8: 'The authorised OECD approach is that the profits to be attributed to a PE are the profits that the PE would have earned at arm's length'.
24. See e.g., Council Resolution of 8 June 2010 on coordination of the Controlled Foreign Corporation (CFC) and thin capitalisation rules within the European Union [2010] OJ C 156/1, preamble: 'thin capitalisation rules which observe the arm's-length principle are capable of preventing tax avoidance, or maintaining the balanced allocation of taxing powers, or both'.
25. See e.g., Art. 12(4) of the 2017 OECD Model Tax Convention.
26. See Council Directive 2006/112/EC of 28 November 2006 on the common system of value added tax [2006] OJ L 347/1, Art. 80. *See also* Case C-103/09, *The Commissioners for Her Majesty's Revenue and Customs v. Weald Leasing Ltd*, ECLI:EU:C:2010:804, para. 45.
27. See e.g., section 22(7) of the Swedish income tax act *Inkomstskattelag* (1999:1229).

Chapter 1: Introduction

The second allocation method considered in this book is transfer pricing safe harbours that supplement a generally formulated arm's length provision. It is further assumed that such safe harbours provide predetermined profit margins, or ranges thereof, that apply to certain intercompany transactions. An example of transfer pricing safe harbour is provided in the 2017 OECD transfer pricing guidelines for certain eligible low value-adding intragroup services, which may be charged with a 5% profit mark-up.[28] Transfer pricing safe harbours may implement the arm's length principle, or they may deviate from it,[29] depending on the material content of the safe harbour (i.e., typically the level of profits prescribed by the safe harbour rule) and the eligibility to such a safe harbour (i.e., the conditions that need to be fulfilled for the safe harbour to be applicable). Transfer pricing safe harbours are usually limited in their scope to companies with less complex functions, or transactions with a low level of complexity,[30] because it is only in such cases that it can be established in advance and with sufficient reliability which level of profits, or which range of profits, should be earned to remunerate the performance of certain functions.

The third allocation method considered in this book is a system of formula apportionment with firm-specific factors. Indeed, the income of the members of a multinational enterprise may be allocated between these members on the basis of a formula with firm-specific apportionment factors such as sales, labour costs, tangible assets, or other factors. The income allocation would not be based on a general principle or on a predetermined profit margin, but on the choice and the relative weight of the apportionment factors, as well as the presence of these factors in the territories of different countries. A system of formula apportionment may constitute the main allocation method; examples are provided at subnational level in certain federal countries such as the United States (US) and Canada, and a system of formula apportionment is suggested within the EU through the common consolidated corporate tax base (CCCTB).[31] A system of formula apportionment may also be implemented in combination with other allocation methods, which could be described as a 'hybrid' system.[32] This is the most likely alternative in case formulaic elements were to be implemented in the current tax systems, without agreeing on a formula-based

---

28. *See* para. 7.61 of the 2017 OECD transfer pricing guidelines.
29. *See* paras 4.111–4.113 of the 2017 OECD transfer pricing guidelines.
30. *See* para. 4.129 of the 2017 OECD transfer pricing guidelines.
31. *See* European Commission, 'Proposal for a Council Directive on a Common Consolidated Corporate Tax Base (CCCTB)' COM(2016) 683 final.
32. *See* Reuven S. Avi-Yonah, 'Between Formulary Apportionment and the OECD Guidelines: A Proposal for Reconciliation' (2010) 2 World Tax Journal 3; Yariv Brauner, 'Formula Based Transfer Pricing' (2014) 42 Intertax 615; Richard Collier and Joseph L. Andrus, *Transfer Pricing and the Arm's Length Principle After BEPS* (Oxford University Press 2017) 286–289; Stefan Greil, 'The Dealing at Arm's Length Fallacy: A Way Forward to a Formula-Based Transactional Profit Split?' (2017) 45 Intertax 624, 627–629. *See also* United Nations, *Practical Manual on Transfer Pricing for Developing Countries* (United Nations 2017) 37, for the example provided by the rules in Brazil: 'the Brazilian transfer pricing rules set out a maximum ceiling on the expenses that may be deducted for tax purposes in respect of imports and lay down a minimum level for the gross income in relation to exports, effectively using a set formula to allocate income to Brazil'.

allocation method at an international level such as a CCCTB.³³ To a certain extent, the 2017 OECD transfer pricing guidelines acknowledge the use of hybrid systems in situations with no reliable comparables on the open market, by recognising the possibility to depart from transfer pricing methods that rely on independent comparables. For example, the benefits under a cost contribution arrangement may be shared between the participants on the basis of an allocation key.³⁴ Another example is the profit split method, which normally aims at implementing the arm's length principle; the application of this method may nevertheless share certain features with a system of formula apportionment, when the profits are split on the basis of firm-specific factors,³⁵ with no direct reliance on independent comparables.³⁶ It has even been argued that Article 9 of the OECD Model Tax Convention does not aim at allocating among multinational enterprises the profits that exceed those that are earned by independent enterprises, something that may speak in favour of relying on a formula-based allocation method in such cases.³⁷ It is impossible to consider all combinations of different allocation methods in this book. Yet the analyses relating to each allocation method are likely to contribute to the selectivity analysis of various combinations of allocation methods, as long as they have features in common with the methods studied in this book.

Now that the three allocation methods have been introduced, I return to the formulation of the problem analysed in this research project. As all domestic or treaty-based tax measures, rules that implement methods for the allocation of the corporate tax base need to comply with State aid law, including the selectivity test. In this respect, it must be emphasised that the compatibility with the rules on State aid of the application of one of the allocation methods – the arm's length principle – has been raised in several decisions of the European Commission relating to certain advance tax rulings granted by several Member States.³⁸ Beyond the questions raised in these

---

33. See Yariv Brauner, 'Formula Based Transfer Pricing' (2014) 42 Intertax 615, 621. It could be argued that one of the main obstacles to the global implementation of formula apportionment, namely the need to agree at an international level on a change of paradigm and amend the existing double taxation conventions, has weakened with the inclusive work conducted by the OECD as part of the Base Erosion and Profit Shifting (hereafter BEPS) project, in particular with the conclusion of the multilateral convention.
34. See para. 8.19 of the 2017 OECD transfer pricing guidelines, which mentions that '(t)he possibilities for allocation keys include sales (turnover), profits, units used, produced, or sold; number of employees, and so forth'.
35. See para. 2.141 of the 2017 OECD transfer pricing guidelines. On this topic see Robert Robillard, 'Profit-Split Methods and the OECD: Leaning Toward Formulary Apportionment?' (2017) 87 Tax Notes International 1005.
36. See para. 3.39 of the 2017 OECD transfer pricing guidelines: '(a) transactional profit split method might in appropriate circumstances be considered without comparable data'.
37. For a presentation of the argument see Mitchell A. Kane, 'Transfer Pricing, Integration and Synergy Intangibles: A Consensus Approach to the Arm's Length Standard' (2014) 6 World Tax Journal 282, 299. However, it should be emphasised that this author does not recommend to split the profits that exceed arm's length profits on the basis of a formula, but rather to let the group decide: see at 304, where the author considers that 'under the fractional interpretation of article 9, the taxpayer has discretion to set prices in a way that allocates the [premium for common control] to whichever jurisdiction it chooses'.
38. See particularly Commission Decision (EU) 2017/502 of 21 October 2015 on State aid SA.38374 (2014/C ex 2014/NN) implemented by the Netherlands to Starbucks [2017] OJ L 83/38; Commission Decision (EU) 2016/2326 of 21 October 2015 on State aid SA.38375 (2014/C ex

Chapter 1: Introduction

decisions, the problem consists in understanding the implications of the selectivity criterion in State aid law on the rules for the taxation of the profits of multinational enterprises, given that a selective measure is likely to be incompatible with the rules on State aid, thus being illegal. It is this interaction that the book focuses on, i.e., the potential *intrinsic* selectivity of the allocation methods, whether it is de jure or de facto selectivity. The potential selectivity of the *application* of these methods in particular cases, for example through the study of the advance pricing arrangements analysed by the European Commission, is not in the scope of the book. Therefore, although the problem analysed in this research project touches upon certain of the questions of principle raised in the decisions taken by the European Commission, the core of this research project concerns rather the study, at a theoretical level, of the implications of the notion of selectivity on the rules for the allocation of the corporate tax base.

Despite being simply formulated, the problem investigated in this book is not a straightforward exercise. This is particularly due to the complexity of the definition of the notion of selectivity.[39] Although the CJEU has provided a method of analysis as well as various applications of the selectivity criterion to tax measures,[40] it remains difficult to precisely determine where and how to draw a line between general and selective tax measures. The difficulty to define the notion of selectivity is also partly explained by the evolution of this notion,[41] which has been widened with certain cases ruled by the CJEU,[42] and had probably not matured at the time of writing this book.[43] Indeed, the concept of selectivity is likely to continue evolving with the decisions taken by the European Commission, and eventually with the case law of the Union courts.[44]

2014/NN) which Luxembourg granted to Fiat [2016] OJ L 351/1; Commission Decision (EU) 2016/1699 of 11 January 2016 on the excess profit exemption State aid scheme SA.37667 (2015/C) (ex 2015/NN) implemented by Belgium [2016] OJ L 260/61; Commission Decision (EU) 2017/1283 of 30 August 2016 on State aid SA.38373 (2014/C) (ex 2014/NN) (ex 2014/CP) implemented by Ireland to Apple [2017] OJ L 187/1.

39. In this respect, *see* Saturnina Moreno González, 'Les aides d'État à caractère fiscal: le critère de sélectivité de la mesure' in Gilbert Orsoni (ed), *Mélanges en l'honneur de Pierre Beltrame* (Presses Universitaires d'Aix-Marseille 2010) 381.
40. *See* e.g., Joined Cases C-20/15 P and C-21/15 P, *European Commission v. World Duty Free Group*, ECLI:EU:C:2016:981, para. 54, with reference to further cases.
41. *See* Claire Micheau, 'Evolution of State Aid Rules: Conceptions, Challenges, and Outcomes' in Herwig C. H. Hofmann and Claire Micheau (eds), *State Aid Law of the European Union* (Oxford University Press 2016) 18. *See also* Case C-236/16, *Asociación Nacional de Grandes Empresas de Distribución (ANGED) v. Generalitat de Catalunya*, ECLI:EU:C:2017:852, Opinion of AG Kokott, para. 85 where the Advocate General seems to see an evolution between the *Gibraltar* and *World Duty Free Group* cases on the need, for a measure to be selective, to identify a category of undertakings; Advocate General Kokott also emphasised at footnote 63 the potential inconsistencies in the case law of the Court.
42. *See* Phedon Nicolaides, 'Excessive Widening of the Concept of Selectivity' (2017) 16 European State Aid Law Quarterly 62, 72; concurring on the wide effect of the *World Duty Free Group* case, *see* Gunnar Rabe, 'Statliga stöd' (2017) Skattenytt 386.
43. Therefore, it has correctly been pointed out that the case law of the CJEU in the area of State aid applied to tax rules is still in search of balance: *see* Georgios Matsos, 'Systematic Misconceptions of State Aid Law in the Area of Taxation' (2014) 13 European State Aid Law Quarterly 491, 504; Marta Villar Ezcurra, 'The Concept of "Environmental Tax" in a State Aid Context When a Fiscal Energy Measure Is Concerned' (2017) 16 European State Aid Law Quarterly 11, 19.
44. On the general relation between the practice of the European Commission and the case law of the CJEU, *see* Melchior Wathelet and Nathalie Bonhomme, 'La Commission et la jurisprudence

Moreover, independently from the evolution of State aid law, the taxation of the profits of multinational enterprises is a complex matter, subject to intense debate. This is especially true in view of the globalisation of trade, the digitalisation of the economy, and the diverging views on the tax policy options to tackle these challenges.[45]

The combination of the evolution of the notion of selectivity in State aid law, on the one hand, and the need to adapt the rules for the taxation of the profits of multinational enterprises to the modern economy, on the other hand, makes it necessary to assess whether existing, as well as alternative rules for the allocation of the corporate tax base might entail a selective treatment. Accordingly, the purpose of this book is to study the application of the selectivity test to different allocation methods.

1.2 PURPOSE OF THE STUDY AND EXPECTED CONTRIBUTION

The purpose of this book is to study the application of the selectivity test to the following three methods for the allocation of the corporate tax base among multinational enterprises: the arm's length principle, transfer pricing safe harbours, and systems of formula apportionment with firm-specific factors. The expected contribution is the suggestion of an analytical framework on the application of the selectivity test, at a theoretical level, to the three allocation methods. Accordingly, the research question investigated in this book can be formulated as follows: what is the outcome of the selectivity test when it applies to the arm's length principle, transfer pricing safe harbours, and systems of formula apportionment with firm-specific factors? The answers brought to this research question are mainly intended at contributing to the academic literature on the consequences of the rules on State aid on the taxation of the income of multinational enterprises. The outcome of this research project may also be relevant for lawmakers who need to reconcile the imperatives of State aid law with the design of rules that match their tax policies, as well as for judges or lawyers who apply the rules on State aid to tax provisions.

This study is conducted at a theoretical level, on the basis of a selection of characteristics that are particular to each allocation method.[46] In other words, the contribution of this book is limited to an abstract consideration of the implications of

---

de la Cour en matière fiscale' in Edoardo Traversa and Vincent Deckers (eds), *Liber Amicorum Jacques Autenne – Promenades sous les portiques de la fiscalité* (Bruylant 2010) 479.

45. In this respect *see* in particular the material published by the OECD as part of the BEPS project: < http://www.oecd.org/tax/beps/beps-actions.htm > accessed 18 February 2018. *See also* e.g., Yariv Brauner, 'Formula Based Transfer Pricing' (2014) 42 Intertax 615, 616–617; Robert J. Danon, 'Treaty Abuse in the Post-BEPS World: Analysis of the Policy Shift and Impact of the Principal Purpose Test for MNE Groups' (2018) 72 Bulletin for International Taxation 31; Martijn L. Schippers and Constantijn E. Verhaeren, 'Taxation in a Digitizing World: Solutions for Corporate Income Tax and Value Added Tax' (2018) 27 EC Tax Review 61.
46. In this vein *see* Thomas Jaeger, 'Tax Incentives Under State Aid Law: A Competition Law Perspective' in Isabelle Richelle, Wolfgang Schön and Edoardo Traversa (eds), *State Aid Law and Business Taxation* (Springer 2016) 45, where the author calls for 'a better understanding of the typical characteristics and effects of tax norms and a better distinction of those effects vis-à-vis the effects of other, common State aid measures'.

Chapter 1: Introduction

the selectivity test on the allocation methods. It is not relied on the domestic rules or on the tax treaties in force in the Member States, apart from a few examples to illustrate certain ideas.[47] This implies that the analyses contained in this book do not provide comprehensive answers to the selectivity test of the allocation methods that are implemented, or contemplated by the Member States; to that end, the analyses included in this book should be completed by the consideration of the relevant national provisions as well as tax treaties.

Although the purpose of this book is limited to the analysis of the selectivity test when it applies to the allocation methods, this research project might also be of relevance in other contexts than the domestic or the treaty-based rules for the allocation of the corporate tax base, in particular the tax rules that share certain similarities with the allocation methods.[48] The analyses included in this book may also be of relevance in case of enactment by the Member States of a CCCTB. Assuming that such a harmonisation of corporate income taxes is implemented through a directive, taxation under the common rules would most likely be an action attributable to the Union, not to the Member States; that would make the rules fall short of one of the criteria of the State aid definition, which is that of an action attributable to a Member State.[49] However, the attribution of aid to the Union or to the Member States is a complex matter,[50] and it cannot be excluded that taxation under domestic provisions that implement a harmonised set of rules be attributable to the Member States, depending on criteria such as the type of rule at hand, the drafting of the directive, the options that could be exercised by the Member States, whether the rules are adopted unanimously or through enhanced cooperation, or the method to transpose the harmonised rules into domestic law. Therefore, the study conducted in this book may also contribute to the selectivity test of the apportionment mechanism of a CCCTB, would the rules on State aid be applicable.

In the following section, I will expose the limitations that apply to this research project.

1.3 LIMITATIONS

The scope of this study is subject to several types of limitations. To start with, this book is written in the field of legal science. It does not include studies in the field of

---

47. Therefore, when it comes to the material content of the arm's length principle, unless mentioned otherwise it is relied on the descriptions of the application of the principle that are included in the 2017 OECD transfer pricing guidelines.
48. An example is the attribution of profits to permanent establishments.
49. For an example in the field of VAT where the condition of intervention by the State was not met, see Case C-460/07, *Sandra Puffer v. Unabhängiger Finanzsenat, Außenstelle Linz*, ECLI:EU:C:2009:254, para. 70.
50. It is not the purpose of this book to investigate the attribution of aid to the Member States or to the Union. For literature devoted to this topic see e.g., Joachim Englisch, 'EU State Aid Rules Applied to Indirect Tax Measures' (2013) 22 EC Tax Review 9, 14–16; Raymond Luja, 'The Attribution of State Aid to Member States in the Exercising of Options in Directives' (2013) 12 European State Aid Law Quarterly 119; Louis Vogel, *European State Aid Law* (Bruylant 2017) 23–26.

economics, although economics is an important parameter for the design of tax rules as well as for the complete application of State aid law.[51]

As already indicated above with respect to the purpose of the study, only three allocation methods are taken into consideration: a generally formulated arm's length provision, transfer pricing safe harbours, and a system of formula apportionment with firm-specific factors. Other allocation methods, or combinations of allocation methods, are not included in the scope of this book. When it comes to systems of formula apportionment, the study is limited to apportionment mechanisms based on firm-specific factors, as suggested in the EU and applied at subnational level in the US and Canada.[52] Other formula-based allocation methods, such as formulas based on macroeconomic factors or industry average ratios, are out of the scope of this study.

The book does not aim at comprehensively analysing and comparing the allocation methods from a tax policy perspective; rather, the allocation methods are analysed to the extent that is necessary to serve the purpose of the book. For each allocation method, it is only the sharing mechanism that is subject to an analysis in the light of the selectivity criterion; other features of the allocation methods, such as the definition of 'associated enterprises' or the determination of the income to be apportioned under a formula-based allocation method, are excluded from this study. The theoretical features of the allocation methods that are analysed in this book are those that I consider as being at the heart of the sharing mechanism of each method.[53]

From the perspective of State aid law, the scope of the book is limited to the application of the selectivity criterion to the allocation methods. The other components of the notion of State aid are out of the scope of this study. In particular, the notion of advantage is not analysed in the book. There is a debate as to the difference between the notions of advantage and selectivity, which is illustrated by the use, in certain cases, of the expression 'selective advantage' by the CJEU[54] as well as by the European Commission.[55] However, the use of this expression, which may create a confusion between the notions of advantage and selectivity, has to do with the difference between

---

51. On the importance of economics for the purpose of State aid control *see* e.g., Hans W. Friederiszick, Lars-Hendrick Röller, and Vincent Verouden, 'European State Aid Control: an Economic Framework' in Paolo Buccirossi (ed), *Handbook of Antitrust Economics* (MIT Press 2008) 625; Michaël Karpenschif, 'Le critère de l'opérateur en économie de marché et la crise financière' in Valérie Giacobbo-Peyronnel and Christophe Verdure (eds), *Contentieux du droit de la concurrence et de l'Union européenne – questions d'actualité et perspectives* (Bruylant 2017) 428–432.
52. *See* European Commission, 'Proposal for a Council Directive on a Common Consolidated Corporate Tax Base (CCCTB)' COM(2016) 683 final, Art. 28.
53. On the need to analyse the main characteristics of certain tax rules in the light of State aid law, *see* Thomas Jaeger, 'Tax Incentives Under State Aid Law: A Competition Law Perspective' in Isabelle Richelle, Wolfgang Schön, and Edoardo Traversa (eds), *State Aid Law and Business Taxation* (Springer 2016) 45.
54. *See* e.g., Case C-524/14 P, *European Commission v. Hansestadt Lübeck*, ECLI:EU:C:2016:971, para. 40; Joined Cases C-20/15 P and C-21/15 P, *European Commission v. World Duty Free Group*, ECLI:EU:C:2016:981, para. 53; Case C-74/16, *Congregación de Escuelas Pías Provincia Betania v. Ayuntamiento de Getafe*, ECLI:EU:C:2017:496, para. 38.
55. *See* e.g., Commission Decision (EU) 2017/1283 of 30 August 2016 on State aid SA.38373 (2014/C) (ex 2014/NN) (ex 2014/CP) implemented by Ireland to Apple [2017] OJ L 187/1, paras 225 and following.

the State aid control of general schemes, and that of individual aid. The CJEU has explained that there is a difference between the notions of advantage and selectivity:[56] 'the requirement as to selectivity under Article 107(1) TFEU must be clearly distinguished from the concomitant detection of an economic advantage'.[57] The Court has also made clear that the concomitance of the notions of advantage and selectivity is limited to the case of individual aid.[58] Given that this book is written from a sole theoretical perspective, without assessing the compatibility with State aid law of an individual aid such as a tax ruling, the selectivity criterion does not coincide with the concept of advantage. Accordingly, it is methodologically correct to study the selectivity criterion alone, without also considering the notion of advantage. This methodological choice is largely observed in the academic literature devoted to the selectivity criterion in State aid law.[59]

1.4 PREVIOUS RESEARCH

There is considerable research in the field of State aid law, including the application of the State aid rules to tax measures.[60] Since the European Commission started to examine the compatibility with the rules on State aid of certain advance tax rulings and of certain international tax rules, numerous publications have focused both on the

---

56. In this sense, see e.g., Hugo López López, 'General Thought on Selectivity and Consequences of a Broad Concept of State Aid in Tax Matters' (2010) 9 European State Aid Law Quarterly 807, 809; U.S. Department of the Treasury White Paper, *The European Commission's recent Investigations of Transfer Pricing Rulings* (2016) 6. However, diverging, see e.g., Rita Szudoczky, *The Sources of EU Law and Their Relationships: Lessons for the Field of Taxation* (IBFD 2014) 580; Richard Lyal, 'Transfer Pricing Rules and State Aid' (2015) 38 Fordham International Law Journal 1017, 1031; Liza Lovdahl Gormsen, 'EU State Aid Law and Transfer Pricing: A Critical Introduction to a New Saga' (2016) 7 Journal of European Competition Law & Practice 369, 376.
57. See most notably Case C-15/14 P, *European Commission v. MOL Magyar Olaj- és Gázipari Nyrt.*, ECLI:EU:C:2015:362, para. 59. See also Case C-522/13, *Ministerio de Defensa and Navantia SA v. Concello de Ferrol*, ECLI:EU:C:2014:2262, para. 34.
58. See Case C-15/14 P, *European Commission v. MOL Magyar Olaj- és Gázipari Nyrt.*, ECLI:EU: C:2015:362, para. 60.
59. For similar limitations see e.g., Claire Micheau, *Tax Selectivity in European Law of State Aid: Legal Assessment and Alternative Approaches* (2015) 40 European Law Review 323; Michael Lang, 'State Aid and Taxation: Selectivity and Comparability Analysis' in Isabelle Richelle, Wolfgang Schön, and Edoardo Traversa (eds), *State Aid Law and Business Taxation* (Springer 2016) 34.
60. For a non-exhaustive list of research projects see Mona Aldestam, *EC State Aid Rules Applied to Taxes* (Uppsala 2005); Claire Micheau, *Droit des Aides d'État et des Subventions en Fiscalité – Droit de l'Union Européenne et de l'OMC* (Larcier 2013); Marilyne Sadowsky, *Droit de l'OMC, droit de l'Union européenne et fiscalité directe* (Larcier 2013); Alexander Rust and Claire Micheau (eds), *State Aid and Tax Law* (Kluwer Law International 2013); Michael Lang, 'Tax Rulings and State Aid Law' (2015) 3 British Tax Review 391; Phedon Nicolaides, 'State Aid Rules and Tax Rulings' (2016) 15 European State Aid Law Quarterly 416; Wolfgang Schön and Edoardo Traversa (eds), *State Aid Law and Business Taxation* (Springer 2016); Alexandre Maitrot de la Motte, 'L'identification des "paramètres pertinents pour établir la sélectivité" des avantages fiscaux' (2017) 26 Revue de Droit Fiscal 37.

decisions taken by the Commission,[61] and on some of the questions of principle that are raised by these decisions.[62] Therefore, certain of the issues analysed in this book have been subject to previous research, especially some of the questions of principle relating to the application of the selectivity test to the arm's length principle. This does not need to imply, however, that the conclusions reached in this book coincide with those drawn by other scholars. Moreover, little research focuses on alternative taxation methods to the arm's length principle. Accordingly, by applying the selectivity criterion to the arm's length principle, transfer pricing safe harbours, as well as systems of formula apportionment with firm-specific factors, and by reconciling the findings with respect to all these allocation methods, the book investigates research questions that have not yet been explored at depth. This calls for an observation in the context of legal theory: while legal research often aims at reconstructing a legal system,[63] the research project undertaken in this book could be described as implying the construction,[64] or the suggestion, of what I perceive as the right application of the selectivity test to the allocation methods.[65]

There is also significant research relating to the three allocation methods analysed in this book. The arm's length principle has since long been subject to analysis and criticism in the literature.[66] Formula apportionment has been considered in the doctrine as an alternative method for the allocation of the corporate tax base,[67]

---

61. *See* e.g., Lee A. Sheppard, 'EU Amazon Case: Is Transfer Pricing Really the Issue?' (2015) 77 Tax Notes International 291; Marc Rasch and Pawel Wroblewski, 'European Commission Decision on Fiat: State Aid Case Explained' (2016) 23 International Transfer Pricing Journal 440.
62. *See* e.g., Richard Lyal, 'Transfer Pricing Rules and State Aid' (2015) 38 Fordham International Law Journal 1017; Liza Lovdahl Gormsen, 'EU State Aid Law and Transfer Pricing: A Critical Introduction to a New Saga' (2016) 7 Journal of European Competition Law & Practice 369; Thomas Jaeger, 'Tax Concessions for Multinationals: In or Out of the Reach of State Aid Law?' (2017) 8 Journal of European Competition Law & Practice 221.
63. *See* Nils Jareborg, *Rättsdogmatik som vetenskap*, (2004) Svensk Juristtidning 1, 4: '*(d)en kortaste beskrivningen av rättsdogmatik är att den består i* rekonstruktion av rättssystem' (emphasis not added); Nils Jansen, 'Making Doctrine for European Law' in Rob van Gestel, Hans-W. Micklitz, and Edward L. Rubin (eds), *Rethinking Legal Scholarship – A Transatlantic Dialogue* (Cambridge University Press 2017) 236.
64. *See* Nils Jareborg, *Rättsdogmatik som vetenskap*, (2004) Svensk Juristtidning 1, who at 4 stresses the legitimacy of the objective of searching for ideal solutions ('*(d)et är helt legitimt för rättsdogmatiker att söka efter ideala lösningar*'). On the notion of 'construction', *see also* Anders Agell, 'Rättsdogmatik eller konstruktiv rättsvetenskap' in Åke Frändberg, Ulf Göranson, and Torgny Håstad (eds), *Festskrift till Stig Strömholm* (Iustus Förlag 1997) 35.
65. From a methodological perspective, this part of the research process resembles what has been described as 'critical legal dogmatic research': *see* Jan Kleineman, 'Rättsdogmatisk Metod' in Fredric Korling and Mauro Zamboni (eds), *Juridisk Metodlära* (Studentlitteratur 2013) 21, 39.
66. *See* e.g., Wolfgang Schön, 'Transfer Pricing, the Arm's Length Standard and European Union Law' in Isabelle Richelle, Wolfgang Schön, and Edoardo Traversa (eds), *Allocating Taxing Powers within the European Union* (Springer 2013) 74, where the author finds that the arm's length principle is under attack 'conceptually, politically and legally'; *see also* Reuven S. Avi-Yonah, 'The Rise and Fall of Arm's Length: A Study in the Evolution of U.S. International Taxation' (1995) 15 Virginia Tax Review 89.
67. *See* e.g., Walter Hellerstein, 'The Case for Formulary Apportionment' (2005) 12 International Transfer Pricing Journal 103; Michael Kobetsky, 'The Case for Unitary Taxation of International Enterprises' (2008) 62 Bulletin for International Taxation 201; Wolfgang Schön, 'Transfer Pricing, the Arm's Length Standard and European Union Law' in Isabelle Richelle, Wolfgang Schön, and Edoardo Traversa (eds), *Allocating Taxing Powers Within the European Union*

although it is still rejected by the OECD as a valid alternative to the arm's length principle.[68] Scholars have also suggested a combination of the arm's length principle and a system of formula apportionment,[69] sometimes arguing that in certain cases there is no fundamental difference between the two,[70] or that the arm's length principle and formula apportionment are not incompatible.[71] Given that the purpose of the book is limited to the selectivity test of the allocation methods, no contribution is made in this study to the tax policy analysis of these methods.

1.5 METHOD OF RESEARCH

It has been written that 'without method, scholarship becomes nothing more than the expression of personal values'.[72] This view is particularly appropriate for the research conducted in this book, which faces several methodological challenges despite a rather traditional purpose. Indeed, this study, which aims at applying the selectivity test to three methods for the allocation of the corporate tax base, pursues an objective common to many areas of national law that are subject to the superior provisions of the primary law of the EU: it consists in understanding how the two fields of the law interact and, when incompatibilities or tensions are identified, they are being investigated to suggest interpretations or wordings of the national law that correctly enforce EU law. Since State aid law binds the Member States, there is a need to understand the

---

(Springer 2013) 75: '(o)n the whole, the economic, political and legal arguments against the arm's length standard seem to press for the introduction of global or regional profit consolidation for corporate groups accompanied by a formulaic apportionment of the tax base'.
68. *See* para. 1.32 of the 2017 OECD transfer pricing guidelines. *See also* Dana L. Glenn, 'Formula Apportionment no Solution to BEPS, OECD Rep Says' (2014) 73 Tax Notes International 692: 'At the outset of the base erosion and profit-shifting project, the OECD analysed the arm's length standard and considered whether a different approach was needed to combat BEPS, but it decided that a switch to formula apportionment would not solve the problem.'
69. For examples of discussions in the doctrine on alternative allocation methods such as combinations of the arm's length principle and formula apportionment *see* J. Scott Wilkie, 'Reflecting on the "Arm's Length Principle": What Is the "Principle"? Where Next?' in Wolfgang Schön and Kai A. Konrad (eds), *Fundamentals of International Transfer Pricing in Law and Economics* (Springer 2012) 152–156. On the feasibility of implementing features of a system of formula apportionment under the arm's length principle *see* Romero J.S. Tavares, 'Multinational Firm Theory and International Tax Law: Seeking Coherence' (2016) 8 World Tax Journal 243, 274. *See also* Reuven S. Avi-Yonah and Ilan Benshalom, 'Formulary Apportionment – Myths and Prospects' (2011) 3 World Tax Journal 371, where the authors at 372 suggest 'a hybrid tax regime which incorporates elements from both ALS (…) and formulary arrangements for the hard-to-source residuals where there are no comparables'.
70. *See* Reuven S. Avi-Yonah, 'Between Formulary Apportionment and the OECD Guidelines: A Proposal for Reconciliation' (2010) 2 World Tax Journal 3, 4: 'Once you do not base the ALS on finding comparables, then it is not very meaningful to say that a particular method is or is not compatible with the ALS, because if there are no comparables you cannot prove that the result reached by that method was not what unrelated parties would have done at arm's length'.
71. *See* e.g., Michael C. Durst, 'Beyond BEPS: A Tax Policy Agenda for Developing Countries' (2014) 18 ICTD Working Paper < https://assets.publishing.service.gov.uk/media/57a089c1ed915d62 2c0003ab/WP18-FINAL.pdf > accessed 11 February 2018, 6.
72. *See* Paul W. Kahn, 'Freedom and Method' in Rob van Gestel, Hans-W. Micklitz, and Edward L. Rubin (eds), *Rethinking Legal Scholarship – A Transatlantic Dialogue* (Cambridge University Press 2017) 499.

implications of the selectivity test on the tax rules implementing the allocation methods, for such rules to be drafted or interpreted in a way that complies with the requirements of Article 107(1) of the TFEU. Accordingly, given the superior value of European law over national or treaty-based tax rules, the research method that is made necessary by the purpose of this study is the legal dogmatic method.[73] This research method aims at clarifying the content of the law on the basis of an analysis of various legal sources, in particular EU primary and secondary law, tax treaties, national rules, national court cases, preparatory works, soft law, and the academic literature.[74]

While the purpose of this book requires relying on the legal dogmatic method, the use of this research method does not come without difficulties. These difficulties are twofold. On the one hand, they are due to the different positions in the hierarchy of norms of the legal sources that are considered in the book. On the other hand, the methodological difficulties faced in this research project come from the lack of precise material content of some of the legal sources that are being investigated. I will explain these methodological difficulties in more details, and expose how I address them in the book. To start with, the selectivity criterion stems from hard law, not from soft law, although useful guidance is provided by various sources of soft law.[75] The sources of hard law in the area of State aid are the provisions of the TFEU, the rulings of the Union courts, as well as the decisions taken by the European Commission in application of the State aid rules. All these sources of law are binding on the Member States, except for the decisions taken by the European Commission that have been annulled by the Union courts.

These sources of hard law provide various levels of guidance with respect to the application of the rules on State aid. Article 107(1) of the TFEU is generally formulated and is not sufficient to fully apply the selectivity test to the allocation methods. Therefore, since the purpose of this study cannot be achieved on the basis of the sole wording of Article 107(1) of the TFEU, the content of the selectivity test needs to be filled with the case law of the Union courts, as well as the practice of the European Commission that is consistent with that case law, so as to find elements of answer to the research question investigated in this book. Yet, little guidance is provided on these

---

73. On the legal dogmatic method, *see* Jan Hellner, *Metodproblem i rättsvetenskapen: studier i förmögenhetsrätt* (Jure 2001) 22–24; Nils Jareborg, *Rättsdogmatik som vetenskap*, (2004) Svensk Juristtidning 1.
74. In this respect, a parallel can be made between the use of legal sources by courts, and in the academic literature: *see* e.g., Roger Persson Österman, *Kontinuitetsprincipen i den svenska inkomstbeskattningen* (Juristförlaget 1997) 18.
75. A relevant source of interpretation is the notice on the notion of State aid issued in 2016 by the European Commission. However, this notice is not binding on the Member States, and cannot constitute more than an informative source to interpret the selectivity criterion: *see* Commission Notice on the notion of State aid as referred to in Art. 107(1) of the Treaty on the Functioning of the European Union [2016] OJ C 262/1. As all the communications issued by the European Commission, the notice is binding only on the Commission, not on the Member States. For an example with respect to the banking communication (Communication from the Commission on the application, from 1 August 2013, of State aid rules to support measures in favour of banks in the context of the financial crisis [2013] OJ C 216/1), *see* Case C-526/14, *Kotnik and others*, ECLI:EU:C:2016:570, para. 45: 'the Banking Communication must be interpreted as meaning that it is not binding on the Member States'.

Chapter 1: Introduction

issues by the case law of the Union courts.[76] Most of the questions analysed in this research project had not been subject to settled case law at the time of writing this book. The case law of the CJEU in the area of State aid is also evolving, and is sometimes difficult to reconcile so as to come to a clear meaning of the notion of selectivity. Several decisions taken by the European Commission include analyses of the questions that are in the scope of this study,[77] but these decisions have been appealed, so the final answers had not been provided by the Union courts at the time of writing this book. Consequently, the interpretation of the rules on State aid by the European Commission is taken into account in this research project, but it is not taken for granted. In the lack of clear guidance provided by the Union courts on several questions of principle, how to achieve the purpose of this book through relying on the legal dogmatic method?

First of all, reliance on the legal dogmatic method is not, per se, precluded by the lack of case law of the Union courts relating to the research question analysed in this book. The primary source of law is Article 107(1) of the TFEU; despite the lack of application of this article by the Union courts to cases concerning the allocation methods, the principle remains, that of prohibition of illegal State aid, as interpreted by the CJEU in various cases. Moreover, even if the Union courts had ruled on all issues included in the scope of this study, that would not prevent research from being dedicated, on the basis of the legal dogmatic method, to the intrinsic meaning of Article 107(1) of the TFEU, or to the analysis of the reasoning of the courts.

If no clear guidance was provided by the Union courts on the selectivity analysis of the allocation methods at the time of writing this book, it must be emphasised that these courts have ruled in numerous State aid cases, some of which concern issues of principle that are similar to those analysed in this book. A methodological question is, accordingly, whether or not State aid cases that have been ruled outside the field of tax law, or in relation to other tax issues than the allocation methods, are at all relevant for this study.

There is no methodological hinder to generally exclude the consideration of cases ruled in other fields of tax law than the allocation methods, or even cases ruled outside the area of tax law. Three types of arguments support the consideration of cases ruled on other matters than the allocation methods for the purpose of this study. The first argument comes from the Treaty itself: all cases applying the rules on State aid need to implement similarly Article 107(1) of the TFEU, since no provision of the Treaty justifies applying differently the rules on State aid to different areas of national law. The

---

76. For example, some guidance, although not sufficient to fully analyse the topic of this book, is provided by Joined Cases C-182/03 and C-217/03, *Kingdom of Belgium and Forum 187 ASBL v. Commission of the European Communities*, ECLI:EU:C:2006:416.
77. *See* particularly Commission Decision (EU) 2017/502 of 21 October 2015 on State aid SA.38374 (2014/C ex 2014/NN) implemented by the Netherlands to Starbucks [2017] OJ L 83/38; Commission Decision (EU) 2016/2326 of 21 October 2015 on State aid SA.38375 (2014/C ex 2014/NN) which Luxembourg granted to Fiat [2016] OJ L 351/1; Commission Decision (EU) 2016/1699 of 11 January 2016 on the excess profit exemption State aid scheme SA.37667 (2015/C) (ex 2015/NN) implemented by Belgium [2016] OJ L 260/61; Commission Decision (EU) 2017/1283 of 30 August 2016 on State aid SA.38373 (2014/C) (ex 2014/NN) (ex 2014/CP) implemented by Ireland to Apple [2017] OJ L 187/1.

second argument stems from the case law of the CJEU and the way the Court has been reasoning when applying State aid law: the CJEU does not limit itself to referring to other cases ruled in the area of tax law, but considers cases issued outside this field, sometimes through reasoning by analogy.[78] The third argument relates to the method of teleological interpretation that is made necessary by the nature of the law of the EU,[79] and that is often – albeit not always – applied by the CJEU.[80] According to the method of teleological interpretation, rules are interpreted in the light of their purpose.[81] Since the purpose of the State aid rules does not change with the area of application, the interpretation of these rules may have a broader reach than the *in casu* applications made by the CJEU in particular rulings.[82]

The above does not mean that all State aid cases are transposable to other areas of application of State aid law. It simply means that the findings of certain rulings may be considered when reasoning in other areas of the law that are also subject to the State aid rules, similarly to how the CJEU is reasoning. To avoid the risk that incorrect parallels are made in this study, and to minimise the subjective dimension that is inherent to research conducted in the field of EU law,[83] the following precautions are taken. Cases that are issued outside the field of tax law are only mentioned as examples when they are relevant from the point of view of principle for the purpose of this study. No conclusions are directly reached based on such non-tax cases. Cases ruled on tax

---

78. On the use of analogies by the CJEU, see Jörgen Hettne and Ida Otken Eriksson, *EU-Rättslig Metod: Teori Och Genomslag i Svensk Rättstillämpning* (2nd edn, Norstedts Juridik 2011) 165–167.
79. In this respect, see the analysis of Gutmann on the exercise of judicial power by the CJEU in tax cases: Daniel Gutmann, 'Some Theoretical Thoughts on Judicial Power and Tax Law, with a Particular Focus on the ECJ' in Luc Hinnekens and Philippe Hinnekens (eds), *A Vision of Taxes Within and Outside European Borders – Festschrift in Honor of Prof. Dr. Frans Vanistendael* (Kluwer Law International 2008) 485; Jane Reichel, 'EU-Rättslig Metod' in Fredric Korling and Mauro Zamboni (eds), *Juridisk Metodlära* (Studentlitteratur 2013) 109, 122.
80. See Jörgen Hettne and Ida Otken Eriksson, *EU-Rättslig Metod: Teori Och Genomslag i Svensk Rättstillämpning* (2nd edn, Norstedts Juridik 2011) 168–170.
81. See particularly Case 283/81, *Srl CILFIT and Lanificio di Gavardo SpA v. Ministry of Health*, ECLI:EU:C:1982:335, para. 20: 'every provision of Community law must be placed in its context and interpreted in the light of the provisions of Community law as a whole, regard being had to the objectives thereof and to its state of evolution at the date on which the provision in question is to be applied'. More generally, it can be observed that the Grand Chamber of the CJEU has adhered to the interpretation of international treaties in the light of the Vienna Convention on the Law of Treaties: see Case C-648/15, *Republic of Austria v. Federal Republic of Germany*, ECLI:EU:C:2017:664, para. 39: 'it follows from the provisions of the Vienna Convention, to which both the Republic of Austria and the Federal Republic of Germany are parties, that a treaty must be interpreted in good faith in accordance with the ordinary meaning to be given to its terms in their context and in the light of its object and purpose, taking into account any relevant rules of international law applicable in the relations between the parties to that treaty'.
82. Poiares Maduro argues even that teleological interpretation in EU law does not 'refer exclusively to a purpose driven interpretation of the relevant legal rules', but also 'to a particular systemic understanding of the EU legal order that permeates the interpretation of all its rules': see Miguel Poiares Maduro, 'Interpreting European Law: Judicial Adjudication in a Context of Constitutional Pluralism' (2007) 1 European Journal of Legal Studies 137, 140.
83. See Jan Komárek, 'Legal Reasoning in EU Law' in Anthony Arnull and Damian Chalmers (eds), *The Oxford Handbook of European Union Law* (Oxford University Press 2015) 28.

Chapter 1: Introduction

issues that do not concern the allocation methods but that relate to matters of principle that are relevant for this study are taken into account. Such cases can support an argumentation, without being decisive.

After considering the lack of guidance in the primary law of the EU, I now turn to the allocation methods. Similarly to the selectivity criterion, the allocation methods lack a precisely determined material content, but for different reasons. The material content that is given in this book to the allocation methods does not stem from hard law but from soft law, doctrine, or even assumptions, given that the study does not consider a body of existing national or treaty-based rules, but different options to legislate or to interpret national law. This is a consequence of the fact that the study is conducted at a theoretical level, without testing whether national rules or tax treaty provisions entail a selective treatment. It is also a consequence of the allocation methods as such, in particular a generally formulated arm's length provision, which is intrinsically abstract, as it relies on a principle. To give some material content to the arm's length principle, and especially to a generally formulated arm's length provision, I rely on the 2017 OECD transfer pricing guidelines. These guidelines are useful but they are not binding,[84] and remain in many respects very general. The material content of the other allocation methods does not, apart from a few exceptions,[85] rely on a comprehensive source like the guidelines; instead, the material content that is given to transfer pricing safe harbours and to systems of formula apportionment relies mostly on the academic literature, examples of provisions found in the systems of formula apportionment existing in the US and Canada, or the proposal for a CCCTB.[86]

The consequence from a methodological perspective of the lack of precisely determined material content of the selectivity criterion and of the allocation methods, is that the analyses included in this book only provide contributions at an abstract level, by reconciling my understanding of the selectivity criterion with the arm's length principle as it is described in the 2017 OECD transfer pricing guidelines, and the assumptions I make with respect to the material content of the two other allocation methods. Therefore, the findings of this study cannot be directly applied to the selectivity test of an allocation method in force in a Member State. To that end, the analyses included in this book need to be supplemented by the consideration of the applicable national laws and tax treaties.

Before concluding this section on the method of research employed in this book, it should be stressed that the methodological difficulties described above are not unique to this project; they are rather common to research dedicated to the application of the primary law of the EU to the principles of direct taxation relied on by the Member

---

84. Although the OECD transfer pricing guidelines represent the most developed guidance for the application of the arm's length principle, and despite the fact that the guidelines are widely relied on, they have no precisely determined material content, and are not legally binding; in this respect, *see* the developments in section 2.3.2 of this book. Even if the guidelines were binding, they could hardly have a precisely determined material content, something that is a consequence of the reliance on a general principle instead of concrete material rules.
85. An exception concerns the transfer pricing safe harbours described in the 2017 OECD transfer pricing guidelines.
86. *See* European Commission, 'Proposal for a Council Directive on a Common Consolidated Corporate Tax Base (CCCTB)' COM(2016) 683 final, in particular at Art. 28.

States when exercising their sovereign power to tax. Similarly to the study performed in this book, scholars have conducted research at a theoretical level on the application of State aid law to various types of tax rules without relying on national law, but rather through considering principles of taxation or typical ways of drafting tax rules at an abstract level.[87] This is partly a consequence of the lack of guidance provided in the case law, and of the dynamic nature of both the State aid rules and tax rules.[88] There are examples of studies relating to the application of the rules on State aid to the arm's length principle,[89] tax treaties,[90] patent boxes,[91] or VAT.[92] These studies include at least some developments at a theoretical level, with no consideration for national rules. Moreover, part of the research in EU law needs to be carried out in a sole theoretical manner, with no direct connection to the domestic law of the Member States, to contribute to the doctrine at the level of the Union.

1.6 OUTLINE

The outline of this study follows the method of analysis that is mostly relied upon by the Union courts when assessing the selectivity of tax measures. Although this methodology has not always been followed by the Union courts,[93] the CJEU applies it in the vast majority of cases.[94] It is also the method described in the 2016 Commission notice on the notion of State aid.

---

87. For a few, non-exhaustive examples of research conducted at an abstract level without relying on national law, see e.g., Mona Aldestam, *EC State Aid Rules Applied to Taxes* (Uppsala 2005); Claire Micheau, *Droit des Aides d'État et des Subventions en Fiscalité – Droit de l'Union Européenne et de l'OMC* (Larcier 2013); Alexander Rust and Claire Micheau (eds), *State Aid and Tax Law* (Kluwer Law International 2013); Marilyne Sadowsky, *Droit de l'OMC, droit de l'Union européenne et fiscalité directe* (Larcier 2013); Wolfgang Schön and Edoardo Traversa (eds), *State Aid Law and Business Taxation* (Springer 2016).
88. On the dynamic nature of EU law, see Jörgen Hettne and Ida Otken Eriksson, *EU-Rättslig Metod: Teori Och Genomslag i Svensk Rättstillämpning* (2nd edn, Norstedts Juridik 2011) 165.
89. See e.g., Richard Lyal, 'Transfer Pricing Rules and State Aid' (2015) 38 Fordham International Law Journal 1017; Liza Lovdahl Gormsen, 'EU State Aid Law and Transfer Pricing: A Critical Introduction to a New Saga' (2016) 7 Journal of European Competition Law & Practice 369.
90. See e.g., Raymond Luja, 'Tax Treaties and State Aid: Some Thoughts' (2004) 44 European Taxation 234; Christiana Panayi, 'Limitation on Benefits and State Aid' (2004) 44 European Taxation 83.
91. See e.g., Cécile Brokelind, 'Intellectual Property, Taxation and State Aid Law' in Isabelle Richelle, Wolfgang Schön, and Edoardo Traversa (eds), *State Aid Law and Business Taxation* (Springer 2016) 221.
92. See e.g., Ben Terra, 'Value Added Tax and State Aid Law in the European Union' (2012) 40 Intertax 101; Joachim Englisch, 'EU State Aid Rules Applied to Indirect Tax Measures' (2013) 22 EC Tax Review 9.
93. See in particular the de facto selectivity analysis applied in the *Gibraltar* case. See also Joined Cases C-20/15 P and C-21/15 P, *European Commission v. World Duty Free Group*, ECLI:EU:C:2016:624, Opinion of AG Wathelet, footnote 45: 'the classification of a tax system as "selective" is not subject to the identification of a reference framework and a derogation from that framework where a tax system which, instead of laying down general rules applicable to all undertakings from which a derogation is made for certain undertakings, achieves the same result by adjusting and combining the tax rules in such a way that their very application results in a different tax burden for different undertakings'.
94. See Wolfgang Schön, 'Tax Legislation and the Notion of Fiscal Aid: A Review of 5 Years of European Jurisprudence' in Isabelle Richelle, Wolfgang Schön and Edoardo Traversa (eds), *State Aid Law and Business Taxation* (Springer 2016) 8.

Chapter 1: Introduction

This method of analysis implies three main steps: first, the reference system is defined. It is the starting point of the selectivity analysis. Second, it is investigated if a tax measure deviates from the reference system and thus treats differently undertakings that are in a comparable situation in the light of the objective of the reference system. If a difference in treatment is found, the tax measure is considered to be prima facie selective. The third and last step of the method of analysis consists in investigating whether a prima facie selective measure may be justified by the nature or the general scheme of the tax system, and, if this is the case, whether the measure does not go beyond what is necessary to attain the objective it pursues.[95] Although this method of analysis has been subject to criticism in the literature,[96] it is applied in this book given the support of the CJEU in its favour.

The research conducted in the book is divided in two main parts. In the first part, I will address the elements of the selectivity test that, in my opinion, are common to the three allocation methods: the determination of the reference system (Chapter 2), the potential relevance of the market economy operator test (Chapter 3), and the comparability analysis (Chapter 4). In the second part of the book, I turn to the investigation of how the selectivity test applies to each of the three allocation methods. This starts by analysing the prima facie selectivity of each allocation method (Chapters 5, 6, and 7), before considering whether prima facie selective measures are able to be justified and, if so, whether they are in line with the principle of proportionality (Chapter 8). The outline of the book is justified and described in more details below.

The book starts with an introductory chapter that describes mainly the problem considered in this book, the purpose and limitations of the study, the method of research, as well as the outline. After the introductory chapter, the first question that needs to be investigated is the reference system that is relevant for the purpose of the selectivity test of an allocation method. That includes the question of the potential intrinsic implications of Article 107(1) of the TFEU on the material content of an allocation method. This is the purpose of Chapter 2 of the book. Next, it is studied in Chapter 3 whether the market economy operator test might be of relevance for the selectivity assessment of the allocation methods. This test, often relied on in the practice of the European Commission and in the case law of the Union courts, requires the Member States to act in certain cases as if they were private operators subject to the market forces. It is studied in this chapter whether the concept of market economy operator test may be relevant for the selectivity assessment of the allocation methods, or if it may guide the interpretation of the arm's length principle under the rules on State aid, given that they both rely on the effects of the market forces. Although the market economy operator test is normally not applicable to the notion of selectivity, certain positions taken by the European Commission make it necessary to raise the

---

95. *See* Joined Cases C-78/08 to C-80/08, *Paint Graphos*, ECLI:EU:C:2011:550, para. 75. The principle of proportionality is also found at Art. 5(4) of the TEU with respect to 'Union action'.
96. *See* e.g., Michael Lang, 'Tax Rulings and State Aid Law' (2015) 3 British Tax Review 391, 393; Thomas Jaeger, 'Tax Incentives Under State Aid Law: A Competition Law Perspective' in Isabelle Richelle, Wolfgang Schön and Edoardo Traversa (eds), *State Aid Law and Business Taxation* (Springer 2016) 50.

question, in particular given the reliance by the Commission on the notion of 'market-based outcomes',[97] which seems close to the market economy operator test.[98]

Chapter 4 is dedicated to the comparability analysis. This supposes to first determine the objective of the reference system, as it is in the light of that objective that the assessment of a difference in treatment and the comparability analysis are made. It is then investigated which undertakings are in a comparable legal and factual situation, in the light of the objective of the reference system.

Chapters 5, 6, and 7 consider whether a generally formulated arm's length provision, transfer pricing safe harbours, and systems of formula apportionment with firm-specific factors might, respectively, be prima facie selective. This supposes to analyse, for each allocation method, whether it deviates from the reference system (de jure selectivity) or, in the lack of explicit difference in treatment in the law,[99] whether the effects of an allocation method may favour certain undertakings (de facto selectivity). In addition, certain aspects of the application of the arm's length principle are analysed in Chapter 5, to consider whether prima facie selectivity may stem from such applications of the principle; indeed, the positions taken by the European Commission imply a preference for certain applications of the arm's length principle, which could make other applications of this principle prima facie selective.

The last step of the selectivity test consists in assessing whether a tax measure that is prima facie selective may be justified by the nature or the general scheme of the system, and whether a measure that is justified is also proportionate in that it does not go beyond what is necessary to attain the objective it pursues. This is the purpose of Chapter 8. The findings of the study are reconciled in Chapter 9 of the book.

The two parts of the book, including the nine chapters, are summarised below:

- Chapter 1: Introduction
  Part I: Elements of the Selectivity Test That Are Common to the Three Allocation Methods
- Chapter 2: Determination of the Reference System
- Chapter 3: Potential Relevance of the Market Economy Operator Test
- Chapter 4: Comparability Analysis
  Part II: Selectivity Assessment of the Three Allocation Methods
- Chapter 5: Prima Facie Selectivity of a Generally Formulated Arm's Length Provision
- Chapter 6: Prima Facie Selectivity of Transfer Pricing Safe Harbours
- Chapter 7: Prima Facie Selectivity of a System of Formula Apportionment with Firm-Specific Factors
- Chapter 8: Justification and Proportionality Tests
- Chapter 9: Conclusion

---

97. *See* Commission Notice on the notion of State aid as referred to in Art. 107(1) of the Treaty on the Functioning of the European Union [2016] OJ C 262/1, paras 171–174.
98. *See* Michael Honoré, 'State Aid and Taxation – All Clear?' (2015) 24 European State Aid Law Quarterly 306.
99. *See* Joined Cases C-106/09 P and C-107/09 P, *European Commission v. Government of Gibraltar*, ECLI:EU:C:2011:732, para. 92.

PART I   Elements of the Selectivity Test That Are Common to the Three Allocation Methods

The first part of this book is devoted to the analysis of the elements of the selectivity test that are common to the three allocation methods: the determination of the reference system (Chapter 2), the potential relevance of the market economy operator test (Chapter 3), and the comparability analysis (Chapter 4).

CHAPTER 2
Determination of the Reference System

2.1 INTRODUCTION

The main method of analysis for assessing prima facie selectivity in tax cases consists in making a comparison between the taxes levied on an undertaking in a given situation, with the 'normal' levy of taxes according to the so-called reference system applicable in a given Member State.[100] The reference system is a set of norms that is used as a benchmark to investigate whether there has been a deviation from the normal application of the tax system that only certain undertakings could benefit from.[101] The identification of the reference system is an important step of a State aid analysis,[102]

---

100. This methodology has not always been clearly established. It is now settled case law that the determination of the reference system, i.e., what is sometimes described as 'normal taxation', is a prerequisite for conducting the selectivity test of a tax measure (*see* particularly Case C-88/03, *Portuguese Republic v. Commission of the European Communities*, ECLI:EU:C:2006:511, para. 56: 'The determination of the reference system has a particular importance in the case of tax measures, since the very existence of an advantage may be established only when compared with "normal" taxation'). Certain cases, however, do not follow the same methodology, when the rules at hand do not include a principle and an exception, but when their effects favour certain undertakings.
101. *See* Commission Notice on the notion of State aid as referred to in Art. 107(1) of the Treaty on the Functioning of the European Union [2016] OJ C 262/1, para. 133.
102. On the importance of the determination of the reference system *see*, among others, Vanessa Hernández Guerrero, 'Defining the Balance Between Free Competition and Tax Sovereignty in EC and WTO Law: The "Due Respect" to the General Tax System' (2004) 5 German Law Journal 87. For a contrary view, whereby the determination of the reference system does not influence the outcome of the analysis, *see* Liza Lovdahl Gormsen 'EU State Aid Law and Transfer Pricing: A Critical Introduction to a New Saga' (2016) 7 Journal of European Competition Law & Practice 369, 377. *See also* Case C-236/16, *Asociación Nacional de Grandes Empresas de Distribución (ANGED) v. Generalitat de Catalunya*, ECLI:EU:C:2017:852, Opinion of AG Kokott, para. 88, where the determination of a normal tax system was found not 'decisive', regard being had to the findings of the CJEU in the *Gibraltar* and *World Duty Free Group* cases.

since the selectivity test may, in certain cases, have different outcomes depending on which reference system is used, and which comparator within the reference system is relied on.[103]

Nevertheless, the identification of the reference system and of an exception to it, is not a necessary step of the selectivity analysis. There are situations where a reference system cannot be clearly identified, or where its correct identification does not influence the outcome of the selectivity analysis. For example, when several rules coexist, each rule may constitute a separate reference system; alternatively, the rules might need to be considered together as a single reference system. In such cases, instead of relying on the identification of a main rule and of an exception to that main rule, the focus of the selectivity test is on the existence of a difference in treatment between undertakings that are in a comparable situation. In such cases, the selectivity test is close to a principle of non-discrimination. In other cases, a rule may be designed with no exception from the normal system of taxation (i.e., the rule is designed in a non-discriminatory manner), apparently treating all undertakings in a similar way; however, the effects of such a rule may be to differentiate between undertakings that are in a comparable situation. There are also cases where a difference in treatment exists, no matter if the reference system is defined in a broader or a narrower manner: a narrow definition would be close to the difference in treatment between certain undertakings, whereas a broad definition would encompass other undertakings, but without eliminating the existence of the difference in treatment; only the derogation itself could constitute a reference system that has a material effect on the selectivity analysis.[104] Accordingly, I agree with the view suggested by Advocate General Kokott that the identification of the reference system is not necessarily 'decisive'.[105] It

---

103. An illustration is a decision of the European Commission relating to the exemption from corporate tax for certain public undertakings, notably for six undertakings that operated Dutch public seaports. If the regime applicable to public undertakings operating seaports is deemed as the reference system, the existence of State aid as a consequence of the exemption is highly unlikely, as this is precisely what the system prescribes. Conversely, if the reference system is the general system of corporate income tax, State aid is more likely as certain undertakings are exempted from this tax: see Commission Decision 2016/634 of 21 January 2016 on aid measure SA.25338 (2014/C) (ex E 3/2008 and ex CP 115/2004) implemented by the Netherlands – Corporate tax exemption for public undertakings [2016] OJ L 113/148, where at para. 71 the Commission considers that the reference system should be the Dutch system for corporate taxation.
104. For example, in the case of the UK CFC rules, no matter if the reference system is defined broadly (the whole CFC regime) or narrowly (the CFC regime applying to 'artificial diversion for (deemed) non-trading finance profits'), a difference in treatment would exist anyway: see State aid SA.44896 (2017/C) (ex 2017/NN) – Potential State aid scheme regarding UK Group Financing Exemption – Invitation to submit comments pursuant to Art. 108(2) of the Treaty on the Functioning of the European Union [2017] OJ C 400/10, footnote 52. Only a very narrow definition of the reference system would result in no difference in treatment, if the reference system consists in the derogation to the main rule in favour of the undertakings that are not subject to the normal CFC taxation: when the reference system consists in the derogation itself, then the choice of the reference system indeed is of relevance, because no difference in treatment stems from the law.
105. See Case C-236/16, *Asociación Nacional de Grandes Empresas de Distribución (ANGED) v. Generalitat de Catalunya*, ECLI:EU:C:2017:852, Opinion of AG Kokott, para. 88. Similarly, see also Case C-100/15 P, *Netherlands Maritime Technology Association, formerly Scheepsbouw Nederland v. European Commission*, ECLI:EU:C:2016:254, para. 76.

Chapter 2: Determination of the Reference System

nevertheless remains an important step of the selectivity test, at least to correctly identify the objective of the measure in the light of which the comparability analysis is performed.[106] There are also cases where the determination of the reference system is decisive, if one considers that an exception to a main rule constitutes a reference system.

The research questions investigated in this chapter relate to the identification of the reference system that is relevant for the selectivity test of different methods for the allocation of the corporate tax base among multinational enterprises. This chapter is divided in two sections. First, it is investigated whether the reference system is made of the domestic rules of a Member State, or if Article 107(1) of the TFEU may constitute, or influence the reference system (section 2.2). This question is indeed raised by the European Commission in several decisions, as well as in the 2016 notice on the notion of State aid, whereby the Treaty could have an impact on the determination of the reference system. Second, it is focused on the determination of the material content of the reference system, based on the conclusions reached in the previous section (section 2.3). The conclusions of this chapter are presented in section 2.4.

2.2 THE RELEVANCE OF ARTICLE 107(1) OF THE TFEU FOR THE DETERMINATION OF THE REFERENCE SYSTEM

2.2.1 Introductory Remarks and Peculiarities of the Allocation Methods

Traditionally, when assessing the potential selectivity of a domestic tax rule, the Union courts have been testing its compatibility with State aid law in the light of the domestic tax system. This seems fully correct, as a Member State may grant an aid or relieve an undertaking from a burden, and thus influence its competitive position, through the exercise of its sovereign prerogatives as a lawmaker. This is a consequence of the principle of legality, which in most Member States is a constitutional principle that implies that taxes may only be levied as a result of a decision made by Parliament or another State body that has the authority to levy taxes.[107] It is logical that the exercise of the sovereign power to tax is subject to State aid control, given the primacy of the rules on State aid over the domestic laws of the Member States: there is a need to test the potential selectivity of the tax rules in force in the Member States to effectively implement the State aid control of national tax measures. Consequently, it is tempting to conclude that the reference system should consist of the domestic tax rules in force

---

106. In this respect, Advocate General Wahl found the identification of the reference system 'of crucial importance' (*see* Case C-203/16 P, *Dirk Andres (administrator of Heitkamp BauHolding GmbH), previously Heitkamp BauHolding GmbH v. European Commission*, ECLI:EU:C:2017:1017, Opinion of AG Wahl, para. 99), emphasising also the different position of Advocate General Kokott (*see* footnote 36 of the Opinion).
107. On the principle of legality in taxation *see* Frans Vanistendael, 'Legal Framework for Taxation' in Victor Thuronyi (ed), 1 *Tax Law Design and Drafting* (International Monetary Fund 1996) 15; Anders Hultqvist, *Legalitetsprincipen vid inkomstbeskattningen* (Juristförlaget 1995).

in a Member State, which would also apply to the allocation methods. This would make Article 107(1) of the TFEU irrelevant as to the determination of the material content of the reference system.

However, when it comes to the tax rules for allocating the corporate tax base among multinational enterprises, there is a certain degree of complexity that needs to be emphasised before reaching conclusions on the relevance of Article 107(1) of the TFEU for the determination of the reference system. The rules on the allocation of the corporate tax base have a special nature, which may need a peculiar analytical framework for the purpose of the application of the rules on State aid. It is especially legitimate to ask whether the selectivity test should only be performed in the light of the domestic law in force in a Member State, or whether the application of the selectivity test to the allocation methods may require an additional or alternative benchmark, so as to enable a full application of the State aid rules. In this respect, the European Commission has argued in several decisions, as well as in the 2016 notice on the notion of State aid,[108] that Article 107(1) of the TFEU has a material content on its own when it comes to the allocation methods. According to the Commission, State aid law would provide an alternative benchmark for the determination of the reference system and imply an obligation to tax associated enterprises in accordance with the arm's length principle, 'independently of whether a Member State has incorporated this principle into its national legal system'.[109] This position, which contrasts with the earlier findings of the European Commission,[110] touches upon a fundamental question, that of the fiscal sovereignty of the Member States in view of the rules on State aid.[111] Important as it is, I will not fully consider the question of the fiscal sovereignty of the Member States, but will only investigate the relevance of Article 107(1) of the TFEU for the determination of the reference system.

To start with, the nature of a corporate income tax requires that the tax system includes certain basic rules that fulfil different functions to capture the income earned by corporations. These rules, which are described here as the basic corporate income tax rules, aim – among other purposes – at defining which entities are subject to tax, which items of income are taxable or exempt from tax, whether or not expenses are deductible, and at what point in time revenues and expenses are taken into account.

---

108. *See* Commission Notice on the notion of State aid as referred to in Art. 107(1) of the Treaty on the Functioning of the European Union [2016] OJ C 262/1, para. 172.
109. *See* Commission Decision (EU) 2017/502 of 21 October 2015 on State aid SA.38374 (2014/C ex 2014/NN) implemented by the Netherlands to Starbucks [2017] OJ L 83/38, para. 264; Commission Decision (EU) 2017/1283 of 30 August 2016 on State aid SA.38373 (2014/C) (ex 2014/NN) (ex 2014/CP) implemented by Ireland to Apple [2017] OJ L 187/1, para. 257.
110. *See* e.g., Commission Decision 2004/76/EC of 13 May 2003 on the aid scheme implemented by France for headquarters and logistics centres [2004] OJ L 23/1, para. 45, where the Commission, to test whether a national measure implemented the arm's length principle, compared it to the domestic law in force in the Member State as well as the tax treaties it had concluded, with no reference to non-binding legal sources.
111. For a comparable position of the European Commission, where the reference system is not the legal system in place in a Member State, but what the Commission considers to be the right system, *see* Commission Decision (EU) 2018/160 of 30 June 2017 on the State aid SA.44351 (2016/C) (ex 2016/NN) implemented by Poland for the tax on the retail sector [2018] OJ L 29/38, para. 49, last sentence.

Chapter 2: Determination of the Reference System

These basic tax rules are inherent to the concept of income, and are thus relevant for the taxation of all undertakings, no matter whether they carry out domestic or cross-border activities, and irrespective of their size or membership in a corporate group.

The application of the selectivity test to the basic tax rules does not need, in most cases, to rely on another benchmark that the one provided by the tax system itself. Of course, certain basic rules may raise difficult selectivity issues, as illustrated by cases such as *Paint Graphos* (in relation to the types of entities subject to the corporate income tax) or *World Duty Free Group* (in relation to the types of acquisitions of shares that may be depreciated). Yet even in these cases the selectivity test does not require that the reference system be extended beyond the domestic law: the selectivity test can be carried out on the sole basis of the corporate income tax system because the difference in treatment stems from the domestic law. The need of the tax system to include a difference in treatment can also be fully assessed as part of the justification analysis, in the light of the principles that are intrinsic to the domestic corporate income tax system.

If we now consider the allocation methods, the need for an additional or alternative benchmark so as to carry out the selectivity test is stronger. The problem that is raised by multinational enterprises that conduct cross-border activities is that the basic corporate income tax rules may not be sufficient to ensure that the members of such enterprises are taxed in accordance with the objective[112] of the corporate income tax system,[113] thereby revealing a potential difference in treatment with other categories of undertakings that are taxed in accordance with that objective. When the members of a multinational enterprise pursue strictly their own interests, or do business only with third parties, the basic corporate income tax rules may suffice to tax each group member on its net income, i.e., in accordance with the objective of the corporate income tax system.[114] If, in contrast, the members of the group enter into cross-border intercompany transactions, the application of the basic corporate income tax rules of each country where the group is established may not enable the taxation of each group member on its net income, mainly because income may be shifted from one country to another through the pricing of the transactions. This shows the peculiar nature of the allocation methods: they are not needed as such to implement the basic functions of a corporate income tax, but they become vital in the presence of multinational enterprises that enter into intercompany transactions. The function of an allocation method is indeed twofold: it aims at: (i) sharing the income of multinational enterprises on a cross-border basis, and at (ii) safeguarding the tax base of the countries where group members are located.[115] These functions are not fulfilled by the

---

112. *See* section 4.2 for the determination of the objective of a corporate income tax system.
113. *See* Commission Notice on the notion of State aid as referred to in Art. 107(1) of the Treaty on the Functioning of the European Union [2016] OJ C 262/1, para. 133, where the Commission defines the reference system through taking into account its scope and objectives.
114. It is indeed suggested in section 4.2 that the objective of most corporate income tax systems is the taxation of corporations on their net income.
115. Concurring, *see* Case C-382/16, *Hornbach-Baumarkt AG v. Finanzamt Landau*, ECLI:EU:C: 2017:974, Opinion of AG Bobek, para. 24.

application of the basic corporate income tax rules. Therefore, from a fiscal perspective, a Member State would normally need an allocation method, if it aims at achieving the objective of its corporate income tax system.

May the above observation change the legal source of the reference system? If the reference system is made of the sole domestic tax rules, with no effect of Article 107(1) of the TFEU on the content of the reference system, the State aid control of the taxation of multinational enterprises will be limited to national law. The *Apple* case provides an interesting illustration of the consequences that may arise as a result of a domestic system that includes the basic corporate income tax rules, but that lacks an allocation method, or has an inappropriate method that does not enable taxation in accordance with the objective of the tax system.[116] In that case, it is clear that limiting the reference system to the domestic law results in a twofold problem. On the one hand, the lack of allocation method (or the existence of an allocation method that is not proper) threatens the objectives of the corporate income tax system: group members may be subject to tax on the basis of an income that does not correspond to their net income. In other words, the objective of a corporate income tax system that aims at taxing all undertakings on their net income may not be achieved with respect to multinational enterprises that are not subject to an allocation method. On the other hand, the objectives of the rules on State aid are also threatened by the lack of allocation method (or the existence of an inappropriately designed allocation method), as there is a risk of difference in treatment between different undertakings, especially between independent and associated enterprises that are members of multinational corporate groups. A difference in treatment between different undertakings is likely to have an impact on their competitive position, and thus on the trade between the Member States.

Consequently, if only certain undertakings, because of the lacks of national law, eventually escape the levy of tax in accordance with the objective of a tax system, such a system might entail a difference in treatment between different undertakings that falls within the scope of the State aid rules because of the inequality created by the system and its potential impact on competition and trade. It could thus be wondered whether Article 107(1) of the TFEU could imply an obligation to legislate in a certain way, to avoid such differences in treatment with respect to the objectives of a corporate income tax system, and the consequences on competition and trade implied by such differences in treatment. In other words, a corporate income tax system might need an additional or alternative reference system to comply with the rules on State aid, when the domestic rules do not enable the similar taxation of all undertakings that are in a comparable situation.

The need for an alternative or additional benchmark that would supplement the domestic rules is precisely what the European Commission has been arguing in several documents and decisions. The Commission has suggested that the reference system, if necessary, be extended beyond the domestic rules to contain, as an allocation method,

---

116. *See* Commission Decision (EU) 2017/1283 of 30 August 2016 on State aid SA.38373 (2014/C) (ex 2014/NN) (ex 2014/CP) implemented by Ireland to Apple [2017] OJ L 187/1.

Chapter 2: Determination of the Reference System

the arm's length principle.[117] This arm's length principle, which may materially deviate from the arm's length principle described in the OECD transfer pricing guidelines,[118] would apply 'independently of whether a Member State has incorporated this principle into its national legal system'.[119] The main argument brought in support of this view is not an economic one, but a legal one.

Before considering this argument, it is worth observing that the economically most efficient method to allocate the corporate tax base is not necessarily the market price, which the arm's length principle to a great extent relies on; other allocation methods have been considered in the doctrine, such as the marginal cost of intercompany transactions.[120] Even in the area of State aid and outside the field of taxes, the

---

117. *See* Commission Notice on the notion of State aid as referred to in Art. 107(1) of the Treaty on the Functioning of the European Union [2016] OJ C 262/1, para. 172; European Commission, 'DG Competition Working Paper on State Aid and Tax Rulings' (2016) < http://ec.europa.eu/competition/state_aid/legislation/working_paper_tax_rulings.pdf > accessed 6 February 2018, para. 4 where it is indicated that 'a fiscal measure that endorses a method for determining an integrated group company's taxable profit in a manner that does not result in a reliable approximation of a market-based outcome in line with the arm's length principle can confer a selective advantage upon its recipient'. *See also* Commission Decision (EU) 2017/502 of 21 October 2015 on State aid SA.38374 (2014/C ex 2014/NN) implemented by the Netherlands to Starbucks [2017] OJ L 83/38, para. 264 (last sentence).
118. An example is provided by the *Apple* decision where the interpretation of the arm's length principle made by the European Commission seems at odds with the OECD transfer pricing guidelines. For instance, in this decision the Commission claims that a large part of the profits of the group shall be taxable in Ireland; however, it has been argued that these profits should normally be taxable in the United States, particularly given the high number of employees performing important functions in the United States as opposed to Ireland: *see* e.g., Romero J.S. Tavares, Bret N. Bogenschneider, and Marta Pankiv, 'The Intersection of EU State Aid and U.S. Tax Deferral: A Spectacle of Fireworks, Smoke, and Mirrors' (2016) 19 Florida Tax Review 121, in particular at 148–149 and 171; Frans Vanistendael, 'Are the EU and U.S. Headed for a Tax War?' (2016) 83 Tax Notes International 1057, 1060; Marc Rasch and Pawel Wroblewski, 'European Commission Decision on Fiat: State Aid Case Explained' (2016) 23 International Transfer Pricing Journal 440; U.S. Department of the Treasury White Paper, *The European Commission's Recent Investigations of Transfer Pricing Rulings* (2016) 19-22. For a diverging view, *see* Alexia Kardachaki and Mart van Hulten, 'Report on the EUCOTAX Conference "State Aid, Intangibles and Rulings"' (2017) 26 EC Tax Review 284, 285, where an argument is reported according to which the arm's length principle under international tax law and under State aid law are 'the same principle'.
119. *See* Commission Notice on the notion of State aid as referred to in Art. 107(1) of the Treaty on the Functioning of the European Union [2016] OJ C 262/1, para. 172; Commission Decision (EU) 2017/502 of 21 October 2015 on State aid SA.38374 (2014/C ex 2014/NN) implemented by the Netherlands to Starbucks [2017] OJ L 83/38, para. 264; Commission Decision (EU) 2017/1283 of 30 August 2016 on State aid SA.38373 (2014/C) (ex 2014/NN) (ex 2014/CP) implemented by Ireland to Apple [2017] OJ L 187/1, para. 257.
120. *See* especially Jack Hirshleifer, 'On the Economics of Transfer Pricing' (1956) 29 The Journal of Business 172, who summarises his arguments by stressing that 'market price is the correct transfer price only where the commodity being transferred is produced in a competitive market, that is, competitive in the theoretical sense that no single producer considers himself large enough to influence price by his own output decision. If the market is imperfectly competitive, or where no market for the transferred commodity exists, the correct procedure is to transfer at marginal cost (given certain simplifying conditions) or at some price between marginal cost and market price in the most general case'. *See also* Bengt Holmström and Jean Tirole, 'Transfer Pricing and Organizational Form' (1991) 7 The Journal of Law, Economics, and Organization 201; Tomáš Buus and Jaroslav Brada, 'Economics of Transfer Pricing Reviewed' (2008) < https://ssrn.com/abstract = 954333 > accessed 18 January 2018.

market forces are not an obligatory and uncontroversial benchmark to assess the existence of a possible departure from the reference system.[121]

I now return to the consideration of the argument supporting the claims of the European Commission. Instead of the possible economic merits of the arm's length principle as such, the argument of the European Commission is a legal one, and it is based on the idea that Article 107(1) of the TFEU prohibits the unequal treatment of undertakings that are in a comparable factual and legal situation, something that would be achieved by relying on the arm's length principle. In other words, Article 107(1) of the TFEU would entail a principle of non-discrimination that is enforced by the implementation of the arm's length principle. I will consider below the relevance of this argument from a legal perspective.[122]

Article 107(1) of the TFEU is part of the primary law of the EU, so if it can be established that this article favours a particular method of taxation, it would be justified to argue that this method is binding on the Member States. The article in itself gives no guidance as to the choice of a method for the allocation of the corporate tax base. The article solely precludes aid granted by a Member State that favours certain undertakings or the production of certain goods. Instead, what justifies the position of the Commission is mainly the *Forum 187* case ruled by the CJEU in 2006, and the idea that Article 107(1) of the TFEU embodies an obligation to provide equal treatment that would be fulfilled by relying on the arm's length principle. Accordingly, to proceed with the analysis, I will first consider whether the *Forum 187* judgment implies an obligation to apply the arm's length principle (section 2.2.2). Second, I will analyse the relevance of the argument pertaining to the principle of equal treatment (section 2.2.3).

2.2.2 Does the *Forum 187* Judgment Imply an Obligation to Apply the Arm's Length Principle as an Allocation Method?

I will now analyse whether the *Forum 187* judgment implies an obligation to apply the arm's length principle. *Forum 187* concerned the transfer pricing method applicable to determine the profit of certain companies established in Belgium assuming, among other conditions, that such companies belong to a multinational enterprise and perform certain preparatory, auxiliary, and centralisation activities. The transfer pricing method implied that the companies that qualified for this special regime would receive as remuneration for their activities an 8% profit margin on their costs,

---

121. *See* the arguments developed in Luca Rubini, *The Definition of Subsidy and State Aid: WTO and EC Law in Comparative Perspective* (Oxford University Press 2009) 246–249.
122. One could also consider the relevance of this argument from an economic perspective, which this book does not attempt at doing. It can simply be observed that research has been conducted on the economic effects of the removal of discriminatory provisions. It has been argued, in the area of the fundamental freedoms applied to direct taxes and on the basis of a study of the reactions of the Member States to the CJEU's case law, that the elimination of discrimination does not necessarily 'lead to increased neutrality and a more level playing-field, but may actually steer the EU further away from establishing an internal market': *see* Rita De La Feria and Clemens Fuest, 'The Economic Effects of EU Tax Jurisprudence' (2016) 41 European Law Review 44, 71.

excluding 'staff costs, financial charges and corporation tax'.[123] This method, inspired by the cost plus method described at paragraphs 2.45 to 2.61 of the 2017 OECD transfer pricing guidelines, was found by the CJEU to be in breach of State aid law, partly because it excluded some expenses from the cost base, and also because it did not provide justification for the 8% profit margin. The Court observed that 'the transfer prices [did] not resemble those which would be charged in conditions of free competition'.[124] The CJEU also considered that State aid control should be performed by comparing the regime at issue 'with the ordinary tax system, based on the difference between profits and outgoings of an undertaking carrying on its activities in conditions of free competition'.[125]

Does the reasoning of the CJEU in the *Forum 187* decision create an obligation to apply the arm's length principle as an allocation method, if necessary by extending the reference system beyond the domestic rules? In my opinion, the findings of the Court cannot be interpreted as a clear obligation to apply the arm's length principle, at least not in the way this principle is described in the OECD transfer pricing guidelines, although the ruling does not preclude the application of the arm's length principle. I consider the argument that the *Forum 187* case implies an obligation to rely on the arm's length principle incorrect, and that for two main reasons: (i) the fact that in this case the deviation from the arm's length principle characterised the existence of an advantage, not its selectivity, and (ii) the lack of clear support for this argument in the wording of the case. I shall consider each of these arguments in turn.

First, the paragraphs of the case that the Commission relies on to support its view relate to the notion of advantage,[126] not selectivity.[127] The Belgian measure was eventually found selective because of its limited scope to certain types of undertakings, not because of an inherent deviation from the arm's length principle or from the treatment of independent enterprises.[128] In contrast, the Commission argues for an obligation to apply the arm's length principle as part of the selectivity criterion in the 2016 notice,[129] and in the section on the existence of a 'selective advantage' in the decisions it took on certain tax rulings issued by the Member States.[130]

Second, the benchmark used to test the method used by Belgium for the allocation of the corporate tax base among associated enterprises is the 'difference between profits and outgoings of an undertaking carrying on its activities in conditions of free competition.' There are two elements in this sentence: the 'difference between

---

123. *See* Joined Cases C-182/03 and C-217/03, *Kingdom of Belgium and Forum 187 ASBL v. Commission of the European Communities*, ECLI:EU:C:2006:416, para. 9.
124. *See* Joined Cases C-182/03 and C-217/03, *Kingdom of Belgium and Forum 187 ASBL v. Commission of the European Communities*, ECLI:EU:C:2006:416, para. 96.
125. *See* Joined Cases C-182/03 and C-217/03, *Kingdom of Belgium and Forum 187 ASBL v. Commission of the European Communities*, ECLI:EU:C:2006:416, para. 95.
126. *See* paras 95 and 97 of the *Forum 187* decision.
127. The analysis of the selectivity criterion starts at para. 119 of the *Forum 187* decision.
128. *See* paras 119 and following of the *Forum 187* decision.
129. *See* Commission Notice on the notion of State aid as referred to in Art. 107(1) of the Treaty on the Functioning of the European Union [2016] OJ C 262/1, paras 169 and following.
130. *See* e.g., Commission Decision (EU) 2017/502 of 21 October 2015 on State aid SA.38374 (2014/C ex 2014/NN) implemented by the Netherlands to Starbucks [2017] OJ L 83/38, para. 264.

profits and outgoings of an undertaking', and the performance of 'activities in conditions of free competition'. The 'difference between profits and outgoings of an undertaking' should reasonably be interpreted as the principle of net taxation, which is intrinsic to the concept of income, as the very notion of income supposes that tax is levied only on the profits that remain after the expenses necessary for obtaining the revenues have been deducted.[131] The reference to the principle of net taxation does not, in my opinion, create an obligation to rely on the arm's length principle, as other methods for the allocation of the corporate tax base may be implemented as part of a corporate income tax system and allocate to different group members profits or losses that do have a connection with the concept of income. I will illustrate this statement with three observations related to the three allocation methods considered in this book:

- If one considers the arm's length principle, although different transfer pricing methods are more[132] or less[133] connected to the concept of income, the strong reliance on the prices set, or the profits earned by independent comparable entities, ensures that the connection with the concept of income is kept.[134]
- Next, transfer pricing safe harbours would normally be implemented as part of a corporate income tax system where group members are taxed on the basis of the net taxation principle. The income earned under a safe harbour is meant to have a connection with the concept of income if the safe harbour implements the arm's length principle. Even safe harbours that deviate from the arm's length principle may have some connection with the concept of income, although the connection becomes weaker as the safe harbour deviates from the arm's length principle.
- Finally, a system of formula apportionment with firm-specific factors has the weakest connection with the concept of income of the three allocation methods, but some connection cannot be excluded. A system of formula apportionment would typically share a net consolidated income earned by several members of a group; the formula that allocates a portion of the consolidated income to each group member may not reflect the actual income of this group member. Depending on the apportionment factors and their

---

131. This statement is only conceptual, it does not aim at establishing a general definition of the concept of income, which depends on the rules of each country for the determination of the taxable revenues and the deductible expenses.
132. The resale price method and the cost plus method rely on the concept of gross margin, while the transactional net margin method relies on the concept of net margin; in either case, it is an item of income after the deduction of certain expenses that is taken into account.
133. The comparable uncontrolled price method relies on the notion of revenue (for the seller) or cost (for the buyer) rather than on the notion of profit, but the consequence of the use of this method will eventually influence the income of the associated enterprises. The profit split method would normally split profits or losses, although they may be computed with different techniques: see para. 2.137 of the 2017 OECD transfer pricing guidelines where it is stated that 'Generally, the combined profits to be split in a transactional profit split method are operating profits.'
134. See e.g., Charles E. McLure, 'Replacing Separate Entity Accounting and the Arm's Length Principle with Formulary Apportionment' (2002) 56 Bulletin for International Taxation 586, 587.

respective weight, a system of formula apportionment has more or less connection with the concept of income. However, when the apportionment factors are firm-specific, such as sales, labour, or tangible assets, some connection with the concept of income must be recognised to exist.[135]

In contrast to what is discussed above, taxation methods that do not form part of an income tax, such as a destination-based cash flow tax, would probably not produce an outcome that is compatible with the findings of the CJEU in the *Forum 187* decision, if only certain undertakings were subject to such a tax. Indeed, a system of taxation based on cash flows is conceptually different from an income tax, as it resembles more a consumption tax.[136] At this stage, we have reached a subconclusion: the arm's length principle is not the only allocation method under which associated enterprises are taxed on an income that is attributable to them and that is connected to the principle of net taxation, although the arm's length principle is likely to be the allocation method that best achieves the objective to tax on a net basis. I now turn to the second element described in *Forum 187*: the notion of 'conditions of free competition'.

The second element described at paragraphs 95 and 96 of the *Forum 187* judgment is that associated enterprises should be taxed on the basis of the income generated by the performance of 'activities in conditions of free competition'. In this respect, as emphasised by Luja, it can be observed that the CJEU did not define the words 'free competition'.[137] The French version of the case, which uses the expression '*conditions de libre concurrence*', does not provide more indications on the meaning of 'conditions of free competition'. This implies that it is not necessarily the conditions that exist between independent enterprises that should be relied on to allocate the corporate tax base among multinational enterprises although this is a possible meaning.[138] Associated enterprises, whether they form domestic or cross-border groups, could also be considered to do business in conditions of 'free competition', as they are freely competing with other enterprises, under the market forces, to reach out to their customers. Moreover, the Court did not indicate what profit mark-up should have been applied,[139] nor did it rely on the profits observed on the open market to assess those of associated enterprises; in other words, the CJEU did not take an opportunity to require the application of the arm's length principle between associated enterprises. This

---

135. In this respect, *see* section 7.3.3.2 of this book.
136. In this respect, it has been observed that a destination-based cash flow tax 'provides consumption treatment for foreign investment but income treatment for domestic investment': *see* Harry Grubert, 'Destination-Based Income Taxes: A Mismatch Made in Heaven?' (2015) 69 Tax Law Review 43, 52.
137. *See* Raymond H.C. Luja, 'Do State Aid Rules Still Allow European Union Member States to Claim Fiscal Sovereignty?' (2016) 25 EC Tax Review 323.
138. Indeed, when looking at how the Court formulates different rulings, it is well possible that the expression 'free competition' means the conditions that exist between independent enterprises. For example, the expression 'fully competitive conditions' seems to be equal to the conditions that exist between companies with no 'relationship of interdependence': *see* Case C-311/08, *Société de Gestion Industrielle (SGI) v. Belgian State*, ECLI:EU:C:2010:26, para. 72; similarly, *see* Case C-318/10, *Société d'investissement pour l'agriculture tropicale SA (SIAT) v. État belge*, ECLI:EU:C:2012:415, para. 52.
139. *See* Phedon Nicolaides, 'State Aid Rules and Tax Rulings' (2016) 15 European State Aid Law Quarterly 416, 418.

means that the words 'free competition' do not have a clear meaning as to which profit margin should be earned by associated enterprises, and it cannot be held with all certainty that the profit that the CJEU had in mind in the *Forum 187* case, if any, matches an analysis under the arm's length principle.

Therefore, the *Forum 187* case provides no irrefutable support to an obligation to apply the arm's length principle as an allocation method.[140] At the same time, the Court did not preclude the application of the arm's length principle, as this allocation method does not contradict the two requirements set by the CJEU at paragraphs 95 and 96 of the ruling, i.e., the notions of net income and of free competition.

Even if the CJEU meant in the *Forum 187* case that State aid law implies an obligation to apply the arm's length principle as an allocation method, this conclusion is not necessarily the one that best implements the State aid rules. The Court may have reached a questionable outcome, and later judgments could contradict this one. Therefore, one should in any case analyse the merits of the arguments put forward by the European Commission in support of its claim that Article 107(1) of the TFEU embodies an obligation to apply the arm's length principle as an allocation method. The rationale of the argument is that Article 107(1) of the TFEU implies a general principle of equal treatment, which would require the application of the arm's length principle. It is the purpose of the following section to analyse whether that argument is convincing.

2.2.3 Does Article 107(1) of the TFEU Imply a General Principle of Equal Treatment That Requires the Application of the Arm's Length Principle?

2.2.3.1 *Introductory Remarks*

The argument put forward by the European Commission relies on two steps, in addition to the reference to the *Forum 187* judgment. The first step is that Article 107(1) of the TFEU implies a general principle of equal treatment.[141] The second step, if one

---

140. Concurring, *see* Phedon Nicolaides, 'State Aid Rules and Tax Rulings' (2016) 15 European State Aid Law Quarterly 416, 420 where the author finds it more likely that the correct interpretation of the *Forum 187* case is that a company should cover all its costs, not necessarily earning an arm's length profit. *See also* Saturnina Moreno González, 'State Aid and Tax Competition: Comments on the European Commission's Decisions on Transfer Pricing Rulings' (2016) 15 European State Aid Law Quarterly 556, 564; Dimitrios A. Kyriazis, 'From Soft Law to Soft Law Through Hard Law: The Commission's Approach to the State Aid Assessment of Tax Rulings' (2016) 15 European State Aid Law Quarterly 428, 435; Tony Joris and Wout De Cock, 'Is Belgium and Forum 187 v. Commission a Suitable Legal Source for an EU "At Arm's Length Principle"?' (2017) 16 European State Aid Law Quarterly 607, 614: 'the Commission uses a very broad interpretation of the wordings of the ECJ by deriving an at arm's length principle from the words "*free competition*"'.
141. *See* Commission Notice on the notion of State aid as referred to in Art. 107(1) of the Treaty on the Functioning of the European Union [2016] OJ C 262/1, para. 172; Commission Decision (EU) 2017/502 of 21 October 2015 on State aid SA.38374 (2014/C ex 2014/NN) implemented by the Netherlands to Starbucks [2017] OJ L 83/38, para. 264; Commission Decision (EU) 2016/1699 of 11 January 2016 on the excess profit exemption State aid scheme SA.37667

accepts the first one, is that the principle of equal treatment is enforced by the arm's length principle. While the first step is uncontroversial, I will argue below that the second one is not indisputable.

It can hardly be argued against the first step of the argument, i.e., that Article 107(1) of the TFEU implies a general principle of equal treatment, although the notion of 'general principle' is a vague one.[142] The CJEU has systematically held that the rules on State aid prohibit that a Member State grants an advantage to certain undertakings in comparison with others which are in a comparable legal and factual situation.[143] By precluding that advantages are being granted to only certain undertakings, the CJEU indeed requires that undertakings that are in a comparable legal and factual situation receive an equal treatment; in this sense, the selectivity test embodies a principle of equal treatment. The difficulty comes from determining what type of equal treatment Article 107(1) requires. This is the second step of the argument of the European Commission.

I will now investigate whether the second step of the argument is convincing, i.e., the idea that the principle of equal treatment is met by applying the arm's length principle.

To begin with, two potential counterarguments are considered, before focusing on the argument that the arm's length principle would enable a similar treatment for independent and associated enterprises. A first potential counterargument to the intrinsic implications of Article 107(1) of the TFEU is the breach of the fiscal sovereignty of the Member States in the area of direct taxation; the consequence of this counterargument would be that the Member States are free to rely on the arm's length principle, or on another allocation method, given that the rules for the allocation of the corporate tax base and the taxation of multinational enterprises have not been harmonised within the EU. As argued elsewhere, I do not find this argument convincing, given the supremacy of EU primary law over domestic law.[144]

A second counterargument that is not either convincing, and that is not relied on by the European Commission, is the potential binding value of the arm's length principle, as a consequence of being part of customary international law. Although it has sometimes been argued that the arm's length principle has become part of binding

---

(2015/C) (ex 2015/NN) implemented by Belgium [2016] OJ L 260/61, para. 150; Commission Decision (EU) 2016/2326 of 21 October 2015 on State aid SA.38375 (2014/C ex 2014/NN) which Luxembourg granted to Fiat [2016] OJ L 351/1, para. 228.

142. In this respect see Anthony Arnull, 'What Is a General Principle of EU Law?' in Rita de la Feria and Stefan Vogenauer (eds), *Prohibition of Abuse of Law – A New General Principle of EU Law?* (Hart Publishing 2011) 7: '(t)he term "general principle" is deceptively anodine'.
143. See e.g., Case C-88/03, *Portuguese Republic v. Commission of the European Communities*, ECLI:EU:C:2006:511, para. 56; Joined Cases C-20/15 P and C-21/15 P, *European Commission v. World Duty Free Group*, ECLI:EU:C:2016:981, para. 54.
144. This argument is developed in Jérôme Monsenego, *Taxation of Foreign Business Income within the European Internal Market* (IBFD 2012) 67–70. For similar views in the area of State aid law see Alexandre Maitrot de la Motte, *Droit fiscal de l'Union européenne* (2nd edn, Bruylant 2016) 285; Massimo Merola, 'The Rebus of Selectivity in Fiscal Aid: A Nonconformist View on and Beyond Case Law' (2016) 39 World Competition 533, 537.

customary international law,¹⁴⁵ I find this argument far from being convincing. Without exposing at length why the arm's length principle is not likely to have become part of binding customary international law, three arguments can be enumerated. First, there are other tax rules or principles (e.g., the principle of worldwide taxation or the principle of net taxation) that are frequently relied on by various States, without such rules being legally binding on these or other States as a consequence of international law.¹⁴⁶ Second, no ruling issued by an international court has found a principle of taxation to be part of binding customary international law; I have accordingly argued that there is no binding customary international tax law that would apply in the area of direct taxation.¹⁴⁷ Third, it is hard to conceive that the arm's length principle is binding under international law, as its material content is indeed variable: there are important divergences in the interpretation of the arm's length principle between different countries, and yet none of these interpretations has been found incompatible with international law. Therefore, I turn now to the main argument that supports the view that Article 107(1) of the TFEU might embody the arm's length principle: the principle of equal treatment. While this claim seems convincing at first sight, it appears disputable upon a closer look. As I see it, there are two main weaknesses in the argument according to which the principle of equal treatment embodied in Article 107(1) of the TFEU requires the application of the arm's length principle: first, the arm's length principle, as it is described in the OECD transfer pricing guidelines, does not always require an identical treatment between independent and associated enterprises (section 2.2.3.2). Second, the arm's length principle is not necessarily the sole allocation method that enables some form of equal treatment (section 2.2.3.3).

2.2.3.2 *The Arm's Length Principle and the Principle of Equal Treatment*

As mentioned above, it is unquestionable that Article 107(1) of the TFEU implies a general principle of equal treatment. It is equally undeniable that the arm's length principle includes a general objective of equal treatment, or at least of sufficiently similar treatment, between associated enterprises and independent enterprises that are in a comparable situation.¹⁴⁸ In addition, there are conceptual similarities between the rules on State aid and the arm's length principle, such as the reliance on the notion of

---

145. *See* e.g., Reuven Avi-Yonah and Zachée Pouga Tinhaga, 'Unitary Taxation and International Tax Rules' (2014) ICTD 26 Working Paper < https://papers.ssrn.com/sol3/Delivery.cfm/SSRN_ID2602240_code572410.pdf?abstractid=2351920&mirid=1 > accessed 6 February 2018. More generally *see also* Pierpaolo Rossi-Maccanico, 'Fiscal State Aids, Tax Base Erosion and Profit Shifting' (2015) 24 EC Tax Review 63, 66.
146. In this respect *see* Cécile Brokelind, 'The Evolution of International Income Tax Law Applied to Global Trade' (2006) 34 Intertax 126.
147. *See* Jérôme Monsenego, *Taxation of Foreign Business Income Within the European Internal Market* (IBFD 2012), Chapter 2.
148. *See* para. 2.6 of the 2017 OECD transfer pricing guidelines: 'The application of the arm's length principle is generally based on a comparison of the price, margin or profits from particular controlled transactions with the price, margin or profits from comparable transactions between independent enterprises'. *See also* Richard Collier and Joseph L. Andrus, *Transfer Pricing and the Arm's Length Principle After BEPS* (Oxford University Press 2017) 2.

comparability,[149] or on the effects of the market forces.[150] Moreover, the arm's length principle provides a form of equality between different associated enterprises that are in a comparable situation, since all of them will be subject to the common benchmark of the effects of the market forces.

Does the resemblance between these two objectives of equal treatment imply that the requirements of Article 107(1) of the TFEU are necessarily met by the arm's length principle? The wording of the article does not provide an answer to this question. At the time of writing this book, the interpretation of the article by the Union courts in tax cases does not either clearly define the type of equal treatment that is required by the article. This may be explained by the fact that the Union courts answer to questions that are specific to the circumstances of the cases they are to rule on, or that the courts regularly stress that what matters is not the purpose or the objectives of national measures, or even the regulatory techniques used, but rather the effects of State measures,[151] which cannot be discriminatory.[152]

Despite the elements of resemblance between Article 107(1) of the TFEU and the arm's length principle, in my opinion these elements do not provide a motivated justification for concluding that State aid law necessarily embodies an obligation to apply the arm's length principle. I will first demonstrate that the arm's length principle does not enable a perfectly similar treatment between independent and associated enterprises, or between different associated enterprises. I will then argue that the arm's length principle is not necessarily the sole allocation method that may enable the similar treatment of different undertakings.

Although the arm's length principle does aim at treating similarly associated and independent enterprises that are in a comparable situation, it does not enable a

---

149. A consequence of the reliance on the notion of comparability in the two fields is that when the arm's length principle results in different tax consequences for situations that are not comparable, no selectivity for State aid purposes should be at hand. For example, if two companies perform research and development activities, but one company does so as a contract R&D while the other is characterised as a fully-fledged researcher, the application of the arm's length principle for the pricing of the cross-border intercompany transactions involving these companies would typically result in different outcomes: the fully-fledged researcher would be entitled to higher profits than the contract R&D (at least if the intangible property created by the research and development activities is profitable), as the former normally owns intangible property to a greater extent than the latter. Under a State aid analysis, a Member State applying the arm's length principle and levying a lower corporate income tax on the contract R&D than on the fully-fledged researcher should not be considered to be providing a selective advantage to the company acting as a contract R&D: although an advantage is provided (the lower amount of tax levied on the contract R&D), there is no selective treatment as the two companies are not in a comparable factual situation. The different levels of remuneration are precisely a consequence of the two companies performing different functions, assuming different levels of risks, and owning or using different assets.
150. In this respect *see* Chapter 3 of this book.
151. *See* Case 173/73, *Italian Republic v. Commission of the European Communities*, ECLI:EU:C: 1974:71, para. 27.
152. *See* e.g., Case C-524/14 P, *European Commission v. Hansestadt Lübeck*, ECLI:EU:C:2016:971, para. 48. *See also* Commission Notice on the notion of State aid as referred to in Art. 107(1) of the Treaty on the Functioning of the European Union [2016] OJ C 262/1, para. 67: 'Only the effect of the measure on the undertaking is relevant, and not the cause or the objective of the State intervention.'

perfectly similar treatment between the two categories of enterprises, or between different associated enterprises. Two main reasons explain this statement, which I will consider in turn. First, the arm's length principle relies to a large extent on approximations,[153] subjective appreciations of various economic factors, and it does not aim at finding single values but rather ranges thereof.[154] This means that the arm's length principle cannot provide full equality between independent and associated enterprises, or between different associated enterprises, but only the approximation, more or less accurate, of an equal treatment. Accordingly, if Article 107(1) of the TFEU embodies an obligation to provide equal treatment, this obligation can only partly be achieved under the arm's length principle.

I now turn to the second argument that supports the idea that the arm's length principle does not enable a perfectly similar treatment between independent and associated enterprises. As the arm's length principle relies heavily on the notion of comparability, while at the same time it is often difficult to find on the open market transactions that are fully comparable to those that are being tested under the arm's length principle, the functioning of this principle intrinsically requires to accept some differences between independent and controlled transactions.[155] In particular, there are certain sources of income – whether revenues or costs – that are exclusive to multinational enterprises, and for which no direct benchmark can be provided by the open market. This is because the same sources of income do not exist, or do not have the same characteristics, outside corporate groups.[156] Under the OECD transfer pricing guidelines, the solution in such cases consists in hypothesising the terms and conditions that would be applied by independent enterprises, but without directly relying on observations from the open market, as suggested e.g., for group synergies[157] or the profit split method.[158] Here follow three examples that illustrate sources of income that are exclusive to multinational enterprises, for which no direct benchmark can be provided by independent enterprises:

---

153. *See* para. 3.55 of the 2017 OECD transfer pricing guidelines where it is emphasised that 'in general the application of the arm's length principle only produces an approximation of conditions that would have been established between independent enterprises'.
154. *See* para. 1.8 of the 2017 OECD transfer pricing guidelines where it is mentioned that 'the arm's length principle provides *broad parity* of tax treatment for members of MNE groups and independent enterprises' so as to put them '*on a more equal footing* for tax purposes' (emphasis added), which shows that no identical treatment is provided.
155. *See* Richard Collier and Joseph L Andrus, *Transfer Pricing and the Arm's Length Principle After BEPS* (Oxford University Press 2017) 106.
156. For an illustration of the impossibility in certain situations to find reliable comparables, *see* US General Accounting Office, 'IRS Could Better Protect U.S. Tax Interests In Determining The Income Of Multinational Corporations' (1981), where at 52–53 it is observed that 'because of the structure of the modern business world, IRS can seldom find an arm's length price on which to base adjustments but must instead construct a price'. A similar view is developed in Luís Eduardo Schoueri, 'Arm's Length: Beyond the Guidelines of the OECD' (2015) 69 Bulletin for International Taxation 690, 712.
157. *See* para. 1.162 of the 2017 OECD transfer pricing guidelines with respect to group synergies, which are to be shared in proportion to the contribution of each party to the creation of a synergy.
158. *See* para. 2.117 of the 2017 OECD transfer pricing guidelines.

– In case of profits that are earned because of the integration between group members,[159] such profits cannot be allocated among the group members based on an analogy with independent enterprises.[160] Instead, the OECD transfer pricing guidelines recommend making the fiction of the arm's length principle stronger, by hypothesising how independent parties would have acted, or would have remunerated the contributions of each party, had they been in a similar situation.[161] In certain cases profit split might be the only reliable transfer pricing method, particularly for highly integrated operations or when both parties to a transaction make unique valuable contributions.[162] From a fiscal perspective, there is a need to depart from the exact application of conditions existing between independent enterprises, because an analogous application of the conditions existing between independent enterprises may result in certain profits being untaxed or taxed in a country with little or no connection to such income. Indeed, if the profit of each group member is benchmarked against the profit of independent enterprises, this last profit may not include the additional income earned by the group thanks to, for example, the synergies it achieves.[163] For that reason, in the absence of comparables data, the guidelines recommend to hypothesise the terms that would be adopted by independent parties, while recognising the effects of the integration between associated enterprises. For example, if the profit split method is to be applied and that no reliable comparables exist, the guidelines recommend to split profits based on the 'relative value of the functions performed' by the parties to a profit split arrangement.[164] In other words, when profits are earned because of the integration between group members, the arm's length

---

159. Since one of the reasons for groups to exist is the higher gains made possible thanks to the integration between group members, the combined profit of a multinational enterprise may exceed the benchmarkable functional return of its members. This is because the profits earned by independent enterprises cannot include the additional gains that the integration between the group members may produce. Examples of such additional profits are synergies and costs savings. The theory of the firm and the reason for conducting inhouse rather than outsourced activities is clearly explained in the UN transfer pricing manual: '(u)sually, the administrative costs of organizing production within a firm are less than the cost of the alternative, which is outsourcing market transactions': see United Nations, *Practical Manual on Transfer Pricing for Developing Countries* (United Nations 2017) para. A.2.3.
160. In this respect is has been argued that Art. 9 of the OECD Model Tax Convention aims only at allocating among the members of a multinational enterprise the profits that 'could have been earned at arm's length', i.e., the article would be 'silent about the allocation of any common control premiums': see Mitchell A. Kane, 'Transfer Pricing, Integration and Synergy Intangibles: A Consensus Approach to the Arm's Length Standard' (2014) 6 World Tax Journal 282, 299. For a similar view, see Hubert Hamaekers, 'Arm's Length – How Long?' (2001) 8 International Transfer Pricing Journal 30, 34.
161. *See* for example, with respect to synergies, para. 1.162 of the 2017 OECD transfer pricing guidelines, which suggests that the benefits of synergies that can be attributed to deliberate concerted group actions 'should generally be shared by members of the group in proportion to their contribution to the creation of the synergy'.
162. *See* para. 2.115 of the 2017 OECD transfer pricing guidelines.
163. *See* Richard Collier and Joseph L. Andrus, *Transfer Pricing and the Arm's Length Principle After BEPS* (Oxford University Press 2017) 125.
164. *See* para. 2.125 of the 2017 OECD transfer pricing guidelines.

principle does not recommend an identical treatment between independent and associated enterprises; the enforcement of conditions existing between independent enterprises is then only a general objective that cannot be fully implemented in practice. Ddifferences in treatment may thus exist between these categories of undertakings as no direct benchmark can be provided by the open market.

- I now move to a second illustration of the income of multinational enterprises for which no direct benchmark may be provided by independent enterprises, this time with respect to the costs incurred by members of multinational enterprises. In that regard, there are certain costs that by definition are not benchmarkable on the open market, i.e., costs that would not be incurred by independent enterprises.[165] Conversely, certain costs may be saved thanks to group membership, something that may 'heighten the aggregate profits earned by group members'.[166] In such cases, there is no other solution than either decreasing the degree of comparability so as to allocate and price such costs on the basis of the most comparable independent transactions, or allocating the costs on the basis of an allocation key,[167] thus departing even more from the conditions existing between independent enterprises. In either case, no identical treatment with independent enterprises is possible, despite the general objective of relying on the arm's length principle.

- A last example is that of risks that materialise and affect a whole group or several group members, while in independent situations the realisation of a risk would affect fewer entities, especially those that are legally bound by the risk.[168] The benchmark provided by independent enterprises is not fully correct in such cases, when the effects the realization of risks are different for independent and associated enterprises. Therefore, the arm's length principle cannot provide an allocation of risks, and an allocation of the consequences of the realization of such risks, that is identical to observations on the open market.

Consequently, it is unquestionable that for certain transactions, reliable comparable independent data cannot exist, at least not without a different conception of the notion of comparability. The neutrality aimed at by the arm's length principle is even more difficult to ensure for business activities that are normally performed by

---

165. An example is the cost for the management function that supervises the activities of a group and takes the strategic decisions that relate to the integration of the activities of a multinational enterprise; such a cost by definition does not exist within independent enterprises, and thus information based on independent enterprises cannot provide guidance as to how to reasonably share such costs among a multinational enterprise, and what profit mark-up should be earned for the performance of these functions.
166. *See* e.g., para. 1.157 of the 2017 OECD transfer pricing guidelines with respect to synergies that may result from the combined purchasing power of group members.
167. Such an allocation key is likely to be based on firm-specific factors, such as the sales, the number of employees, the levels of wages, the number of IT platforms, the ownership of tangible assets, etc.
168. An example would be the reputational risk to which the members of a group are exposed, even when the members are not legally bound by such a risk.

multinational enterprises only, as opposed to independent enterprises, such as global trading.[169] In such cases, there are no independent transactions that provide a reliable benchmark to attribute income to associated enterprises.

The conclusion from the above analysis is that the argument according to which the principle of equal treatment would be enforced by the arm's length principle is not entirely true, given that: (i) this principle does not provide full equality between independent and associated enterprises, or between different associated enterprises, and (ii) in certain cases no reliable benchmark is provided by independent enterprises or transactions, thus preventing that a complete equal treatment is provided.

2.2.3.3 *The Principle of Equal Treatment and Alternative Allocation Methods*

After demonstrating that the arm's length principle does not always enable a perfectly similar treatment between independent and associated enterprises or between different associated enterprises, I will now consider whether the arm's length principle is the sole allocation method that may be required by the principle of equal treatment, or if other allocation methods may also provide for some form of equal treatment. In the latter case, Article 107(1) of the TFEU could not justify the view according to which the principle of equal treatment necessarily requires the application of the arm's length principle. The two main alternatives to a generally formulated arm's length provision that are studied in this book are transfer pricing safe harbours, and a system of formula apportionment with firm-specific factors. It is argued below that these allocation methods are not clearly at odds with the principle of equal treatment, would it be required under Article 107(1) of the TFEU.

A transfer pricing safe harbour may be in line with the arm's length principle or depart from it, depending on the level of the margins that it prescribes, and the circumstances in which the regime applies. In the former case, i.e., a system of fixed margins that are in line with the arm's length principle, this allocation method would enable a more accurate achievement of the principle of equal treatment, both towards independent enterprises and other associated enterprises, as the margins are fixed and thus avoid the approximative nature of the arm's length principle when it is generally formulated. The flaw of the arm's length principle with respect to transactions that do not exist between independent enterprises would, of course, remain. In the latter case, i.e., a system of fixed margins that depart from the arm's length principle, equal treatment is achieved only between the associated enterprises to which the safe harbour applies; no equal treatment would be achieved with independent enterprises, as the regime would precisely depart from the conditions that exist between independent enterprises. Differences in treatment would also exist between associated enterprises that are, or are not, eligible to the safe harbour. In other words, it is only when transfer pricing safe harbours implement the arm's length principle that they provide

---

169. *See* the arguments developed in Peter H. Blessing, 'Divergence of Third Party Pricing from Arm's Length Results' in Philip Baker and Catherine Bobbett (eds), *Tax Polymath: A Life in International Taxation – Essays in Honour of John F. Avery Jones* (IBFD 2011) 153.

for an equal treatment between independent and associated enterprises, as well as between different associated enterprises, to a greater extent than a generally formulated arm's length provision.

A system of formula apportionment is theoretically different from an allocation method based on the arm's length principle. Despite the lack of a single way to implement formula apportionment,[170] the basic sharing mechanism underlying this allocation method remains the same: it implies allocating income among the members of a group on the basis of an allocation key. Such a key includes one or more elements, and in case there are several elements, the formula may also include a method to weigh the elements against each other. If one assumes that there is in a Member State a single allocation key that applies similarly to all companies that are in the scope of the rule, formula apportionment does enable – with respect to the mechanism to share income – equal treatment between the companies to which it applies.[171] If all multinational enterprises are subject to formula apportionment, they will all be treated alike. In addition, there is much less room for subjectivity and interpretation under formula apportionment than under the arm's length principle, as a formula provides objective elements to share the income without having to rely significantly on subjective considerations. Accordingly, a higher degree of equality is achieved for the taxation of multinational enterprises with formula apportionment than with the arm's length principle. However, and contrary to the arm's length principle, a different treatment remains with independent companies, which are solely taxed on the basis of the rules for the determination of the corporate income, without being subject to the effects of the formula.

The result from the above analysis is that if one assumes that Article 107(1) of the TFEU implies an obligation to provide equal treatment, the three allocation methods studied in this book all achieve some degree of equal treatment, and thus partly comply with the obligation to provide equal treatment. At the same time, the three allocation methods do not fully achieve the principle of equal treatment, and differences in treatment vary with the allocation methods. This means that the arm's length principle is not clearly superior to the other allocation methods when it comes to the achievement of the objective of equal treatment. Since no allocation method achieves a perfectly equal treatment towards all other types of undertakings, it may be distinguished between two categories of allocation methods, depending on the type of equality that is achieved. On the one hand, equality between independent and associated enterprises may be achieved – although not completely – by the arm's length principle, whether it is generally formulated or implemented through a system of safe harbours; on the other hand, equality between different associated enterprises is best achieved by a system of formula apportionment and transfer pricing safe harbours that implement the arm's length principle, albeit in this last case only with respect to the intercompany transactions that are eligible to the safe harbour.

---

170. A system of formula apportionment may be designed in various ways, especially with respect to the apportionment factors and the weight given to each factor.
171. This does not mean that formula apportionment necessarily is compatible with State aid law. In this respect, *see* Chapter 7 of this book.

2.2.3.4 Concluding Remarks

To conclude, it follows from the above observations that the principle of equal treatment embodied in Article 107(1) of the TFEU does not imply an obligation for the Member States to tax members of multinational enterprises on the basis of the arm's length principle. Indeed, on the one hand, the arm's length principle as it is described in the OECD transfer pricing guidelines does not provide for a full equality between independent and associated enterprises, and such equality is not desirable given that independent and associated enterprises may be in different situations. On the other hand, the principle of equal treatment, depending on what type of equal treatment is sought, may also be achieved with other allocation methods.

Additionally, it can be observed that there are certain technical arguments that would make it difficult for Article 107(1) of the TFEU to imply an obligation to apply the arm's length principle: in particular, there is no single understanding of the material content of the arm's length principle.[172] Moreover, the interaction of an allocation method implied by Article 107(1) of the TFEU with other domestic rules in force in the actual Member State would also be problematic.[173] As a result, I am of the opinion that Article 107(1) of the TFEU should not constitute or supplement the reference system.[174] This finding could be supported by parallels with cases in the area of free movement law where the CJEU has recognised the right of the Member States to depart from the arm's length principle, which could support the idea that several allocation methods, including non-arm's length methods, may be compatible with State aid law. For instance, in the *Lankhorst-Hohorst* case the Court did not accept an argument put forward by some Member States consisting in justifying a breach of the fundamental freedoms by a provision that would implement the 'internationally recognised' arm's length principle, something that would ensure the coherence of the applicable tax system.[175] Also, the CJEU accepted in the *Thin Cap GLO* case that non-arm's length

---

172. Quite the contrary, as illustrated by the differences in the interpretations of this principle reached by the tax administrations and courts of various countries, or the fact that countries have varying positions as to the inclusion of Art. 9(2) of the OECD Model Tax Convention in their tax treaties.
173. For instance, a general anti-avoidance rule may be in force and influence the normal application of an allocation method; how would such an anti-avoidance rule interact with an allocation method implied by Art. 107(1) of the TFEU? From the opening decision in the *Engie* case, it seems that the European Commission considers that the non-application of a domestic general anti-avoidance rule may constitute State aid, something that could require its application even if Art. 107(1) of the TFEU already implies an obligation to apply the arm's length principle (*see* State aid SA.44888 (2016/NN) (ex 2016/EO) – Luxembourg – Possible State aid in favour of GDF Suez – Invitation to submit comments pursuant to Art. 108(2) of the Treaty on the Functioning of the European Union [2017] OJ C 36/13, para. 158.
174. For a similar conclusion, although it is reached on different grounds, *see* Michael Lang, 'Tax Rulings and State Aid Law' (2015) 3 British Tax Review 391, 394; Wolfgang Schön, 'Tax Legislation and the Notion of Fiscal Aid: A Review of 5 Years of European Jurisprudence' in Isabelle Richelle, Wolfgang Schön, and Edoardo Traversa (eds), *State Aid Law and Business Taxation* (Springer 2016) 9: 'the relevant benchmark treatment cannot be derived autonomously from European law and it cannot be determined by reference to fiscal standards as applied in other States inside or outside the European Union'.
175. *See* Case C-324/00, *Lankhorst-Hohorst GmbH and Finanzamt Steinfurt*, ECLI:EU:C:2002:749, paras 39–42.

terms be justified by producing evidence of their commercial justification.[176] These cases contradict the idea that the arm's length principle is embodied in the law of the EU.

The conclusions reached in this section of the book could also be supported, from a conceptual perspective, by drawing a parallel with Article 345 of the TFEU, which requires EU law to be neutral with regard to the system of property ownership in the Member States:[177] if one assumes that income can be compared to 'property', the neutrality required by Article 345 of the TFEU would imply that Article 107(1) of the TFEU cannot include an inherent preference for a given method of taxation, as such a preference would jeopardise the right of the Member States to freely govern the system of property ownership in their territory, i.e., their tax systems. This argument is, however, only suggested at a conceptual level.

The next step of the analysis of the reference system is the determination of its material content.

2.3 THE DETERMINATION OF THE MATERIAL CONTENT OF THE REFERENCE SYSTEM

This section focuses on the determination of the material content of the reference system. This step is necessary, as part of the selectivity analysis, for the identification of the existence of a deviation from the reference system: without defining what the material content of the reference system is, it is impossible to accurately identify whether a State measure implies a deviation from such a reference system.[178]

To precisely determine the material content of the reference system, two questions need to be investigated. First, the scope of the reference system needs to be established, in particular with respect to the question of whether the reference system is made of the whole corporate income tax system or of an allocation method (section

---

176. *See* Case C-524/04, *Test Claimants in the Thin Cap Group Litigation v. Commissioners of Inland Revenue*, ECLI:EU:C:2007:161, para. 87: 'Whilst, at first sight, the criteria laid down by those provisions appear to require a consideration of objective and verifiable elements in order to determine whether a purely artificial arrangement, entered into for tax reasons alone, is involved, it is for the national court to determine whether those provisions allow taxpayers, where the transaction does not satisfy the arm's-length criterion, to produce evidence of the commercial justifications for that transaction, under the conditions referred to in the preceding paragraph.'
177. According to Art. 345 TFEU, which has been described as implementing the concept of 'capitalisme d'État' in the law of the European Union (*see* Michaël Karpenschif, *Droit européen des aides d'État* (Bruylant 2015) 71, with further references to publications by the European Commission), 'The Treaties shall in no way prejudice the rules in Member States governing the system of property ownership'. In its 2016 notice the Commission mentions that 'The Union legal order is neutral with regard to the system of property ownership and does not in any way prejudice the right of Member States to act as economic operators' (*see* Commission Notice on the notion of State aid as referred to in Art. 107(1) of the Treaty on the Functioning of the European Union [2016] OJ C 262/1, para. 73). For an overview of the implications of Art. 345 TFEU *see* Bram Akkermans and Eveline Ramaekers, 'Article 345 TFEU (ex Article 295 EC), Its Meanings and Interpretations' (2009) 15 European Law Journal 292.
178. The determination of the material content of the reference system is also relevant to quantify an illegal aid, something that is not studied in this book.

2.3.1). Second, it is investigated what legal sources the reference system is made of, something that is especially relevant so as to establish whether or not the reference system may include non-binding legal sources (section 2.3.2).

2.3.1 Determination of the Scope of the Reference System

The determination of the scope of the reference system, in particular whether the reference system should have a broad or narrow scope, is an important question that may influence the outcome of the selectivity test. A broad reference system enlarges the scope of the selectivity test, thereby making exceptions to the system more likely to constitute illegal State aid,[179] whereas a narrow reference system allows the Member States to implement differences of treatment to a greater extent, thereby decreasing the scope of the selectivity test. In this respect, two alternatives are relevant for an allocation method: either the reference system is made of the whole corporate income tax system, or the reference system is made of the sole allocation method. In this last case, i.e., if an allocation method constitutes, alone, the reference system against which the selectivity test is performed, the Member States might tax multinational enterprises differently from independent enterprises and domestic groups.

The case law of the Union courts and the decisions of the Commission tend to adopt a broad definition of the reference system,[180] although the guidance in this respect is not entirely clear.[181] In several cases the Union courts found a general tax regime (e.g., the corporate income tax, the VAT, an environmental levy, or a tax on

---

179. In this respect, it has been argued that 'a broad definition of State aid is necessary in order to cover possible alternative barriers to trade created by the States through financially effective regulatory and fiscal measures': see Herwig Hofmann, 'Activity in a Multi-level System: Motivations for Aid, Why Control It, Evolution of Aid in the EU' in Herwig C. H. Hofmann and Claire Micheau (eds), *State Aid Law of the European Union* (Oxford University Press 2016) 9.
180. Concurring, *see* Humbert Drabbe, 'The Test of Selectivity in State Aid Litigation: The Relevance of Drawing Internal and External Comparisons to Identify the Reference Framework' in Alexander Rust and Claire Micheau (eds), *State Aid and Tax Law* (Kluwer Law International 2013) 98; Case C-203/16 P, *Dirk Andres (administrator of Heitkamp BauHolding GmbH), previously Heitkamp BauHolding GmbH v. European Commission*, ECLI:EU:C:2017:1017, Opinion of AG Wahl, para. 106. However, a potentially more narrow approach can be observed from the opening decision regarding the UK CFC rules: *see* State aid SA.44896 (2017/C) (ex 2017/NN) – Potential State aid scheme regarding UK Group Financing Exemption – Invitation to submit comments pursuant to Art. 108(2) of the Treaty on the Functioning of the European Union [2017] OJ C 400/10, paras 60–63, where the reference system is not made of the whole corporate income tax system, but only of the CFC rules; however, in this case the breadth of the reference system does not change the outcome of the selectivity analysis, unless it is the particular derogatory treatment that constitutes the reference system (in this respect, *see* footnote 52 of the opening decision).
181. *See* Phedon Nicolaides, 'State Aid Rules and Tax Rulings' (2016) 15 European State Aid Law Quarterly 416, who at 424 finds surprising that despite 'the pivotal role of the reference system, the case law offers hardly any guidance'. Concurring on the lack of guidance, but disagreeing on the surprising character of such a lack, *see* Advocate General Wahl, Opinion delivered on 20 December 2017, Case C-203/16 P, *Dirk Andres (administrator of Heitkamp BauHolding GmbH), previously Heitkamp BauHolding GmbH v. European Commission*, ECLI:EU:C: 2017:1017, paras 100 and 101.

Jérôme Monsenego

travels by flight[182]) to constitute the reference system, as opposed to the actual measure that was at hand, especially when the measure constituted an exception to the main rule. In certain cases, State aid control may even require that a given tax be considered together with another tax, something that strengthens the broad character of the reference system.[183]

What is particularly relevant for the topic of this book is the view taken by the Court in the *Forum 187* case, where the CJEU considered that the rules applying for the determination of the profits of coordination centres had to be assessed against the benchmark of 'the ordinary tax system' in force in the Member State,[184] something that I interpret as meaning that the whole corporate income tax system constituted the reference system. However, this broad approach does not mean that the Court necessarily chooses the broadest reference system; the Court still appreciates which reference system is the most relevant one in the case at hand.[185] This is summarised by Advocate General Wahl, who emphasised that 'the Court has endorsed an approach that seeks to identify the entire body of rules that influence the tax burden weighing on undertakings'.[186]

The European Commission has also regularly taken a broad approach as to the determination of the reference system. Before the publication of the 2016 notice on the notion of State aid, the 1998 notice provided little guidance, but the mention of the 'tax system' and the 'common system' were indications of a broad approach.[187] In the decisions that followed the adoption of the Code of conduct in 1997, the Commission relied several times on the departure from 'normal' taxation to characterise an

---

182. See e.g., Case C-143/99, *Adria-Wien Pipeline GmbH*, ECLI:EU:C:2001:598, para. 55; Joined Cases C-78/08 to C-80/08, *Paint Graphos*, ECLI:EU:C:2011:550, para. 50; Case T-500/12, *Ryanair Ltd*, ECLI:EU:T:2015:73, para. 90 (the position of the General Court was later confirmed by the CJEU: see Joined Cases C-164/15 P and C-165/15 P, *European Commission v. Aer Lingus Ltd*, ECLI:EU:C:2016:990, paras 49–53).
183. An illustration is provided by the *GIL* case where an insurance premium tax and the value added tax were considered together with respect to the need to prevent the avoidance of taxes (see Case C-308/01, *GIL Insurance Ltd and Others v. Commissioners of Customs & Excise*, ECLI:EU:C:2004:252).
184. See Joined Cases C-182/03 and C-217/03, *Kingdom of Belgium and Forum 187 ASBL v. Commission of the European Communities*, ECLI:EU:C:2006:416, para. 95: 'In order to decide whether a method of assessment of taxable income such as that laid down under the regime for coordination centres confers an advantage on them, it is necessary (...) to compare that regime with the ordinary tax system, based on the difference between profits and outgoings of an undertaking carrying on its activities in conditions of free competition'. See also Joined Cases C-78/08 to C-80/08, *Paint Graphos*, ECLI:EU:C:2011:550, para. 50.
185. See e.g., Case C-524/14 P, *European Commission v. Hansestadt Lübeck*, ECLI:EU:C:2016:971, where at para. 62 the Court narrowed down the scope of the reference system to the rules for the levy of landing fees applied to the operation of a given airport. However, this case does not seem to be directly transposable to the area of direct taxes: see Phedon Nicolaides, 'Selectivity Requires Comparison' (2018) < http://stateaidhub.eu/blogs/stateaiduncovered/post/9125 > accessed 24 January 2018.
186. See Case C-203/16 P, *Dirk Andres (administrator of Heitkamp BauHolding GmbH), previously Heitkamp BauHolding GmbH v. European Commission*, ECLI:EU:C:2017:1017, Opinion of AG Wahl, para. 109.
187. See Commission notice on the application of the State aid rules to measures relating to direct business taxation [1998] OJ C 384/3, para. 16.

Chapter 2: Determination of the Reference System

advantage,[188] or on other relatively broad descriptions.[189] The 2016 notice applies a broad definition of the reference system, it being 'composed of a consistent set of rules that generally apply – on the basis of objective[190] criteria – to all undertakings falling within its scope as defined by its objective'.[191] Specific guidance is provided for the field of tax law, which confirms this broad approach.[192] A similar approach is found in the Commission decisions relating to the transfer pricing rulings issued by several Member States, in which the reference system consisted in the general corporate income tax regime.[193]

In my opinion, a broad definition of the reference system is consistent with the general objectives of the State aid rules.[194] Too narrow an approach would tend to consider certain exceptions to a main rule as general measures on their own, thereby emptying the notion of State aid of its meaning.[195] For example, if in *Paint Graphos* the rules applying to cooperative companies (i.e., the exemption from corporate income tax) would constitute the reference system (as opposed to the general regime for the taxation of commercial companies), such rules would be considered as general

---

188. *See* e.g., Commission Decision 2003/601/EC of 17 February 2003 on aid scheme C54/2001 (ex NN55/2000) Ireland – Foreign Income [2003] OJ L 204/51, para. 33 ('the measure must afford the beneficiaries an advantage that reduces the costs they normally bear in the course of their business').
189. *See* e.g., Commission Decision 2009/809/EC of 8 July 2009 on the groepsrentebox scheme which the Netherlands is planning to implement [2009] OJ L 288/26, para. 75, where the Commission referred to a 'particular legal system'.
190. The objective nature of the determination of the reference system is questioned by Advocate General Wahl: *see* Case C-203/16 P, *Dirk Andres (administrator of Heitkamp BauHolding GmbH), previously Heitkamp BauHolding GmbH v. European Commission*, ECLI:EU:C:2017:1017, Opinion of AG Wahl, para. 105.
191. *See* Commission Notice on the notion of State aid as referred to in Art. 107(1) of the Treaty on the Functioning of the European Union [2016] OJ C 262/1, para. 133. That paragraph does not rely on the explicit findings of the Union courts; it is rather the own interpretation of the Commission. However, as indicated above, the case law of the Union courts tends to adopt a broad definition of the reference system. Therefore, the definition suggested by the Commission is consistent with the findings of the Union courts.
192. *See* Commission Notice on the notion of State aid as referred to in Art. 107(1) of the Treaty on the Functioning of the European Union [2016] OJ C 262/1, para. 134: 'In the case of taxes, the reference system is based on such elements as the tax base, the taxable persons, the taxable event and the tax rates. For example, a reference system could be identified with regard to the corporate income tax system, the VAT system, or the general system of taxation of insurance.'
193. *See* e.g., Commission Decision (EU) 2016/2326 of 21 October 2015 on State aid SA.38375 (2014/C ex 2014/NN) which Luxembourg granted to Fiat [2016] OJ L 351/1, para. 215; Commission Decision (EU) 2017/502 of 21 October 2015 on State aid SA.38374 (2014/C ex 2014/NN) implemented by the Netherlands to Starbucks [2017] OJ L 83/38, para. 251; Commission Decision (EU) 2016/1699 of 11 January 2016 on the excess profit exemption State aid scheme SA.37667 (2015/C) (ex 2015/NN) implemented by Belgium [2016] OJ L 260/61, para. 129; State aid SA.44888 (2016/NN) (ex 2016/EO) – Luxembourg – Possible State aid in favour of GDF Suez – Invitation to submit comments pursuant to Art. 108(2) of the Treaty on the Functioning of the European Union [2017] OJ C 36/13, para. 100, with reference not to the general system, but to provisions of the system that apply generally.
194. Concurring, *see* Case C-203/16 P, *Dirk Andres (administrator of Heitkamp BauHolding GmbH), previously Heitkamp BauHolding GmbH v. European Commission*, ECLI:EU:C:2017:1017, Opinion of AG Wahl, para. 109.
195. Concurring, *see* Conor Quigley, *European State Aid Law and Policy* (3rd edn, Hart Publishing 2015) 113.

measures, thereby giving Italy the possibility to tax cooperative and commercial companies differently without the rules being subject to State aid scrutiny; however, cooperative and commercial companies may be performing comparable activities, they may even be competitors, and thus the grant of aid to either category of undertaking may affect competition and trade in the internal market. It follows from that observation that, in my opinion, the CJEU was right to consider that the general corporate income tax system constituted the reference system in the *Paint Graphos* case. In addition, a broad approach as to the determination of the reference system does not necessarily imply that an exception to the normal rule will constitute State aid, as the justification analysis may – as it did in *Paint Graphos* – result in the rules being compatible with State aid law.

A second argument supporting a broad definition of the reference system is the principle developed in the case law according to which the regulatory technique used by a Member State should not play a decisive role as part of a State aid analysis, focus being first and foremost on the effects of a measure.[196] A third argument relates to the interaction between different tax rules, as part of a given tax system. The coherence of a corporate income tax system relies on different types of rules, which cannot be separated from each other, for the system to function properly. In many cases, even a specific provision that could be described as *lex specialis* is still interacting with other provisions of the same tax system, despite the special nature of this rule: such a specific measure would be part of a consistent whole from which it cannot be separated, as the special rule has a function that is relevant only in the context in which it operates. For example, a special anti-avoidance rule such as a limitation to the deduction of interest expenses needs to be considered together with other types of rules, such as the general provision on the deductibility of business-related expenses, or the rules providing a definition of the notion of interest expenses. In such cases it is necessary to consider different provisions together, to obtain the full picture of a tax system and understand its internal consistency. *A fortiori*, rules that cannot be described as *lex specialis* and that belong to the more basic rules of a tax system cannot be isolated from the others for the purpose of State aid control.

Certain types of tax rules could, however, constitute a separate reference system. As part of a system of income taxation, although there may be a single objective to tax income, the method to realise such taxation may vary depending on the type of income. For example, within an income tax system, the taxation of capital gains often differs from the taxation of business profits or income from employment.[197] In such cases, it might be reasonable that such rules constitute a separate reference system.

---

196. *See* Case C-487/06 P, *British Aggregates Association v. Commission of the European Communities and United Kingdom*, ECLI:EU:C:2008:757, para. 89 *in fine*: 'Article [107(1) of the TFEU] defines State interventions on the basis of their effects, and thus independently of the techniques used'; Joined Cases C-106/09 P and C-107/09 P, *European Commission v. Government of Gibraltar*, ECLI:EU:C:2011:732, para. 87; Case C-524/14 P, *European Commission v. Hansestadt Lübeck*, ECLI:EU:C:2016:971, para. 48; Joined Cases C-164/15 P and C-165/15 P, *European Commission v. Aer Lingus Ltd*, ECLI:EU:C:2016:990, para. 58.
197. Various reasons may explain why capital gains are likely to be taxed differently from business profits or employment income, such as inflation, the need to prevent multiple taxation, or the fact that despite the constant evolution of the value of an asset, the realisation of capital gains

Chapter 2: Determination of the Reference System

A subsidiary argument in favour of a broad definition of the reference system relates to the fact that when a Member State acts not as a regulator but as a market operator, the assessment of whether an advantage has been granted is normally done by comparing the treatment of an undertaking with that of its competitors, the latter being considered as the 'normal' treatment.[198] For example, if a State intervention relieves an undertaking of certain costs, the assessment of State aid is done by comparison to the costs that would normally be borne by the competitors to this undertaking. It might be a consistent reading of the rules on State aid to also take into account the tax rules that apply to an undertaking's competitors to perform the selectivity test: a broad definition of the reference system would make it more likely that what is considered as 'normal' taxation corresponds to the tax rules that apply to all undertakings.

This being said, I now turn to determining whether an allocation method is part of the general corporate income tax system, or if an allocation method is a separate reference system that should be assessed individually in the light of the selectivity test. As already mentioned in section 2.2.1, the allocation methods are peculiar measures that do not have the same purpose as most other corporate income tax rules. In the paragraphs below, I will argue that the two types of rules, i.e., the basic principles of the corporate income tax system and an allocation method have different purposes that are not mutually exclusive, but are rather to be combined for the taxation of the profits of a multinational enterprise.

It was stated above that any corporate income tax system needs certain basic rules that define the income earned by corporations that the system aims at taxing. This is what the CJEU seems to have in mind when it refers to the 'ordinary'[199] or the 'general'[200] tax system, or what the Commission describes as the 'corporate income tax system'.[201] These basic rules apply to all undertakings, no matter whether they carry out domestic or cross-border activities, and irrespective of their size or ownership. The purpose of the rules is mainly to define which entities are subject to tax, which items of income are taxable or exempt from tax, whether or not expenses are deductible, and at what point in time revenues and expenses are taken into account. In contrast, an allocation method has a more specific purpose, which comes on the top of the

---

or losses is normally recognised only at the time of the sale of an asset. Therefore, a tax system would typically tax capital gains differently from business profits or employment income, for example with respect to how to compute income, when income is realised, and what tax rate applies, although both capital gains, employment income and business profits qualify as income. The conclusion is that the taxation of capital gains may constitute a separate reference system, as emphasised by the European Commission: *see* Commission Decision 2008/711/EC of 11 March 2008 on State aid C 15/07 (ex NN 20/07) implemented by Italy on the tax incentives in favour of certain restructured banks [2008] OJ L 237/70.

198. *See* Phedon Nicolaides, 'What Is Normal?' (2017) 16 European State Aid Law Quarterly 146.
199. *See* Joined Cases C-182/03 and C-217/03, *Kingdom of Belgium and Forum 187 ASBL v. Commission of the European Communities*, ECLI:EU:C:2006:416, para. 95.
200. *See* e.g., Case C-88/03, *Portuguese Republic v. Commission of the European Communities*, ECLI:EU:C:2006:511, para. 81; Joined Cases C-78/08 to C-80/08, *Paint Graphos*, ECLI:EU:C: 2011:550, para. 65.
201. *See* Commission Notice on the notion of State aid as referred to in Art. 107(1) of the Treaty on the Functioning of the European Union [2016] OJ C 262/1, para. 134.

corporate income tax system. I mentioned earlier that in my view, an allocation method has two functions, a policy function and an anti-avoidance function, these being two faces of the same coin.[202] The policy function lies in the distributive effect of an allocation method,[203] and may be influenced by considerations relating to tax competition[204] or fairness[205] in the cross-border allocation of the taxing rights. The anti-avoidance function is mainly motivated by the need for a State to safeguard the objective of its corporate income tax system. Consequently, allocation methods are peculiar tax rules given their twofold function.

Despite the peculiar nature of an allocation method, it is normally not independent from the rest of the corporate income tax system. In other words, an allocation method in most Member States does not constitute 'a consistent set of rules'[206] that would make it a separate reference system. Instead, the income of group members is normally subject to the basic principles of the corporate income tax system, both for the items of income that are in the scope of an allocation method, and for the remaining items of income. For example, if the allocation method is a generally formulated arm's length provision, it would apply together with certain other rules in the case of a payment connected to a business restructuring: in addition to the application of the arm's length principle for the determination of the amount to be possibly paid by one party to the other, the payment is normally subject to the remaining rules of the countries concerned with respect to issues such as the deductibility of the payment, or the classification of the receipt as capital gains or other types of income. Other rules would also be applicable, such as indirect taxes.[207] To take another example, when two associated enterprises conclude an intercompany loan, the borrower will be charged an interest expense by the lender. Assuming that the domestic tax provisions in the country of the borrower include both a generally formulated arm's length provision and rules on the limitation of the deduction of interests, the interest expense will be subject to the cumulative application of the two rules: first, the arm's length test would

---

202. It can be observed that these two functions were acknowledged by the CJEU as justifications of the compatibility with the fundamental freedoms of a measure implementing the arm's length principle: *see* Case C-311/08, *Société de Gestion Industrielle (SGI) v. Belgian State*, ECLI:EU:C:2010:26, para. 69.
203. According to Schön, this policy function could also be divided into two subfunctions: '(u)nder current international tax rules, the application of the "arm's length" standard fulfils two functions at the same time. It allocates income to the involved parties and it allocates taxing rights to the involved countries': *see* Wolfgang Schön, 'International Tax Coordination for a Second-Best World (Part III)' (2010) 3 World Tax Journal 227, 230.
204. A policy function of an allocation method may include a tax competition dimension to attract certain investments or encourage certain activities, such as an advantageous safe harbour rule.
205. A policy function of an allocation method may aim at allocating to group members a 'fair' share of the global profits to safeguard the taxing rights of a Member State on the activities conducted by a multinational enterprise on its territory.
206. *See* Commission Notice on the notion of State aid as referred to in Art. 107(1) of the Treaty on the Functioning of the European Union [2016] OJ C 262/1, para. 133.
207. In this respect, the OECD transfer pricing guidelines stress that the rules on business restructurings are concerned with the application of the arm's length principle, with no prejudice for the application of other rules (*see* para. 9.8 of the 2017 OECD transfer pricing guidelines: '(t)he domestic tax treatment of an arm's length payment, including rules regarding the deductibility of such a payment and how domestic capital gains tax provisions may apply to an arm's length capital payment, are […] not within the scope of this chapter').

apply, and for the interest expense that is at arm's length and is potentially deductible, the second test would apply. The same is true if an allocation method is a transfer pricing safe harbour: for example, if the safe harbour rule consists in a net margin on revenues earned by distribution activities, the revenues would be computed by relying on the rules that establish which items of income are taxable and which items of income are exempt from tax. The profit of this company would thus be subject to the combined application of the basic principles of the corporate income tax system and the allocation method.[208] In contrast to the foregoing, if a Member State were to apply a system of formula apportionment that includes all the rules necessary for the determination of the income to be apportioned, such a system might qualify for a 'consistent set of rules' that could constitute a reference system on its own, if there were no need to rely on other rules. However, that would not necessarily preserve a system of formula apportionment from being incompatible with State aid law: a difference in treatment would be created between different categories of undertakings by the coexistence of different reference systems, so the measure may still be selective; nevertheless, this case is an example of situation where the notion of reference system is not 'decisive'.[209]

Consequently, in the case of a generally formulated arm's length provision or a transfer pricing safe harbour, the allocation method and the basic rules of the corporate income tax system are normally not mutually exclusive, given that the application of either rule would typically not exclude the other. The two rules are rather to be combined in the presence of a multinational enterprise, as the sole application of either type of rule would prevent the determination of the taxable income of a group member consistently with the objective of the system: neither the sole application of the basic principles of the corporate income tax system, nor the sole application of an allocation method, is likely to result in an outcome that is consistent with the objective of a corporate income tax system. In other words, a comprehensive corporate income tax system *needs* rules that fulfil the two functions, i.e., basic principles for the determination of the corporate income, and allocation methods that share the income of multinational enterprises among their members and protect the domestic tax base: it is by combining allocation methods to the basic corporate income tax principles that a general corporate income tax system becomes consistent with its objective.

Moreover, it may not be technically correct, in a given Member State, to isolate the allocation method from the rest of the tax system. The allocation method may very well rely on concepts or assumptions that are dealt with in other provisions. The allocation method may also need to be compatible with other rules of the same tax system or certain of its general principles. For example, whether an arm's length

---

208. Indeed, if the group member earns foreign income, such income will not necessarily be included in the revenues that constitute the basis for the computation of the net margin: it needs first to be investigated whether foreign income is subject to tax or exempt. Similarly, if the group member earns royalty income, such income will be included in the revenues that constitute the basis for the computation of the net margin only if royalties are taxable under the corporate income tax system of this Member State.
209. *See* Case C-236/16, *Asociación Nacional de Grandes Empresas de Distribución (ANGED) v. Generalitat de Catalunya*, ECLI:EU:C:2017:852, Opinion of AG Kokott, para. 88.

provision allows the recharacterisation of transactions or solely the correction of transfer prices may depend on whether or not the Member State applies a general anti-avoidance rule or a principle of substance-over-form, and how such a rule is interpreted by domestic courts. Therefore, the basic principles of a corporate income tax system and the allocation method are likely to be cumulative not only from a functional perspective, but also from a technical perspective.

In view of the foregoing, I draw the conclusion that the basic corporate income tax principles and the allocation methods would normally form a single reference system. After the determination of the scope of the reference system, the focus is on the legal sources that constitute the reference system.

2.3.2 Determination of the Sources of Law That Constitute the Reference System

The conclusions from the previous sections are twofold: on the one hand, Article 107(1) of the TFEU cannot inherently impose a given allocation method as a reference system. This implies that the reference system is made not of what the Treaty would prescribe, but of domestic or treaty-based rules. On the other hand, I argued that the reference system should comprise the whole corporate income tax system, as opposed to the sole allocation method. These conclusions are not, however, sufficient to precisely determine the material content of the reference system, something that is necessary for a correct assessment of the existence of a selective treatment: if the sources of law that constitute the reference system are not precisely identified, it becomes impossible to assess whether a deviation from the reference system is at hand. Moreover, the quantification of illegal aid requires also to precisely determine the material content of the reference system and the sources of law that are comprised by the reference system.[210]

To determine the sources of law that constitute the reference system, I find it convincing to have in mind that the notion of aid supposes, in the area of tax law, an alleviation from the obligation to pay tax. In other words, for illegal aid to be at hand, there needs to be a relief from the coercive effect of the law. It is because taxes are legally imposed by a State, that a relief from an obligation to pay tax may result in an illegal aid. Thus, the content of the reference system should be dependent on what is legally binding in a Member State. Which sources are legally binding cannot be described for all the Member States in a general and exhaustive manner; it has, instead, to be determined on a case-by-case basis. What seems necessary is to include in the reference system all the sources of law that have a binding effect in a given case. A comprehensive analysis of the relevant legal sources is needed, together with the interaction between such sources. In most Member States the main source of law is made of the legal provisions enacted by Parliament. Therefore, the domestic tax rule implementing an allocation method, together with the rest of the corporate income tax system, constitutes the main source of law of the reference system.

---

210. The issue of quantification of illegal aid is left outside the scope of this book.

Chapter 2: Determination of the Reference System

However, in many cases domestic tax provisions are binding only if a constitutional rule or an international commitment does not provide otherwise. Therefore, the study of the domestic reference system should be completed with additional provisions. In particular, allocation methods, as numerous international tax rules, are often considered together with tax treaties. Tax treaty provisions should thus be part of the reference system, as long as they are in force and applicable.[211] Consistently with what was argued above with respect to the combination of the allocation method and the basic principles of the corporate income tax system, the entire tax treaty – to the extent it is applicable – should be taken into consideration to determine the content of the reference system, not the sole allocation method such as an arm's length provision drafted along the lines of Article 9 of the OECD Model Tax Convention. A tax treaty indeed includes a set of rules that are intended to be considered together, not separately.[212] Moreover, domestic court cases may also be binding, at least those issued in matters of principle by the highest national courts. Foreign court cases, on the contrary, are often lacking a binding effect in other States. Last, administrative guidance may need to be taken into account, depending on their legal standing in the actual Member State.[213] In my view, the combination of these different legal sources should be performed according to the hierarchy of norms in force in the actual Member State, because the normal application of the law can only be assessed by considering how the tax system should be applied in the particular case of a given country.

Consequently, no comprehensive answer can be provided as to the determination of the sources of law that constitute the reference system, only a single way of reasoning: the reference system should include all the legal sources that are binding, as it is a relief from the obligation to apply such legal sources that implies a deviation from the normal treatment under the domestic and treaty-based rules. Non-binding sources cannot be part of the reference system, although they may be useful for the purpose of the interpretation of the reference system and the assessment of a deviation from it.[214] In addition, relying on sources that are not binding in the legal order of a Member State would breach the principles of legality and of equality before the law; it would also create an issue of foreseeability.[215]

---

211. Not all tax treaty provisions are applicable in a given case, even when the treaty has entered into force. For example, in countries where it is considered that a tax treaty cannot create a taxing right in the absence of a domestic rule, it cannot be argued that the treaty provision is binding and thus part of the reference system when a tax liability is lacking under the domestic law. Therefore, for a tax treaty provision to be part of the reference system, it has to be applicable in the situation at hand.
212. Examples of provisions that need to be taken into account are the residence article (as this article may preclude a company from being resident in a Member State), the non-discrimination article (as it may grant certain rights to taxpayers), or the mutual agreement article (e.g., in case the competent authorities of a Member State have concluded an interpretative mutual agreement with another State in accordance with Art. 25(3) of the OECD Model Tax Convention).
213. This may be a complex issue, as even in countries where administrative guidance is in principle binding on taxpayers and tax administrations, courts may be empowered to find the administrative guidance illegal.
214. In this respect see section 5.4.2 of this book.
215. See Pierre Marie Sabbadini, *Les aides d'État – Aspects juridiques et économiques* (Larcier 2015) 148.

This proposal *ratione materiae* has also consequences *ratione temporis*. If one accepts the idea that the reference system can only consist of legal sources that are binding, the existence of a deviation from it should be assessed on the basis of the reference system that is relevant for the year(s) under scrutiny. In other words, it is submitted that the material content of the reference system should be identified for the period of time during which a tax measure is subject to State aid control. It is not satisfactory to use as a benchmark the reference system as it was at another point in time,[216] such as the time of State aid control. This is because the reference system may, at that time, have a different material content than when the taxes were levied. An example is provided by the evolution over time of the material content of the arm's length principle as it is described in the OECD transfer pricing guidelines.[217] This evolution is acknowledged in the guidelines: the 2017 update implemented not only 'clarifications', but also 'revisions'.[218] Such revisions might change the material content of the guidelines, as compared to the previous wording.[219] To take one example, the recognition of the assumption of a risk has evolved between the 2010 and 2017 guidelines: while the 2010 update was more lenient[220] (with, in particular, no systematic obligation to have the financial capacity to assume a risk[221]), the 2017 update puts higher expectations on the risk bearer to be assigned a risk as well as the income connected to it.[222]

The above statement *ratione temporis* is the direct consequence of the previous reasoning *ratione materiae*: a tax relief at a given point in time can be granted only by departing from what was binding at that point in time, as opposed to what was not binding. The principles of protection of legitimate expectations and of legal certainty support this view, as they normally preclude the retroactive application of the law.[223]

---

216. For a similar view *see* Wolfgang Schön, 'State Aid in the Area of Taxation' in Leigh Hancher, Tom Ottervanger, and Piet Jan Slot (eds), *EU State Aids* (5th edn, Sweet & Maxwell 2016) para. 13-053.
217. *See* Jacques Malherbe, *Les États-Unis au secours de leurs multinationales* (2016) 37 Revue de Droit Fiscal 3, where the author considers that the arm's length principle '*a eu un contenu variable dans le temps*'; Anja Taferner and Jurjan Wouda Kuipers, 'Tax Rulings: In Line with OECD Transfer Pricing Guidelines, but Contrary to EU State Aid Rules?' (2016) 56 European Taxation 134, 137.
218. *See* para. 19 of the preface to the 2017 OECD transfer pricing guidelines.
219. *See* Richard Collier and Joseph L Andrus, *Transfer Pricing and the Arm's Length Principle After BEPS* (Oxford University Press 2017) 155–156.
220. *See* paras 9.21 and following of the 2010 OECD transfer pricing guidelines.
221. *See* para. 9.29 of the 2010 OECD transfer pricing guidelines.
222. *See* paras 1.56 and following of the 2017 OECD transfer pricing guidelines, and especially para. 1.65 with regard to the notion of 'control over risk'.
223. *See* the analysis of Advocate General Wathelet: Case C-303/13 P, *European Commission v. Jørgen Andersen*, ECLI:EU:C:2015:340, Opinion of AG Wathelet, particularly at paras 12–29, with references to several cases issued by the Union courts. On this topic *see also* Vittorio Di Bucci and Agnieszka Stobiecka-Kuik, 'The Temporal Application of the State Aid Rules' in *EC State Aid Law – Le Droit des Aides d'Etat dans la CE – Liber Amicorum Francisco Santaolalla Gadea* (Kluwer Law International 2008) 311–345; Julia Lipinsky and Jan Wolters, 'Time will Tell – A Brief Contemplation on the Temporal Application of Substantive State Aid Rules in the Light of the Recent *Andersen*-Judgment of the CJEU' (2016) 15 European State Aid Law Quarterly 193; Liza Lovdahl Gormsen and Clement Mifsud-Bonnici, 'Legitimate Expectation of Consistent Interpretation of EU State Aid Law: Recovery in State Aid Cases Involving Advanced Pricing Agreements on Tax' (2017) 8 Journal of European Competition Law & Practice 423, 433.

Chapter 2: Determination of the Reference System

2.4 CONCLUSION

The conclusion from this chapter is that the reference system that is relevant for the selectivity test of the allocation methods is made of the binding elements of the corporate income tax system of a given Member State, which includes both the basic principles of the tax system and the allocation method.[224] In other words, it is the whole corporate income tax system that constitutes the reference system.[225] It was found in this chapter that Article 107(1) of the TFEU cannot intrinsically imply an obligation to apply the arm's length principle or any other allocation method, and that such an obligation cannot either be deducted from the sole *Forum 187* judgment. At the same time, it was emphasised that the basic corporate income tax rules may not be sufficient to ensure that the members of such enterprises are taxed in accordance with the objective of the corporate income tax system, thereby revealing a potential difference in treatment with other categories of undertakings that are taxed in accordance with that objective.

This lack of binding effect of Article 107(1) of the TFEU on the content of the reference system is consistent with the right of the Member States to decide on their tax systems, including the right to decide not to levy an income tax. Support to this view is provided by certain scholars who consider that State aid law does not impose an obligation to levy a tax on income.[226] Support to this view is also provided by cases issued by the CJEU with respect to other issues that also relate to the principle of legality: a case where the Court found that State aid law did not impose an obligation on a local authority to charge a fee for the use of routes and bus lanes,[227] and a case where the CJEU did not require a Member State to enact an anti-avoidance measure.[228] These views respect the principle of legality in areas of the law that have not been harmonised.

See also U.S. Department of the Treasury White Paper, *The European Commission's Recent Investigations of Transfer Pricing Rulings* (2016) 14; Ulf Bernitz and Anders Kjellgren, *Europarättens Grunder* (7th edn, Norstedts Juridik 2018) 168–170.

224. A similar view is held by Lang, who considers that the State aid control of tax rulings 'must be addressed separately against the background of each legal system': *see* Michael Lang, 'Tax Rulings and State Aid Law' (2015) 3 British Tax Review 391, 394.
225. Concurring, *see* Edoardo Traversa and Pierre M. Sabbadini, 'State-Aid Policy and the Fight Against Harmful Tax Competition in the Internal Market: Tax Policy in Disguise?' in Werner Haslehner, Georg Kofler, and Alexander Rust (eds), *EU Tax Law and Policy in the 21st Century* (Kluwer Law International 2017) 129.
226. For example, Luja argues that 'no Member State or autonomous region is obliged to have a general tax on profits at all', considering that the possible consequences of the lack of income tax should be a matter of harmful tax competition rather than a matter of State aid (*see* Raymond H.C. Luja, 'The Selectivity Test: The Concept of Sectoral Aid' in Alexander Rust and Claire Micheau (eds), *State Aid and Tax Law* (Kluwer Law International 2013) 112). Similarly, Szudoczky emphasises that the Member States should be allowed to design systems that do not rely on the concept of income: *see* Rita Szudoczky, *The Sources of EU Law and Their Relationships: Lessons for the Field of Taxation* (IBFD 2014) 490.
227. *See* Case C-518/13, *Eventech Ltd v. The Parking Adjudicator*, ECLI:EU:C:2015:9, para. 44.
228. *See* Case C-417/10, *Ministero dell'Economia e delle Finanze, Agenzia delle Entrate v. 3M Italia SpA*, ECLI:EU:C:2012:184, para. 32.

The findings of this chapter do not imply that a reference system cannot fall short of the selectivity test. On the one hand, the State aid rules demand the non-discriminatory application of the reference system. On the other hand, even the consistent application of the reference system may still prove selective, on the basis of the de facto selectivity test. In both cases, selectivity may nevertheless be justified by the nature or the logic of the tax system. I will return to all these issues in Chapters 4–8 of this book. However, before embarking on the analysis of these issues, I will study a question that supplements the analysis of the reference system made in this chapter, namely whether the market economy operator test might be of relevance for the selectivity assessment of the allocation methods. This is the purpose of Chapter 3 of this book.

CHAPTER 3
Potential Relevance of the Market Economy Operator Test

3.1 INTRODUCTION

In the practice of the European Commission and in the case law of the Union courts, a concept has developed requiring the Member States, when they participate in certain economic activities, to act as if they were private operators subject to the market forces. This concept, often described as the 'market economy operator test',[229] implies under certain circumstances an obligation to subject the economic terms of the transactions between the Member States or public undertakings, on the one hand, and private operators, on the other hand, to the effects of the market forces. This test normally applies for the assessment of an advantage, not for the selectivity test. However, the practice of the European Commission raises the question of the applicability of the market economy operator test as part of the selectivity assessment of certain fiscal

---

229. For analyses of the market economy operator test *see* e.g., Matthew Parish, 'On the Private Investor Principle' (2003) 28 European Law Review 70; Conor Quigley, *European State Aid Law and Policy* (3rd edn, Hart Publishing 2015) 153–192; Małgorzata Agnieszka Cyndecka, 'The Applicability and Application of the Market Economy Investor Principle' (2016) 15 European State Aid Law Quarterly 381. The expression 'market economy operator test' is used in this chapter. No distinction is made between this principle and other principles such as the market economy investor principle, the private creditor test, or the private investor test, although differences may exist. In this respect, *see* e.g., Leigh Hancher, 'The General Framework' in Leigh Hancher, Tom Ottervanger, and Piet Jan Slot (eds), *EU State Aids* (5th edn, Sweet & Maxwell 2016) 97–106. The differences between the various formulations and meanings of the market economy operator test have, in my view, no important significance on the application of this test to the allocation methods, the relevant question being whether or not the expectations put on the Member States when they act as market operators also apply when they exercise their right to tax. Therefore, there is no need making a distinction between the market economy operator test and the other formulations of this test, for the purpose of this chapter.

measures,[230] especially given the requirement to search for a 'reliable approximation of a market-based outcome'[231] when the Member States are taxing the income of multinational enterprises. The search for 'market-based outcomes' may imply an obligation to apply the arm's length principle, or an obligation to interpret the arm's length principle consistently with the interpretation of the market economy operator test.[232] Accordingly, in section 3.2 I will address whether the market economy operator test may have a binding effect on the selectivity assessment of the allocation methods.

Irrespective of the binding effect of the market economy operator test in relation to the selectivity assessment of the allocation methods, this notion is interesting at a conceptual level, as it reflects the interpretation by the Union courts and the European Commission of the effects of the market forces. The Union courts could, for example, assess the correct application of the arm's length principle by a Member State in the light of the interpretation of the market economy operator test, since both rules rely on the market forces. Accordingly, in section 3.3 I will investigate the interpretation of the market forces under the market economy operator test, in particular through a comparison with the arm's length principle as it is interpreted in the 2017 OECD transfer pricing guidelines. On the basis of the findings of sections 3.2 and 3.3, in section 3.4 I will consider the relevance of the interpretation of the effects of the market forces under the market economy operator test, for the selectivity assessment of the allocation methods. Finally, I will present the conclusions of this chapter in section 3.5.

3.2 MAY THE MARKET ECONOMY OPERATOR TEST HAVE A BINDING EFFECT ON THE SELECTIVITY ASSESSMENT OF THE ALLOCATION METHODS?

The market economy operator test, which has been recognised explicitly by the CJEU since the so-called *Meura* case,[233] and regularly relied on by the European

---

230. *See* European Commission, 'Draft Commission Notice on the notion of State aid pursuant to Article 107(1) TFEU' (2014) 23. On the possible relevance of the market economy operator test to assess the compatibility with State aid law of advance tax rulings, *see* Alexandre Maitrot de la Motte, 'L'identification des "paramètres pertinents pour établir la sélectivité" des avantages fiscaux' (2017) 26 Revue de Droit Fiscal 37, where the author at 44 suggests the idea that the lawfulness of advance tax rulings could be assessed in view of what the Members States obtain (e.g., jobs created, indirect taxes levied) in return for the tax reliefs they provide.
231. *See* Commission Notice on the notion of State aid as referred to in Art. 107(1) of the Treaty on the Functioning of the European Union [2016] OJ C 262/1, paras 171–174, as well as the references to the concept of 'market-based outcomes' in the decisions concerning *Starbucks, Fiat*, or *Apple*.
232. *See* James Kavanagh and Nicole Robins, 'Corporate Tax Arrangements Under EU State Aid Scrutiny – The Application of the Market Economy Operator Principle' (2015) 14 European State Aid Law Quarterly 358, 366.
233. *See* Case 234/84, *Kingdom of Belgium v. Commission of the European Communities*, ECLI:EU:C:1986:302, para. 14. In its case law the CJEU has used different wordings, depending on the context in which the Court has ruled. The material content of these different wordings is not studied here. For example, when a Member State acts in its capacity as shareholder, the CJEU uses the expression 'private investor test' (*see* Case C-124/10 P, *Commission v. Électricité de France (EDF)*, ECLI:EU:C:2012:318, para. 78).

Chapter 3: Potential Relevance of the Market Economy Operator Test

Commission,[234] implies that the conditions of the transactions between public authorities and private undertakings should correspond to the conditions existing between private operators acting under 'normal market conditions'.[235] 'Normal market conditions' are defined as 'the conditions applying to the economy of a Member State where it does not intervene in favour of certain undertakings'.[236] This means, according to Quigley, that the market economy operator test is satisfied where a private operator transacting with a public authority 'could theoretically have derived the same benefits from the mere functioning of the market'.[237] Consequently, under the rules on State aid, an intervention by a Member State shall produce no advantage to a private operator: public authorities are expected to act as if they were private operators that are subject to the market forces.

The European Commission has, at certain occasions, relied on the logic of the market economy operator test, although formulated differently, to assess the behaviours of the Member States in relation to tax matters.[238] The Commission has argued at paragraph 55 of the opening decision in the Amazon case that '(w)hen accepting a calculation method of the taxable basis proposed by the taxpayer, the tax authorities should compare that method to the prudent behaviour of a hypothetical market operator, which would require a market conform remuneration of a subsidiary or a branch, which reflect normal conditions of competition. For example, a market operator would not accept that its revenues are based on a method which achieves the lowest possible outcome if the facts and circumstances of the case could justify the use of other, more appropriate methods'. The reference to a 'hypothetical market operator' seems to have been replaced, in later documents, by the need to reach 'market-based outcomes'.[239] The concept of 'market-based outcomes' has been considered in the

---

234. *See* Commission Notice on the notion of State aid as referred to in Art. 107(1) of the Treaty on the Functioning of the European Union [2016] OJ C 262/1, para. 75. For an illustration of the communications issued by the European Commission where it provides its view on what constitutes a behaviour that is in line with the market economy operator test, *see* e.g., Communication from the Commission to the Member States on the application of Arts 107 and 108 of the Treaty on the Functioning of the European Union to short-term export-credit insurance [2012] OJ C 392/1, particularly at para. 15 for the material elements of State aid in the area of short-term export-credit insurance.
235. *See* Case C-39/94, *Syndicat français de l'Express international and others v. La Poste and others*, ECLI:EU:C:1996:285, para. 60. The CJEU confirmed this view several times, which is now considered settled case law (*see* e.g., Case C-280/00, *Altmark Trans and Regierungspräsidium Magdeburg*, ECLI:EU:C:2003:415, para. 84).
236. *See* Case C-131/15 P, *Club Hotel Loutraki AE and Others v. European Commission*, ECLI:EU:C:2016:989, para. 72.
237. *See* Conor Quigley, *European State Aid Law and Policy* (3rd edn, Hart Publishing 2015) 154.
238. *See* e.g., State aid – Ireland – State aid SA.38373 (2014/C) (ex 2014/NN) – Alleged aid to Apple – Invitation to submit comments pursuant to Art. 108(2) of the Treaty on the Functioning of the European Union [2014] OJ C 369/22, para. 56. *See also* State aid – Luxembourg – State aid SA.38944 (2014/C) (2014/NN) – Alleged aid to Amazon – Invitation to submit comments pursuant to Art. 108(2) of the Treaty on the Functioning of the European Union [2015] OJ C 44/13, para. 55.
239. *See* Commission Notice on the notion of State aid as referred to in Art. 107(1) of the Treaty on the Functioning of the European Union [2016] OJ C 262/1, paras 171 and 172. In the 2014 draft notice on the notion of State aid the Commission made clear that the market economy operator test might apply to tax measures, as it stated that 'the applicability of the [market economy

doctrine to constitute 'a new hybrid' of the market economy operator test, as it would apply between private companies, whereas the test normally applies to assess the conduct of public authorities.[240] The question raised by this reference to the market economy operator test in the area of taxation is straightforward: may the market economy operator test have a binding effect on the selectivity assessment of the allocation methods? I will argue below that this question should be answered negatively.

The market economy operator test is normally relevant for the assessment of the existence of an advantage, not for the test of its possible selectivity. For instance, in the case *SFEI*, the CJEU stated that 'in order to determine whether a State measure constitutes aid, it is necessary to establish whether the recipient undertaking receives an *economic advantage* which it would not have obtained under normal market conditions' (emphasis added).[241] Therefore, at first sight the market economy operator test does not seem to be applicable as part of the selectivity assessment of a fiscal measure. However, given that advantages may be granted through fiscal measures such as tax reliefs, it is relevant to ask whether the market economy operator test may apply to tax measures. If the test does apply, the Member States would need to act under the influence of the market forces when they are legislating and levying taxes. Examples of consequences of the application of the market economy operator test to the area of tax law could be an obligation to levy tax on the basis of the arm's length principle (whether as part of an allocation method, or for other purposes), or an obligation to maximise the levy of taxes by analogy to a private operator who would seek to maximise its profits.

Normally, the market economy operator test applies only when a Member State takes part in economic activities with State resources, and in an area where it is in competition with private operators. This contrasts with situations where a Member State exercises prerogatives that are exclusive to public authorities, such as legislating.[242] Indeed, as emphasised by Advocate General Léger, 'the Court distinguishes between two categories of situation: those where the intervention of the State is of an economic nature and those where it forms part of the exercise of public powers'.[243]

---

operator test] cannot be ruled out simply because the means employed by the State are fiscal': see European Commission, 'Draft Commission Notice on the notion of State aid pursuant to Article 107(1) TFEU' (2014) 23.
240. See Michael Honoré, 'State Aid and Taxation – All Clear?' (2015) 24 European State Aid Law Quarterly 306.
241. See Case C-39/94, *Syndicat français de l'Express international and others v. La Poste and others*, ECLI:EU:C:1996:285, para. 60.
242. See in this respect Vivien Rose and David Bailey, 'State Aids' in Vivien Rose and David Bailey (eds) *Bellamy and Child: European Union Law of Competition* (7th edn, Oxford University Press 2013), para. 17.012: '(t)he need to compare the State's actions with those of a hypothetical or actual71 private investor in an equivalent position means that the market economy investor principle can be applied only where the State is acting as an undertaking (that is, as an economic actor), and not where it is acting as a public authority'. See also Commission Notice on the notion of State aid as referred to in Art. 107(1) of the Treaty on the Functioning of the European Union [2016] OJ C 262/1, para. 77.
243. See Opinion delivered on 14 January 2003, Case C-280/00, *Altmark Trans and Regierungspräsidium Magdeburg*, ECLI:EU:C:2002:188, Opinion of AG Léger, para. 20.

Chapter 3: Potential Relevance of the Market Economy Operator Test

Therefore, as put by the General Court, 'a public investor is not in the same situation as a private investor'.[244] It is only when a Member State exercises regulatory power in an area that is not exclusive to the public sphere, that the acts of a Member State may generally be assessed in the light of the market economy operator test.[245] This should imply that taxes are clearly outside the scope of the market economy operator test, given that a State normally has an exclusive right to levy taxes on its territory; the levy of tax is indeed a prerogative that stems from statehood.[246]

Yet fiscal measures are not fully outside the scope of the market economy operator test. The question of the applicability of this test to fiscal measures was at issue in the *EDF* case, which is about a Member State that granted certain tax reliefs to a company in which it held shares. Although taxes as such are normally levied by a Member State as a regulator, in this case the reason justifying the tax relief was rather the fact that the Member State was a shareholder of the recipient of the aid. Therefore, the CJEU considered that the acts of the Member State could be assessed in the light of the market economy operator test, even when these acts took the form of fiscal measures. The Court thus found the market economy operator test relevant for the State aid control of a tax relief.[247] The CJEU considered in particular that 'an economic advantage must – even where it has been granted through fiscal means – be assessed inter alia in the light of the private investor test, if (...) it appears that, notwithstanding the fact that the means used were instruments of State power, the Member State concerned conferred that advantage in its capacity as shareholder'.[248]

The *EDF* decision has been criticised by part of the doctrine.[249] It has also been observed that the Court solely accepted the possibility of the test applying to taxes,

---

244. *See* Joined Cases T-228/99 and T-233/99, *Westdeutsche Landesbank Girozentrale v. European Commission*, ECLI:EU:T:2003:57, para. 272.
245. For an illustration of the application of the market economy operator test to areas where public authorities have regulatory powers that are not exclusive to the public sphere, *see* e.g., Case T-196/04, *Ryanair Ltd v. Commission of the European Communities*, ECLI:EU:T:2008:585, para. 101: 'The mere fact that, in the present case, the Walloon Region has regulatory powers in relation to fixing airport charges does not mean that a scheme reducing those charges ought not to be examined by reference to the private investor principle, since such a scheme could have been put in place by a private operator.'
246. *See* Joined Cases T-228/99 and T-233/99, *Westdeutsche Landesbank Girozentrale v. European Commission*, ECLI:EU:T:2003:57, where at para. 272 the General Court found that a public investor 'has access to resources flowing from the exercise of public power, in particular from taxation'. Concurring *see* Wolfgang Schön, 'Tax Legislation and the Notion of Fiscal Aid: A Review of 5 Years of European Jurisprudence' in Isabelle Richelle, Wolfgang Schön, and Edoardo Traversa (eds), *State Aid Law and Business Taxation* (Springer 2016) 6. This does not prevent a Member State from deciding which part of the State organisation should levy the taxes. Therefore, aids not granted by a Member State itself may still be in the scope of the State aid rules, such as regional aids.
247. *See* Case C-124/10 P, *Commission v. Électricité de France (EDF)*, ECLI:EU:C:2012:318.
248. *See* Case C-124/10 P, *Commission v. Électricité de France (EDF)*, ECLI:EU:C:2012:318, para. 92.
249. *See* e.g., Thomas Jaeger, 'From Santander to LuxLeaks – and Back' (2015) 24 European State Aid Law Quarterly 345, 348 where the author observes that there are no normal market conditions for decisions over taxes given that a State has 'no individual, case-by-case discretion whether to collect taxes or whether to use the revenue from taxpayer A for purpose X'; Wolfgang Schön, 'State Aid in the Area of Taxation' in Leigh Hancher, Tom Ottervanger, and Piet Jan Slot (eds), *EU State Aids* (5th edn, Sweet & Maxwell 2016) para. 13-043, with further references at footnote 153.

without considering whether this test was actually applicable in that case.[250] However, it can be concluded from *EDF* that the market economy operator test is not applicable to the area of taxes, unless a tax advantage is granted by a State not in its public capacity, but rather in a capacity that could be exercised by a private operator, such as being a shareholder. Accordingly, the market economy operator test can have no general binding effect on the levy of taxes, and, for the purpose of this study, on the choice of an allocation method.[251] This means that the market economy operator test can only be applied to fiscal measures on a case-by-case basis, as opposed to being generally and *in abstracto* applicable to (parts of) a tax system.

Therefore, although it can be agreed with the statement that '(t)he market investor test is an arm's length test'[252] (because it relies on the effects of the market forces), the market economy operator test and the arm's length principle 'obey two different logics',[253] so that the former can have no binding effect on the latter. Accordingly, the market economy operator test cannot oblige the Member States to include in their domestic tax laws a given allocation method, not even the arm's length principle, although this allocation method shares a common rationale with the market economy operator test.[254] This also means, in my view, that the objective mentioned by the European Commission to implement taxation methods that ensure 'market-based outcomes' cannot be legally supported by the market economy operator test.

Despite the lack of binding effect of the market economy operator test on the design of the allocation methods, it is legitimate to ask whether the interpretation by the Union courts and the Commission of the effects of the market forces under the

---

250. *See* Laurence Idot, 'Notion d'aide et critère de l'investisseur privé en économie de marché' (2012) 8–9 Europe 335.
251. Concurring *see* Thomas Jaeger, 'From Santander to LuxLeaks – and Back' (2015) 24 European State Aid Law Quarterly 345, 348; Werner Haslehner, 'Double Taxation Relief, Transfer Pricing Adjustments and State Aid Law' in Isabelle Richelle, Wolfgang Schön, and Edoardo Traversa (eds), *State Aid Law and Business Taxation* (Springer 2016) 154.
252. *See* Paris Anestis and Stephen Mavroghenis, 'The Market Investor Test' in Michael Sánchez Rydelski (ed), *The EC State Aid Regime: Distortive Effects of State Aid on Competition and Trade* (Cameron May 2006) 112.
253. *See* Saturnina Moreno González, 'State Aid and Tax Competition: Comments on the European Commission's Decisions on Transfer Pricing Rulings' (2016) 15 European State Aid Law Quarterly 556, 563. I agree with this statement, particularly given that while the market economy operator test is more of a one-sided test (because it assesses the behaviour of a State), the arm's length principle is more of a two-sided test (because it takes into consideration the positions of the two parties to a transaction). The application of the market economy operator test to tax measures could threaten the balance in the allocation of the corporate tax base among the Member States, because if the Member States were to act as market operators when levying taxes, they could be expected to maximise their fiscal revenues. Since the allocation of the corporate tax base among the Member States is by definition a cross-border issue, the combination of the claims of the Member States concerned by the allocation of the corporate tax base of a multinational enterprise – assuming that such claims should imply a maximisation of their fiscal revenues – may lead to situations of multiple taxation. In other words, the interpretation that is made of what the market forces require in the context of the market economy operator test obeys to a logic that is not transposable to the context of the taxation of the income of multinational enterprises.
254. Concurring *see* Wolfgang Schön, 'State Aid in the Area of Taxation' in Leigh Hancher, Tom Ottervanger, and Piet Jan Slot (eds), *EU State Aids* (5th edn, Sweet & Maxwell 2016) para. 13-045.

market economy operator test might be relevant for the assessment of potential deviations from the arm's length principle. I will address this question in the following section.

3.3 INTERPRETATION OF THE EFFECTS OF THE MARKET FORCES UNDER THE MARKET ECONOMY OPERATOR TEST

3.3.1 Introduction

It was concluded in the section above that the market economy operator test should have no binding effect on the *design* of the tax rules of the Member States. However, when tax rules (e.g., an allocation method implementing the arm's length principle) rely on the effects of the market forces, the State aid control of such rules may, or perhaps even should, be inspired by the *interpretation* of the effects of the market forces under the market economy operator test, if the effect of the market forces are interpreted differently between these two sources.[255] The position taken by the European Commission points to the relevance of the market economy operator test as guidance for the interpretation of the effects of the market forces.[256] This position is motivated by referring to the mention of conditions of 'free competition' by the CJEU.[257] These are close, if not similar, to 'normal market conditions', and thus to the market economy operator test.[258] From a theoretical standpoint it would indeed seem consistent that a given benchmark (the need to rely on the market forces) produces the same consequences under the State aid rules, no matter which type of rule is subject to State aid control. Therefore, it should be investigated whether the interpretation of the effects of the market forces has the same material content under the market economy operator test as under the arm's length principle, which is the purpose of the following section (section 3.3.2).

---

255. Indeed, if the interpretation of the effects of the market forces is the same under the market economy operator test and the arm's length principle, there is no point in asking whether the former may, or should influence the latter: the two would have similar material contents as to the effects of the market forces.
256. *See* e.g., State aid – Ireland – State aid SA.38373 (2014/C) (ex 2014/NN) – Alleged aid to Apple – Invitation to submit comments pursuant to Art. 108(2) of the Treaty on the Functioning of the European Union [2014] OJ C 369/22, para. 56; State aid – Luxembourg – State aid SA.38944 (2014/C) (2014/NN) – Alleged aid to Amazon – Invitation to submit comments pursuant to Art. 108(2) of the Treaty on the Functioning of the European Union [2015] OJ C 44/13, para. 55. *See also* Commission Notice on the notion of State aid as referred to in Art. 107(1) of the Treaty on the Functioning of the European Union [2016] OJ C 262/1, paras 171 and 172.
257. *See* Joined Cases C-182/03 and C-217/03, *Kingdom of Belgium and Forum 187 ASBL v. Commission of the European Communities*, ECLI:EU:C:2006:416, para. 96.
258. *See* Case C-131/15 P, *Club Hotel Loutraki AE and Others v. European Commission*, ECLI:EU:C:2016:989, where at para. 72 the Court defines 'normal market conditions' as 'covering the conditions applying to the economy of a Member State where it does not intervene in favour of certain undertakings'.

3.3.2 Comparison Between the Market Economy Operator Test and the Arm's Length Principle

From a conceptual perspective, the market economy operator test resembles the arm's length principle as it is interpreted in the OECD transfer pricing guidelines. However, although the two tests partly overlap, I will show that certain differences remain.

To start with, it can be observed that the aims of the two notions are comparable, as both the market economy operator test and the arm's length principle apply to transactions that need to be regulated. Indeed, whether in the context of transactions between public authorities and private undertakings, or in the context of transactions between associated enterprises, the terms of the transactions may have an impact on the profitability and on the competitive position of the parties. The terms of the transactions may also have an impact on the public resources of the Member States involved. Accordingly, the two types of situations to which the market economy operator test and the arm's length principle apply need to be regulated, so as to ensure a correct allocation of resources between the parties to a transaction.

While the transactions described above need to be regulated, it can be observed that the two tests rely on similar principles to regulate such transactions. This is the strongest resemblance between the market economy operator test and the arm's length principle. The two concepts have a common rationale, and use a common benchmark for assessing the terms of transactions: both tests rely on the market forces when setting expectations on the Member States or on associated enterprises, thereby aiming at a form of neutrality[259] between the situation that is being tested,[260] and what the market forces command.[261] The reliance on the market forces is so strong under the two tests, that even in the lack of reliable comparable information, the two tests imply making an assumption as to how the market forces would react to a given situation.[262]

In addition to the reliance on the market forces as a general benchmark, there are other important similarities between the market economy operator test and the arm's length principle. I will address three of them below. However, there are also certain

---

259. The concept of neutrality is referred to, for instance, in the Commission Communication on the application of the State aid rules to public undertakings in the manufacturing sector: *see* Commission communication to the Member States – Application of Arts 92 and 93 of the EEC Treaty and of Art. 5 of Commission Directive 80/723/EEC to public undertakings in the manufacturing sector [1993] OJ C 307/3, in particular at point 11 where the Commission refers to the need '(t)o ensure respect for the principle of neutrality'. The principle of neutrality stems also from Art. 345 of the TFEU, as this article implies that the Treaties shall in no way prejudice the rules in Member States governing the system of property ownership.
260. The situation that is being tested consists in the terms of transactions between public authorities and private operators, on the one hand, and the terms of transactions between associated enterprises, on the other hand.
261. Concurring *see* Liza Lovdahl Gormsen, 'EU State Aid Law and Transfer Pricing: A Critical Introduction to a New Saga' (2016) 7 Journal of European Competition Law & Practice 369, 378.
262. An example of such assumption in the application of the arm's length principle is the need to assume how independent parties would have acted in the circumstances that are being tested, although no reliable comparable information exists: *see* paras 9.109 and 9.113 of the 2017 OECD transfer pricing guidelines, and para. 9.19 of the 2010 OECD transfer pricing guidelines.

differences between the two tests, in particular with respect to the interpretation of what the market forces require. I will return to these differences later on.

First, the two tests rely on the notion of comparability. This comes as a corollary of transposing the effects of the market forces to the situation that is being tested. In other words, the two tests require that the effects of the market forces be transposed to a situation that is comparable to the one observed on the open market. A fundamental characteristic of the arm's length principle is indeed the notion of comparability between controlled and uncontrolled transactions.[263] In addition to stating that principle,[264] the OECD transfer pricing guidelines devote a whole chapter on how to conduct a comparability analysis.[265] The Union courts also rely on the notion of comparability when applying the market economy operator test: the conduct of a Member State and the terms of transactions with private operators are assessed in the light of the respective position of each party.[266] Moreover, both the arm's length principle and the market economy operator test require that comparability adjustments be made to the terms of the transactions that are being tested, to ensure that the effects of the market forces are correctly transposed to comparable situations.[267] For example, it was mentioned above in section 2.2.3.2 that the arm's length principle (as it is described in the 2017 OECD transfer pricing guidelines) does not always require an identical treatment to situations observed on the open market; the same reasoning applies under the market economy operator test, which accepts some discrepancy

---

263. The first OECD report on transfer pricing, issued in 1979, already emphasised the importance of the notion of comparability, and provided parameters to take into account when using various transfer pricing methods: see OECD, *Transfer Pricing and Multinational Enterprises* (OECD 1979) paras 48 and following.
264. See para. 1.33 and following of the 2017 OECD transfer pricing guidelines.
265. See Chapter 3 of the 2017 OECD transfer pricing guidelines.
266. Examples are provided in several areas of application of the market economy operator test. In the case of contributions by the public authorities to the capital of private companies, the CJEU found that 'it must be considered whether, in similar circumstances, a private investor of a stature comparable to that of the bodies administering the public sector might have been induced to provide contributions of capital to a like extent' (see Case C-261/89, *Italian Republic v. Commission of the European Communities*, ECLI:EU:C:1991:367, para. 8). See also Case T-296/97, *Alitalia – Linee aeree italiane SpA v. Commission of the European Communities*, ECLI:EU:T:2000:289, where the General Court at para. 81 used as a benchmark the situation of a private investor 'in comparable circumstances'; the same notion of 'comparable circumstances' is frequently used in the OECD transfer pricing guidelines. The CJEU has used other expressions when referring to the concept of comparability, such as the investigation of situations that are 'as close as possible' to each other: see Case C-300/16 P, *European Commission v. Frucona Košice a.s.*, ECLI:EU:C:2017:706, para. 60.
267. See paras 3.47 and following of the 2017 OECD transfer pricing guidelines. On the need to make adjustments upon the application of the market economy operator test to strengthen the comparability between two situations, see Davide Grespan and Sandro Santamato, '"Favouring Certain Undertakings or the Production of Certain Goods": Advantage' in Wolfgang Mederer, Nicola Pesaresi, and Marc Van Hoof (eds), 4 *EU Competition Law: State Aid* (Claeys & Casteels 2008) para. 2.350: 'the closest market reference should be suitably corrected to take into account any specificity related to the position of the investor, the characteristics of the operation, and any other factor that is capable of influencing the choices of an investor'.

between private and public operators, for example by expecting the Member States to seek for profitability in the long term, whereas private operators may be more interested in short term profits.[268]

Second, the two tests rely on a link between the activity performed by an enterprise, and the economic outcome that should be attributed to that activity. This is a central consequence of the so-called functional analysis in the context of the arm's length principle. Indeed, a central part of the arm's length principle relies on a direct link between the functions performed, the risks assumed, and the assets used by an enterprise (as evidenced by a functional analysis), and the exposure of an enterprise to the economic outcome of a business activity,[269] whether it is profits or losses. Similarly, the Union courts have recognised the idea of a connexion between the level of return that should be expected by a public authority acting as a market participant, and the level of involvement of that authority in terms close to those described in the OECD transfer pricing guidelines.[270] In addition to profits, the Union courts have applied the same reasoning to the assumption of losses,[271] and the allocation of costs.[272]

---

268. *See* e.g., Case C-305/89, *Italian Republic v. Commission of the European Communities*, ECLI:EU:C:1991:142, para. 20. Such a discrepancy seems indeed logical, as States and private operators are not in a fully comparable situation, the former having an incentive and the financial capacity to make long term investments, the latter having an incentive to make shorter term investments given the expectations of their shareholders and their more limited financial capacity.
269. *See* paras 1.51 and following of the 2017 OECD transfer pricing guidelines, and particularly the second sentence of para. 1.56 where it is indicated that '(u)sually, in the open market, the assumption of increased risk would also be compensated by an increase in the expected return, although the actual return may or may not increase depending on the degree to which the risks are actually realised'.
270. Examples are provided by cases where the Union courts considered that the level of return that is expected by a public investor should be connected to the level of risk that is assumed when making the investment. *See* for instance Cases T-228/99 and T-233/99, *Westdeutsche Landesbank Girozentrale v. Commission of the European Communities*, ECLI:EU:T:2003:57, para. 255: 'the use of an average return must be consistent with the notion that an informed private investor, that is, an investor who wishes to maximise his profits but without running excessive risks in comparison with other participants in the market, would, when calculating the appropriate return to be expected for his investment, in principle require a minimum return equivalent to the average return for the sector concerned'.
271. The market economy operator test indeed determines whether or not a State-owned company may support the losses of its subsidiaries, something that takes into account the contributions of and expectations from each party in a manner that closely resembles the arm's length principle. An example is provided by a case where the CJEU accepted the support of losses similarly to the possibility under the arm's length principle for an entrepreneur to support the losses of its limited-risk counterpart: *see* Case 303/88, *Italian Republic v. Commission of the European Communities*, ECLI:EU:C:1991:136, para. 21, where the Court considered that a parent company may, 'for a limited period, bear the losses of one of its subsidiaries in order to enable the latter to close down its operations under the best possible conditions. Such decisions may be motivated not solely by the likelihood of an indirect material profit but also by other considerations, such as a desire to protect the group's image or to redirect its activities'. *See also* Communication from the Commission – European Union framework for State aid in the form of public service compensation [2012] OJ C 8/15, para. 33. For comparable ideas developed in the application of the arm's length principle, *see* para. 1.129–1.131 of the 2017 OECD transfer pricing guidelines.
272. *See* e.g., Case T-375/15, *Germanwings GmbH v. European Commission*, ECLI:EU:T:2017:289.

Chapter 3: Potential Relevance of the Market Economy Operator Test

Third, the methods that put in practice the ideas described above are also relatively similar when comparing the arm's length principle and the market economy operator test. For the purpose of finding a market value when relying on the market economy operator test, it is often relied on benchmarking studies as well as on ranges of values.[273] This reminds of the recommendations made in the OECD transfer pricing guidelines,[274] which is not surprising as in both cases the objective is to come as close as possible to a market value through the most relevant statistical tools. There seems also to be a preference for applying the market economy operator test through making direct comparisons (the so-called *pari passu* approach),[275] which reminds of the preference described in the OECD transfer pricing guidelines for the Comparable Uncontrolled Price (CUP) method.[276] Another example relates to the approximation of the value of an asset, which is subject to similar valuation methods in the two contexts.[277]

Moreover, as a consequence of the important similarities between the market economy operator test and the arm's length principle, the two tests share certain common issues. For example, whereas the arm's length principle struggles with the comparability between independent and associated enterprises, the market economy operator test struggles with the comparability between public and private undertakings.[278] Another common problem concerns the difficulty to accurately determine and

---

273. *See* for example Case T-163/05, *Bundesverband deutscher Banken v. Commission*, ECLI:EU:T:2010:59, para. 195. *See also* Conor Quigley, *European State Aid Law and Policy* (3rd edn, Hart Publishing 2015) 155; Samuel Cornella, 'The "Market Economy Investor Principle" to Evaluate State Aid: Latest development and New Perspectives' (2015) 22 Maastricht Journal of European and Comparative Law 553, 569–570.
274. *See* paras 3.55 and following of the 2017 OECD transfer pricing guidelines.
275. *See* e.g., Commission decision of 7 July 2015 in State Aid SA.36574 (2015/NN, ex 2013/CP) – France – Alleged aid to Altrad [2015] OJ C 369/1, paras 45–52; Case T-296/97, *Alitalia – Linee aeree italiane SpA v. Commission of the European Communities*, ECLI:EU:T:2000:289, para. 81. *See also* Vivien Rose and David Bailey, 'State Aids' in Vivien Rose and David Bailey (eds) *Bellamy and Child: European Union Law of Competition* (7th edn, Oxford University Press 2013), para. 17.012 at footnote 71: 'Reliance on the principle is easiest where there is direct evidence that a rational private investor would be prepared to invest on the same terms as the State, e.g., where the State is investing in *pari passu* to a private investor. Other evidence, such as expert opinions, can, however, also be relied upon'; on this point *see also* Samuel Cornella, 'The "Market Economy Investor Principle" to Evaluate State Aid: Latest Development and New Perspectives' (2015) 22 Maastricht Journal of European and Comparative Law 553, 567.
276. *See* para. 2.15 of the 2017 OECD transfer pricing guidelines.
277. In particular, the method consisting in computing the net present value of an asset by calculating the total future cash flows that this asset may generate, often described as the discounted cash flow method, is used both by the European Commission when quantifying aid in non-tax cases (*see* e.g., Commission decision of 18 July 2007 State aid NN 34/2007 (ex CP 189/2004) – Germany Capital contributions NORD/LB [2008] OJ C 4/1, para. 46), and in the OECD transfer pricing guidelines when describing valuation techniques (*see* paras 6.158 and following of the 2017 OECD transfer pricing guidelines).
278. *See* e.g., the *Chronopost* case, in which the CJEU acknowledged that in certain cases public undertakings may act differently from private undertakings (in this case, a private undertaking would not have created and maintained a network such as that created by the French post office, which operated as a legal monopoly): Joined Cases C-83/01 P, C-93/01 P and C-94/01 P, *Chronopost SA, La Poste and French Republic v. Union française de l'express (Ufex), DHL International, Federal express international (France) SNC and CRI.E. SA*, ECLI:EU:C:2003:388, para. 36. *See also* Cases T-228/99 and T-233/99, *Westdeutsche Landesbank Girozentrale v.*

quantify the consequences of the effects of the market forces, when such effects are to be transposed to a situation that is being tested under the arm's length principle or the market economy operator test.[279]

However, despite the resemblance at a conceptual level between the market economy operator test and the arm's length principle, the interpretation of what the market forces require under these two tests does not exactly match. To start with, despite the apparent objective nature of the market forces, there is not necessarily a single correct interpretation of the effects of the market forces. The market economy operator test and the arm's length principle, as it is described in the OECD transfer pricing guidelines, may thus be diverging, although they rely on a similar benchmark. In this respect, it is argued in a study made on behalf of the European Commission, that the arm's length principle and the concept of market value are not necessarily similar.[280] Several examples actually show a discrepancy between the market economy operator test as it is interpreted by the Union courts, and the arm's length principle as it is described in the 2017 OECD transfer pricing guidelines. I will consider three cases of discrepancies below. These examples are not meant to be exhaustive, they simply illustrate the differences in the interpretation of the effects of the market forces between the market economy operator test and the arm's length principle as it is described in the 2017 OECD transfer pricing guidelines.

First, the market economy operator test implies that the conduct of a Member State is assessed at the time of this conduct, not on the basis of later facts.[281] This does

---

European Commission, ECLI:EU:T:2003:57, para. 272, where the General Court considered that 'a public investor is not in the same situation as a private investor'; Case 234/84, *Kingdom of Belgium v. Commission of the European Communities*, ECLI:EU:C:1986:151, Opinion of AG Lenz, at 2271, where the Advocate General considers that a State 'has the possibility of procuring the necessary capital resources on a substantial scale – through taxation or compulsory loans'. On this point *see also* Malcolm Ross, 'State Aids and National Courts: Definitions and Other Problems – A Case of Premature Emancipation?' (2000) 37 Common Market Law Review 401, 407: 'difficulties remain in both conceptualizing and applying appropriate comparators'.

279. In this respect it can be observed that because of this complexity, the CJEU does not aim at performing a full control of the correctness of the conclusions reached by the European Commission: *see* Joined Cases C-328/99 and C-399/00, *Italian Republic and SIM 2 Multimedia SpA v. Commission of the European Communities*, ECLI:EU:C:2003:252, para. 39.
280. *See* European Commission/Deloitte, 'Study on the Application of Economic Valuation Techniques for Determining Transfer Prices of Cross Border Transactions between Members of Multinational Enterprise Groups in the EU' (European Commission 2016) 28–33; *see also* at 90 for an analysis of the strengths and weaknesses of different valuation standards, where it can be observed that the OECD transfer pricing guidelines are considered not consistent with other valuation standards. For a comment on this study *see* Olivier Treidler and Samuel Jung, 'Economic Valuation Techniques for Transfer Pricing' (2017) 85 Tax Notes International 561.
281. *See* e.g., Case C-482/99, *French Republic v. Commission of the European Communities*, ECLI:EU:C:2002:294, para. 71: 'in order to examine whether or not the State has adopted the conduct of a prudent investor operating in a market economy, it is necessary to place oneself in the context of the period during which the financial support measures were taken in order to assess the economic rationality of the State's conduct, and thus to refrain from any assessment based on a later situation'. Confirming, *see* Case C-124/10 P, *Commission v. Électricité de France (EDF)*, ECLI:EU:C:2012:318, para. 85; Case T-303/10, *Wam Industriale SpA v. European Commission*, ECLI:EU:T:2012:505, para. 158. *See also* Małgorzata Agnieszka Cyndecka, 'The Applicability and Application of the Market Economy Investor Principle' (2016) 15 European State Aid Law Quarterly 381, 396, with further references at footnote 213.

Chapter 3: Potential Relevance of the Market Economy Operator Test

not mean that ex-post evaluation is forbidden under State aid law: there are areas where ex-post evaluation is recommended, such as regional aid,[282] or certain schemes with an annual budget exceeding EUR 150 million.[283] However, the position of the Union courts when they interpret the market economy operator test does contrast with an important paragraph of the 2017 OECD transfer pricing guidelines where, under certain circumstances and subject to the exceptions described at the following paragraph, a possibility is given to tax administrations to consider '*ex post* outcomes as presumptive evidence about the appropriateness of the *ex ante* pricing arrangements' (emphasis not added).[284] The purpose of this paragraph is to compensate for information asymmetry between taxpayers and tax administrations with respect to 'hard-to-value intangibles'.[285] In contrast to what the OECD transfer pricing guidelines recommend (albeit in a limited number of cases), *ex post* evaluations for information asymmetry purposes are not generally accepted by the Union courts when they apply the market economy operator test.[286]

A second illustration of the differences between the market economy operator test and the arm's length principle as to the interpretation of what the market forces require, relates to the extent of the obligations that are imposed by such market forces, with one alternative being the test of the *terms* of a transaction, the other alternative being a test of the *purpose* of a transaction. On the one hand, the market economy operator test, as it is interpreted by the Union courts, applies not only to the terms of a transaction between a Member State and a private undertaking, but also to the purpose of this transaction. It is a business purpose test that creates an obligation on the Member States to enter into transactions with private undertakings only if that makes commercial sense, something that has even been considered as 'self-evident'.[287]

---

282. In this respect *see* European Commission, 'Communication from the Commission to the European Parliament, the Council, the European Economic and Social Committee and the Committee of the Regions – EU State Aid Modernisation' COM(2012) 209 final, especially at para. 21; Guidelines on regional State aid for 2014-2020 [2013] OJ C 209/1, paras 142–144.; for an illustration of an *ex post* evaluation of an aid scheme with respect to regional aid, *see* Commission Decision of 18 February 2016 State Aid SA.42225 (2015/N) – Lithuania, Regional aid scheme for the promotion of the development of strategic information and communication technology (ICT) projects on strategic ICT sites [2016] OJ C 142/1.
283. *See* Commission Regulation (EU) No 651/2014 of 17 June 2014 declaring certain categories of aid compatible with the internal market in application of Arts 107 and 108 of the Treaty [2014] OJ L 187/1, Art. 1(2)(a).
284. *See* para. 6.192 of the 2017 OECD transfer pricing guidelines.
285. *See* para. 6.191 of the 2017 OECD transfer pricing guidelines.
286. *See* e.g., Case T-16/96, *Express Ltd v. Commission of the European Communities*, ECLI:EU:T:1998:78, para. 76, where the General Court applied the market economy operator test 'having regard to the information available and developments foreseeable' at the time of the investment. In other words, the General Court did not seek to compensate for information asymmetry between public authorities and private operators.
287. *See* Nicholas Khan and Klaus-Dieter Borchardt, 'The Private Market Investor Principle: Reality Check or Distorting Mirror?' in *EC State Aid Law: Liber Amicorum in Honour Francisco Santaolalla* (Kluwer Law International 2008) 117 at footnote 24, with references to Commission decisions that relied on the idea that enforcing market terms are not sufficient to ensure compliance with the market economy operator test.

On the other hand, the arm's length principle, at least as it is described in the 2017 OECD transfer pricing guidelines, does not imply a general test of the commercial rationality of a transaction, the idea being that multinational enterprises are free to organise their business operations 'as they see fit',[288] i.e., with no need to demonstrate a business purpose in addition to the arm's length character of a transaction (although the arm's length character of a transaction implies, as such, a test of rationality). So the difference between the market economy operator test as it is interpreted by the Union courts and the arm's length principle as it is described in the OECD transfer pricing guidelines, seems to consist in a more far-reaching obligation under the former test to take into account the strategic aspects that are relevant for a Member State (that would be a subjective approach),[289] while the latter test would be more focused on the sole terms of the transactions (which would be a more objective approach).[290]

A third illustration of the discrepancy between the market economy operator test and the arm's length principle concerns the methods for the approximation of the results commanded by the market forces. The arm's length principle relies primarily on the notion of range, which is understandable as the pricing of intercompany transactions takes into account the bilateral perspective of the two parties to a transaction. It is a two-sided approach (although the transfer pricing methods are either one-sided or two-sided), so the result has to be acceptable to both parties. The market economy operator test is a test of the results achieved by a Member State or a public undertaking, which considers to a lesser extent the perspective of the counterpart. Therefore, although the market economy operator test also relies on benchmarking studies and ranges of values, the outcome of this test tends to expect a Member State to maximise its profits when dealing with private actors in order not to be granting illegal State

---

288. *See* para. 9.34 of the 2017 OECD transfer pricing guidelines. An exception to this rule exists, however, 'where the arrangements made in relation to the transaction, viewed in their totality, differ from those which would have been adopted by independent enterprises behaving in a commercially rational manner in comparable circumstances' (para. 1.122). In such cases, the guidelines do accept that tax administrations disregarded certain transactions for transfer pricing purposes.
289. The case law on the so-called owner effect confirms that strategic aspects may be taken into account for the application of the market economy operator test, when assessing the rationality of an investment made with public funds: *see* e.g., Cases T-228/99 and T-233/99, *Westdeutsche Landesbank Girozentrale v. European Commission*, ECLI:EU:T:2003:57, para. 222.
290. Here it can be observed that certain tax rules, in particular general anti-avoidance rules, do rely on subjective approaches to a greater extent than the arm's length principle: *see* e.g., Art. 29(9) of the 2017 OECD Model Tax Convention under which a benefit under a tax treaty may be denied if the obtention of that benefit was one of the principal purposes of an arrangement, or Art. 6(2) of the anti-tax-avoidance directive (Council Directive (EU) 2016/1164 of 12 July 2016 laying down rules against tax avoidance practices that directly affect the functioning of the internal market [2016] OJ L 193/1) under which a Member State shall ignore an arrangement that provides a tax advantage with no valid commercial reasons.

aid,[291] although this is not a general obligation.[292] This contrasts with the approach of the OECD transfer pricing guidelines, according to which any value within an arm's length range is likely to be acceptable,[293] with no expectation on a particular party to maximise its profits.

The foregoing analysis leads me to the following conclusion. Although from a conceptual perspective the market economy operator test and the arm's length principle have a common rationale and largely overlap, the content given to the effects of the market forces is partly diverging between these two tests. How to explain the divergences observed between the market economy operator test and the arm's length principle? In my view, the differences between the two tests as to the interpretation of the effects of the market forces may, to some extent, be explained by an element that is intrinsic to the reliance on the market forces, which is the notion of comparability. Indeed, the peculiarities of States,[294] on the one hand, and of integrated but private multinational groups,[295] on the other hand, put them in different – and thus hardly comparable – situations. This calls for different consequences under the market forces, and more generally for different ways of reasoning when transposing the effects of the market forces to the transactions that are being tested.[296] Beyond the notion of comparability, there can simply be differences of views between the Union courts and

---

291. The 'market price' looked for when interpreting the market economy operator test is defined as 'the highest price which a private investor acting under normal competitive conditions [is] ready to pay': see e.g., Case C-390/98, *H.J. Banks & Co. Ltd v. The Coal Authority*, ECLI:EU:C:2001:456, para. 77. Confirming, see Joined Cases C-214/12 P, C-215/12 P and C-223/12 P, *Land Burgenland v. European Commission*, ECLI:EU:C:2013:682, para. 92 and para. 99 ('the private market-economy vendor will opt in principle for the highest offer, where that offer is binding and credible, regardless of the reasons which led the potential buyer to submit that offer').
292. In particular, when a Member State pursues the realisation of a public policy objective laid down in its own legislation, it may not be under the obligation to maximise its profits. See e.g., Case C-518/13, *Eventech Ltd v. The Parking Adjudicator*, ECLI:EU:C:2015:9, where the Court at paras 47–48 found that a Member State that pursues the objective to ensure a safe and efficient transport system does not necessarily confer an economic advantage.
293. See paras 3.60 and 3.62 of the 2017 OECD transfer pricing guidelines. See also European Commission, 'EU Joint Transfer Pricing Forum Report on the use of Comparables in the European Union' (European Commission 2016) 12, point c).
294. Certain of the special features of States are the long-term perspective of their different actions, their virtually endless financial capacity, the national perspective of the public revenues and expenditures, or certain functions they need to perform such as the protection of their citizens.
295. Certain of the special features of privately-owned multinational enterprises may include the global interests that are pursued, the global objective to maximise profits (as opposed to a maximisation of profits per country or company; in this respect see the mention at para. 6.114 of the 2017 OECD transfer pricing guidelines of the 'assumption that MNE groups seek to optimise resource allocations'), the integration of certain functions between different group members, or the synergy effects that may be achieved thanks to group features such as the volume of purchases.
296. For example, whereas a Member State has a virtually indefinite borrowing capacity, a private undertaking is bound to have a lower capacity to borrow money. This affects the risk profile of the borrowers, and thus the risks taken by the lenders as well as the amounts lent and interests rates applied. Therefore, although the benchmark is in appearance the same to test the terms of the transactions entered into by public authorities or associated enterprises, the outcome of this benchmark, i.e., the expectations put on public authorities or on associated enterprises when they enter into transactions with private undertakings or other associated enterprises, is likely to differ depending on the test that is being carried out.

the OECD transfer pricing guidelines, when they interpret the effects of the market forces. Indeed, as mentioned above, the benchmark to test the terms of the two types of transactions does not need to match, neither as a consequence of the rules on State aid, nor as a consequence of the market forces, even if the market economy operator test and the arm's length principle apparently rely on a similar benchmark.

Based on the findings of this chapter, the next section contains conclusions on the consequences of the interpretation of the effects of the market forces under the market economy operator test, for the selectivity assessment of the allocation methods.

3.4 THE RELEVANCE OF THE MARKET ECONOMY OPERATOR TEST FOR THE SELECTIVITY ASSESSMENT OF THE ALLOCATION METHODS

Given the resemblances and differences between the market economy operator test and the arm's length principle, what is the relevance – if any – of the interpretation of the effects of the market forces under the market economy operator test, for the selectivity assessment of the allocation methods? This question may only concern the *interpretation* of the allocation methods used by the Member States, not their *design*; indeed, as argued in section 3.2 above, the market economy operator test should have no binding effect on the design of the tax rules of the Member States.

At first sight, the interpretation of the effects of the market forces under the market economy operator test seems particularly relevant for the selectivity assessment of a generally formulated arm's length provision, given that it too relies on the market forces, without providing for predetermined prices or margins: the approximative nature of the arm's length principle could thus benefit from interpretative guidance under the market economy operator test. It could be argued that given that the two tests rely on similar benchmarks, the interpretation of the effects of the market forces under the market economy operator test in the decisions made by the Commission, and *a fortiori* in the cases ruled by the Union courts, could influence the selectivity assessment of an allocation method based on the arm's length principle, especially the State aid control of a potential deviation from the reference system of a generally formulated arm's length provision.

However, I believe that the interpretation of the effects of the market forces under the market economy operator test may only provide an informative, non-binding illustration of the application of the market forces, with a low relevance for purposes of interpretation.[297] Three arguments support this view. The first reason explaining this

---

297. For a contrary view *see* James Kavanagh and Nicole Robins, 'Corporate Tax Arrangements Under EU State Aid Scrutiny – The Application of the Market Economy Operator Principle' (2015) 14 European State Aid Law Quarterly 358, 366 where the authors consider that not only the market economy operator test but also 'other areas of competition law and regulation can provide useful insights to help identify whether there are sufficiently similar comparators to be able to apply the comparable uncontrolled price method, and the other OECD methods that rely on comparator analysis, to assess whether tax arrangements are in line with the MEOP'. For a more nuanced view *see* Wolfgang Schön, 'Tax Legislation and the Notion of Fiscal Aid: A Review of 5 Years of European Jurisprudence' in Isabelle Richelle, Wolfgang Schön, and Edoardo Traversa (eds), *State Aid Law and Business Taxation* (Springer 2016) 6, where the

statement lies in the analysis of the reference system, which I suggest in section 2.3.2 of this book should only include the binding legal sources in force in a Member State. If only a deviation from what the binding legal sources prescribe may constitute a selective measure, the appreciation of selectivity could not be based on non-binding sources, such as the interpretation of the market forces under the market economy operator test. Second, it was demonstrated in section 3.3 that the market economy operator test and the arm's length principle are to some extent diverging, which implies that it would be difficult to determine objectively in which situations the former may help interpret the latter. Third, decisions applying the market economy operator test provide only an example of what the market forces may require. Such an example may not be the only interpretation of the effects of the market forces.[298]

Moreover, it was emphasised above that the market economy operator test and the arm's length principle are diverging with respect to the approximation of results, in particular concerning the notion of range and the one-sided or two-sided method of analysis. This speaks for not relying on the market economy operator test when interpreting the arm's length principle, as the latter requires some flexibility. Indeed, economic operators may behave in various ways under the same circumstances: too much generalising the behaviour expected from a person is not in conformity with the idea of relying on the market forces, since on the open market different reactions to the same situation may be observed. For instance, independent undertakings acting on a given market may have different aversion to risks or appetite for profits, even under the same circumstances. Whereas an undertaking may be willing to take on risks, another one may be more averse to risks; whereas one undertaking may be interested in quick profits, another one may favour long-term investments.[299] This idea is partly acknowledged in the OECD transfer pricing guidelines through the notion of range, the account being taken of both parties' positions, the mention that transfer pricing is not an exact science, as well as the emphasis put on analysing the 'business strategies'[300] of associated enterprises and their comparators, including 'risk aversion' and 'timing issues'.[301] Therefore, the interpretation of the effects of the market forces under the market economy operator test should not, in my opinion, be relied on to assess a potential deviation from a reference system that includes the arm's length principle. The OECD transfer pricing guidelines, despite their lack of binding effect, have a greater legitimacy and relevance for the interpretation of an arm's length provision, in

---

author suggests that relying on the market economy operator test for the assessment of fiscal State aid 'can only work by analogy' (as opposed to providing a binding source of interpretation), something that would also imply 'intricate measurement issues'.

298. This is to some extent recognised in the OECD transfer pricing guidelines with the statement that transfer pricing is not an exact science (*see* particularly paras 1.13 and 3.55 of the 2017 OECD transfer pricing guidelines), and the notion of range that is advocated in the guidelines as opposed to the search for a perfect value. The arm's length principle may also be subject to certain diverging interpretations between different countries.
299. In this respect, *see* Jérôme Monsenego, 'The Substance Requirement in the OECD Transfer Pricing Guidelines: What Is the Substance of the Substance Requirement?' (2014) 21 International Transfer Pricing Journal 9, 16.
300. *See* paras 1.114 and following of the 2017 OECD transfer pricing guidelines.
301. In addition to the views expressed in Chapter 1 of the 2017 OECD transfer pricing guidelines (in particular para. 1.114), *see also* para. 3.67 with respect to timing issues.

particular when the domestic arm's length provision and the treaty article on business profits are drafted along the lines of Article 9 of the OECD Model Tax Convention.

What about other allocation methods? The interpretation of the effects of the market forces under the market economy operator test seems clearly immaterial for the assessment of a potential deviation from the reference system of other allocation methods, whether they do not rely on the market forces (formula apportionment), or when they do rely on the market forces but provide for fixed values (transfer pricing safe harbours that implement the arm's length principle). However, the market economy operator test could generally imply a preference for market-based outcomes in the assessment of the effects of other allocation methods as part of the de facto selectivity test. This is, in essence, what the European Commission argues in the 2016 notice on the notion of State aid as well as in several decisions.[302] From a theoretical perspective, this argument is not deprived of any relevance: given that the market economy operator test is now an established yardstick of State aid law, it would be consistent that the assessment of the normality[303] of tax measures as part of the de facto selectivity test be relying on some connection to the effects of the market forces. However, no legal argument supports this view. The CJEU has not relied on a general preference for market-based outcomes when performing the de facto selectivity test of tax measures. Consequently, the interpretation of the effects of the market forces under the market economy operator test may only provide an informative, non-binding illustration of the application of the market forces, with a low relevance for purposes of interpretation, given the existence of divergences of principle between the market economy operator test and the arm's length principle.

3.5 CONCLUSION

The conclusion of this chapter is that the market economy operator test can have no binding effect on the design or on the interpretation of the allocation methods, whether or not such methods are relying on the arm's length principle. The market economy operator test provides no legal support to a general requirement to search for a 'reliable approximation of a market-based outcome'[304] when the Member States are taxing the income of multinational enterprises.

After having analysed the determination of the reference system, and investigated whether the reference system may be completed by the notion of market economy operator test, the next step of the selectivity test is dedicated to the comparability analysis. This is the purpose of Chapter 4 of this book.

---

302. *See* Commission Notice on the notion of State aid as referred to in Art. 107(1) of the Treaty on the Functioning of the European Union [2016] OJ C 262/1, paras 171–174.
303. *See* Michaël Karpenschif, *Droit européen des aides d'État* (Bruylant 2015), who at 72 quotes Rials according to whom the market economy operator test is 'un pur instrument de mesure des comportements et des situations en termes de normalité'.
304. *See* Commission Notice on the notion of State aid as referred to in Art. 107(1) of the Treaty on the Functioning of the European Union [2016] OJ C 262/1, para. 171.

CHAPTER 4
Comparability Analysis

4.1 INTRODUCTION

Once the reference system has been determined, the next step of a selectivity analysis is the investigation of whether a tax measure favours certain undertakings over others which, in the light of the objective pursued by the tax system, are in a comparable factual and legal situation.[305] Accordingly, this chapter is structured as follows: first, I will address the determination of the objective of a corporate income tax system, as it is in the light of that objective that the assessment of a difference in treatment and the comparability analysis are made (section 4.2). I will then investigate which undertakings are in a comparable legal and factual situation, in the light of the objective of the corporate income tax system (section 4.3). The conclusions of this chapter are presented in section 4.4.

4.2 DETERMINATION OF THE OBJECTIVE OF THE TAX SYSTEM

It is settled case law that comparability has to be established with regard to the objective of the corporate income tax system; that is, the determination of this objective comes before the comparatility test.[306] The first step of the analysis consists in determining which tax rule is being investigated. There is no need to ask this question when it is the measure as such that constitutes the reference system, as illustrated by

---

305. *See* Joined Cases C-20/15 P and C-21/15 P, *European Commission v. World Duty Free Group*, ECLI:EU:C:2016:981, para. 54, with further references. *See also* Commission Notice on the notion of State aid as referred to in Art. 107(1) of the Treaty on the Functioning of the European Union [2016] OJ C 262/1, para. 135. On the importance of performing a thorough comparability analysis, *see* Case C-70/16 P, *Comunidad Autónoma de Galicia and Redes de Telecomunicación Galegas Retegal, SA (Retegal) v. European Commission*, ECLI:EU:C:2017:1002, para. 61.
306. *See* Case C-524/14 P, *European Commission v. Hansestadt Lübeck*, ECLI:EU:C:2016:971, para. 60.

the case of air travel taxes.³⁰⁷ Yet, given that it is suggested in Chapter 2 that it is not the allocation method as such, but the whole corporate income tax system that constitutes the reference system for the purpose of the topic analysed in this book, it does matter to ask whether it is the tax measure at hand (in our case, the allocation method), or the whole corporate income tax system, for which the objective needs to be determined.

One could take a broad perspective and look at the objective of the reference system, or a narrower perspective through investigating the objective of the tax measure in question, in this case an allocation method. The choice is important, as the objectives of the two do not need to match. On the one hand, the general corporate income tax system and a measure that is part of it may have objectives that are consistent and complementary: for example, if the objective of the tax system is to levy tax on the net income, a measure that allows the deduction of expenses that are connected to earning income would have an objective that is consistent with that of the system.³⁰⁸ On the other hand, certain measures may have a different objective than the general system of which they form part: for example, a measure that implies faster depreciation for certain assets has no necessary link with the general objective of taxing the net income of taxpayers, as in the end the amount deducted is the same. The rules providing for the faster depreciation of certain assets have a policy dimension (e.g., the incentive given to the acquisition of certain assets) that has no necessary link with the objective of the system (the taxation of corporations on their net income). Therefore, there is a need to determine whether it is the objective of the corporate income tax system, or that of the measure subject to the selectivity test, that should be taken into account for State aid purposes.

The position of the CJEU has been evolving through different cases.³⁰⁹ The Court found in *Adria-Wien* that the investigation of whether or not undertakings are in a comparable legal and factual situation is done 'in the light of the objective pursued *by the measure in question*' (emphasis added).³¹⁰ That could be described as a narrow

---

307. *See* Joined Cases C-164/15 P and C-165/15 P, *European Commission v. Aer Lingus Ltd*, ECLI:EU:C:2016:990.
308. Indeed, as emphasised by Schön, 'the ability-to-pay principle requires the full deductibility of cost incurred in the context of an income-generating activity': *see* Wolfgang Schön, 'International Tax Coordination for a Second-Best World (Part I)' (2009) 1 World Tax Journal 67, 74. If a tax system aims at levying tax on the basis of the ability-to-pay principle, then as long as an expense has a connection with the earning of income it should be deductible for corporate income tax purposes, so as to ensure that the tax is levied on the net income (i.e., the increased wealth or consumption capacity) of the taxpayer.
309. In this respect *see* Rita Szudoczky, 'Convergence of the Analysis of National Tax Measures under the EU State Aid Rules and the Fundamental Freedoms' (2016) 15 European State Aid Law Quarterly 357, who at 366 emphasises that 'the case law is not clear on the question whether it is the objective of the measure under review or the objective of the system of which the measure forms part which needs to be taken as the yardstick of comparison in the selectivity analysis'.
310. *See* Case C-143/99, *Adria-Wien Pipeline GmbH, Wietersdorfer & Peggauer Zementwerke GmbH*, ECLI:EU:C:2001:598, para. 41.

Chapter 4: Comparability Analysis

perspective. Later cases favour a broader approach,[311] where it is the objective pursued by a 'particular legal regime'[312] or the 'ordinary' or 'general' tax system that is being investigated.[313] A broader approach is clearly evidenced by the *Gibraltar* case, where the measure at hand was examined in the light of the general objective of taxing corporations on their income, although the measure in effect did not achieve this objective;[314] rather, it resulted in a tax exemption for companies with no physical presence on the territory of Gibraltar, even if they earned income there.

The broad perspective taken by the Court to determine the measure for which the objective is being considered is consistent with the position, argued at Chapter 2 above, that the reference system should be defined in a broad way, as opposed to choosing a particular measure as a reference system. It also shows that the CJEU may not accept that the Member States are at full liberty to set the objectives of their tax systems and design tax measures to reach such objectives,[315] as illustrated by the *Gibraltar* case where the Court refused the right of a Member State to design a tax system that, with no open discrimination, pursued the objective of taxing companies on the basis of their physical presence on the territory of Gibraltar.[316]

Two objections can be made to the broad approach according to which it is the objective pursued by the general tax system that should be taken into account. First, it

---

311. This has also been described as a 'different dogmatic construction': *see* Roland Ismer and Sophia Piotrowski, 'The Selectivity of Tax Measures: A Tale of Two Consistencies' (2015) 43 Intertax 559.
312. *See* Joined Cases C-106/09 P and C-107/09 P, *European Commission v. Government of Gibraltar*, ECLI:EU:C:2011:732, para. 75.
313. *See* Joined Cases C-20/15 P and C-21/15 P, *European Commission v. World Duty Free Group*, ECLI:EU:C:2016:981, paras 57 and 60. This position of the CJEU in State aid cases contrasts with cases issued on the basis of the freedoms of movement, where the Court takes into account the aim pursued by the actual measure, not by the whole tax system: *see* e.g., Case C-252/14, *Pensioenfonds Metaal en Techniek v. Skatteverket*, ECLI:EU:C:2016:402, para. 48, as well as para. 53 where the Court takes into account the objective of 'neutral taxation' for pension funds. *See also* Case C-319/02, *Petri Manninen*, ECLI:EU:C:2004:484, para. 33; Case C-418/07, *Société Papillon v. Ministère du Budget, des Comptes publics et de la Fonction publique*, ECLI:EU:C:2008:659, para. 27.
314. *See* Cases C-106/09 P and C-107/09 P, *European Commission v. Government of Gibraltar*, ECLI:EU:C:2011:732, para. 101, where the Court found that the objective of the proposed tax reform was to 'introduce a general system of taxation for all companies established in Gibraltar'.
315. To what extent the Member States may decide over their fiscal policy is a complex matter. In this respect *see* Case C-308/01, *GIL Insurance Ltd*, ECLI:EU:C:2003:481, Opinion of AG Geelhoed, where at para. 74 the Advocate General considered that preventing the introduction of a special rate of VAT would entail a risk to 'extend the substantive scope of the prohibition on State aid far beyond the limits contemplated by the framers of the Treaty'. More generally *see* Case C-237/04, *Enirisorse SpA v. Sotacarbo SpA*, ECLI:EU:C:2006:21, Opinion of AG Poiares Maduro, para. 45: '(t)he Court is seeking to guard against the scope of the Community rules being broadened to cover distortions of competition that are simply the result of differences in legislative policy between Member States'.
316. There are, however, cases where the Court did accept the objectives or the inherent mechanisms of a national system, despite the potentially negative consequences on various undertakings; *see* e.g., C-353/95 P, *Tiercé Ladbroke SA v. Commission of the European Communities*, ECLI:EU:C:1997:596, where the Court at para. 34 accepted that a system of levy on bets taken on horse-races relied on the rate of the State in which the race is run. Moreover, objectives that are of interest for the Union are, however, recognised and accepted to a greater extent. *See* e.g., the *British Aggregates* case, where the Court found that the 'protection of the environment

is settled case law that the technicalities of a measure should not influence the selectivity test, so as to focus on the effects of a measure.[317] However, if one is bound to the objectives of the reference system solely because the measure at hand has been implemented as part of this system, the outcome of the selectivity test is eventually influenced by the regulatory technique employed by a Member State, i.e., the choice made by a Member State to include a tax measure in a given reference system, whereas the same tax measure could be implemented in another reference system. For example, an anti-avoidance measure may be implemented in the corporate income tax system or in a separate anti-avoidance act, something that may change the relevant reference system and the objective attached to it.

A second objection to the broad perspective favoured by the CJEU is that it may be difficult to precisely identify the objective of the tax system. Although it is true that the objective of a tax system is often 'to raise public finance',[318] it may not be the only objective,[319] especially in the Member States where taxes are used as a means to influence behaviours and achieve various policy goals.[320] Moreover, in most Member States, corporate income taxes do not contribute to a major part of the fiscal revenues,[321] which minimises the public finance objective of such taxes and opens for other objectives, such as considerations of equity. As already emphasised above, the objective of the reference system does not need to match the objective of a tax measure that is part of that system. The fact that the Member States may pursue various objectives as part of a single tax system is particularly true for the Member States that have an interventionist tradition, as opposed to the Member States that design their tax systems with a strive for neutrality. In addition, complex tax regimes such as income taxes may pursue different objectives,[322] whereas other taxes that are less complex may pursue fewer objectives.

---

constitutes one of the essential objectives of the Community': see Case C-487/06 P, *British Aggregates Association v. Commission of the European Communities and United Kingdom*, ECLI:EU:C:2008:757, para. 91.

317. *See* e.g., Case C-487/06 P, *British Aggregates Association v. Commission of the European Communities and United Kingdom*, ECLI:EU:C:2008:757, para. 89 *in fine*; Joined Cases C-106/09 P and C-107/09 P, *European Commission v. Government of Gibraltar*, ECLI:EU:C:2011:732, para. 87.
318. *See* Conor Quigley, *European State Aid Law and Policy* (3rd edn, Hart Publishing 2015) 114.
319. *See* Peter Melz, 'General Legal Report: Legal Aspects of Taxation for Non-fiscal Purposes' in Jane Bolander (ed), *Yearbook for Nordic Tax Research 2009: The Non-fiscal Purposes of Taxation* (DJØF 2009); Case C-203/16 P, *Dirk Andres (administrator of Heitkamp BauHolding GmbH), previously Heitkamp BauHolding GmbH v. European Commission*, ECLI:EU:C:2017:1017, Opinion of AG Wahl, para. 162.
320. *See* Richard Lyal, 'Transfer Pricing Rules and State Aid' (2015) 38 Fordham International Law Journal 1017, 1030.
321. It can be observed that the share of revenues from corporate income taxes amounted to 9% of total tax revenues in 2014: *see* OECD, *Revenue Statistics 2016 – Tax revenue trends in the OECD* (OECD 2016). The tax mix varies from one Member State to another, but in many countries, value added tax or personal income tax would stand for a higher share of the total tax revenues than corporate income tax.
322. In the field of income taxes, certain measures may not (solely) pursue the objective of raising public revenue or taxing in relation to the ability-to-pay of taxpayers. Instead, certain income tax measures may favour other objectives based on, for example, the redistribution of resources, family policies, or environmental considerations.

Chapter 4: Comparability Analysis

Despite these objections, it is settled case law that a deviation from the reference system has to be considered by comparing undertakings with respect to the objective of the reference system, not that of the actual tax measure. For that reason, I will consider the comparability analysis consistently with the position of the CJEU, i.e., by considering the objective of the tax system. Here, it should first be asked whether it is the main objective of the tax system that should be relied on for the purpose of the comparability analysis, or if one should rely on all the objectives pursued by the system. It can be observed that the CJEU and the Commission do not use the exact same language. The Court refers to 'the objective pursued' by the tax system,[323] i.e., it uses the singular. It is also in this way that the Union courts have been reasoning, through looking for what I interpret as the main objective of the tax system. The Commission, in contrast, mentions at some instances the 'objectives' of the system,[324] i.e., it uses the plural. It is the language of the CJEU that is used in this book, not only because it is that of the Court, but also because it appears difficult, if not impossible to precisely identify several objectives pursued by a corporate income tax system.[325] Since the reference system is defined broadly, by including several types of tax measures that may pursue different objectives, it is logical to only attribute a single objective to the reference system, as the different objectives pursued by the components of the reference system may be diverging. It would also be problematic to assess with accuracy the comparability of different undertakings with regard to several objectives pursued by a tax system. Accordingly, it is the main objective of a corporate income tax system that is investigated below.

How to determine the main objective of a corporate income tax system? The CJEU seems to assume that the main objective of the corporate income tax systems of the Member States is to tax the net income earned by corporations, i.e., the difference

---

323. *See* e.g., Case C-524/14 P, *European Commission v. Hansestadt Lübeck*, ECLI:EU:C:2016:971, para. 41; Joined Cases C-20/15 P and C-21/15 P, *European Commission v. World Duty Free Group*, ECLI:EU:C:2016:981, para. 54.
324. *See* Commission Notice on the notion of State aid as referred to in Art. 107(1) of the Treaty on the Functioning of the European Union [2016] OJ C 262/1, para. 128. *See also* Commission Decision (EU) 2017/1283 of 30 August 2016 on State aid SA.38373 (2014/C) (ex 2014/NN) (ex 2014/CP) implemented by Ireland to Apple [2017] OJ L 187/1, paras 224 and 226.
325. For example, among many questions, one may ask if the objectives of a corporate income tax system include raising public revenues, ensuring a form of equality between legal and natural persons, the promotion of a given principle such as the principle of neutrality, or the competitiveness of a country. In addition, one may wonder how to determine the objectives of a corporate income tax system: one may rely on the sole wording of the law, on a preamble (*see* e.g., Case C-236/16, *Asociación Nacional de Grandes Empresas de Distribución (ANGED) v. Generalitat de Catalunya*, ECLI:EU:C:2017:852, Opinion of AG Kokott, para. 6), on preparatory works, on the interpretation of the tax system made by courts or the doctrine, or on other means. In this respect, it seems that at least the preparatory works constitute a source of information that should be taken into account to establish the objective of a tax system: *see* e.g., Case C-5/14, *Kernkraftwerke Lippe-Ems GmbH v. Hauptzollamt Osnabrück*, ECLI:EU:C:2015:354, para. 78 (case related to a duty on the use of nuclear fuel for the commercial production of electricity).

between revenues and deductible expenses.[326] The European Commission is apparently of the same view.[327] Indeed, without attempting at exhaustively defining the concept of 'income',[328] a common denominator to most corporate income tax systems is the taxation of the net income of corporations.[329] Although the concept of income is vague, especially because it relies on different policies in different countries that also evolve with time,[330] what generally characterises the concept of income is indeed an increase or decrease in wealth or consumption capacity, as a consequence of the pursuance of a given activity or the ownership of certain assets.[331] The increase or decrease in wealth or consumption capacity is normally measured in most countries by deducting from the revenues of a corporation the expenses that are necessary to obtain such revenues.[332] The difference between the revenues and the deductible expenses results in a net income before tax, which could also be described as an ability-to-pay income tax, to the extent the income is positive.[333] Moreover, the Court seems to have

---

326. The notion of net income is acknowledged by the CJEU when referring to 'the difference between profits and outgoings of an undertaking' (see Joined Cases C-182/03 and C-217/03, *Kingdom of Belgium and Forum 187 ASBL v. Commission of the European Communities*, ECLI:EU:C:2006:416, para. 95).
327. See State aid SA.44888 (2016/NN) (ex 2016/EO) – Luxembourg – Possible State aid in favour of GDF Suez – Invitation to submit comments pursuant to Art. 108(2) of the Treaty on the Functioning of the European Union [2017] OJ C 36/13, para. 104.
328. In this respect see e.g., Kevin Holmes, *The Concept of Income* (IBFD 2001).
329. For an example of definition of the concept of net income as taxable income, see European Commission, 'Proposal for a Council Directive on a Common Corporate Tax Base' COM(2016) 685 final, Art. 7: '(t)he tax base shall be calculated as revenues less exempt revenues, deductible expenses and other deductible items'.
330. In this respect, a trend consisting in broadening the tax base and lowering the tax rate is observed in many countries, for example as a consequence of limiting the deductibility of interest expenses and preventing hybrid mismatches, sometimes with a concomitant lowering of the tax rate to make such a change neutral in terms of fiscal revenues. This makes the concept of income impossible to precisely define. On the trends observed in the OECD member countries, see OECD, *Tax Policy Reforms 2017* (OECD 2017) 54.
331. In this case it is the yield that is derived from an asset, not the ownership of the asset as such, that is normally taxed as part of a corporate income tax system.
332. See e.g., European Commission, 'Proposal for a Council Directive on a Common Corporate Tax Base' COM(2016) 685 final, Art. 9(1): '(e)xpenses shall be deductible only to the extent that they are incurred in the direct business interest of the taxpayer'.
333. See Case C-279/93, *Finanzamt Köln-Altstadt v. Roland Schumacker*, ECLI:EU:C:1995:31, paras 32-33, where the Court refers to the notion of ability-to-pay tax. See also Ana Paula Dourado, 'The Interest Limitation Rule in the Anti-Tax Avoidance Directive (ATAD) and the Net Taxation Principle' (2017) 26 EC Tax Review 112, 114: '(n)et income taxation in each sovereign State is a manifestation of the ability-to-pay principle and was designed under a symmetric condition'. In this respect, Schön argues that 'the ability-to-pay principle is reflected in the very idea that the income tax (including corporate income tax) should look at the consumption power of particular taxpayers (while indirect taxes look at a continuum of market transactions and acts of consumption), that it should take into account all items of revenue and expenditure connected to a source of income in a symmetrical fashion and that the income should be subject to a progressive tax rate (at least at the level of natural persons)': see Wolfgang Schön, 'International Tax Coordination for a Second-Best World (Part I)' (2009) 1 World Tax Journal 67, 72; Rita Szudoczky, 'Convergence of the Analysis of National Tax Measures under the EU State Aid Rules and the Fundamental Freedoms' (2016) 15 European State Aid Law Quarterly 357, 363; Case C-203/16 P, *Dirk Andres (administrator of Heitkamp BauHolding GmbH), previously Heitkamp BauHolding GmbH v. European Commission*, ECLI:EU:C:2017:1017, Opinion of AG Wahl, para. 125. For a similar reasoning, where taxes on profits were considered to

developed in the *Gibraltar* case a form of presumption that the tax systems of the Member States should contain a corporate income tax, given that the regime at hand was found selective partly because it did not generally tax companies on their income; this strengthens the view that the objective of a corporate income tax system, whether it is explicit or presumed, is the taxation of the net income of corporations.

In the light of the above analysis, I draw the conclusion that the CJEU attributes to a corporate income tax system the main objective of taxing the net income of corporations. At the same time, it must be acknowledged that several other rules than the ones that determine which profits are taxable, and which expenses are deductible, are often part of a corporate income tax system, and influence the annual taxable income without necessarily pursuing the objective to tax the net income of corporations. It is thus legitimate to ask whether such rules may affect the general objective pursued by a corporate income tax system. For example, there are certain rules that connect items of income with timing aspects, such as depreciation rules.[334] Controlled foreign corporation (CFC) rules could be described as pursuing more a fiscal objective (that of preventing tax deferral), than the objective of taxing corporations on their net income.[335] There are also rules that provide thresholds for the existence of a tax liability.[336] Do such rules affect the general objective pursued by the corporate income tax? I believe not, as long as the tax effectively paid by corporations is mainly determined by the difference between the gross revenues, and the expenses that are necessary to obtain such revenues.[337] Since the case law of the CJEU points to identifying the main objective of a tax system, the Court at the same time accepts that a system includes rules that pursue other, secondary, objectives.

---

mirror the ability-to-pay of taxpayers as opposed to taxes on turnover, *see* Commission Decision (EU) 2017/329 of 4 November 2016 on the measure SA.39235 (2015/C) (ex 2015/NN) implemented by Hungary on the taxation of advertisement turnover [2017] OJ L 49/36, paras 67–68; Commission Decision (EU) 2016/1846 of 4 July 2016 on the measure SA.41187 (2015/C) (ex 2015/NN) implemented by Hungary on the health contribution of tobacco industry businesses [2016] OJ L 282/43 para. 44, where the European Commission finds that taxes on profits do reflect the ability-to-pay of the taxpayers, since these taxes – as opposed to turnover taxes – take into account the costs incurred by the taxpayers to determine the taxable income. In contrast, 'turnover taxes hit companies in respect of their size rather than their profitability or ability to pay': *see* e.g., Commission Decision (EU) 2018/160 of 30 June 2017 on the State aid SA.44351 (2016/C) (ex 2016/NN) implemented by Poland for the tax on the retail sector [2018] OJ L 29/38 para. 58.

334. Such rules would typically precise the temporal elements of the concept of net income, with the objective to assign to each taxable year the right usage of an asset; depreciation rules may also pursue tax policy objectives, e.g., to encourage the investment in a given type of asset.
335. *See* Mattias Dahlberg and Bertil Wiman, *The Taxation of Foreign Passive Income for Groups of Companies – General Report* (IFA Cahiers Volume 98A, Sdu 2013).
336. For example, rules on the definition of corporate residence or the existence of a permanent establishment do not, as such, contribute to the definition of the concept of net income. They rather define when legal subjects become liable to tax.
337. It is reasonable to rely on the effects of the system, not only because of the emphasis regularly put by the CJEU on the need to take into account the effects of State measures, but also because a tax system may be labelled as an income tax but may actually rely on a weak connection to the concept of income, for example if it focuses more on cash flows or revenues than on the net income.

It can also be observed that the twofold function of an allocation method (*see* section 2.2.1 above) is consistent with the objective to tax the net income of corporations. The anti-avoidance function is clearly consistent with the general objective to tax corporations on their net income: there is a need to supplement the basic corporate income tax rules with an allocation method to ensure that the income earned in a given country is not eroded by the prices of intercompany transactions; this anti-avoidance function preserves the notion of income. The second function of an allocation method is to share between different countries the income of a multinational enterprise. This function has not necessarily a direct connection to the concept of net income, but it is likely to approximate the income earned in each country by a multinational enterprise; therefore, the sharing function of an allocation method may also have a connection to the objective to tax the net income of corporations.

Accordingly, it is in the light of the objective to tax corporations on their net income that the comparability test should be performed. The concept of net income is, in my opinion, more precise in relation to an income tax than the general concept of ability-to-pay tax,[338] given that this ability may come from other factors than income, such as wealth. However, the two concepts are close.

Now that the objective of a corporate income tax system has been identified, one may proceed with the next step of the selectivity test: the analysis of the comparability between different categories of undertakings.

4.3 THE COMPARABILITY BETWEEN DIFFERENT CATEGORIES OF UNDERTAKINGS

4.3.1 Introduction

The selectivity concept, whether it applies to tax or non-tax measures, relies strongly on the notion of non-discrimination, and thus on the notion of equal treatment.[339] However, a prerequisite for a requirement of equal treatment is the notion of comparability: it is settled case law that the rules on State aid require the equal treatment of undertakings, but only for those that are 'in a comparable factual and legal situation'.[340] The CJEU made clear in *World Duty Free Group* that the question is 'whether the situation of operators benefitting from [a] measure is comparable with that of operators excluded from it'.[341] Similar requirements of comparability apply in

---

338. *See* e.g., Wolfgang Schön, 'Taxation and State Aid Law in the European Union' (1999) 36 Common Market Law Review 911, 925. Generally, on the notion of ability-to-pay tax, *see* Yves Hougardy, 'La capacité contributive' in Edoardo Traversa and Vincent Deckers (eds), *Liber Amicorum Jacques Autenne – Promenades sous les portiques de la fiscalité* (Bruylant 2010) 135.
339. *See* e.g., Case C-524/14 P, *European Commission v. Hansestadt Lübeck*, ECLI:EU:C:2016:971, para. 53.
340. *See* e.g., Joined Cases C-78/08 to C-80/08, *Paint Graphos*, ECLI:EU:C:2011:550, para. 49; Case C-524/14 P, *European Commission v. Hansestadt Lübeck*, ECLI:EU:C:2016:971, para. 41. For an earlier expression of that principle, *see* Case C-353/95 P, *Tiercé Ladbroke SA v. Commission of the European Communities*, ECLI:EU:C:1997:596, para. 33.
341. *See* Joined Cases C-20/15 P and C-21/15 P, *European Commission v. World Duty Free Group*, ECLI:EU:C:2016:981, para. 94.

other legal orders that also provide for equal treatment,[342] although the content of the notion of comparability may be diverging depending on the legal order at stake. In the area of State aid law, the notion of comparability is unfortunately not precisely defined.[343] Nevertheless, what is clear is that the notion of comparability in the field of State aid is a broad one, as the Union courts found in the vast majority of tax cases that different undertakings were in a comparable situation.

The comparability analysis is of particular importance for the topic covered by this book. This is because the outcome of the selectivity test is highly dependent on which categories of undertakings are being compared to each other, and whether or not such categories of undertakings are in a comparable situation. The critical question is whether or not independent and associated enterprises, as well as members of domestic and cross-border groups, are in a comparable situation. If these undertakings are in a comparable situation, the Member States would need to tax them similarly, or to justify any differences of treatment. If, in contrast, these undertakings are not in a comparable situation, the Member States could tax them differently without infringing on the rules on State aid. The question of comparability is thus critical, and it is also a highly relevant one because the Member States would typically need to tax independent and associated enterprises differently, as well as members of domestic and cross-border groups.

The outline of this section follows the two components of the notion of comparability as it is defined by the CJEU. Accordingly, I will study the notion of comparability from a factual perspective (section 4.3.3). I will also analyse comparability from a legal perspective (section 4.3.4). However, before delving into comparability in State aid law, a parallel with free movement law appears relevant, as this area of EU law relies also on the notion of comparability. For that reason, I will start by assessing the relevance of the notion of comparability in free movement law for State aid law purposes (section 4.3.2).

4.3.2 Assessment of the Relevance of the Notion of Comparability in Free Movement Law for State Aid Law Purposes

Given the importance of the comparability analysis for the purpose of the selectivity test, and in view of the lack of detailed guidance on how to conduct the comparability analysis for State aid law purposes, it is relevant to ask whether one may – or even should – rely on the comparability analysis performed by the CJEU in cases ruled on the basis of the freedoms of movement. Indeed, the case law on the application of the freedoms of movement to discriminatory tax measures relies strongly, similarly to State

---

342. For example, tax treaties often include an article on the prohibition of discrimination: *see* Art. 24 of the OECD Model Tax Convention.
343. *See* e.g., the *3M Italia* case, where the CJEU simply stated that two categories of undertakings where not in a factual and legal comparable situation, without explicitly considering the reasons leading to this conclusion: Case C-417/10, *Ministero dell'Economia e delle Finanze, Agenzia delle Entrate v. 3M Italia SpA*, ECLI:EU:C:2012:184, para. 42.

aid law, on the notion of comparability: discriminations can arise only through the application of different rules to comparable situations, or the application of the same rule to different situations.[344]

It is important to observe that when the CJEU applies free movement law to corporate taxation measures, there is little point comparing the situation of members of multinational enterprises with that of independent enterprises. Instead, the relevant comparison is between domestic and cross-border groups, as it is this comparator that can evidence a possible difference in treatment between domestic and cross-border situations, the latter being the result of the exercise of the freedom of movement. In that respect, the Court does consider that associated enterprises can be compared to each other, including members of domestic and multinational groups. For example, in *SGI* – a case assessing the compatibility with the freedom of establishment of the transfer pricing rules of Belgium – the Court compared the situation of a company resident of Belgium having 'a relationship of interdependence' with a company resident of another Member State, to that of a Belgian resident having such a relationship with a domestic company.[345] Similar comparisons were made in cases relating to other types of tax rules, such as group taxation,[346] or withholding taxes.[347] A different opinion was, however, held by Advocate General Bobek, who argued that 'for the specific purpose of making sure that tax does not escape the jurisdiction of a Member State, foreign and domestic subsidiaries are not comparable'.[348]

Now that it was recalled that the CJEU finds members of domestic and cross-border groups to be in a comparable situation for free movement law purposes, it can be asked if the comparability test in free movement law is relevant for State aid law purposes. It is important to stress that the application of the freedoms of movement builds on the prerequisite of the exercise of such freedoms. Free movement law aims at protecting cross-border activities from various discriminations that exist because of the exercise of the freedom of movement. It is logical that the comparability test be conducted between cross-border and domestic situations, as it is a prerequisite to make the freedoms of movement effective and assess whether cross-border activities are treated less favourably than domestic activities. At the same time, free movement law supposes comparing domestic and cross-border situations that have, apart from their territorial connections, the most similar characteristics, i.e., situations that are the most comparable to each other. This makes, in my view, the comparability test in free movement law conceptually different from that of State aid law.[349] State aid law does

---

344. *See* e.g., Case C-279/93, *Finanzamt Köln-Altstadt v. Roland Schumacker*, ECLI:EU:C:1995:31, para. 30.
345. *See* Case C-311/08, *Société de Gestion Industrielle SA v. État belge*, ECLI:EU:C:2010:26, paras 42 and 43.
346. *See* e.g., Case C-446/03, *Marks & Spencer plc v. David Halsey (Her Majesty's Inspector of Taxes)*, ECLI:EU:C:2005:763.
347. *See* e.g., Case C-319/02, *Petri Manninen*, ECLI:EU:C:2004:484.
348. *See* Case C-382/16, *Hornbach-Baumarkt AG v. Finanzamt Landau*, ECLI:EU:C:2017:974, Opinion of AG Bobek, para. 60.
349. For a different opinion *see* Luc de Broe, 'Can Tax Treaties Confer State Aid?' (2017) 5 EC Tax Review 228, 229 (*see* particularly footnote 12, *in fine*). *See also* Rita Szudoczky, *The Sources of EU Law and Their Relationships: Lessons for the Field of Taxation* (IBFD 2014), where the

not compare domestic to cross-border situations, but the situation of undertakings in the same Member State, with a view to preventing distortions of competition and trade. Without the cross-border prerequisite in State aid cases, the notion of comparability appears wider in the field of State aid law. Moreover, while comparability in free movement law is assessed in the light of the objective of the measure at hand,[350] in the area of State aid law comparability is assessed in the light of the objective of the reference system,[351] which is arguably broader than a given tax measure. Finally, I observe that while the CJEU in State aid cases requires that undertakings are in a comparable factual and legal situation (i.e., the criteria are cumulative),[352] in free movement cases the criteria seem to rather be alternative: certain cases rely on legal comparability,[353] but others rely on factual comparability.[354] In view of the arguments analysed above, I conclude that the comparability test in free movement law cannot be relied on for the purpose of a State aid analysis. There is, accordingly, a need to perform a comparability analysis that is specific to State aid law.

Since an allocation method applies in most cases solely to companies that are members of multinational enterprises, the question is whether such companies should be compared to other members of multinational enterprises, to members of domestic groups, or to independent enterprises. To investigate this question, comparability is analysed from a factual (section 4.3.3) as well as from a legal perspective (section 4.3.4), in the light of the objective pursued by the tax system.[355]

4.3.3 Comparability from a Factual Perspective

Before embarking on the study of the factual comparability between undertakings that are either independent, members of domestic groups, or members of multinational groups, it is important to emphasise that the OECD transfer pricing guidelines do not provide a definition of comparability that is suitable for State aid law purposes. I will first explain why, and will then return to the determination of comparability from a factual perspective.

---

author at 471 considers that the 'comparative approach to selectivity is similar to the discrimination analysis which is aimed at ascertaining whether or not a Member State measure infringes the free movement provisions'.
350. See Case C-418/07, *Société Papillon v. Ministère du Budget, des Comptes publics et de la Fonction publique*, ECLI:EU:C:2008:659, para. 27; Case C-18/11, *The Commissioners for Her Majesty's Revenue & Customs v Philips Electronics UK Ltd*, ECLI:EU:C:2012:532, para. 17.
351. See Joined Cases C-20/15 P and C-21/15 P, *European Commission v. World Duty Free Group*, ECLI:EU:C:2016:981, para. 77.
352. See e.g., Joined Cases C-20/15 P and C-21/15 P, *European Commission v. World Duty Free Group*, ECLI:EU:C:2016:981, para. 57.
353. See e.g., Case 270/83, *Commission of the European Communities v. French Republic*, ECLI:EU: C:1986:37, paras 19–20.
354. See e.g., Case C-279/93, *Finanzamt Köln-Altstadt v. Roland Schumacker*, ECLI:EU:C:1995:31, paras 36–37.
355. See e.g., Joined Cases C-20/15 P and C-21/15 P, *European Commission v. World Duty Free Group*, ECLI:EU:C:2016:981, para. 57. The general objective of the tax system is analysed in section 4.2 above.

There are differences at the level of principle between the notion of comparability used in State aid law, and that described in the OECD transfer pricing guidelines. The main difference is one of purpose: whereas the OECD transfer pricing guidelines aim at defining a standard for the taxation of the profits of multinational enterprises, State aid law aims at preventing distortions of competition between different undertakings. The large purpose of the State aid rules requires a large understanding of the notion of comparability that does not, per se, exclude certain types of undertakings from the comparison. By contrast, since the purpose of the OECD transfer pricing guidelines and of the arm's length principle is to find a standard to tax multinational enterprises especially with respect to the tax planning opportunities created by transactions between associated enterprises, the standard used to prevent such tax planning opportunities can, by definition, not be provided by observations from other associated enterprises: for the standard to be relevant for fiscal purposes, it needs to be based on another benchmark than that provided by associated enterprises. The arm's length principle supposes to disregard the legal differences between groups and independent enterprises, so as to use the benchmark provided by independent enterprises to set the standard of taxation for multinational enterprises. Despite certain obvious differences, groups and independent enterprises are, through a fiction, deemed to be in a comparable situation. Other differences exist between State aid law and the OECD arm's length principle when it comes to the notion of comparability, such as the relevance of legal elements,[356] or the geographical scope of the comparability test.[357] Consequently, the OECD transfer pricing guidelines do not provide a definition of comparability that is suitable for State aid law purposes.

I now return to the determination of comparability from a factual perspective. It is not clear how to exactly define factual comparability in State aid law, at least when a comparison is made between undertakings that are independent, members of domestic groups, and members of multinational groups. The notion of factual comparability is certainly a broad one, as illustrated by the *Adria-Wien* case where the CJEU found that national measures do not constitute State aid if they apply to all undertakings 'regardless of their activity'.[358] By 'activity' the Court referred in this case to the manufacture of goods, but in the context of the selectivity assessment of the allocation

---

356. In particular, whereas State aid law relies on both legal and factual elements, the arm's length principle relies mostly on facts. Although legal elements such as the contracts that are concluded between associated enterprises are the starting point of a transfer pricing analysis (*see* paras 1.42 and following of the 2017 OECD transfer pricing guidelines), these legal elements need to be supplemented by facts or economic considerations to be able, when necessary, to implement between associated enterprises the terms of comparable transactions between independent enterprises.
357. For State aid law purposes, the comparability test is national, whereas comparability under the OECD transfer pricing guidelines does not necessarily rely on enterprises resident of the same country. The limitation of the geographical scope to the territory of one Member State is consistent with the purpose of the State aid rules. The opposite would result in effectively controlling the economic policies of the Member States. Comparability for transfer pricing purposes focuses more on the functions performed by the enterprises that are being compared, than on their country of residence: the residence of the enterprises that are being compared does not necessarily affect whether or not they are comparable to each other.
358. *See* Case C-143/99, *Adria-Wien Pipeline GmbH*, ECLI:EU:C:2001:598, para. 36.

Chapter 4: Comparability Analysis

methods, this concept may be interpreted differently, and is thus imprecise: the term 'activity' could, for instance, refer to the functional profile of an undertaking, or to the industry in which an undertaking is selling its goods or services. Advocate General Wathelet in his opinion in the *World Duty Free Group* case also insisted on the breadth of the notion of factual comparability, by considering that undertakings performing 'similar operations' were in a comparable situation. There was no need for the undertakings to share additional similarities, which in this case could imply acquiring similar levels of shareholdings, to support similar levels of risks when investing in certain shares, or to own shareholdings for similar periods of time.[359] The CJEU did not even reflect on this notion, simply considering that undertakings acquiring shares in domestic or foreign companies were in a comparable situation. It follows from the foregoing that the notion of factual comparability is a broad one, although it is not precisely defined by the Court.

Some guidance exists, however, on the notion of factual comparability. What is settled case law is that there is no need for undertakings to be competitors or to be doing business within the same sector, to be in a comparable factual situation. This implies that a measure may be selective even if it applies to undertakings in different sectors.[360] Accordingly, the notion of *comparability* is to be distinguished from that of *competition*, although the State aid rules are included in the chapter of the TFEU on the rules of competition.[361] In my opinion, it is understandable that the CJEU does not require undertakings to be competitors to be in a comparable factual situation, as the opposite would enable the Member States to grant aid to certain sectors. This seems justified as the purpose of the selectivity criterion is both to prevent undue comparative advantages, and a distortion in the international allocation of resources.[362] At the same time, there are arguments against the position of the Court: as pointed out by Temple Lang, 'if two groups of companies are in "comparable situations" but are not in competition with each other, there may be no distortion of competition, and so no infringement of the Treaty'.[363] This argument could nevertheless be countered based

---

359. *See* Joined Cases C-20/15 P and C-21/15 P, *European Commission v. World Duty Free Group*, ECLI:EU:C:2016:624, Opinion of AG Wathelet, para. 91.
360. *See* Case C-524/14 P, *European Commission v. Hansestadt Lübeck*, ECLI:EU:C:2016:971, para. 58.
361. *See* Conor Quigley, *European State Aid Law and Policy* (3rd edn, Hart Publishing 2015) 7.
362. In this respect *see* Luca Rubini, *The Definition of Subsidy and State Aid: WTO and EC Law in Comparative Perspective* (Oxford University Press 2009) 359–377, with further references.
363. *See* John Temple Lang, 'Autogrill España and Banco Santander: The Concept of "General" Tax Measures Clarified for State Aid' (2015) 5 European Law Review 763, 767. On a possible lack of analysis of the breach of equality between competitors *see* Francesco de Cecco, *State Aid and the European Economic Constitution* (Hart 2013), 100: 'Member State A may decide to increase the corporation tax rate for all sectors except one, sector x. Even if undertakings in sector x do not have competitors in A, and even if they are subject to the same rate of taxation as undertakings in sector x in Member State B, they are nonetheless regarded as recipients of State aid. This is one of the most puzzling aspects of selectivity, which may, arguably, only be explained in light of the absence of detailed microeconomic analysis where regulatory measures are concerned. It may well be that an increase in tax for other sectors may have indirect benefits for x, which derive from the fact that, while x does not have direct competitors in the output market, it may gain a competitive edge on the input market, which may in turn produce an advantage over its competitors in Member State B.'

on the objective of the rules on State aid to protect the competition between the Member States, which is not the main objective of these rules but is not either, it has been argued, outside their scope.[364] Despite the criticisms that may be raised against the interpretation of the notion of factual comparability, it is the interpretation favoured by the CJEU that is relied on in this book, so as to analyse the issue of factual comparability consistently with the case law of the Court.

Based on the broad notion of factual comparability that is systematically applied by the CJEU, one may be tempted to argue that, if the objective of the corporate income tax is to tax corporations on their net income, the fact that different types of undertakings are earning income through pursuing a commercial activity is enough to place them in a comparable factual situation. This view is supported by the finding of the Court that the comparability test is performed in the light of the objective of the reference system:[365] all types of undertakings would be potentially in a comparable situation, as long as they are in the scope of application of the reference system. Such a view could be supported by an interpretation *a contrario* of the *Paint Graphos* case, where the Court considered that cooperative societies and commercial companies were not in a comparable situation because of their differences with respect to earning profits; *a contrario*, pursuing a commercial activity could be sufficient to place different undertakings in a comparable factual situation. If one applies this way of reasoning, whereby all companies pursuing a commercial objective are in a comparable factual situation, then members of multinational enterprises would be comparable to both independent enterprises and domestic groups, assuming they all pursue such an objective.

Although the above argument is appealing, it is not sufficient to conclude that all types of undertakings earning income through pursuing a commercial activity are in a comparable factual situation. One needs to address the factual features of members of multinational enterprises, to conclude whether or not they really are comparable to independent enterprises or domestic groups. To that end, I will consider below three of the most important characteristics of members of multinational enterprises. These characteristics are the cross-border organisation of multinational enterprises, the control that may exist between different group members, and the common interests that may be pursued by group members. These three characteristics are addressed subsequently.

---

364. In this respect Hancher insists on the fact that the State aid rules relate 'to competition between Member States, and not just competition between undertakings': *see* Leigh Hancher, 'EU State Aid Law – Déjà Vu All Over Again?' in Leigh Hancher, Tom Ottervanger, and Piet Jan Slot (eds), *EU State Aids* (5th edn, Sweet & Maxwell 2016) para. 1-029. *See also* Herwig Hofmann, 'Activity in a Multi-level System: Motivations for Aid, Why Control It, Evolution of Aid in the EU' in Herwig C. H. Hofmann and Claire Micheau (eds), *State Aid Law of the European Union* (Oxford University Press 2016) 6, with respect to negative externalities.
365. *See* Joined Cases C-20/15 P and C-21/15 P, *European Commission v. World Duty Free Group*, ECLI:EU:C:2016:981, para. 77.

Chapter 4: Comparability Analysis

First, the concept of 'multinational enterprise' can be defined as a group of companies that are not all resident of the same country.[366] In other words, multinational enterprises have, from a legal perspective, a cross-border organisation. However, not only are the members of multinational enterprises resident of different countries (this is a legal aspect that is analysed below as part of the legal comparability), but also their organisation (or their 'value chain'[367]) is, in many cases, spread over several jurisdictions. In contrast, independent enterprises and domestic groups are likely to have their value chain mostly located in one country; if this is not the case, i.e., if independent enterprises and domestic groups have elements of their value chain located abroad, such elements may lead to the existence of a permanent establishment,[368] which in turn leads to the need to attribute profits to such a permanent establishment and thus to apply an allocation method, with the result of a clear resemblance with a multinational enterprise. If we assume that independent enterprises and domestic groups have no permanent establishment abroad, does the cross-border organisation of a multinational enterprise preclude the factual comparability with independent enterprises or domestic groups, or can they be in a factual comparable situation despite having different organisations?

As I see it, it is doubtful that the cross-border organisation, as opposed to the domestic organisation of undertakings, precludes them from being in a factual comparable situation. The argument would be valid if multinational enterprises would always have a cross-border, well-integrated value chain, while independent enterprises or domestic groups would have purely domestic value chains. But this is not necessarily the case. Of course, there are cases where multinational enterprises are organised through value chains that would not exist between independent enterprises, such as situations where the activities of different group members are very specialised and form part of a consistent, well-integrated whole. However, no general distinction can be made between multinational enterprises and other undertakings with respect to their value chains; it cannot be generally stated that multinational enterprises always have a cross-border integrated value chain, whereas independent enterprises or domestic groups would never have one. For example, independent enterprises may export and have significant presence abroad without having a permanent establishment; independent enterprises may also outsource certain elements of the value chain to third parties, thus avoiding the characterisation as a multinational enterprise while still relying on organisational elements present in different countries to maximise their profits. What is more, whether companies pursue domestic or cross-border activities does not necessarily affect their objective to earn income, as they in either case develop

---

366. *See* the definition provided in the glossary of the 2017 OECD transfer pricing guidelines, where a multinational enterprise is defined as '(a) group of associated companies with business establishments in two or more countries'.
367. For the definition of a 'value chain' *see* Koen D. Backer and Sébastien Miroudot, *Mapping Global Value Chains* (OECD Trade Policy Papers 159, OECD 2013) 7, citing Gereffi and Fernandez-Stark: '(a) value chain can be simply defined as the "full range of activities that firms and workers do to bring a product from its conception to its end use and beyond"'. *See also* Michael E. Porter, *Competitive Advantage* (Free Press 1985) 11–15.
368. That would be the case if, for example, manufacturing or distribution activities were performed abroad.

an ability-to-pay tax through earning profits; the choice of the location of the elements of the value chain is likely to be influenced by various factors such as costs, taxes, or the proximity to suppliers or to clients, but all of these factors are eventually connected to the objective to maximise profits. Since the comparability analysis is made in the light of the objective of the tax system, which we assume is the taxation of the net income of corporations, the capacity of undertakings to earn income and the need of the tax systems to tax such income are not fundamentally affected by the more or less cross-border character of their organisations. In addition, the CJEU has found that State measures should not treat differently undertakings that have a domestic and a cross-border activity,[369] which means that the cross-border organisation of multinational enterprises does not prevent them from being in a factual comparable situation to domestic groups or independent enterprises.

I now turn to the second feature of members of multinational enterprises, namely the factual (as opposed to the legal) control that may exist between different undertakings. This aspect does not distinguish multinational groups from domestic groups (because factual control may exist independently from the geographical organisation of a group), but it does distinguish groups (whether multinational or domestic) from independent enterprises. Apart from the legal control that results from the ownership of shares (which is studied below at section 4.3.4), it is indeed likely that there are greater possibilities of factual control between associated enterprises than between independent enterprises, possibly precluding the two from being in a comparable situation. Factual control may exist in different situations, such as – with no ambition of being exhaustive – when several group members are managed by the same (group of) persons,[370] when decisions of certain enterprises need to be approved by employees of other associated enterprises, or when one group member is economically dependent on another, for example because it sells to this associated enterprise most of its goods or services.

At the same time, one needs to acknowledge that situations of factual control are not exclusive to associated enterprises. Although there are frequent situations of factual control exercised by certain group members over other group members, factual control may also exist between legally independent enterprises, for example when one undertaking needs the services of another undertaking to perform its activities, or when one undertaking has few clients and becomes economically dependent on such clients. In these examples, certain undertakings may have a factual control over other unrelated undertakings, as a consequence of their bargaining power or scientific knowledge, without being legally entitled to any form of control. The fact that some form of control may exist without necessarily owning shares or having rights in another company is illustrated by the definition of the concept of 'associated enterprises' at

---

369. *See* Joined Cases C-20/15 P and C-21/15 P, *European Commission v. World Duty Free Group*, ECLI:EU:C:2016:981, para. 119.
370. For an example where factual dependence was found in such a situation, thus triggering the application of the transfer pricing rules, *see* the ruling issued by the French Conseil d'État, Case 372097, *Société LifeStand Vivre Debout*, 15 April 2016. For a comment on this case *see* Caroline Silberztein and Benoît Granel, 'La dépendance de fait en matière de prix de transfert' (2016) 51–52 Revue de Droit Fiscal 47.

Article 9 of the OECD Model Tax Convention, which includes factual control such as the participation in the management of a company as a criterion that characterises the association between different companies, with no requirement of legal ownership. It is also illustrated by the change made to Article 5 paragraph 6 of the OECD Model Tax Convention as part of the 2017 update to the Model, which creates a presumption of economic dependency as a consequence of group membership, where a person acts exclusively or almost exclusively on behalf of one or more enterprises to which it is closely related.[371]

As situations of factual control are not exclusive to groups, it cannot be held that the notion of factual control in all cases precludes the factual comparability between groups (whether domestic or multinational) and independent enterprises. It seems only likely that situations of factual control occur more frequently between associated enterprises than between independent enterprises, and that the degree of control is higher within associated enterprises. Therefore, the factual control that exists between different categories of undertakings does not *a priori* preclude the comparability between multinational enterprises, domestic groups, and independent enterprises, but is likely to result in group members (whether belonging to domestic or international groups) being more comparable to each other than to independent enterprises. In addition, no matter the frequency and the degree of control that may exist between various undertakings, the existence of some form of control does not necessarily affect the objective of earning profits: whether one considers a controlling or a controlled entity, both may be willing to maximise their profits. This speaks for independent and associated enterprises being in a comparable factual situation. The only situation where the existence of control might affect the objective of earning profits is when certain entities do not pursue their own interests. It is to this aspect that I now turn.

The third factual aspect that is analysed here relates to what intrinsically characterises most corporate groups (whether domestic or multinational), as opposed to independent enterprises: the pursuance of a common interest. There is considerable research in the field of economics on this topic – often described as the 'theory of the firm' – and it is my understanding that most scholars find groups and independent enterprises to be in different situations.[372] While independent enterprises pursue mostly – if not exclusively – their own interest (and ultimately the interest of their owners), associated enterprises may be pursuing an interest that is common to the whole group. This last interest does not necessarily match that of each and every

---

371. *See* Art. 5(6) of the 2017 OECD Model Tax Convention.
372. It is impossible to provide in this book an exhaustive reference of the literature dealing with the differences between groups and independent enterprises. For a few examples *see* Oliver Williamson, 'The Theory of the Firm as Governance Structure: From Choice to Contract' (2002) 16 Journal of Economic Perspectives 171; Michael Porter, 'The Five Competitive Forces that Shape Competitive Theory' (2008) 86 Harvard Business Review 78 (the forces identified by Porter are influenced by the integration within firms); Harry Grubert, 'Destination-Based Income Taxes: A Mismatch Made in Heaven?' (2015) 69 Tax Law Review 43, 46; Isabel Verlinden and Bram Markey, 'From Compliance to the C-Suite: Value Creation Analysed Through the Transfer Pricing Lens' (2016) 44 Intertax 774; Ulrich Schreiber and Lisa Maria Fell, 'International Profit Allocation, Intangibles and Sales-Based Transactional Profit Split' (2017) 9 World Tax Journal 1, 3.

member of the group.³⁷³ For example, a group might have an interest in being present on various markets, although some of these markets might not be profitable. Group membership may also affect the willingness to earn profits,³⁷⁴ or the readiness to assume risks,³⁷⁵ of each group member. An example would be the case where certain group companies responsible for manufacturing activities receive the instruction not to produce according to their full capacity, because other manufacturers located in less expensive places have an excess of production capacity.³⁷⁶

To achieve the common interest of a group, the business activities of an integrated firm are often organised differently than those of an independent enterprise: for example, certain group members may be specialised in certain well-defined functions, so as to maximise their productivity and save costs; groups may control all the steps of the value chain through owning the companies that are responsible for these different steps; groups may also decide to pursue activities that would be impossible for independent enterprises, and thus develop sources of profits that are not available to them.

The integration between group members may have consequences both on earning profits, and on making losses.³⁷⁷ Different positive economic effects such as synergies or costs savings may occur thanks to group membership, something that tends to increase the profits derived by integrated firms, thus explaining the choice to conduct business activities through integrated rather than independent organisations.³⁷⁸ Conversely, risks that materialise within integrated groups may negatively affect more enterprises than the ones legally bound by the realisation of a risk, as a consequence of group membership.³⁷⁹ Accordingly, group membership and the

---

373. Different reasons might justify this group interest, such as the possibility of making economies of scales by increasing production volumes, or marketing arguments through exposing the highest number of potential consumers to a given brand.
374. In contrast, in the absence of factual control, the earning of profits and the willingness to earn such profits are under the influence of other factors, in particular the requirements of the owners and the effects of the market forces.
375. In this respect *see* the parallel made by Nicolaides between the assessment of the comparability between integrated firms and independent enterprises, and a case where the General Court accepted that a State guarantee reduced the level of risks assumed by the beneficiary of that guarantee (Joined Cases T-479/11 and T-157/12, *French Republic and IFP Énergies nouvelles v. European Commission*, ECLI:EU:T:2016:320). The author mentions that 'by analogy, control of one company over another reduces the risk which is inherent in the transactions between different companies' (*see* Phedon Nicolaides, 'State Aid Rules and Tax Rulings' (2016) 15 European State Aid Law Quarterly 416, 422).
376. In such cases, the factual control that exists within groups does not guarantee that each group member always seeks to maximise its profits, although the strategy decided by the group may very well contribute in the best possible manner to the overall profit of the group.
377. For example, group membership may have positive effects for many entities without the participation of each member, in case a group obtains an authorisation to sell medication in a given country.
378. Synergy effects may explain certain mergers or acquisitions. The European Commission recognises the search for, and the existence of such effects: *see* e.g., Commission Decision 2000/392/EC of 8 July 1999 on a measure implemented by the Federal Republic of Germany for Westdeutsche Landesbank – Girozentrale [2000] OJ L 150/1, where at para. 224 the Commission mentions that 'Synergy effects are normal consequences of a merger.'
379. For example, the realisation of an environmental risk may impact a whole group with no responsibility or mistake being imputable to each member.

Chapter 4: Comparability Analysis

pursuance of a common interest are likely to impact the profitability of the activities carried out by a group. On the basis of the research conducted by Coase and Musgrave, Andresen concluded that '(t)he combined profit of two independent entities from a common transaction is, by definition, *ceteris paribus* smaller than the combined profit of two members of an MNE from the same, then related-party, transaction'.[380] Indeed, group membership opens certain business opportunities that are not available to independent enterprises; if each business decision is also made rationally so that the most profitable alternative is chosen between outsourcing an activity and performing it internally, the effect at the level of a group is the maximisation of profits.

In the light of the three characteristics of multinational enterprises that were discussed above, I consider that independent and associated enterprises are not in the same situation, mainly given the difference in the interests they pursue. Other arguments, not mentioned here, confirm this view.[381] The result would be that the recommendations developed in the OECD transfer pricing guidelines to use the market forces as a benchmark to set the prices of intercompany transactions are potentially economically incorrect – although they may be fiscally desirable.[382] As pointed out by Wilkie, the statement of the arm's length principle in the guidelines 'necessarily misses the mark, though by how much is hard to tell'.[383] The result from the foregoing analysis would also be that associated enterprises with a high level of intercompany control and that pursue a common interest, may not be in a comparable situation to independent enterprises from a State aid law perspective, if the comparability analysis focuses only on the characteristics of each group of undertakings. This statement is not necessarily valid in all situations as it is purely theoretical. In certain circumstances it cannot be excluded that a group member faces circumstances that are highly similar to those faced by an independent enterprise with respect to its interests, organisation, and profit potential. Therefore, if a general conclusion cannot be drawn, it can at least be stated that integrated firms are more likely to be in a comparable situation with other integrated firms, than with independent enterprises.

Yet, despite the factual differences existing between associated and independent enterprises, we have to remember that in the field of State aid law, the factual comparison itself is not sufficient. It should be performed in the light of the objective of

---

380. *See* Ulf Andresen, 'Comments on Professor Schoueri's Lecture "Arm's Length: Beyond the Guidelines of the OECD"' (2015) 69 Bulletin for International Taxation 717, 720, with further references at footnote 38.
381. Among various issues, one is the difference in the cost structures of independent and associated enterprises. In this respect, it has been argued that multinational enterprises may have the financial capacity to invest in the long run so as to, in the end, earn income that exceeds that of independent enterprises, but that in the short run multinational enterprises may be exposed to higher levels of costs: *see* Yariv Brauner, 'Formula Based Transfer Pricing' (2014) 42 Intertax 615, 626.
382. In this respect it is mentioned in the OECD transfer pricing guidelines that 'The arm's length principle is viewed by some as inherently flawed because the separate entity approach may not always account for the economies of scale and interrelation of diverse activities created by integrated businesses': *see* para. 1.10 of the 2017 OECD transfer pricing guidelines.
383. *See* J. Scott Wilkie, 'Reflecting on the "Arm's Length Principle": What Is the "Principle"? Where Next?' in Wolfgang Schön and Kai A. Konrad (eds), *Fundamentals of International Transfer Pricing in Law and Economics* (Springer 2012) 143.

the tax system. Against the background of the case law of the CJEU and the logic of the State aid rules, the factual differences between independent and associated enterprises do not, in my opinion, preclude their comparability for the purpose of the selectivity test. If it is true that these categories of undertakings may pursue different interests and eventually earn different levels of profits, it does not affect the goal of a tax system to tax such profits; it only affects, to some extent, the means employed to achieve this goal. The *P Oy* case tends to evidence that a difference in profitability does not preclude the comparability between these categories of undertakings, as the CJEU found that a State measure cannot aim at favouring undertakings that are in financial difficulty.[384] This supposes that undertakings that are more or less profitable are in a comparable situation. By analogy, the integration existing within multinational enterprises, as far as it may enable them to be more profitable than independent enterprises, should not preclude their comparability. In addition, it is clear that the Member States do not need fundamentally different rules to tax the profits of independent and associated enterprises, with the important exception of an allocation method and of various antiavoidance rules. A Member State would normally aim at taxing the profits of all companies, whether or not they are part of a group. The general objective of corporate groups can also be assumed to be the maximisation of profits earned at the group level (though not necessarily at the level of each group member), similarly to independent enterprises. In other words, I see no reason in the factual differences mentioned above to conclude that they are not in a comparable situation in view of the objective of a corporate income tax system to tax the net income of all corporations.

I also find support to the above conclusion in a parallel with the case law of the CJEU relating to the right of the Member States to apply different tax rules to different industries. The factual differences observed above between independent and associated enterprises in terms of profitability and interests pursued, could be compared to the differences that exist between more or less profitable industries, or industries subject to various economic cycles. All undertakings active in different industries are normally aiming at earning profits, and a Member State that aims at taxing such profits does not need to generally subject these different categories of undertakings to different income tax rules, although certain rules may be needed to effectively tax all types of industries. The opposite would, from the start, create a breach in the competitive conditions between the different categories of undertakings.[385] This view is supported by several cases. For example, in *Italy v. Commission*, the Court did find companies in the textile industry to be comparable to other companies, although their cost structures or competitive positions were different.[386] The same reasoning was applied by the CJEU in cases relating to different types of taxes. For example, in *Adria Wien*, the environmental objective of a rebate on an energy tax for undertakings manufacturing

---

384. *See* Case C-6/12, *P Oy*, ECLI:EU:C:2013:525.
385. At the same time, the differences between various categories of undertakings may justify certain differences in the technical design of the tax rules, something that may be taken into account as part of the justification and proportionality analysis. In this respect, *see* Chapter 8 of this book.
386. *See* Case 173/73, *Italian Republic v. Commission of the European Communities*, ECLI:EU:C:1974:71.

tangible goods did not prevent them from being in a factual comparable situation, despite the different activities, cost structures, and environmental impact of the two categories of undertakings.[387]

There are examples where the Court reached a different outcome, but when one analyses why, the outcome appears motivated and consistent with the previously mentioned cases. A relevant example is the *Kernkraftwerke* case, which related to a duty on the use of nuclear fuel for the commercial production of electricity. The CJEU found that undertakings relying on different methods for electricity production were not in a comparable situation with respect to the objective of the duty, which was clearly linked to the method of production of energy.[388] The Court found that methods of producing electricity based on nuclear fuel were not comparable to other methods, as only the latter generated radioactive waste, which is likely to trigger particular costs. In other words, the scope of the tax made sense only for undertakings producing electricity based on nuclear fuel. In contrast, an income tax system has a broader scope that does not intrinsically need to differentiate between multinational enterprises, domestic groups, and independent enterprises. The corporate income tax targets all undertakings, and the fiscal revenues generated by the tax are not financing certain costs borne in relation to certain undertakings. Rather, the fiscal revenues generated by the corporate income tax would typically contribute to the national treasury of a Member State, or perhaps the treasury of a municipality, with no direct link between the levy of the tax and the use of the revenues generated by the tax. Moreover, the corporate income tax has, if not solely, at least partly a fiscal purpose; an excise duty such as that at hand in the *Kernkraftwerke* case may have a fiscal purpose, but it is likely to also have a political or regulatory purpose; the specificity of such a political or regulatory purpose makes it less relevant, or even not relevant, to compare undertakings that have different characteristics in regard of the duty, such as different methods to produce electricity. No such need for differentiation exists with a tax that has a more fiscal purpose and applies indistinctly to all undertakings, such as an income tax.

The conclusion is that, from a factual perspective, the arguments discussed above indicate that independent enterprises, domestic groups, and multinational enterprises are in a factual comparable situation in the light of the objective to tax companies on their net income. The next section considers comparability from a legal perspective.

4.3.4 Comparability from a Legal Perspective

Comparability from a legal perspective is difficult to precisely define, however its scope is more limited than factual comparability where any circumstance may come into play and influence the outcome of the comparability analysis. The study of comparability from a legal perspective reveals several differences between independent and associated enterprises, especially when associated enterprises have a cross-border

---

387. *See* Case C-143/99, *Adria-Wien Pipeline GmbH, Wietersdorfer & Peggauer Zementwerke GmbH*, ECLI:EU:C:2001:598, para. 41, and more generally how the Court reasoned in this case.
388. *See* Case C-5/14, *Kernkraftwerke Lippe-Ems GmbH v. Hauptzollamt Osnabrück*, ECLI:EU:C:2015:354, para. 79.

organisation. However, I believe that such differences do not prevent the legal comparability between these categories of undertakings, when it is assessed in the light of the objective of a corporate income tax system. I will explain why below.

To start with, let us consider the case of the membership in domestic (as opposed to cross-border) groups of companies. Group membership is often recognised in the field of tax law, even at a domestic level. The association between firms creates needs from a fiscal perspective that may be based on various objectives such as, to name two examples, the willingness to implement the principle of neutrality, or the need to prevent tax avoidance. With respect to the former, there are various types of rules that apply to domestic groups of companies and that aim at implementing, to a more or less important extent, similar tax outcomes irrespective of the organisation of a group. Examples are participation exemption regimes (to avoid multiple taxation in the corporate sector and ensure a neutral treatment of profit distributions in different corporate structures), the transfer of assets below market value, or systems that achieve the net taxation of corporate income through mechanisms such as group relief, tax unity, or group contribution. With respect to the prevention of tax avoidance, depending on the group taxation rules existing within a country, different rules will be needed to effectively prevent the avoidance of the levy of tax that a system aims at implementing. For example, in a Member State where the aim for neutrality is important, efficient anti-avoidance provisions are needed to prevent various forms of abuse, such as limitations to the transfer of losses in the case of corporate reorganisations with loss-making companies.

It follows from the above – very general – observations that the association between enterprises is, in many cases, likely to be acknowledged and produce consequences in the area of tax law. This differs from what can be observed in civil law, as illustrated by the diverging approaches between civil law and tax law with respect to the freedom to contract: tax law sometimes needs to question the freedom to contract as a consequence of the association between enterprises, in contrast to civil law that is likely to respect the freedom to contract to a greater extent. There is an explanation to this difference, which is the need of tax law to depart from various legal arrangements to fulfil the purpose of certain rules.[389] In other words, to achieve the objective of the corporate income tax and subject all companies to a tax on their net income, tax systems need to treat dependent and independent enterprises differently with respect to the freedom to contract. In this respect, Vann considered that 'freedom of contract needs to be constrained to produce a robust and meaningful allocation of profit within the firm'.[390] The points made in this paragraph emphasise that civil law and tax law may draw different consequences from the association between enterprises. This speaks for independent and associated enterprises being in a different situation from a legal perspective.

---

389. For an analysis of the effects of group membership on the freedom to contract in the contexts of civil law and tax law, *see* Jérôme Monsenego, 'La correction des prix de transfert entre sociétés apparentées au regard du concept civiliste de liberté contractuelle – Vers un renforcement de la théorie de l'autonomie du droit fiscal?' (2012) 9 Revue de Droit Fiscal 30.
390. *See* Richard J. Vann, 'Taxing International Business Income: Hard-Boiled Wonderland and the End of the World' (2010) 2 World Tax Journal 291, 333.

I now turn to the peculiarities of multinational enterprises. When associated enterprises are resident of different countries, it becomes obvious that they are not in the same position as domestic groups or independent enterprises with respect to their tax liabilities. In particular, it can be observed that while resident companies – whether or not they are part of a group – are, in many countries, subject to an unlimited tax liability in their State of residence, non-resident companies are either not subject to tax, or they are subject to a limited tax liability when they have a permanent establishment or earn income sourced in a given country. This is a consequence of the concept of residence, and of the legal principle of personality.[391] Tax treaties would most often preclude a country from taxing non-resident companies, unless a permanent establishment exists on its territory and a profit can be allocated to such a permanent establishment.[392] Thus, the taxing rights of the Member States are not similar for independent enterprises and domestic groups (which are subject to an unlimited tax liability), and multinational enterprises (the foreign members of which are not fully liable to tax). This basic difference triggers various types of consequences. To mention two examples, the lack of taxing rights on foreign group members opens up for arbitrage mechanisms through transfer pricing arrangements, or hybrid mismatches that exploit the differences in the legal and tax provisions of different countries.[393]

It follows from the foregoing considerations that tax rules are different for resident and non-resident companies. This puts independent and associated enterprises in different legal situations (although not necessarily from a State aid perspective), when associated enterprises are resident of different countries. Indeed, in view of the limited taxing rights on non-resident companies, independent enterprises and domestic groups can be taxed on their net income with limited possibilities to mitigate their tax burden, whereas multinational enterprises have greater opportunities to decrease their tax burden through various cross-border arbitrage mechanisms. At the same time, multinational enterprises also carry the risk of being subject to multiple taxation, as a consequence of the different tax claims of the countries to which they have a connection. Double taxation may also occur in the context of domestic groups, but to a different extent than for multinational enterprises given that the income of domestic group members stays within the tax jurisdiction of their State of residence. This creates a need for rules that are peculiar to members of multinational enterprises, such as allocation methods, rules on the limitation of the deduction of certain expenses, foreign tax credits, or dispute resolution mechanisms.

The arguments presented above reveal certain legal differences between independent enterprises, associated enterprises, and members of domestic groups. We now need to consider this comparison in the context of the rules on State aid, where the

---

391. Here, it is assumed that companies are opaque and not subject to CFC rules or to the tax rules applying to fiscally transparent entities.
392. *See* Art. 7 of the OECD Model Tax Convention.
393. For an overview of different tax planning techniques, *see* Philippe Lion, 'Comprendre la planification fiscale internationale et le cadre dans lequel elle s'opère' in Sami Douénias (ed), *Mélanges Pascal Minne – Fiscalité internationale et patrimoniale* (Bruylant 2017) 351. *See also* Sami Douénias, 'Défense et illustration ... de la fiscalité internationale' in Sami Douénias (ed), *Mélanges Pascal Minne – Fiscalité internationale et patrimoniale* (Bruylant 2017) 269.

comparison is made in the light of the objective of the corporate income tax system. In my opinion, all commercial undertakings are in a comparable legal situation when being compared in the light of the objective to tax their net income. To start with, it can be observed that apart from certain specific tax rules such as allocation methods, group taxation schemes, or anti-avoidance provisions, there is no general need as part of a corporate income tax system to subject members of multinational enterprises, members of domestic groups, and independent enterprises to a totally different set of income tax rules.[394] If such a general need existed, the CJEU might recognise it and accept that the three categories of undertakings are not in a comparable situation from a legal perspective, as the Court did in several other contexts.[395] Instead, the three categories of undertakings can very well be subject to the same corporate income tax system, which in certain cases needs to be supplemented by specific rules that ensure the eventual achievement of the objective of the system. The fact that the Member States may subject the three categories of undertakings to partly different tax rules with a specific purpose such as an allocation method or a group taxation scheme cannot, alone, put them in different situations for State aid law purposes. Were it to be the case, the choice of a national norm also entail a right to keep such a norm free of State aid control, something that would undermine the effect of the rules on State aid.[396]

If a Member State did not subject all commercial undertakings to the same basic corporate income tax rules, it would certainly contravene the rules on State aid, as demonstrated by the *Paint Graphos* case where only the special features of cooperative

---

394. A common consolidated corporate tax base would be different than the current tax systems based on the separate entity approach. However, while it might be argued that the common consolidated corporate tax base could improve the conditions for the taxation of multinational enterprises, it is not an absolute condition to tax their income, but rather a different way to achieve this objective.
395. *See* the example of the *Tiercé Ladbroke* case, where the Court recognised that the systems for betting on horse-races may be subject to different regulatory conditions in different countries: see Case C-353/95 P, *Tiercé Ladbroke SA v. Commission of the European Communities*, ECLI:EU:C:1997:596, para. 35. The difference between residents and non-residents may also lead to consequences that are acceptable from the perspective of EU law: for example, the CJEU found that non-resident pension funds were not in a situation comparable to resident pension funds. For resident pension funds, a yearly lump sum tax could be levied to reflect the yield of their assets. In contrast, no such tax could be levied on foreign pension funds, because of the limited taxing rights of the Member State of source, which prevented it from levying the same lump sum tax. Instead, non-resident pension funds were subject to a withholding tax on outbound dividends, which the CJEU did not find in breach of EU law: *see* Case C-252/14, *Pensioenfonds Metaal en Techniek v. Skatteverket*, ECLI:EU:C:2016:402, paras 56 and 63.
396. For example, if two companies are independent and are competing on a given market, one company could set up a fully-owned subsidiary in another country with some business activities; this newly built group would be subject to the allocation methods in force in the two countries. If multinational enterprises and independent enterprises are, from the start, not in a comparable situation for State aid law purposes, and assuming that the allocation methods result in a different tax burden than the basic principles of the corporate income tax system, the simple act of creating a group would suffice to escape the normal application of the corporate income tax rules, with a possible negative impact on the competition between these undertakings, and more generally, on the trade throughout the internal market. In this example, adding a cross-border element may be to the benefit of the taxpayer. There is a comparable discussion in the field of free movement law, where the addition of a cross-border element to a domestic situation may (abusively or not) entitle a person to the protection of EU law: *see* Stephen Weatherill, *The Internal Market as a Legal Concept* (Oxford University Press 2017) 131–133.

Chapter 4: Comparability Analysis

companies could put them in a different legal situation from commercial companies. To illustrate this argument, we can consider the example of rules on the depreciation of assets. If independent enterprises, domestic groups, and members of multinational enterprises were in a different legal situation, these categories of undertakings could be subject to different depreciation rules without infringing on the rules on State aid. However, there is no general need to subject, *a priori*, these categories of undertakings to different depreciation rules. If there is a need, in certain cases, to subject different undertakings to different rules on depreciation, I believe that this assessment cannot be accurately made as part of the comparability analysis. This is because the comparability analysis provides a general answer to the question of comparability, with no consideration for the actual rule at hand, since it is the objective of the system, not that of the rule, that is taken into account. Instead, the need for an exception to the main rules on depreciation suits better the justification analysis. Similarly, since the issues raised by the taxation of multinational enterprises do not generally demand a totally different tax system than what applies to independent enterprises or members of domestic groups, in my opinion the need of a tax system for certain additional provisions such as allocation methods or group taxation schemes does not prevent them from being in a comparable legal situation to the other categories of undertakings.

In addition, if the characteristics of members of multinational enterprises require certain particular rules such as allocation methods or anti-avoidance provisions to achieve the objective of a corporate income tax system, the characteristics of domestic groups require also – albeit to a different extent – certain specific rules. The taxation of domestic groups is often subject to provisions that deviate from those of independent enterprises, to implement a form of neutrality between different organisations. However, this does not preclude the legal comparability between members of domestic groups and independent enterprises.

Finally, when one takes into account the objective of a corporate income tax system, the case law of the CJEU and the practice of the European Commission confirm the points that were made above. The *Paint Graphos* case supports the view that members of multinational enterprises, members of domestic groups, and independent enterprises are in a comparable situation in the light of the objective of the corporate income tax. In this case, the Court found cooperative and commercial companies not to be in a comparable situation with respect to several of the differences that existed between the two, in the light of the objective of the Italian corporate income tax. It can be agreed with this outcome, assuming that cooperative companies actually do not pursue a lucrative objective.[397] In contrast, it can reasonably be assumed that members of multinational enterprises, members of domestic groups, and independent enterprises that are pursuing commercial activities are all aiming at the realisation of profits; if a Member State intends at taxing such profits, the *Paint Graphos* case implies, when it is interpreted *a contrario*, that all these categories of undertakings should be deemed

---

397. This assumption cannot, however, be generalised so that cooperative companies never are deemed to have a lucrative objective. The activity of a cooperative company may very well be commercial and aimed at earning profits, even though such profits may not be to the benefit of the owner, but to the benefit of, for instance, a foundation.

to be in a comparable legal situation. This is a consequence of the general objective of the corporate income tax system to tax the income earned by the commercial activities of commercial companies, irrespective of their ownership, the possible association with other companies, and the possible foreign residence of certain group members. Moreover, the large understanding of the notion of comparability has at least been confirmed, perhaps even broadened, in a later case where the CJEU ruled on the compatibility with State aid law of a tax exemption for the Spanish Catholic Church. The Court did not analyse at depth whether the Spanish Catholic Church was in a comparable situation to other undertakings, but simply compared the treatment of the Church to that of 'all economic operators'.[398] This broad understanding of the notion of comparability speaks in favour of comparing members of multinational enterprises to other types of undertakings, not just to other multinational enterprises.

This conclusion is strengthened by the position taken in the Commission notice with respect to undertakings for collective investments.[399] Such undertakings act as intermediary vehicles for collective investments, as opposed to private investments. To promote a neutral treatment of investments, whether they are made by private investors directly or through undertakings for collective investment, the Commission found that it was justified not to subject such undertakings to corporate income taxation. This conclusion was reached on the basis of the justification analysis, which means that undertakings for collective investments were in the first place considered to be in a comparable situation to other commercial undertakings. Indeed, undertakings for collective investments do pursue a commercial activity, though not for their own benefit but for the benefit of the investors. The Commission found these two categories of undertakings to be in a comparable situation in the light of the objective of the corporate income tax, although it was justified to exempt undertakings for collective investments from the corporate tax liability given their ultimate objective and the need to avoid the taxation in chain of their profits. Accordingly, if undertakings for collective investments are in a comparable situation to commercial companies, despite their particular role as intermediary vehicles for collective investments, then members of multinational enterprises, members of domestic groups, and independent enterprises should *a fortiori* be in a comparable situation, given that they have no such diverging roles. This conclusion could also be strengthened by a parallel to the *Navantia* case, where the CJEU found that private and State-owned companies were in a comparable situation with respect to the levy of property tax, despite the legal difference between shares owned by private shareholders or by a State.[400] In this case, the different characteristics of private and State-owned companies did not prevent them from being in a comparable situation for the purpose of levying tax on immovable property, as the Court paid mostly attention to the differences in the purpose (civil or military) of the use of land.

---

398. *See* Case C-74/16, *Congregación de Escuelas Pías Provincia Betania v. Ayuntamiento de Getafe*, ECLI:EU:C:2017:496, para. 70.
399. *See* Commission Notice on the notion of State aid as referred to in Art. 107(1) of the Treaty on the Functioning of the European Union [2016] OJ C 262/1, paras 161–163.
400. *See* Case C-522/13, *Ministerio de Defensa and Navantia SA v. Concello de Ferrol*, ECLI:EU:C:2014:2262, paras 40–41.

In the light of the foregoing, my conclusion is that independent enterprises, members of domestic groups, and members of multinational enterprises are in a legally comparable situation, when this assessment is made in the light of the objective to tax these undertakings on their net income.[401]

4.4 CONCLUSION

There are numerous factual and legal aspects that are peculiar to members of multinational enterprises, members of domestic groups, and independent enterprises. These three categories of undertakings are in different situations in several respects. However, when the comparison is made in the light of the objective of a corporate income tax, these three categories of undertakings appear to be in a comparable situation. Several authors argue the contrary, considering that members of multinational enterprises and independent enterprises are not in a comparable situation.[402] The arguments raised with respect to the differences between these two categories of undertakings are correct, but I believe that they do not preclude the comparability in the context of the objective of the corporate income tax. Indeed, despite the particular features of these categories of undertakings, they are most likely to aim at the realisation of profits, and a corporate income tax system should aim, under the control of the State aid rules, at taxing such profits in a similar manner, no matter the ownership or organisation of the respective undertakings. It is true that, to achieve the objective of taxation of companies on their net income, the corporate income tax systems need to include certain rules that are specifically targeting different undertakings or transactions. Without such rules, the objective of the corporate income tax systems can be more difficult, if not impossible to achieve. However, it is precisely because the objective of taxation of independent and associated enterprises is the same that despite the different tools that are necessary to achieve this objective, these categories of undertakings are in a comparable situation for State aid law purposes. This position is also that of the European Commission,[403] although it considered in

---

401. For a contrary view *see* Phedon Nicolaides, 'State Aid Rules and Tax Rulings' (2016) 15 European State Aid Law Quarterly 416, 425.
402. See e.g., Wolfgang Schön, 'Transfer Pricing, the Arm's Length Standard and European Union Law' in Isabelle Richelle, Wolfgang Schön, and Edoardo Traversa (eds) *Allocating Taxing Powers Within the European Union* (Springer 2013) 94–96; Phedon Nicolaides, 'State Aid Rules and Tax Rulings' (2016) 15 European State Aid Law Quarterly 416, 421–423; Raymond Luja, 'State Aid Benchmarking and Tax Rulings: Can We Keep It Simple?' in Isabelle Richelle, Wolfgang Schön, and Edoardo Traversa (eds), *State Aid Law and Business Taxation* (Springer 2016) 114.
403. *See* e.g., Commission Decision (EU) 2016/2326 of 21 October 2015 on State aid SA.38375 (2014/C ex 2014/NN) which Luxembourg granted to Fiat [2016] OJ L 351/1, para. 199; Commission Decision (EU) 2016/1699 of 11 January 2016 on the excess profit exemption State aid scheme SA.37667 (2015/C) (ex 2015/NN) implemented by Belgium [2016] OJ L 260/61, para. 126. It must be pointed out, however, that the Commission does not provide a convincing motivation for finding independent and associated enterprises to be in a comparable situation. The Commission seems to consider that the comparability between these categories of undertakings can be assumed based on the scope of the reference system: since the system applies to all undertakings that earn income, they would be in a comparable factual and legal

earlier decisions that the association between enterprises and the existence of common interests might place them in different situations.[404]

Moreover, reaching the opposite conclusion would lead to consequences that, in my opinion, are at odds with the logic of the rules on State aid: if multinational enterprises, domestic groups, and independent enterprises were generally deemed not to be in a comparable situation, the Member States would have the right, under the State aid rules, to tax these three categories of undertakings differently, despite the potential breaches in the competitive conditions that this may imply for various undertakings. Corporations could choose their regime of income taxation by organising themselves in different manners,[405] thus breaching competitive conditions between different categories of undertakings.

With the conclusions to Chapter 4 comes also the end of the first part of this book, which is devoted to the analysis of the elements of the selectivity test that are common to the three allocation methods. This first part sets the scene for the selectivity assessment of each allocation method, which is the subject of the second part of the book.

---

situation. That is clearly put at footnote 87 of the *Fiat* decision: '(i)n general, all undertakings having an income are considered to be in a similar legal and factual situation from the perspective of direct company taxation'. For a similar position, *see* Commission Decision (EU) 2017/2116 of 27 July 2017 on aid scheme SA.38398 (2016/C, ex 2015/E) implemented by France – Taxation of ports in France [2017] OJ L 332/24, para. 71, where the criterion for finding different undertakings to be in a comparable situation is the fact that they all 'generate profits'.

404. *See* Commission Decision 2009/809/EC of 8 July 2009 on the groepsrentebox scheme which the Netherlands is planning to implement [2009] OJ L 288/26, para. 103; Commission Decision of 28 October 2009 on State aid C 10/07 (ex NN 13/07) implemented by Hungary for tax deductions for intra-group interest [2010] OJ L 42/3, para. 111.

405. For example, if a Member State would implement an allocation method that deviates from the taxation of independent enterprises, a standalone company could simply set up a subsidiary in another Member State and enter in a few intercompany transactions to qualify as a multinational enterprise to escape the rules applying to independent enterprises.

PART II Selectivity Assessment of the Three Allocation Methods

It is settled case law that a measure is prima facie selective if it favours certain undertakings over other undertakings which, in the light of the objective pursued by the tax system, are in a comparable factual and legal situation.[406] In the first part of the book I analysed the elements of the selectivity test that are common to the three allocation methods. It can now be investigated how the selectivity test applies to these methods. Since the three allocation methods have different characteristics that raise different issues in the light of the selectivity test, I shall examine each allocation method individually. Accordingly, the second part of the book is devoted to the prima facie selectivity assessment of a generally formulated arm's length provision (Chapter 5), transfer pricing safe harbours (Chapter 6), and a system of formula apportionment with firm-specific factors (Chapter 7). It is then considered whether the prima facie selective measures that have been identified in Chapter 5 through 7 are able to be justified and, if so, whether they are in line with the principle of proportionality (Chapter 8).

Before embarking on the selectivity test of each allocation method, it should be distinguished between the different types of material selectivity that are considered in this part of the book. The first type of material selectivity concerns differences in treatment that stem from the *design* of the law: if the tax system includes a main rule and an exception to it (in which case there is a deviation from the reference system), or if certain rules are drafted so that they have a limited scope of application that excludes certain undertakings (in which case the reference system is not designed in a non-discriminatory manner), the law implies a difference in treatment. As a result of this difference in treatment, certain undertakings may be favoured over others. The tax

---

406. *See* Joined Cases C-20/15 P and C-21/15 P, *European Commission v. World Duty Free Group*, ECLI:EU:C:2016:981, para. 54, with further references. *See also* Commission Notice on the notion of State aid as referred to in Art. 107(1) of the Treaty on the Functioning of the European Union [2016] OJ C 262/1, para. 135.

measure would then be considered de jure selective, because the selectivity stems from the design of the law. There are several difficulties that are specific to the de jure selectivity test. One of these consists in correctly identifying whether or not there is a deviation from the reference system. While in certain cases a difference in treatment is obvious,[407] it may prove difficult to identify, for instance when several rules coexist and no levy appears clearly as the main rule.[408]

Second, selectivity may stem from the *application* of the law, when a measure is applied differently between undertakings, to the benefit of some. This type of selectivity arises on a case-by-case basis, such as when a Member State decides how to tax an undertaking in an advance tax ruling; examples are provided by the *Starbucks*[409] and *Fiat*[410] cases. The case-by-case application of the allocation methods as such is outside the scope of the book. However, the design of the law does have an influence on how the application of the law is assessed in the light of the selectivity test. Measures that contain room for interpretation are more likely to be applied differently for different undertakings, than measures that have a more mechanistic application. Among the three allocation methods studied in this book, selectivity that stems from the *application* of the law concerns mainly a generally formulated arm's length provision, as this method lies on an abstract principle that needs to be interpreted on a case-by-case basis, something that opens for different interpretations. The other allocation methods are not solely based on an abstract principle, but have a more objective and mechanistic character. Therefore, while certain aspects of the application of the arm's length principle are analysed in the second part of the book,[411] the application of the other methods is left out of the scope of this study.

Third, in the lack of an explicit difference in treatment that stems from the design of the law, or of different applications of the law, a tax measure is at first sight general, i.e., non-selective. Yet, it is settled case law that a tax measure that is generally designed may be selective, if 'in practice'[412] and despite the lack of any explicit

---

407. That would typically be the case where a lower tax rate applies in certain exceptional cases, while in all other cases a higher tax rate applies.
408. In the literature is has been emphasised that the CJEU does not, in its discriminatory-based case law, provide criteria for the identification of the main rule and the exception: *see* Wolfgang Schön, 'Tax Legislation and the Notion of Fiscal Aid: A Review of 5 Years of European Jurisprudence' in Isabelle Richelle, Wolfgang Schön, and Edoardo Traversa (eds), *State Aid Law and Business Taxation* (Springer 2016) 13, with reference to the choice between two tax rates for taxes on flights with different lengths. It has also been argued that different rules may have different scopes and objectives, something that would make it difficult to identify the rule and the exception: *see* Michael Lang, 'State Aid and Taxation: Selectivity and Comparability Analysis' in Isabelle Richelle, Wolfgang Schön, and Edoardo Traversa (eds), *State Aid Law and Business Taxation* (Springer 2016) 34.
409. *See* Commission Decision (EU) 2017/502 of 21 October 2015 on State aid SA.38374 (2014/C ex 2014/NN) implemented by the Netherlands to Starbucks [2017] OJ L 83/38.
410. *See* Commission Decision (EU) 2016/2326 of 21 October 2015 on State aid SA.38375 (2014/C ex 2014/NN) which Luxembourg granted to Fiat [2016] OJ L 351/1.
411. It is not the application of the principle in concrete cases that is studied, but rather *how* to apply the principle. The aspects of the application of the arm's length principle that are analysed in this part of the book appear as controversial in the light of the positions taken by the European Commission in certain of its decisions. In this respect, *see* section 5.4 of the book.
412. *See* Joined Cases C-106/09 P and C-107/09 P, *European Commission v. Government of Gibraltar*, ECLI:EU:C:2011:732, para. 101.

Part II: Selectivity Assessment of the Three Allocation Methods

discriminatory element, it favours certain undertakings. This is especially the case when the difference in treatment is not 'a random consequence of the regime at issue, but the inevitable consequence' of the way the measure is designed, i.e., if the intent of the lawmaker was to favour certain undertakings.[413] This is the third type of material selectivity, often described as de facto selectivity,[414] because the selectivity stems from the *effects* of the law. It is this type of selectivity that would be the most relevant in case the reference system is made of an allocation method (instead of the whole corporate income tax system), or if the comparability test should be conducted different associated enterprises (instead of comparing associated enterprises with independent enterprises and domestic groups), because the reference system would not include an explicit difference in treatment between undertakings that are in a comparable situation.

De facto selectivity is difficult to assess, partly because it necessarily includes a subjective dimension.[415] This contrasts with de jure selectivity, which is more straightforward to assess as it mainly implies the identification of a deviation from the reference system, although this identification does not exclude all subjective elements. Consequently, I will present the de facto selectivity test in more details, before delving into the selectivity assessment of each allocation method in Chapters 5, 6, and 7 of the book. It can first be observed that the methodology to carry out the selectivity test has been evolving with the case law of the CJEU, so as to give increasing importance to the effects of a measure.[416] Whereas in the early cases the Court found certain measures selective on the basis of their purpose,[417] thereby being a subjective test, the notion of selectivity evolved to rather focus on the effects of State measures (the so-called effects doctrine),[418] thereby moving to a more objective test, without however fully departing

---

413. *See* Joined Cases C-106/09 P and C-107/09 P, *European Commission v. Government of Gibraltar*, ECLI:EU:C:2011:732, para. 106.
414. *See* e.g., Joined Cases C-20/15 P and C-21/15 P, *European Commission v. World Duty Free Group*, ECLI:EU:C:2016:981, para. 74.
415. The de facto selectivity test lies on certain subjective elements, such as the determination of the benchmark against which the de facto selectivity test is carried out, or the assessment of arguments that may justify a State measure that is *a priori* selective. Moreover, the de facto selectivity test is arguably not solely carried out on the basis of the effects of a State measure; the aims of a measure may have to be taken into account. Indeed, the CJEU at para. 101 of the *Gibraltar* case did pay attention to 'the objective of the proposed tax reform, namely to introduce a general system of taxation for all companies established in Gibraltar'. In the doctrine, Rubini argued that the de facto selectivity test should build on 'two cumulative steps', the effect and the objective of a measure: *see* Luca Rubini, *The Definition of Subsidy and State Aid: WTO and EC Law in Comparative Perspective* (Oxford University Press 2009) 374.
416. The position of the European Commission on the notion of State aid has also evolved over time: *see* e.g., Frans Vanistendael, 'Are the EU and U.S. Headed for a Tax War?' (2016) 83 Tax Notes International 1057', who at 1058 emphasises the 'sweeping change in the concept of state aid' that can be observed in the work of the European Commission.
417. *See* e.g., Joined Cases 6/69 and 11/69, *Commission of the European Communities v. French Republic*, ECLI:EU:C:1969:68, para. 20. *See also* Case 30/59, *De Gezamenlijke Steenkolenmijnen in Limburg v. High Authority of the European Coal and Steel Community*, ECLI:EU:C:1960:41, Opinion of AG Lagrange, at 43, where the Advocate General considered that one could look for the 'real object' of a measure in regard of the charges that an undertaking would 'normally have to bear'.
418. *See* Case 173/73, *Italian Republic v. Commission of the European Communities*, ECLI:EU:C:1974:71, para. 27, for the now famous formula: 'article [107(1) of the TFEU] does not

from a subjective approach. This evolution is understandable, as a State measure may have distortive effects on competition and trade even if it is not the aim pursued by a Member State. De facto selectivity has been applied to various non-tax measures.[419] In the area of taxes, the 'effects doctrine' has led the CJEU to rely on the concept of de facto selectivity in several cases, especially the landmark *Gibraltar* case,[420] which has been considered to put 'effects over form'.[421] Later cases, in particular *World Duty Free Group*, confirm the application to tax measures of the concept of de facto selectivity developed in *Gibraltar*.[422] Nevertheless, the de facto selectivity test does not have a clear scope, in particular when it comes to the identification of the beneficiaries of a measure. In *Gibraltar* the CJEU seemed to require that, in order to be potentially de facto selective, a measure must identify with sufficient precision a privileged category of undertakings that benefits from it,[423] but in *World Duty Free Group* the Court found that there is no requirement to identify a particular category of undertakings as an additional step of the method to assess the selectivity of tax measures,[424] the main focus being on the effects of such measures.[425] The problem is that tax measures that have really general effects are few.[426] The level of a tax rate is often mentioned,

---

distinguish between the measures of State intervention concerned by reference to their causes or aims but defines them in relation to their effects'.

419. See e.g., the *GEMO* case, where a public carcass disposal service that was available to any undertaking was found, in practice, to essentially benefit farmers and slaughterhouses (*see* Case C-126/01, *Ministre de l'économie, des finances et de l'industrie v. GEMO SA*, ECLI:EU:C:2003:622, para. 38). *See* Case T-55/99, *Confederación Española de Transporte de Mercancías (CETM) v. Commission of the European Communities*, ECLI:EU:T:2000:223, para. 40, for a clear explanation of why a general measure may be selective. *See also* Case T-468/08, *Tisza Erőmű kft v. European Commission*, ECLI:EU:T:2014:235, para. 164.
420. In this respect, some scholars consider *Gibraltar* as implying a methodological change. *See* e.g., Édouard Dubout and Alexandre Maitrot de la Motte, 'Normalité, sélectivité et légitimité des régimes fiscaux dans l'Union européenne: les paradis fiscaux au purgatoire des aides d'État?' (2012) 5 Revue de Droit Fiscal 44, 50–52; John Temple Lang, "The Gibraltar State Aid and Taxation Judgment – A "Methodological Revolution"?' (2012) 11 European State Aid Law Quarterly 805, 807. Other scholars find the *Gibraltar* case in line with the previous case law of the Court: *see* e.g., Rita Szudoczky, *The Sources of EU Law and Their Relationships: Lessons for the Field of Taxation* (IBFD 2014) 488.
421. *See* Thomas Jaeger, 'From Santander to LuxLeaks – and Back' (2015) 24 European State Aid Law Quarterly 345, 350.
422. *See* Joined Cases C-20/15 P and C-21/15 P, *European Commission v. World Duty Free Group*, ECLI:EU:C:2016:981, in particular at para. 74. *See also* Joined Cases T-92/00 and T-103/00, *Territorio Histórico de Álava – Diputación Foral de Álava v. Commission of the European Communities*, ECLI:EU:T:2002:61, especially at para. 39.
423. *See* Joined Cases C-106/09 P and C-107/09 P, *European Commission v. Government of Gibraltar*, ECLI:EU:C:2011:732, para. 104.
424. *See* Joined Cases C-20/15 P and C-21/15 P, *European Commission v. World Duty Free Group*, ECLI:EU:C:2016:981, para. 71.
425. *See* Joined Cases C-20/15 P and C-21/15 P, *European Commission v. World Duty Free Group*, ECLI:EU:C:2016:981, paras 76–77.
426. *See* Jean-Yves Chérot, *Les aides d'État dans les Communautés européennes* (Economica 1998), who at 24 stresses that 'la notion même de mesures générales est peu significative tant il est exceptionnel de se trouver en présence de mesures indistinctement applicables à l'ensemble de l'économie sans nuances'.

including by the Commission,[427] as an example of general measure. In contrast, the rules that define the concept of income cannot be purely abstract and general; they need to have some material content and be relying on elements that have, to give a few examples, an economic, organisational, territorial, or accounting nature.

Eventually, the scope of the de facto selectivity concept appears broad[428] and difficult to determine, as virtually any tax measure that defines the tax base needs to build on certain material aspects. Such aspects will have various effects on different undertakings, whether they are positive or negative. Indeed, neither the application of a measure to a great number of undertakings, nor its application to an entire economic sector or several economic sectors, may prevent such a measure from being de facto selective.[429] How to conduct the de facto selectivity test is not obvious, as it does not rely on the mechanic assessment of a deviation from the reference system that stems from the design of the law or from the application of the law, but rather on the subjective assessment of the design of the boundaries of a tax system, including the intent of the lawmaker when deciding these boundaries. Therefore, although the focus on the effects of State measures seems at first sight objective, the assessment of these effects has necessarily a subjective dimension. To that end, de facto selectivity needs to rely on a benchmark to determine what measures produce general or selective effects. Such a benchmark has been described in the academic literature as an assessment of the normality of a reference system,[430] i.e., an investigation of whether the effects of

---

427. *See* Commission notice on the application of the State aid rules to measures relating to direct business taxation [1998] OJ C 384/3, para. 13; the 2016 notice removed reference to tax rates as general measures.
428. *See* Phedon Nicolaides, 'Excessive Widening of the Concept of Selectivity' (2017) 16 European State Aid Law Quarterly 62; Gunnar Rabe, 'Statliga stöd' (2017) Skattenytt 386. The Commission seems in its notice to have a narrower vision of the concept of de facto selectivity, as it considers that this criterion should apply in 'exceptional cases', when 'the structure of the measure is such that its effects significantly favour a particular group of undertakings': *see* Commission Notice on the notion of State aid as referred to in Art. 107(1) of the Treaty on the Functioning of the European Union [2016] OJ C 262/1, para. 121. The Commission also emphasises in the notice the need to 'evaluate whether the boundaries of the system of reference have been designed in a consistent manner or, conversely, in a clearly arbitrary or biased way, so as to favour certain undertakings which are in a comparable situation with regard to the underlying logic of the system in question' (*see* para. 129 of the notice). However, this is only a notice, and it was published before the CJEU ruled in several important cases, particularly the *World Duty Free Group* case, on 21 December 2016.
429. *See* Case C-75/97, *Kingdom of Belgium v. Commission of the European Communities*, ECLI:EU:C:1999:311, para. 32: 'Neither the high number of benefiting undertakings nor the diversity and importance of the industrial sectors to which those undertakings belong warrant the conclusion that the (...) scheme constitutes a general measure of economic policy'. *See also* Case 248/84, *Federal Republic of Germany v. Commission of the European Communities*, ECLI:EU:C:1987:437, para. 18.
430. *See* particularly the use of the word 'abnormal' in the Opinion of Advocate General Jääskinen in the *Gibraltar* case: Joined Cases C-106/09 P and C-107/09 P, *European Commission v. Government of Gibraltar*, ECLI:EU:C:2011:215, Opinion of AG Jääskinen, para. 178. *See also* Édouard Dubout and Alexandre Maitrot de la Motte, 'Normalité, sélectivité et légitimité des régimes fiscaux dans l'Union européenne: les paradis fiscaux au purgatoire des aides d'État?' (2012) 5 Revue de Droit Fiscal 44, 54: 'considérer que des mesures générales sont sélectives présuppose un élargissement du cadre de référence de la normalité, qui n'est plus la politique fiscale de l'État ou l'entité envisagée, mais la pratique fiscale des autres États membres de l'Union'. Similarly, Engelen and Gunn have argued in favour of taking into account the

the reference system are normal[431] or abnormal.[432] Certain authors consider that the benchmark is set by reference to the tax systems of the other Member States.[433] This view is however not undisputed,[434] for instance with respect to the fiscal sovereignty of the Member States in tax matters.[435] The benchmark has even been considered in the doctrine as impossible to define.[436] A comparison between the effects of various tax systems seems at least consistent with one of the purposes of the rules on State aid,

---

objective of the measure so that only measures that have a 'legitimate' objective may be compatible with State aid law: see Frank Engelen and Anna Gunn, 'State Aid: Towards a Theoretical Assessment Framework' in Alexander Rust and Claire Micheau (eds), *State aid and Tax Law* (Kluwer Law International 2013) 144.

431. This is when the system does not favour certain undertakings.
432. This is when the system does favour certain undertakings.
433. See e.g., Édouard Dubout and Alexandre Maitrot de la Motte, 'Normalité, sélectivité et légitimité des régimes fiscaux dans l'Union européenne: les paradis fiscaux au purgatoire des aides d'État?' (2012) 5 Revue de Droit Fiscal 44, 54: 'considérer que des mesures générales sont sélectives présuppose un élargissement du cadre de référence de la normalité, qui n'est plus la politique fiscale de l'État ou l'entité envisagée, mais la pratique fiscale des autres États membres de l'Union'. These authors find a possible justification to this broadening of the reference system in the objective of the State aid rules, which is suggested to consist in the protection of the competition throughout the internal market, not within the Member States. *See also* Luca Rubini, *The Definition of Subsidy and State Aid: WTO and EC Law in Comparative Perspective* (Oxford University Press 2009) 362–363, with further references at footnote 16; Rubini argues that the concept of selectivity would be 'more meaningful' if it were extended to the treatment of competitors in other countries, although such a concept of selectivity would be 'very difficult to administer'; Marilyne Sadowsky, *Droit de l'OMC, droit de l'Union européenne et fiscalité directe* (Larcier 2013), who concludes at 409 that the tax systems of the Member States constitute a point of reference, i.e., a standard against which the State aid control of various tax measures is performed. Concurring on the need for a point of reference *see* Jean-Yves Chérot, *Les aides d'État dans les Communautés européennes* (Economica 1998), who at 23 considers that '(l)'aide apparaît avec le caractère anormal de la mesure adoptée. L'anormalité renvoie nécessairement à une norme de référence'; John Temple Lang, 'The Gibraltar State Aid and Taxation Judgment – A "Methodological Revolution"?' (2012) 11 European State Aid Law Quarterly 805, who at 808 found that the effects of a rule 'can only be identified and assessed in the light of some standard of comparison'.
434. *See* Frank Engelen and Anna Gunn, 'State Aid: Towards a Theoretical Assessment Framework' in Alexander Rust and Claire Micheau (eds), *State Aid and Tax Law* (Kluwer Law International 2013) 141: '(w)e thus reject the notion that there could exist a framework of reference for assessing the existence of an advantage *outside* the actual tax system of the Member State itself'; concurring *see* Leigh Hancher, 'The General Framework' in Leigh Hancher, Tom Ottervanger, and Piet Jan Slot (eds), *EU State Aids* (5th edn, Sweet & Maxwell 2016) para. 3-107. For a view according to which the *Gibraltar* case implies not the assessment of a departure from a 'theoretical international standard' but from the actual domestic system, *see* Pierpaolo Rossi-Maccanico, 'Fiscal State Aids, Tax Base Erosion and Profit Shifting' (2015) 24 EC Tax Review 63, 68. A case ruled by the GC, and confirmed by the CJEU, took the position that the benchmark cannot be constituted of the rules of other Member States: *see* Case T-308/00, *Salzgitter AG v. European Commission*, ECLI:EU:T:2013:30, para. 81; Case C-408/04 P, *Commission of the European Communities v. Salzgitter AG*, ECLI:EU:C:2008:236.
435. *See* Wolfgang Schön, 'Taxation and State Aid Law in the European Union' (1999) 36 Common Market Law Review 911, 923.
436. *See* Marilyne Sadowsky, 'Vers un système fiscal standard?' (2013) 25 Revue de Droit Fiscal 57, at 61: '(l)es systèmes juridiques sont donc à la recherche d'une norme de référence fiscale introuvable'. Similarly, as put by Karpenschif, the problem is 'l'impossibilité de définir un standard juridique sans recourir à d'autres standards': *see* Michaël Karpenschif, *Droit européen des aides d'État* (Bruylant 2015) 74.

Part II: Selectivity Assessment of the Three Allocation Methods

which is to protect the competition between the Member States, on the top of the protection of the competition between various undertakings.[437]

Moreover, even if one has identified a possible benchmark, it is not given that the benchmark should be accepted: one way of reasoning consists in accepting the benchmark, which would imply that a measure that departs from it is de facto selective. Another way of reasoning consists in arguing that there is no reason to accept the existing benchmark; instead, one could replace it with a new, more acceptable, or more 'normal' standard.[438] No clear guidance is available in the case law of the Union courts. Since there is no objective definition of what constitutes 'normal taxation', while at the same time the de facto selectivity test needs to rely on a benchmark, the analyses made in this chapter can hardly avoid a subjective dimension.

The following chapters test whether, and if so under what circumstances, a generally formulated arm's length provision (Chapter 5), transfer pricing safe harbours (Chapter 6), and a system of formula apportionment with firm-specific factors (Chapter 7) might be prima facie selective. These three chapters are completed by the justification and proportionality tests in Chapter 8.

---

437. Indeed, as emphasised by Hancher, 'the Treaty state aid provisions essentially aim at reducing if not eliminating distortions of production and location decisions across Member States – this regime relates to competition between Member States, and not just competition between undertakings': *see* Leigh Hancher, 'EU State Aid Law – Déjà Vu All Over Again?' in Leigh Hancher, Tom Ottervanger, and Piet Jan Slot (eds), *EU State Aids* (5th edn, Sweet & Maxwell 2016) para. 1-029.
438. *See* Wolfgang Schön, 'Destination-Based Income Taxation and WTO Law: A Note' in Heike Jochum, Peter Essers, Michael Lang, Norbert Winkeljohann, and Bertil Wiman (eds), *Practical Problems in European and International Tax Law – Essays in Honour of Manfred Mössner* (IBFD 2016) 429, for a similar reasoning in the area of international trade law.

CHAPTER 5
Prima Facie Selectivity of a Generally Formulated Arm's Length Provision

5.1 INTRODUCTION

This chapter starts by testing a generally formulated arm's length provision in the light of the de jure selectivity test (section 5.2). It is then focused on the effects of a generally formulated arm's length provision, i.e., the de facto selectivity test (section 5.3). Last, three aspects of the application of the arm's length principle are considered, in the light of certain of the positions taken by the European Commission (section 5.4). The conclusions of this chapter are presented in section 5.5.

5.2 DE JURE SELECTIVITY

In the case of a generally formulated arm's length provision, and assuming that it is drafted along the lines of Article 9 of the OECD Model Tax Convention, at first sight there is no difference in treatment implied by the drafting of this allocation method, whether associated enterprises are compared to other associated enterprises or to independent enterprises. Indeed, the purpose of the arm's length principle is to ensure a similar tax treatment between comparable independent and associated enterprises,[439] something that would prevent a difference in treatment between these two categories of undertakings.[440] Moreover, the drafting of the arm's length principle provides in

---

439. *See* the drafting of Art. 9 of the OECD Model Tax Convention. *See also* Luís Eduardo Schoueri, 'Arm's Length: Beyond the Guidelines of the OECD' (2015) 69 Bulletin for International Taxation 690, where the author at 695 stresses the original intent of the arm's length principle to be a 'need for equality between related and unrelated firms'.
440. In this respect, it has been argued that the arm's length principle places independent and associated enterprises on 'equal footing', something that would prevent this allocation method from being selective: *see* Romero J.S. Tavares, Bret N. Bogenschneider, and Marta Pankiv, 'The Intersection of EU State Aid and U.S. Tax Deferral: A Spectacle of Fireworks, Smoke, and

theory a similar treatment between all comparable associated enterprises, because they are all are subject to the same benchmark, i.e., the benchmark provided by the open market.

If at first sight the arm's length principle seems not to carry the risk of being de jure selective, a deeper analysis points to a more nuanced conclusion. Indeed, as already argued at section 2.2.3.2 above, the arm's length principle, as it is described in the 2017 OECD transfer pricing guidelines, does not always implement an equal treatment between associated and independent enterprises. Moreover, there are two aspects of a generally formulated arm's length provision that speak for the de jure selectivity of this allocation method. These aspects are the limited corrective effect of the arm's length principle (section 5.2.1), and the assumed correctness of the benchmark provided by the average effect of the market forces, which would result in the generalisation of the outcomes reached under this allocation method with little consideration for the diversity of the possible behaviours of associated enterprises (section 5.2.2).

5.2.1 The Limited Corrective Effect of the Arm's Length Principle

First, the corrective effect of a generally formulated arm's length provision is, in most countries, limited to intercompany transactions between associated enterprises that are resident of different countries. In other words, the arm's length principle works as an anti-avoidance rule that only applies to multinational enterprises.[441] The arm's length principle would normally not apply for the pricing of transactions between domestic group companies, or between independent enterprises. A clear illustration of the limited corrective effect of the arm's length principle is provided in the OECD transfer pricing guidelines with respect to the recognition of income attributable to intangible property, when certain functions have been outsourced. The guidelines state that if the legal owner of an intangible has outsourced certain functions (as opposed to performing all functions by itself), but 'neither controls nor performs the functions related to the development, enhancement, maintenance, protection or exploitation of the intangible', then 'the legal owner would not be entitled to any ongoing benefit attributable to the outsourced functions'.[442] This illustrates that the arm's length principle, as it is described in the guidelines, starts from a different end than the rules applicable to independent enterprises or members of domestic groups, since the latter do not have to prove that they perform such functions to be able to earn profits on similar intangibles.

Indeed, in many cases, no correction is made to the terms of the transactions between independent enterprises, even if these terms are not rational or do not mirror the market forces. Independent companies may take decisions that deviate from the

---

Mirrors' (2016) 19 Florida Tax Review 121, 174. As explained later in this paragraph as well as in section 2.2.3.2, I do not fully agree with this position.
441. Concurring, *see* Yariv Brauner, 'Formula Based Transfer Pricing' (2014) 42 Intertax 615, 626.
442. *See* para. 6.54 of the 2017 OECD transfer pricing guidelines. *See also* para. 6.63 of the 2017 OECD transfer pricing guidelines, last sentence.

average effect of the market forces, with no income adjustment being performed.[443] It is simply assumed that independent enterprises are facing the market forces, and that there is no need from a fiscal perspective to amend the prices of their transactions. Moreover, many countries that provide for some form of fiscal neutrality for domestic groups would not adjust the terms of intercompany transactions that are carried out below or above market value, assuming certain conditions are fulfilled, such as the level of ownership existing between the associated enterprises or the non-abusive purpose of the intercompany transactions.[444] Accordingly, although in substance the arm's length principle aims at providing a similar treatment between independent and associated enterprises, the corrective effects of a generally formulated arm's length provision are normally limited to associated enterprises. This reveals a difference in treatment to the detriment of members of multinational enterprises, which are the sole undertakings subject to the anti-avoidance effect of the arm's length principle.

Of course, there are explanations to these differences. In the case of independent enterprises, the transfer prices are driven by the own interest of each contracting party, not by a tax incentive. There is no need for the lawmaker to introduce a general rule that would correct the prices of transactions entered into between independent enterprises, as it can be assumed that the average effect of the market forces produces an outcome that is, on a general level, fiscally acceptable. In the case of domestic groups, profits are taxed by the same jurisdiction, no matter which group member earns them. It is true that intercompany transactions between domestic group members may produce a tax arbitrage effect (e.g., to offset the profits of certain group members against the losses of others), but that is not necessarily an issue – except in cases of abuse – in countries with a group taxation regime providing for the neutral taxation of groups. In such cases, it is the purpose of the regime to tax the group on its net income, as opposed to taxing each group member on its own income. Intercompany transfers may thus be undertaken below market value without triggering tax consequences.

The above explanations to differences in treatment to the detriment of members of multinational enterprises may very well be convincing, but they come into play at the level of the justification analysis:[445] the fact remains that multinational enterprises

---

443. There are exceptions to this statement. For example, there are certain tax systems where companies are expected to make rational choices, with the implication that the tax consequences of irrational choices could be disregarded or amended, e.g., under a general anti-abuse doctrine. Another example is the rule in certain tax systems under which transactions that do not reflect market terms and that benefit the owners of a company may be adjusted for corporate income tax purposes, if the result is a transfer of resources to the owner without adequate compensation for the company.
444. The difference in treatment to the detriment of members of multinational enterprises can be illustrated by considering changes to the organisation of a multinational enterprise, which are often described as 'business restructurings'. The effect of the application of the arm's length principle to business restructurings is the obligation to subject a group company to an exit tax upon the transfer of functions, risks or assets to a foreign associated enterprise, in case a capital gain is made on the transfer. In contrast, intercompany transfers made between domestic group member are, in several countries, undertaken with no tax consequences, assuming certain conditions are fulfilled.
445. *See* section 8.3 of this book.

are likely to receive a worse treatment than both independent enterprises and domestic groups of companies, as a consequence of the limited corrective effect of the arm's length principle. The effect is that of an anti-avoidance rule that only targets undertakings that are members of a multinational enterprise. That would make a generally formulated arm's length provision prima facie de jure selective, as it is likely to favour independent enterprises as well as members of domestic groups.

The second aspect of a generally formulated arm's length provision that speaks for the de jure selectivity of this allocation method is the assumed correctness of the benchmark provided by the average effect of the market forces.

5.2.2 The Assumed Correctness of the Benchmark Provided by the Average Effect of the Market Forces

The arm's length principle lies on the assumed correctness of the benchmark provided by the average effect of the market forces, something that results in a generalisation of the outcomes reached under this allocation method. There is a general assumption in the OECD transfer pricing guidelines that observations from the open market provide a correct benchmark of the behaviour that should be expected in a given situation. The arm's length principle implies that the income of the members of multinational enterprises be reassessed if it is lower than the profits generally observed on the open market, with little consideration for the diversity in the possible behaviours of associated enterprises. The notion of 'options realistically available' described in the guidelines illustrates the lack of consideration for the possibility that choices are not always rational.[446] It is assumed in the guidelines that independent parties act in a rational manner,[447] and that the same behaviours should be expected from all associated enterprises that are in a comparable situation; as a result, the outcome of this allocation method is an expectation to act as generally observed on the open market. In other words, the arm's length principle assumes that the correct benchmark is the average or the general effect of the market forces.

This expectation would be convincing if economic behaviours were purely rational, i.e., if the same decisions would typically be made by independent enterprises under the same circumstances. However, certain scholars argue that business decisions are not always rational.[448] Different companies facing the same circumstances

---

446. See particularly para. 1.38 of the 2017 OECD transfer pricing guidelines, where it is stated that '(i)ndependent enterprises, when evaluating the terms of a potential transaction, will compare the transaction to the other options realistically available to them, and they will only enter into the transaction if they see no alternative that offers a clearly more attractive opportunity to meet their commercial objectives'. See also para. 9.27 of the 2017 OECD transfer pricing guidelines.
447. See e.g., para. 6.113 of the 2017 OECD transfer pricing guidelines, for a generalisation of the expectation to act rationally in transactions involving intangibles.
448. See e.g., Stefan Greil, 'The Dealing at Arm's Length Fallacy: A Way Forward to a Formula-Based Transactional Profit Split?' (2017) 45 Intertax 624, who at 626 argues that a prudent business manager may incorporate 'irrelevant information' in the decision-making process. See also at 624, with references to further sources. Among various observations, this author stresses at 627 that 'normative ideas, i.e., how a manager should behave, do not have to coincide with decision-making in reality'.

may not act in the same manner. The actual impact of the market forces on the profitability of independent enterprises is likely to vary from one company to another. This should be true both for independent and associated enterprises, especially in the presence of a rule such as the arm's length principle that aims at harmonising the treatment of the two categories of undertakings. Of course, the reliance on a comparability analysis under the arm's length principle may capture the diversity of behaviours observed on the open market,[449] but it cannot be taken for granted that such average behaviours correspond to those of the parties to a given intercompany transaction.[450] Accordingly, an analysis under a generally formulated arm's length provision – assuming it is interpreted in the light of the 2017 OECD transfer pricing guidelines – implies some level of approximation or even of judgment about the choices made by the associated enterprises to which this allocation method applies.[451] Approximation or judgment necessarily implies, eventually, a risk of incorrectness.[452]

The incorrectness that is created by the generalisation of the expectation to act in line with the average effects of the market forces may result in differences in treatment between independent and associated enterprises, the former acting as they wish and sometimes in an irrational manner, the latter being forced to act in line with the average effect of the market forces. Such differences do not generally favour either category of undertakings, and thus do not make a generally formulated arm's length provision necessarily prima facie de jure selective; instead, it is on a case-by-case basis that the arm's length principle might prove selective to the advantage of either category of undertakings, if there are convincing reasons to believe that associated enterprises would not act as observed from the average effect of the market forces.

Consequently, the two arguments presented above show that a generally formulated arm's length provision might imply a difference in treatment that stems from the design of the law between associated enterprises, on the one hand, and independent enterprises as well as members of domestic groups, on the other hand. This makes a generally formulated arm's length provision likely to be prima facie de jure selective, especially when associated enterprises would not act as observed from the average effect of the market forces, because in this case the benchmark provided by the market forces would simply be incorrect.

---

449. For a similar reasoning with respect to local market features, *see* the last sentence of para. 1.145 of the 2017 OECD transfer pricing guidelines.
450. The diversity in the situations observed on the market is taken into account in the comparability analysis, which reflects the variety of possible outcomes. However, when several observations from the market are aggregated as part of a comparability analysis, it is this combined effect of the market forces that is applied to the tested intercompany transaction. The effect is a generalisation of the behaviours expected, with only little consideration for the particular circumstances of a case.
451. On the approximation and the judgment needed under the arm's length principle, *see* particularly para. 3.81 of the 2017 OECD transfer pricing guidelines, which emphasises that '(t)axpayers and tax administrations should exercise judgment to determine whether particular comparables are reliable'. The notion of 'judgment' is used in several paragraphs of the guidelines.
452. As mentioned at para. 3.57 of the 2017 OECD transfer pricing guidelines, 'while every effort has been made', 'some comparability defects' may remain as part of a comparability analysis.

After investigating whether a generally formulated arm's length provision may be de jure selective, I now turn to investigating whether this allocation method may imply a de facto selective treatment.

5.3 DE FACTO SELECTIVITY

As already observed above, the arm's length principle aims at achieving an allocation of the corporate tax base through an approximation of what transfer prices comparable independent enterprises would charge, or what profit margins independent enterprises would earn. At first sight, this objective of equality between independent and associated enterprises, consecrated at Article 9 of the OECD Model Tax Convention, seems not to provide an advantage or a disadvantage to any undertaking, since in all cases the taxable income is subject to the market forces. This speaks for the arm's length principle being a general measure. In addition, the arm's length principle is not unique to a Member State, but has been relied on for a long time by numerous countries; it expresses such a broad compromise that it can hardly be argued that a Member State has specifically implemented it to favour certain undertakings. Therefore, at a theoretical level and based on the rationale of the arm's length principle, no de facto selectivity is at hand.

This statement is confirmed by analysing the functioning of the arm's length principle. The arm's length principle relies mainly on a functional and a comparability analysis, so as to lay the ground for the allocation of the corporate tax base among a multinational enterprise.[453] This supposes investigating how the functions, risks and assets that are relevant for a given intercompany transaction are shared between the parties to this transaction, which is described in the 2017 OECD transfer pricing guidelines as the accurate delineation of the actual intercompany transactions. Based on the relative importance of the functions, risks and assets attributable to each party to a transaction, prices are set or profits are allocated by analogy with what is observed between independent enterprises.[454] This method seems neutral, as it relies on objective observations from both the tested parties and the comparable independent transactions that serve as a benchmark and are subject to the market forces. The method is also neutral as it does not openly give preference to any type of undertaking. Rather, it is the relative importance of the functions, risks, and assets that are attributable to each party to a transaction, i.e., the substance that supports the transaction, that will determine the arm's length allocation of the corporate tax base.[455] In addition, virtually any business activity involves the performance of some functions, the assumption of certain risks, and the use of certain assets. This contrasts with the tax system at hand in *Gibraltar*, under which it was clear which undertakings did, or did

---

453. *See* paras 1.33 and following of the 2017 OECD transfer pricing guidelines.
454. This is the comparability analysis.
455. This aspect of the arm's length principle is emphasised in the 2017 OECD transfer pricing guidelines through seeking the contribution of each party to the 'creation of value': *see* the references to this expression in Chapter 6 of the guidelines, e.g., at para. 6.12.

Chapter 5: Prima Facie Selectivity of the ALP

not benefit from the tax system.[456] Accordingly, this observation confirms the view expressed in the previous paragraph, i.e., the lack of de facto selectivity of a generally formulated arm's length provision: the effects of the principle would be the same for all undertakings, and thus the principle would be a general measure.

Yet upon a closer look, I believe that a generally formulated arm's length provision might contain some de facto selective features by favouring certain associated enterprises over others. Two arguments are discussed here: the importance given to the parameters chosen in the OECD transfer pricing guidelines (section 5.3.1), and the approximation of results for intercompany transactions with no direct benchmark provided by the open market (section 5.3.2). I will address these arguments successively.

5.3.1 The Importance Given to the Parameters Chosen in the OECD Transfer Pricing Guidelines

Under the 2017 OECD transfer pricing guidelines, the effect of a generally formulated arm's length provision will be to allocate income in relation to the 'economically relevant characteristics or comparability factors' that are identified in the commercial or financial relations between associated enterprises.[457] These factors are the contractual terms of the transaction, the functions performed by each of the parties to the transaction,[458] the circumstances surrounding the transaction as well as industry practices, the characteristics of property transferred or services provided, the economic circumstances of the parties and of the market in which the parties operate, and, finally, the business strategies pursued by the parties.

Companies for which these characteristics are relatively more represented will tend to be allocated a greater share of the income generated by an intercompany transaction than companies that have a lower representation of these factors. Consequently, the effect of a generally formulated arm's length provision is to differentiate between undertakings on the basis of certain economic characteristics: associated enterprises that have a relatively low level of the characteristics described in the guidelines are likely to be subject to a lower tax burden than other associated enterprises that have relatively more important characteristics of the same nature. In particular, when an intercompany transaction generates profits, the parties to the transaction that are performing relatively important functions, assume and control the most significant risks, and own or use the most valuable assets will generally be allocated a greater share of the profits (and thus be subject to a higher tax burden) than

---

456. In *Gibraltar* the features of the tax system were – similarly to the elements of the functional analysis under the arm's length principle – designed in a general manner, they were equally available to any undertaking, and yet the tax system was de facto selective. However, this may be due, in my opinion, to the foreseeability of the application of the criteria of the tax system.
457. *See* paras 1.36 and following of the 2017 OECD transfer pricing guidelines.
458. Account is taken of the assets used and risks assumed, including how the functions relate to the wider generation of value by the group to which the parties belong: *see* para. 1.36, second indent, of the 2017 OECD transfer pricing guidelines.

other companies with fewer of these factors. The opposite would apply in case a transaction is not profitable: companies with the most important role would be more exposed to losses.

It may be questioned whether the relation described above between the economically relevant characteristics of various undertakings, and their right to earn income under the arm's length principle, is a de facto selective feature. On the one hand, the pure effect of this relation is a difference in treatment, to the detriment or to the benefit of certain undertakings, depending on the relative importance of their contributions. This would speak for the de facto selectivity of the arm's length principle, when different members of multinational enterprises are being compared to each other. For example, a company performing more strategic functions than another would be more likely under the arm's length principle to earn higher profits, and to pay higher taxes than a company performing less strategic functions; the latter company could thus be seen as enjoying a selective treatment. On the other hand, it could be argued that the arm's length principle reconstructs the effects of the market forces on the earning of income by providing certain criteria that, on the open market, would typically generate profits that are subject to an income tax. Indeed, in my view, the economically relevant characteristics or comparability factors that were mentioned above are connected with the concept of income, i.e., the presence of these factors reveal an income-generating activity.[459] This would speak for the lack of de facto selectivity of the arm's length principle: all multinational enterprises would, thanks to the arm's length principle, be equally subject to a tax that is proportionate to their capacity to generate income, i.e., their ability-to-pay tax.

In my opinion, as a generally formulated arm's length provision has a close connection to the concept of income, the choice of the parameters described in the OECD transfer pricing guidelines does not entail a selective treatment. This is because the notion of income is in itself neutral: if the parameters that guide the allocation of the tax base among multinational enterprises are closely connected to the concept of income, the profit allocation will not favour a given category of undertakings; the effect would merely be to tax in proportion to the generation of income. That is precisely the objective of a corporate income tax system, and it is a neutral one as the concept of income is neutral. Support to this view is indirectly provided by the case law of the CJEU, since an income tax has never been found as such to be de facto selective, although the effect of the tax is to impose a higher burden on the more profitable taxpayers. The CJEU seems also to have sought for an income tax when applying the de facto selectivity test in the *Gibraltar* case, implicitly blaming Gibraltar for not implementing a regime that levied tax in proportion to the income earned by all undertakings.

---

459. Concurring on the connection between the arm's length principle and the concept of income, *see* Charles E. McLure and Joann M. Weiner, 'Deciding Whether the European Union Should Adopt Formulary Apportionment of Company Income' in Sijbren Cnossen (ed), *Taxing Capital Income in the European Union: Issues and Options for Reform* (Oxford University Press 2000) 258; Charles E. McLure, 'Replacing Separate Entity Accounting and the Arm's Length Principle with Formulary Apportionment' (2002) 56 Bulletin for International Taxation 586, 587.

To conclude, at this stage a generally formulated arm's length provision has no de facto selective features. I shall discuss below whether the approximation of results for intercompany transactions with no direct benchmark provided by the open market may entail a risk that this allocation method is de facto selective.

5.3.2 The Approximation of Results for Intercompany Transactions with No Direct Benchmark Provided by the Open Market

The second reason why a generally formulated arm's length provision might contain de facto selective features relates to the situations where an intercompany transaction has to be priced, while there is no direct benchmark on the open market. Depending on how the arm's length principle is interpreted, certain categories of undertakings might be advantaged in such situations. The starting point of this issue is the fact that multinational enterprises and independent enterprises are not always conducting comparable activities. Multinational enterprises may, for example, perform unique activities that cannot be carried out by independent enterprises.[460] Multinational enterprises may also be involved in activities that generate profits that are in excess of those earned by independent enterprises, for instance thanks to the synergy effects that are derived by the association between the group members.[461] Conversely, associated enterprises may be exposed to higher losses than independent enterprises, for example when they share a risk such as the reputational risk. The OECD transfer pricing guidelines acknowledge these situations, by stressing that when multinational enterprises engage in transactions that independent enterprises would not undertake, there is by definition 'little or no direct evidence of what conditions would have been established by independent enterprises'.[462]

In the presence of intercompany transactions that are not fully comparable to independent transactions, such as in the situations mentioned above, the question is how to rely on the market forces, since it is assumed that the open market provides no sufficiently reliable benchmark because of the lack of comparability. Here, my point is that the treatment of associated enterprises in situations that lack a direct benchmark on the open market might imply, depending on the interpretation of the arm's length principle, a difference in treatment with independent enterprises and domestic groups, for the simple reason that these categories of undertakings are not in a comparable situation. This does not mean that either category of undertakings is systematically

---

460. That would be the case where a business activity is so global that it cannot be performed by an independent enterprise. *See* para. 1.122 of the 2017 OECD transfer pricing guidelines, where it is observed that '(a)ssociated enterprises may have the ability to enter into a much greater variety of arrangements than can independent enterprises, and may conclude transactions of a specific nature that are not encountered, or are only very rarely encountered, between independent parties, and may do so for sound business reasons'.
461. For example, it is emphasised at para. 1.157 of the 2017 OECD transfer pricing guidelines that synergies amongst group members 'are often favourable to the group as a whole and therefore may heighten the aggregate profits earned by group members'. *See* Ulf Andresen, 'Comments on Professor Schoueri's Lecture "Arm's Length: Beyond the Guidelines of the OECD"' (2015) 69 Bulletin for International Taxation 717, 720.
462. *See* para. 1.11 of the 2017 OECD transfer pricing guidelines.

favoured. Rather, the arm's length principle may prove de facto selective on a case-by-case basis, depending on the interpretation of this principle. My position is explained by the analysis of two possible interpretations of the arm's length principle, when there is no direct benchmark provided by the open market: no matter if one interprets the arm's length principle as a strict obligation to apply between associated enterprises the conditions observed on the open market, or if deviations from the open market are accepted, the arm's length principle might favour certain undertakings, despite the theoretical neutrality of the principle. I shall start by considering an interpretation of the arm's length principle according to which the conditions existing between independent enterprises have to be strictly implemented between associated enterprises. I will then consider the case of an interpretation of the arm's length principle that accepts deviation from the open market, which is the interpretation recommended in the OECD transfer pricing guidelines.

First, if the arm's length principle is interpreted as a strict obligation to rely on the conditions existing between independent enterprises, without fully taking into account the peculiarities of the intercompany transactions that are being priced and thus without taking into account the potential lack of comparability between the transactions that are being compared, such a strict interpretation of the arm's length principle would result in a selective treatment to the benefit of either category of undertakings. For example, in case a multinational enterprise derives synergy benefits that cannot be earned by independent enterprises, strictly relying on the profits observed between independent enterprises would result in part of the group's profits not being allocated to any of the group members: each transaction would be remunerated on the basis of what independent enterprises earn, thus disregarding the profits in excess of those earned by independent enterprises that are a consequence of the synergy benefits.[463] Such an interpretation of the arm's length principle would be at odds with the notion of comparability described in the OECD transfer pricing guidelines. It would favour certain multinational enterprises over independent enterprises, especially the more profitable and integrated ones, because they would be particularly likely to earn profits in excess of those earned by independent enterprises. Under this interpretation, the arm's length principle would be de facto selective as it would provide a more beneficial treatment to certain associated enterprises, only part of the profits of which would be subject to tax, as opposed to independent enterprises and domestic groups, which are normally subject to tax on all their income. The opposite effect would be observed in case associated enterprises are less profitable, or more exposed to risks, than independent enterprises. Consequently, if the arm's length principle is interpreted as a strict obligation to rely on the conditions existing between independent enterprises with no sufficient comparability adjustments, differences of treatment will necessarily appear to the benefit of either category of undertakings, as soon as no direct benchmark is provided by the open market.

I now turn to the second reason why a generally formulated arm's length provision might imply a de facto selective treatment. De facto selectivity may occur in

---

463. Concurring, *see* Richard Collier and Joseph L Andrus, *Transfer Pricing and the Arm's Length Principle After BEPS* (Oxford University Press 2017) 125.

situations where the arm's length principle is interpreted so that deviations from the open market are accepted when no reliable information can be obtained from independent enterprises, which is what the OECD transfer pricing guidelines recommend. In some of these situations, the guidelines suggest hypothesising how independent parties would allocate profits among them, something that might require some degree of approximation and lacks direct support from observations of independent enterprises. Deviations from observations of the open market imply two potential types of differences in treatment. On the one hand, associated enterprises may be treated differently from independent enterprises, precisely because of the need to account for the peculiarities of multinational enterprises. On the other hand, different associated enterprises may be treated differently, because of the approximation that is inherent to the application of a generally formulated arm's length provision. An example could be the case of a cost contribution arrangement where each party performs research and development functions, with the result that unique intangible property is commonly owned by the participants to the arrangement in a manner that would not occur between independent enterprises. Chapter 8 of the 2017 OECD transfer pricing guidelines cannot but recommend hypothesising how independent parties would allocate profits among them; this is the least possible departure from observations on the open market, while still keeping the objective to share income on the theoretical basis of the arm's length principle. As a result, the solution applied in a given case does not exist in reality, it is only inspired by it. In such cases, there is by definition a difference in treatment with independent enterprises, since there is a difference in the characteristics of the transactions that are being compared. The determination of the deviations from the open market is, in addition, likely to include some degree of error given the high degree of subjectivity and approximation that is needed to strengthen the fiction of the arm's length principle and apply to intercompany transactions conditions that are inspired by the open market. Such approximations may trigger differences in treatment, this time between different associated enterprises. Accordingly, I agree with the scholars who describe the efficiency of the arm's length principle to correctly allocate profits in such situations as 'illusory'.[464]

The risk for differences in treatment appears even more clearly when one is considering the allocation of the residual income among multinational enterprises, assuming such a residual income is not observed on the open market.[465] Indeed, there is no established methodology under the arm's length principle to allocate the residual income among the group members, and yet the residual must be allocated, to avoid the

---

464. *See* Reuven Avi-Yonah and Zachée Pouga Tinhaga, 'Unitary Taxation and International Tax Rules' (2014) ICTD 26 Working Paper < https://papers.ssrn.com/sol3/Delivery.cfm/SSRN_ID 2602240_code572410.pdf?abstractid = 2351920&mirid = 1 > accessed 6 February 2018, 9.
465. On the notion of 'residual' *see* the developments in Chapter 6 of the 2017 OECD transfer pricing guidelines (in particular para. 6.133) as well as the distinction made by Schön, who stresses that '(f)rom an economic point of view, business income can be divided into notional rents on the invested human and financial capital on the one hand and the (positive or negative) residual for the investor on the other hand': Wolfgang Schön, 'International Tax Coordination for a Second-Best World (Part I)' (2009) 1 World Tax Journal 67, 74. *See also* Mitchell. B. Carroll, *Taxation of National and Foreign Enterprises: Volume 4 Methods of Allocating Taxable Income* (League of Nations 1933) 192, para. 677.

situation described above whereby the residual is not taxed as a consequence of the lack of such residual in transactions between independent enterprises. In this respect, Schön stresses that although the residual 'reflects the risks taken by the involved companies', 'there is no "true" or "natural" allocation of risk'.[466] The same difficulty arises for economies of scale or benefits of integration: it is recognised in the guidelines that there are 'no widely accepted objective criteria for allocating between associated enterprises the economies of scale or benefits of integration resulting from group membership'.[467] In all these situations, the difficulty stems from the lack of benchmark provided by the open market.

How to then allocate residual profits, economies of scale, or benefits of integration, when independent enterprises cannot be in a comparable situation? In certain cases, the methodology recommended in the guidelines resembles more a system of formula apportionment than a system that builds on comparable independent transactions. For example, the benefits of group synergies that can be attributed to deliberate concerted group actions may need to be shared by members of the group 'in proportion to their contribution to the creation of the synergy'.[468] Here, the interpretation of the arm's length principle does not necessarily rely on observations from the open market. Another example concerns situations where 'important functions' are outsourced: in this respect, the guidelines mention that 'it may be necessary to utilise transfer pricing methods not directly based on comparables'.[469] In contrast, when important functions are not outsourced, the guidelines estimate that the legal owner of an intangible 'will be entitled to all of the anticipated, *ex ante*, returns derived from the MNE group's exploitation of the intangible';[470] this generalisation may weaken the connection with the effects of the market forces, because it tends to share with a system of formula apportionment a mechanistic character.

The clearest example of potential deviations from observations on the open market concerns the profit split method. Although this method is, as all the other transfer pricing methods, meant to be consistent with Article 9 of the OECD Model[471] and thus to implement the arm's length principle (in particular by relying on the outcome of the functional analysis[472]), it applies mainly when both parties to an intercompany transaction make unique and valuable contributions.[473] The division of

---

466. *See* Wolfgang Schön, 'International Tax Coordination for a Second-Best World (Part III)' (2010) 3 World Tax Journal 227, 242. Similarly, *see* Stefan Greil, 'The Dealing at Arm's Length Fallacy: A Way Forward to a Formula-Based Transactional Profit Split?' (2017) 45 Intertax 624, 625.
467. *See* para. 1.10 of the 2017 OECD transfer pricing guidelines.
468. *See* para. 1.162 of the 2017 OECD transfer pricing guidelines. An illustration is provided where the benefits of economies of scale result from high volume of purchase; in this case, the guidelines recommend sharing the benefits of the synergies in proportion to the purchase volumes of the group members.
469. *See* para. 6.57 of the 2017 OECD transfer pricing guidelines.
470. *See* para. 6.71 of the 2017 OECD transfer pricing guidelines.
471. *See* para. 2.121 of the 2017 OECD transfer pricing guidelines.
472. *See* para. 3.39 of the 2017 OECD transfer pricing guidelines, which emphasises that 'even in cases where comparable data are scarce and imperfect, the selection of the most appropriate transfer pricing method should be consistent with the functional analysis of the parties'.
473. As opposed to simpler contributions that can be priced on the basis of the other transfer pricing methods.

profits can be supported by comparables data when such data are 'available',[474] but this may not be the most frequent situation. As a result, the profit split method necessarily relies on a weaker link to independent transactions than the other transfer pricing methods, precisely because this method applies in cases where it is unlikely to find independent comparables that can be directly relied on.[475] In certain cases, the division of profits cannot rely on observations from the open market, and can only be achieved by using one or more allocation keys in a manner that 'approximates'[476] the division of profits that would have been anticipated and reflected in an agreement made at arm's length.[477] Such allocation keys may rely on concrete elements such as assets, costs, sales, headcount, etc.[478] Therefore, the effects of the choice of these elements are close to systems of formula apportionment,[479] which are studied in Chapter 7 below, and which point to the de facto selectivity of formulas based on firm-specific factors. In addition, the allocation keys are normally not pre-determined,[480] something that entails a risk of applying different formulas in various cases and thus treat different undertakings differently. The drawbacks of not having pre-determined formulas have been discussed in the doctrine, and certain scholars have suggested the introduction of fixed formulas, or fixed elements in formulas.[481] For example, Wilkie finds that 'there could be a "middle ground" that imports some of the objectivity and commercial reality associated with formulary's identification of factors of production and measures of return, to establish uniform expectations about the elements of business meant to be measured by a profit-oriented method within the parameters of the (OECD transfer pricing guidelines) and more generally according to the "principle" part of the "arm's length principle"'.[482] The introduction of fixed

---

474. *See* para. 2.125 of the 2017 OECD transfer pricing guidelines.
475. *See* para. 2.116 of the 2017 OECD transfer pricing guidelines.
476. *See* the frequent use of the verb 'approximate' at para. 2.6 and paras 2.114 and following of the 2017 OECD transfer pricing guidelines.
477. *See* para. 2.140 of the 2017 OECD transfer pricing guidelines.
478. *See* para. 2.141 of the 2017 OECD transfer pricing guidelines.
479. It can be observed that although the objective of the profit split method is to enforce the arm's length principle, in at least certain cases a profit split arrangement may rely on factors that are close to a system of formula apportionment to share profits. This could be the case when part of the residual profit earned by several associated enterprises cannot be split on the basis of transactions, in a scheme where the associated enterprises make comparable contributions to the creation of value. In such cases, the residual profit could be shared based on objective factors that are close to a system of formula apportionment. With respect to the need, in certain cases, to rely on the profit split method or on alternative methods to the arm's length principle *see* Reuven S. Avi-Yonah, 'Splitting the Unsplittable: Toward a Formulary Approach to Allocating Residuals Under Profit Split' (2013) 12 University of Michigan Public Law Research Paper 378 < https://papers.ssrn.com/sol3/papers.cfm?abstract_id=2369944 > accessed 18 January 2018.
480. This is the main difference with a system of formula apportionment: *see* para. 1.18 of the 2017 OECD transfer pricing guidelines.
481. *See* e.g., Michael C. Durst, 'Beyond BEPS: A Tax Policy Agenda for Developing Countries' (2014) 18 ICTD Working Paper < https://assets.publishing.service.gov.uk/media/57a089c1ed915d622c0003ab/WP18-FINAL.pdf > accessed 11 February 2018, who at 11 argues that the profit split method needs, in order to be effective, to provide 'uniform apportionment keys'.
482. J. Scott Wilkie, 'Reflecting on the "Arm's Length Principle": What Is the "Principle"? Where Next?' in Wolfgang Schön and Kai A. Konrad (eds), *Fundamentals of International Transfer Pricing in Law and Economics* (Springer 2012) 155, footnote 32.

formulas, or fixed elements of formulas, would remove the risk that different results are reached under similar circumstances. It would also decrease the subjective nature of a profit split methodology, and the risk for arbitrary results. At the same time, the selective effects of the elements of the chosen allocation keys would remain, and the connection with the concept of income, which is rather preserved under the arm's length principle, would be weakened.

In the light of the foregoing, I draw the following conclusion: the treatment of associated enterprises in situations that lack a direct benchmark in the open market may imply differences in treatment with independent enterprises and members of domestic groups, when the arm's length principle is interpreted so that certain deviations from the open market are accepted or even required by the lack of comparability between independent and associated enterprises. Differences in treatment between different associated enterprises may also exist as a consequence of the approximation made necessary by the arm's length principle, in particular when the application of that principle cannot directly rely on observations from the open market. There may be convincing reasons explaining these differences,[483] but it is undeniable that associated enterprises are, in such cases, treated differently from independent enterprises or members of domestic groups, simply because they are in a different situation. Under this interpretation of the arm's length principle, it cannot be generally concluded that either category of undertakings is systematically favoured.

The conclusion from this section is that the arm's length principle is not *intrinsically* de facto selective. At the same time, it may prove de facto selective on a *case-by-case* basis, depending on how it is interpreted. After the consideration of the prima facie selectivity of a generally formulated arm's length provision with respect to the design as well as the effects of the law, focus is now on the prima facie selectivity that may stem from certain aspects of the application of the law.

5.4 PRIMA FACIE SELECTIVITY THAT STEMS FROM CERTAIN ASPECTS OF THE APPLICATION OF THE LAW

There are different legislative methods to implement the arm's length principle in a Member State's domestic law. Among various wordings of an arm's length provision, it can be mentioned that while some Member States have only enacted a general provision stating the arm's length principle,[484] others have enacted more detailed provisions, e.g., including guidance in relation to different types of intercompany transactions, industries, or transfer pricing methods.[485] However, unless an allocation

---

483. *See* in particular the developments in section 2.2.3 of this book. The deviation from the treatment of independent enterprises may very well be necessary, and thus justified by the logic of the tax system. It may also be proportionate to the objectives pursued by that system. The justification and proportionality tests are analysed in Chapter 8 of this book.
484. *See* e.g., Commission Decision (EU) 2016/2326 of 21 October 2015 on State aid SA.38375 (2014/C ex 2014/NN) which Luxembourg granted to Fiat [2016] OJ L 351/1, paras 74 and following.
485. For an overview *see* e.g., Jens Wittendorff, 'The Arm's-Length Principle and Fair Value: Identical Twins or Just Close Relatives?' (2011) 62 Tax Notes International 223, 238.

Chapter 5: Prima Facie Selectivity of the ALP

method provides for material interpretations of the arm's length principle (in which case the selectivity issues are similar to those raised by safe harbours), what is common to all types of arm's length provisions is the reliance on an abstract principle, rather than on rules having a precise material content. This makes the assessment of a difference in treatment a difficult exercise, something that is an intrinsic consequence of the methodological choice of legislating on the basis of a principle.[486] By essence, a principle may be interpreted in different manners.[487] This is particularly true for the arm's length principle, which inherently contains some level of approximation and subjectivity, although the reliance on observations provided by the open market is, as such, an objective method.

The abstract nature of a generally formulated arm's length provision makes it possible, even when the principle has been correctly interpreted, that differences in treatment remain between independent and associated enterprises, or between different associated enterprises, when the arm's length principle is being applied in a particular case. This type of prima facie selectivity in concrete cases can only be analysed on a case-by-case basis. It is, thus, outside the scope of this book. The purpose of this section is, instead, to analyse at an abstract level certain aspects of the arm's length principle that may trigger a prima facie selective treatment in the application of this allocation method. The choice of these aspects is based on the decisions made by the European Commission relating to certain advance tax rulings issued by the Member States, where three parameters for the application of the arm's length principle appear particularly controversial.

This section is structured in the following way. I will first address the choice of a transfer pricing method (section 5.4.1). Indeed, it may be wondered whether State aid law requires relying on certain transfer pricing methods rather than on others, for an application of the arm's length principle not to be selective. Second, I will consider how to approximate values, given that the logics of State aid law and of the arm's length principle seem to be different (section 5.4.2); here, the main question is whether State aid law requires that values be approximated in a certain manner. Finally, attention is put on the relevance of sources of interpretation such as the OECD transfer pricing guidelines for the purpose of the assessment of a correct application of a generally formulated arm's length provision (section 5.4.3).

5.4.1 The Choice of a Transfer Pricing Method

The question may be asked whether the choice of a transfer pricing method should be of importance in the assessment of a deviation from a reference system that includes a

---

486. Moreover, it can be observed that given the implications of the arm's length principle in terms of fiscal revenues, States may have a natural incentive to interpret this principle in a manner that is advantageous to their treasuries.
487. For example, not only may different legal sources interpret the arm's length principle in different manners (e.g., different domestic arm's length provisions), but also different persons interpreting the same legal source (e.g., two judges in the same country interpreting the same domestic arm's length provision) may reach different outcomes as to the interpretation of the arm's length principle.

generally formulated arm's length provision, or in the application of this reference system. Both the CJEU[488] and the European Commission[489] seem to be of the opinion that the choice of a transfer pricing method may have an impact on the selectivity test, although there is no clear position of the Court on this point.[490] The answer to this question depends on another question, that of knowing whether or not different transfer pricing methods produce similar outcomes: if this is the case, there can be no deviation from the reference system as a consequence of the choice of a given transfer pricing method, because it would produce the same fiscal effects as other methods. Indeed, there is no reason for *a priori* rejecting the use of any transfer pricing method without bringing the evidence that the application of such a method entails a deviation from the reference system; the choice of a transfer pricing method would be a mere formal question. This statement is supported by the case law issued in other areas than tax law, such as cases where the CJEU has considered that various valuation methods may be relied on, as long as they achieve the same result. An example is provided by a case related to the determination of the market value of a piece of land: while the CJEU considered that 'the best bid or an expert report are likely to provide prices

---

488. *See* particularly paras 94–101 of the *Forum 187* decision, where the CJEU seems to have found the functioning of the cost plus method to be in breach of the State aid rules, mostly because the Court refused the methodology consisting in excluding from the cost base certain expenses; this finding may contradict the cost plus method as it is described in the OECD transfer pricing guidelines, where no exclusion of principle is advocated for certain types of expenses. However, this is only a possible interpretation of the case, as the Court did not clearly reject the use of the method as such. In the area of free movement law, the CJEU accepted in *SGI* and *Thin Cap GLO* the arm's length principle as a possible method to curb tax avoidance practices, without providing guidance as to how to interpret and apply this principle. This does not mean, however, that the CJEU considers that the choice of a transfer pricing method plays no role in the area of free movement law, as these cases did not give the Court an opportunity to analyse transfer pricing methods at depth.
489. In the 2016 notice the Commission is expressing preference for the traditional transfer pricing methods, and particularly the CUP method. The Commission finds it likely that a favourable treatment was granted if a ruling 'allows its addressee to use alternative, more indirect methods for calculating taxable profits, for example the use of fixed margins for a cost-plus or resale-minus method for determining an appropriate transfer pricing, while more direct ones are available': *see* Commission Notice on the notion of State aid as referred to in Art. 107(1) of the Treaty on the Functioning of the European Union [2016] OJ C 262/1, para. 174(c). *See also* Commission Decision 2003/81/EC of 22 August 2002 on the aid scheme implemented by Spain in favour of coordination centres in Vizcaya C 48/2001 (ex NN 43/2000) [2003] OJ L 031/26, para. 28; Commission Decision (EU) 2016/2326 of 21 October 2015 on State aid SA.38375 (2014/C ex 2014/NN) which Luxembourg granted to Fiat [2016] OJ L 351/1, para. 245; European Commission, 'DG Competition Working Paper on State Aid and Tax Rulings' (2016) < http://ec.europa.eu/competition/state_aid/legislation/working_paper_tax_rulings.pdf > accessed 6 February 2018, paras 17–19. For a different position, whereby the choice of a transfer pricing method does not seem to matter, *see* Commission Decision 2004/76/EC of 13 May 2003 on the aid scheme implemented by France for headquarters and logistics centres [2004] OJ L 23/1, para. 46.
490. Here, it can be observed that the CJEU did not accept the consequences, for the determination of the customs value, of a year-end adjustment based on the residual profit split method: *see* CJEU, Case C-529/16, *Hamamatsu Photonics Deutschland GmbH v. Hauptzollamt München*, ECLI:EU:C:2017:984, in particular at paras 26–30. Although the Court did not dispute the validity of the profit split method as such, or its consistency with the arm's length principle, this case might be interpreted as a preference for more direct valuation methods.

corresponding to actual market values', the Court found that 'it cannot be ruled out that other methods may also achieve the same result'.[491]

On the other hand, if different transfer pricing methods produce different outcomes, the question of a possible priority between the methods becomes relevant: the method that would best enforce the reference system, i.e., the method that would produce a result that is the most in line with the arm's length principle, would be the one that deviates the least from the reference system. All the other methods would entail a more important deviation from the reference system, because they would provide a worse approximation of the effects of the market forces.

Consequently, the question is whether different transfer pricing methods produce similar outcomes. It is to this question that I now turn. I will limit the analysis to the transfer pricing methods described in the OECD transfer pricing guidelines. At first sight, there is no difference between the transfer pricing methods, which would imply that the choice is irrelevant for the selectivity test. Indeed, the methods described in the guidelines, although having different characteristics, do share a common goal, which is to implement the arm's length principle.[492] This goal is not connected to a particular transfer pricing method, and could theoretically be achieved with any method. Therefore, a consequence of this common goal is that irrespective of which transfer pricing method is chosen, the result should be the same. This is why the OECD transfer pricing guidelines no longer establish a fixed hierarchy between the different transfer pricing methods that they describe. Moreover, independent parties do not rely on transfer pricing methods when they do business with each other;[493] a transfer pricing method is just a translation, in financial terms, of the conditions existing between independent enterprises. This argues for the choice of a transfer pricing method being irrelevant for the selectivity test, as long as all methods under consideration share the same objective of reaching an outcome consistent with the market forces.

The above is valid, however, only in theory. Several arguments tend to evidence that in reality, different transfer pricing methods are not likely to produce the same results. I shall consider three arguments. First, the OECD transfer pricing guidelines describe various obstacles to the correct application of the methods, which makes them more or less reliable in a given case,[494] or even inapplicable. Transfer pricing methods that prove less reliable in a given case are likely to entail a higher degree of error, something that would result in outcomes that are at variance with those reached under

---

491. *See* Case C-239/09, *Seydaland Vereinigte Agrarbetriebe GmbH & Co. KG v. BVVG Bodenverwertungs- und -verwaltungs GmbH*, ECLI:EU:C:2010:778, para. 39.
492. *See* para. 2.1 of the 2017 OECD transfer pricing guidelines. Methods that do not share the same goal would not lead to similar outcomes. For example, valuation methods based on costs are not likely to produce a result that is consistent with other methods, e.g., those that are based on income.
493. Independent enterprises make business decisions that are not guided by transfer pricing principles or transfer pricing methods, but by the objective of maximising their profits. Therefore, the market can provide no evidence of a preference for a given method.
494. For example, different parameters such as the access to information, the existence of different accounting standards, or the peculiarities of certain industries or intercompany transactions, make the transfer pricing methods described in the OECD transfer pricing guidelines more or less reliable in a particular case.

more reliable methods. In other words, the less reliable methods are likely to produce an incorrect approximation of the effects of the market forces, and thus to deviate from the arm's length principle prescribed by the reference system. Second, despite having the common objective of implementing the arm's length principle, the different transfer pricing methods recognised in the OECD transfer pricing guidelines imply, in their application, more or less room for appreciation, something that entails a risk for diverging outcomes,[495] and potentially for discretionary assessments.[496] In this respect, it should be recalled that, in State aid law, the discretionary power of public authorities is likely to increase the selective nature of a State measure:[497] it is settled case law, both within[498] and outside[499] the field of taxes, that discretionary assessments are likely to entail selectivity. Consequently, transfer pricing methods that give more room for appreciation are more likely to entail a selective treatment. Third, different transfer pricing methods have different ways of functioning, and have a more or less direct connection with information provided by the market. This means that different methods may produce different results.[500] Even assuming that all transfer pricing methods are equally reliable and are applied correctly, the risk exists that different transfer pricing methods produce outcomes that partly overlap, but also partly differ from each other.[501] In other words, it is possible that the arm's length ranges under different transfer pricing methods do not result in similar levels of income.

The arguments mentioned above lead me to the conclusion that, despite the theoretical irrelevance of the question, the choice of a transfer pricing method does play a role in the assessment of a deviation from the reference system. Now that it was argued that the choice of a transfer pricing method matters, the question is raised how to assess whether the choice of a method entails a deviation from the reference system.

---

495. An example is provided with respect to the methods to value intangible assets: it is recognised at para. 6.158 of the 2017 OECD transfer pricing guidelines that 'the estimates of value based on [valuation techniques] can be volatile'.
496. In particular, the risk for discretionary assessments is higher with less direct transfer pricing methods, assuming different methods are equally reliable. For instance, the most direct transfer pricing method – the CUP – gives less room for interpretation than the least direct method – the profit split method – assuming that the CUP relies on sufficiently comparable transactions. The profit split method indeed provides room for interpretation with respect to, among other aspects, the determination of the income that is subject to the split, the choice of an allocation key, or the evaluation of the relative contribution of each party to the profit split arrangement. Nevertheless, the profit splitting factors are supposed to be objective, verifiable, and reliable.
497. *See* Case C-256/97, *Déménagements-Manutention Transport SA (DMT)*, ECLI:EU:C:1999:332, para. 27; Case C-6/12, *P Oy*, ECLI:EU:C:2013:525, para. 25.
498. *See* e.g., Case C-6/12, *P Oy*, ECLI:EU:C:2013:525.
499. *See* e.g., Case C-241/94, *French Republic v. Commission of the European Communities*, ECLI:EU:C:1996:353.
500. To illustrate this statement, *see* e.g., European Commission/Deloitte, 'Study on the Application of Economic Valuation Techniques for Determining Transfer Prices of Cross Border Transactions between Members of Multinational Enterprise Groups in the EU' (European Commission 2016) 28.
501. In this respect, the European Commission observed that '(t)he different methods explained in the OECD Guidelines can result in a wide range of outcomes as regards the amount of the taxable basis': *see* State aid – Luxembourg – State aid SA.38944 (2014/C) (2014/NN) – Alleged aid to Amazon – Invitation to submit comments pursuant to Art. 108(2) of the Treaty on the Functioning of the European Union [2015] OJ C 44/13, para. 55.

Chapter 5: Prima Facie Selectivity of the ALP

Considering the arguments described above, the OECD transfer pricing guidelines provide recommendations to choose a transfer pricing method that best approximates the effects of the market forces. The starting point is the need to find the 'most appropriate method'.[502] To identify the most appropriate method, the guidelines recommend that where a traditional transaction method and a transactional profit method can be applied in an equally reliable manner, the former is preferable to the latter; moreover, in case the CUP method and other transfer pricing methods may be applied in an equally reliable manner, the guidelines indicate that the CUP method is to be preferred.[503]

Therefore, the guidelines give the highest priority not to a method as such, but to the reliability of a method,[504] although a general priority is established in favour of transaction methods (especially the CUP) when different methods are equally reliable.[505] This means that to assess a possible deviation from the reference system, the selectivity test would require one to first assess the reliability of all the transfer pricing methods, and then rank them from the least to the most reliable method. Assuming different methods are equally reliable, the preference would go to traditional transaction methods, and in particular the CUP. In my view, the preference given in the guidelines to the CUP method – assuming several methods, including the CUP, are equally reliable – seems particularly suitable from a State aid perspective, because State aid law entails a need for objectivity and precision that matches the transactional and direct character of the CUP method. More generally, the guidelines recognise that the arm's length principle should ideally be applied 'on a transaction-by-transaction basis'.[506] The findings of the CJEU in the *Forum 187* case seem to also express a preference for the CUP method.[507] The European Commission is of the same opinion,[508]

---

502. *See* para. 2.2 of the 2017 OECD transfer pricing guidelines.
503. *See* para. 2.3 of the 2017 OECD transfer pricing guidelines.
504. I agree with this view, which is the only way to achieve the purpose of any transfer pricing method, namely to provide the best estimate of an arm's length outcome. Which transfer pricing method is the most reliable in a given case is, however, a factual issue, and is thus excluded from the scope of this study.
505. This priority has been subject to criticism. For example, on the basis of the wording of Art. 9 of the OECD Model Tax Convention, which puts emphasis on the correction of profit distortions, Wilkie argues that the arm's length principle should require the assessment of profits, rather than the assessment of transfer prices on a transactional basis: *see* J. Scott Wilkie, 'Reflecting on the "Arm's Length Principle": What is the "Principle"? Where Next?' in Wolfgang Schön and Kai A. Konrad (eds), *Fundamentals of International Transfer Pricing in Law and Economics* (Springer 2012) 144-147.
506. *See* para. 3.9 of the 2017 OECD transfer pricing guidelines.
507. At para. 100 of the *Forum 187* case, the CJEU found that the fixed aspect of the transfer pricing method used in the Belgian coordination centres regime (i.e., the predetermined profit markup of 8% applied to the cost base, described in this case as 'flat-rate amounts') is likely to grant an advantage. If a fixed and predetermined profit markup grants an advantage, the CUP method would be the most-favoured method under State aid law. Indeed, other methods rely, to some extent, on the approximations of profits, be it the margin on costs (resale price method and cost-plus method), the net margin (transactional net margin method), or how certain profits are shared according to a formula (profit split method).
508. In this respect *see* Commission Decision (EU) 2016/2326 of 21 October 2015 on State aid SA.38375 (2014/C ex 2014/NN) which Luxembourg granted to Fiat [2016] OJ L 351/1, para. 132, as well as para. 245, where the Commission observed that '(c)ompared to the other four

something that might be explained by the use of the *pari passu* approach when it is testing State measures in the light of the market economy operator test.[509]

The conclusion reached above does not, however, imply an absolute preference for the transactional methods, and in particular the CUP. The position held in the OECD transfer pricing guidelines should also lead to accepting the less direct transfer pricing methods, when they are the only ones reliable, or when they are more reliable than direct methods such as the CUP. Indeed, in numerous cases the CUP is not applicable, because of the lack of sufficiently comparable information. Various factors such as the growing complexity of business models,[510] the globalisation and the integration of value chains,[511] the intensification of the importance of intangible property, or the developments of the digital economy, contribute to the difficulty of finding reliable comparable independent transactions,[512] thus resulting in the less direct methods being the best possible option, including the profit split method.[513]

In this respect, profit split is a special transfer pricing method that deserves particular consideration in the light of the rules on State aid. It appears quite difficult to assess a deviation from the reference system, when the transfer pricing method chosen is the profit split method. This is because it is unlikely, although not impossible, to find comparable independent arrangements that provide a direct benchmark for splitting

---

methods described in the OECD TP Guidelines, the CUP is more direct and would, if applicable, provide for a more reliable approximation of a market-based outcome'.

509. The *pari passu* approach is one of the methods for the application of the market economy operator test. For an illustration of the use of the *pari passu* approach, see e.g., Commission decision of 7 July 2015 in State Aid SA.36574 (2015/NN, ex 2013/CP) – France – Alleged aid to Altrad [2015] OJ C 369/1, paras 45–52. The *pari passu* approach resembles the CUP method as under this test, a Member State acting in conditions and terms similar to that of a private operator acting in comparable circumstances does not grant State aid. In this respect, *see* e.g., Case T-296/97, *Alitalia – Linee aeree italiane SpA v. Commission of the European Communities*, ECLI:EU:T:2000:289, para. 81: '(a) capital contribution from public funds must (...) be regarded as satisfying the private investor test and not constituting State aid if, inter alia, it was made at the same time as a significant capital contribution on the part of a private investor made in comparable circumstances'.
510. *See* paras 9.6 and 9.35 of the 2017 OECD transfer pricing guidelines. *See also* Andrew Hickman, 'The Application of Revised Transfer Pricing Rules to Aspects of Business Models' (2016) 44 Intertax 730.
511. *See* Koen D. Backer and Sébastien Miroudot, *Mapping Global Value Chains* (OECD Trade Policy Papers 159, OECD 2013).
512. *See* Isabel Verlinden and Bram Markey, 'From Compliance to the C-Suite: Value Creation Analysed Through the Transfer Pricing Lens' (2016) 44 Intertax 774, 776.
513. This may partly explain why the profit split method, which in the 1995 OECD transfer pricing guidelines was a method of 'last resort' (*see* para. 2.49 of the 1995 OECD transfer pricing guidelines), no longer has this status. *See also* OECD, *Addressing the Tax Challenges of the Digital Economy, Action 1 – 2015 Final Report* (OECD 2015) 92; OECD, *BEPS Action 10 – Revised Guidance on Profit Splits* (OECD 2017), para. 21: 'Another example may be where the integration between the parties takes the form of a high degree of inter-dependency. For example, profit split approaches may be used by independent enterprises engaged in long-term arrangements where each party has made a significant contribution (e.g., of an asset) whose value depends on the counterparty to the arrangement. In this kind of case, where each party makes such a contribution, and is dependent on the other party, some form of flexible pricing that takes into account the risks assumed by each party arising from its dependence on the other party may be observed'.

profits among associated enterprises.[514] The profit split method is, indeed, the least direct transfer pricing method. In many cases, a profit split arrangement needs to rely on a methodology that is only to a little extent directly connected to information on profit sharing that is available on the open market, because what the multinational enterprise is doing is either unique, or can only exist in an integrated, and possibly cross-border context.[515] In such cases, the profit split method needs to rely on assumptions to provide a basis for splitting profits that approximates the effects of the market forces. In many cases, profits will have to be split through an allocation key, based on factors such as assets or costs.[516] This does not make the profit split method necessarily selective, as this method is not intrinsically in breach of the reference system: the distance with observations on the open market does not, as such, suffice to necessarily reveal a deviation from the reference system, at least when it is the best option to apply the profit split method. However, considering the distance between observations from the open market and the transaction that is priced on the basis of the profit split method, this transfer pricing method is the most difficult to apply in the light of the selectivity test. As argued above at section 5.3.2, the profit split method is potentially the transfer pricing method that entails the highest risk of being de facto selective, because of the approximation that it implies for transactions with no direct benchmark provided by the open market. Accordingly, the need for precision implied by the selectivity test makes profit split – from a State aid law perspective – a method of last resort that, I submit, should apply when the other, more direct methods cannot be reliably applied.[517]

The conclusion from this section is that the choice of a transfer pricing method does matter. This conclusion is not based on an abstract preference for a given method, although with equal reliability the CUP seems the most in line with the logic of the rules on State aid. The conclusion from this section is rather based on the need to choose the most reliable method to ensure the best possible enforcement of the reference system.

---

514. A direct benchmark could be provided by the terms of a joint-venture arrangement that is comparable to an arrangement between associated enterprises.
515. For example, when development activities are being carried out by R&D entities located in different jurisdictions, the profit split method may be the only applicable transfer pricing method. The sharing methodology would then not rely on data from comparable independent enterprises, but it would need to be based on firm-specific factors when the contribution of each participant to the profit split arrangement is so specific that it would not be performed by an independent party.
516. For example, employee remuneration may be a well-suited allocation key for certain enterprises where the performance of functions by key employees is the main factor contributing to earning income: *see* OECD, *BEPS Action 10 – Revised Guidance on Profit Splits* (OECD 2017), para. 66 *in fine*: '(e)mployee remuneration may be relevant in situations where functions relating to the skills and experience of staff are the primary factor in generating the relevant profits'. However, the chance is low to find independent enterprises sharing profits between them on the basis of the remuneration of their employees. Such an allocation key would thus by relying on a weak connection to observations from the open market.
517. In this respect, it was considered at para. 2.49 of the 1995 OECD transfer pricing guidelines, that the profit split method is a method of 'last resort'. This status was later removed from the guidelines.

After considering the choice of a transfer pricing method, the next section considers the relevance of sources of interpretation for the assessment of deviations from the reference system.

5.4.2 The Relevance of Sources of Interpretation for the Assessment of Deviations from the Reference System

It is difficult to assess a deviation from the reference system when the allocation method is a generally formulated arm's length provision, because this allocation method lies on an abstract principle. Several sources of interpretation exist and are often used by tax administrations and taxpayers, but this does not necessarily mean that State aid law tolerates that such sources are used to apply the reference system, or to assess deviations from it.

Examples of sources of interpretation are the statements of practice published by national tax authorities, the OECD and United Nations (UN) Model Tax Conventions together with their commentaries, the OECD transfer pricing guidelines, the UN practical manual on transfer pricing,[518] or the work of the EU joint transfer pricing forum,[519] which in certain cases may be endorsed by the European Commission or by the European Council. As the OECD transfer pricing guidelines constitute the most developed source of interpretation of the arm's length principle, and given that it is of clear relevance for the Member States of the EU since most of them are also members of the OECD, the analysis below considers mainly the relevance for interpretation purposes of these guidelines for the assessment of a deviation from the reference system. It is also assumed that the OECD transfer pricing guidelines are not granted a binding value through the reference system: the guidelines would then be part of the reference system, and they would need to be taken into account for the assessment of deviations from the reference system. The question I will address in this section can be simply formulated: may one rely on the OECD transfer pricing guidelines to assess the correct interpretation of the arm's length principle for the purpose of the selectivity test?

To start with, it is recalled that binding legal sources may, in certain cases, be interpreted in the light of certain non-binding sources.[520] It is tempting to rely on the OECD transfer pricing guidelines for the assessment of deviations from a reference system that includes a generally formulated arm's length provision. Indeed, it is common ground that the guidelines are both widely relied on,[521] and quite comprehensive. They are referred to in the commentary to Article 9 of the OECD Model Tax

---

518. *See* United Nations, *Practical Manual on Transfer Pricing for Developing Countries* (United Nations 2017).
519. *See* < http://ec.europa.eu/taxation_customs/taxation/company_tax/transfer_pricing/forum/index_en.htm > accessed 20 February 2018.
520. For instance, in the area of international law the Vienna Convention on the Law of Treaties encourages, in certain cases, the interpretation of international treaties in the light of supplementary means of interpretation (*see* Art. 32 of the Convention).
521. *See* Sergio André Rocha, *The Future of Transfer Pricing – General Report* (IFA Cahiers Volume 102B, Sdu 2017) 28.

Chapter 5: Prima Facie Selectivity of the ALP

Convention,[522] something that makes the guidelines a relevant source of interpretation when the business profits article of a double taxation convention is drafted along the lines of the model. Moreover, interpreting the arm's length principle in the light of the OECD transfer pricing guidelines may be particularly useful when the Member States provide limited guidance in their domestic law on the application of the arm's length principle; it would otherwise be difficult to assess a deviation from the reference system.[523] Last, the notice on the notion of State aid mentions that the Commission 'may have regard' to the guidelines.[524]

Yet, the arguments mentioned above do not necessarily make the OECD transfer pricing guidelines a valid source of interpretation for the purpose of the assessment of deviations from the reference system. In my opinion, unless the domestic law refers to the guidelines through giving them a binding value,[525] one cannot rely on this source of interpretation without investigating its applicability. The main argument to support this view is the risk that the material content of the version of the OECD transfer pricing guidelines that is being relied on, differs from that of the reference system. Besides, it was concluded in section 2.3.2 of this book that the reference system should only consist of the binding elements of the corporate income tax system of a given Member State, which includes both the basic principles of the tax system and the allocation method, but – it is assumed here – not the guidelines. Therefore, a source of interpretation that is not binding and thus not part of the reference system cannot, from the outset, be relied on to assess the correctness of the application of the reference system. It is not enough that a domestic rule uses the expression 'arm's length principle', or relies on the rationale of the principle, for the OECD transfer pricing guidelines to necessarily be fully applicable. The 'arm's length principle' described in the guidelines does not need to fully match the 'arm's length principle' enacted in the legislation of a Member State.[526]

In the extreme case, although the OECD transfer pricing guidelines claim not to,[527] it may be wondered whether they always implement the arm's length principle, or if they actually depart from it. First, at the level of principle, the OECD has recognised the possibility to introduce 'special measures either within or *beyond* the arm's length principle' (emphasis added),[528] although such special measures were finally not adopted as part of the final Base Erosion and Profit Shifting (BEPS)

---

522. *See* para. 1 of the commentary on Art. 9 of the 2017 OECD Model Tax Convention.
523. Indeed, the very mention of the arm's length principle does not, in itself, provide a concrete answer as to how to allocate the corporate tax base among associated enterprises.
524. *See* Commission Notice on the notion of State aid as referred to in Art. 107(1) of the Treaty on the Functioning of the European Union [2016] OJ C 262/1, para. 173.
525. In this case the source of interpretation would become part of the reference system.
526. For example, the provisions at paras 1.122–1.124 of the 2017 OECD transfer pricing guidelines enable tax administrations to disregard an intercompany transaction and replace it by an alternative transaction. That may be tolerated by certain domestic laws, but not necessarily by all of them: in certain countries, the domestic law may favour an adjustment of the transfer prices instead of a recharacterisation of the transaction.
527. As emphasised by Brauner, the OECD may 'de facto divorce' from the arm's length principle, 'while keeping its rhetoric alive': *see* Yariv Brauner, 'Formula Based Transfer Pricing' (2014) 42 Intertax 615, 618.
528. *See* OECD, *Action Plan on Base Erosion and Profit Shifting* (OECD 2013) 20.

package.[529] Second, there are examples of measures that may deviate from the arm's length principle. One such measure concerns the determination of the participants to a cost contribution agreement. In this case, the guidelines require that a participant exercises control over the specific risks it assumes.[530] Although this statement is understandable in view of the general logic of the guidelines to require sufficient substance to recognise the entitlement to profits, in my view it cannot be generally assumed that, in all circumstances, an independent party that invests in a project with other unrelated parties would control the risks it financially assumes.[531] Another example of possible deviation from the arm's length principle is the possibility recognised at paragraph 6.192 of the 2017 OECD transfer pricing guidelines for tax administrations to consider '*ex post* outcomes as presumptive evidence about the appropriateness of the *ex ante* pricing arrangements': although the guidelines claim to still apply the arm's length principle, it could be argued that independent parties will not necessarily include in an agreement for the sale of an asset a provision that changes the price of the transaction if the value of the asset, after a certain period of time, does not correspond to what could be expected at the time the contract was concluded. In certain cases, the uncertainty may be subject to a provision that allows for an adjustment of the price, whereas in other cases the parties may accept the uncertainty, possibly taking it into account in setting the price of the asset.[532] Accordingly, I believe that if the guidelines do depart from the arm's length principle, or suggest an interpretation of the principle that is not compatible with the domestic law or the positions of the domestic courts of a Member State, applying them would be in conflict with the reference system.

Several other arguments support the view that the OECD transfer pricing guidelines are not necessarily a valid source of interpretation for the purpose of the application of the reference system, or the assessment of deviations from it. A Member State may have made a reservation to the commentary on Article 9 of the OECD Model Tax Convention,[533] enacted rules that are in conflict with the OECD transfer pricing

---

529. *See* OECD, *Aligning Transfer Pricing Outcomes with Value Creation, Actions 8-10 – 2015 Final Reports* (OECD 2015) 9.
530. *See* para. 8.15 of the 2017 OECD transfer pricing guidelines.
531. For instance, a venture capitalist that invests in a project may have little or no control in the project, but an entitlement to an important profit in case the project is successful.
532. For similar views *see* Hubert Hamaekers, 'Arm's Length – How Long?' (2001) 8 International Transfer Pricing Journal 30, 35; Yariv Brauner, 'Value in the Eye of the Beholder: The Valuation of Intangibles for Transfer Pricing Purposes' (2008) 28 Virginia Tax Review 79, who at 100–101 considers with respect to the US commensurate with income rule that it is 'a major deviation from the arm's length standard'.
533. For example, in the 2017 update to the OECD Model Tax Convention, four Member States of the European Union had made reservations on Art. 9 of the Model. Here, a parallel could also be made to the attribution of profits to permanent establishments. In my opinion, it can certainly not be considered that the reference system for the assessment of the taxation of permanent establishments in the light of State aid law is necessarily made of the authorised OECD approach, given the deviations in many double taxation conventions from the latest Art. 7 of the OECD Model Tax Convention, the reservations made in the commentary on Art. 7, and the lack of domestic provisions explicitly referring to the authorised OECD approach.

guidelines,⁵³⁴ or implemented an arm's length provision that is subject to the precedence of other rules such as special anti-abuse measures.⁵³⁵ In addition, different countries may have different positions as to the material content of the arm's length principle, although they have similarly formulated arm's length provisions.

I conclude from the foregoing considerations that it is legally incorrect to necessarily rely on a given source of interpretation such as the OECD transfer pricing guidelines for the purpose of the application of a generally formulated arm's length provision, or the assessment of a deviation from the reference system. At the same time, this does not generally exclude the right, under the rules on State aid, to rely on the guidelines for the interpretation of a generally formulated arm's length provision. The OECD transfer pricing guidelines may very well be compatible with the reference system, and thus their use may be both legally correct and relevant for a State aid analysis. It is likely that a Member State that has implemented the arm's length principle in its domestic law will accept numerous parts of the OECD transfer pricing guidelines as a source of interpretation, without explicitly referring or adhering to them; the two sources indeed rely on the same principle, and may largely overlap.

Accordingly, when it comes to deciding whether or not, and if so to what extent the OECD transfer pricing guidelines or any other non-binding source of interpretation may be relied on for the purpose of the interpretation of the reference system, the first question to ask is what legal status a source of interpretation has in the domestic law of a given Member State. In case a source of interpretation is not part of the reference system, one should draw a line between what is compatible with the reference system, and what is not. Only the sources of interpretation that are compatible with the reference system may be used to assess a potential deviation from it, something that may include several sources of interpretation.⁵³⁶ Although it may be difficult to draw such a line, ignoring this distinction carries the risk of giving to the reference system a wrong material content.

A last question needs to be considered before concluding this section, that of conflicting sources of interpretation. In case of conflict between several sources of interpretation that are not legally binding, I find no convincing reason for *a priori* giving priority to a given source of interpretation over another. It is true that the OECD transfer pricing guidelines are approved by the OECD Council, which recommends their

---

534. An example is the situation where a Member State considers that the performance of functions has a value such that the transfer of functions would, in itself, constitute a taxable event. In contrast to this position, the OECD transfer pricing guidelines would normally require that risks and assets are also transferred to recognise the transfer of 'something of value': *see* paras 9.10 and 9.48 and following of the 2017 OECD transfer pricing guidelines.
535. For example, a Member State may enact a rule that limits the deductibility of interest expenses, even if the allocation of such expenses is in line with the arm's length principle.
536. For instance, in many cases the OECD transfer pricing guidelines and the work of the EU joint transfer pricing forum are not incompatible with each other, the latter providing additional guidance to certain parts of the former. In such a case, there is no conflict between the sources of interpretation; the cumulated application of these sources does not create a legal issue.

application.[537] Yet this does not give them a binding effect.[538] It does not either give them a superior interpretative value, as other sources may also be approved by the Member States of the EU, or the organisations of which they are members. Therefore, in my opinion one would need to have recourse to traditional legal methods of interpretation by considering, for instance, the preparatory works of the domestic arm's length provision, to solve conflicts between various equally valuable sources of interpretation.

I now turn to the last of the three aspects of the application of the arm's length principle that are considered in this chapter: the assessment of deviations from the reference system in relation to the approximation of values.

5.4.3 The Assessment of Deviations from the Reference System in Relation to the Approximation of Values

State aid law and the arm's length principle seem to be diverging with respect to the approximation of values: while State aid law requires precision and objectivity, the arm's length principle has an approximative and subjective nature.[539] It is an intrinsic and necessary consequence of the choice to rely on an abstract principle. This divergence is analysed below, and it is followed by a reflection on how to reconcile the

---

537. See OECD, Recommendation of the Council on the Determination of Transfer Pricing between Associated Enterprises [C(95)126/Final, as amended].
538. Diverging, see Romero J.S. Tavares, Bret N. Bogenschneider, and Marta Pankiv, 'The Intersection of EU State Aid and U.S. Tax Deferral: A Spectacle of Fireworks, Smoke, and Mirrors' (2016) 19 Florida Tax Review 121, 179–180. On the non-binding effect of the OECD transfer pricing guidelines, see e.g., Jose Calderón, 'The OECD Transfer Pricing Guidelines as a Source of Tax Law' (2007) 37 Intertax 4, 9; Richard Lyal, 'Transfer Pricing Rules and State Aid' (2015) 38 Fordham International Law Journal 1017, 1022. Similarly to the area of transfer pricing, the OECD Council recommends the interpretation of double taxation conventions in the light of the commentary on the OECD Model Tax Convention (see OECD, Recommendation of the Council concerning the Model Tax Convention on Income and on Capital [C(97)195/FINAL], but this does not make such a commentary legally binding. On the lack of binding effect of the commentary on the OECD Model Tax Convention, see David Ward, Luc de Broe, Juergen Killius, Jean-Pierre Le Gall, Toshio Miyatake, Kees van Raad, John F. Avery Jones, Maarten J. Ellis, Sanford H. Goldberg, Gugliemo Maisto, Henri Torrione and Bertil Wiman, *The Interpretation of Income Tax Treaties with Particular Reference to the Commentaries on the OECD Model* (IFA/IBFD 2005).
539. On the subjective nature of the arm's length principle, see para. 3.46 of the 2017 OECD transfer pricing guidelines, which with respect to the selection of potential comparables stresses that '(c)omplete elimination of subjective judgments from the selection of comparables would not be feasible'. For a similar view, see European Commission, 'EU Joint Transfer Pricing Forum Report on the use of Comparables in the European Union' (European Commission 2016) para. 7. It is impossible to provide an exhaustive list of examples in the guidelines to evidence the approximative nature of the arm's length principle. I will only mention one example, concerning the allocation of risk. In case several companies exercise control over risk and have the financial capacity to assume a risk, they all meet the expectations described at para. 1.65 of the 2017 OECD transfer pricing guidelines; however, as the risk (and the income connected to it) cannot be attributed equally to all risks bearers, para. 1.98 allocates the risk 'to the associated enterprise or group of associated enterprises exercising the *most* control' (emphasis added). However, no guidance is provided – and indeed, no guidance can be provided – as to how to determine which enterprise exercises the 'most' control. This assessment is necessarily subjective and approximative.

logics of the selectivity test and of the arm's length principle, to assess deviations from the reference system. It can be observed that in addition to being theoretically important, these questions have a practical relevance with respect to the quantification and the recovery of illegal State aid, although these questions are not in the scope of this book.

The selectivity test requires an accurate identification of a State measure and of the reference system, to assess whether the former deviates from the latter. At first sight, the selectivity test does not seem to require a precise approximation of values: the assessment of a deviation from the reference system for the purpose of the selectivity test is merely a discrimination test, which, as such, does not involve quantification. The extent of a deviation from the reference system does not affect the conclusion of whether or not a State measure is selective, although it may influence the compatibility of an aid with Article 107(1) of the TFEU.[540] It is only if a State measure deviates from the reference system, and all the other criteria of Article 107(1) of the TFEU are fulfilled, that the illegal aid will need to be quantified to correct the distortion of competition.[541]

Moreover, in many cases where it is the application of the law that is subject to the selectivity test, the content of the law can be clearly established with no need to approximate or quantify any economic values; the selectivity test will then consist in assessing whether the State measure follows the requirements set by the law. Even in the area of tax law, numerous tax measures do not require the approximation of values to assess whether or not a measure deviates from the reference system: the assessment of a deviation from the reference system as a consequence of the application of a tax measure may be a rather 'straightforward exercise',[542] once the reference system has been identified. For example, when the duration of the depreciation of an asset is established in the tax or accounting rules, it can easily be assessed whether the amount of depreciation that is deducted for taxation purposes is in conformity with what the reference system prescribes.

---

540. For example, under the rules relating to *de minimis* aid, aids granted below a given threshold are deemed not to have an effect on trade between the Member States, and not to distort or threaten to distort competition: *see* Commission Regulation (EU) No 1407/2013 of 18 December 2013 on the application of Arts 107 and 108 of the Treaty on the Functioning of the European Union to de minimis aid [2013] OJ L 352/1.
541. The actual calculation of the amount of aid to be recovered is a matter that falls within the scope of national law (*see* e.g., Case T-459/93, *Siemens SA v. Commission of the European Communities*, ECLI:EU:T:1995:100, para. 83). In this respect, it can be observed that although 'no provision of EU law requires the Commission, when ordering the recovery of aid declared incompatible with the common market, to fix the exact amount of the aid to be recovered', a decision of recovery needs to 'include information enabling the addressee of the decision to work out itself, without overmuch difficulty', the amount that should be recovered (*see* e.g., Case C-403/10 P, *Mediaset SpA v. European Commission*, ECLI:EU:C:2011:533, para. 126; Case C-81/10 P, *France Télécom SA*, ECLI:EU:C:2011:811, para. 102; Joined Cases C-164/15 P and C-165/15 P, *European Commission v. Aer Lingus Ltd and Ryanair Designated Activity Company*, ECLI:EU:C:2016:990, para. 78).
542. This expression is used by Advocate General Wahl: *see* Case C-203/16 P, *Dirk Andres (administrator of Heitkamp BauHolding GmbH), previously Heitkamp BauHolding GmbH v. European Commission*, ECLI:EU:C:2017:1017, Opinion of AG Wahl, para. 102.

The arm's length principle is, in contrast, a peculiar tax measure that relies on an abstract principle. Tax measures based on the arm's length principle rely in most cases on approximations and ranges of values that may be deemed in line with the principle,[543] as opposed to a single value.[544] The European Commission recognises the uncertainty inherent to the arm's length principle.[545] Besides, despite the objectivity of relying on the market forces, several subjective appreciations are made as part of an arm's length analysis, something that increases its imprecise character,[546] and also creates a risk of error.[547] Through various methods, a range may be refined so as to accurately apply the arm's length principle, but there is in most cases no single market value as a result of an arm's length analysis. An exception would be the case of a perfect comparable, no matter which transfer pricing method is used, something that is particularly rare.[548] The OECD transfer pricing guidelines actually emphasise that the application of the arm's length principle is not 'an exact science'.[549] Moreover, with a similar set of facts, the arm's length principle may still be interpreted differently and produce different or only partly overlapping results, without the principle being clearly infringed. That would be the case, for instance, when two comparability analyses rely on different geographical areas, given that the arm's length principle does not intrinsically indicate the geographical scope of a comparability analysis. Diverging

---

543. *See* paras 3.60 and 3.62 of the 2017 OECD transfer pricing guidelines. *See also* European Commission, 'EU Joint Transfer Pricing Forum Report on the use of Comparables in the European Union' (European Commission 2016) 12, point c).
544. *See* e.g., paras 1.13 and 3.55 of the 2017 OECD transfer pricing guidelines. For an example of the approximative nature of the application of the arm's length principle *see* the US case *Bausch & Lomb* where the court, using its 'best judgment', found that at arm's length an Irish company would have been willing to invest in a production facility 'even if required to share *approximately* 50 percent of the profits therefrom' (emphasis added) with a US company as consideration for use of its intangibles (*see* US Court of Appeals for the Second Circuit, Case 933 F.2d 1084, *Bausch & Lomb Incorporated and Consolidated Subsidiaries*, 14 May 1991).
545. *See* Commission Notice on the notion of State aid as referred to in Art. 107(1) of the Treaty on the Functioning of the European Union [2016] OJ C 262/1, para. 171.
546. *See* Richard Collier and Joseph L. Andrus, *Transfer Pricing and the Arm's Length Principle After BEPS* (Oxford University Press 2017) 140.
547. Examples of subjective elements that are part of the application of the arm's length principle are the appreciation of business strategies, the evaluation of the relative importance of the elements of a functional analysis, or the assumptions made for the purpose of the valuation of intangible property.
548. The arm's length principle as it is widely applied, builds on the idea of an approximation of a market value through different statistical methods. The reason for that is easily understandable: as in most cases a perfect comparable cannot be found (*see* para. 3.38 of the 2017 OECD transfer pricing guidelines), the most reliable method is to compile the best available comparables in a range of values that is determined through different statistical methods. The reconciliation of the conditions surrounding the tested party and the sample of comparables will then allow choosing, among the values of the comparables, a value or a range of values that is deemed to be the best estimate of an arm's length value. Thus, the methodology that is inherent to the arm's length principle supposes making approximations in the most reliable manner, and in the vast majority of cases one cannot arrive at a better result than a well-refined range of values. *See* para. 1.13 of the 2017 OECD transfer pricing guidelines.
549. *See* paras 1.13, 3.55, and 4.8 of the 2017 OECD transfer pricing guidelines.

interpretations may also exist with regard to the core meaning of the arm's length principle, for example with respect to the treatment of synergies or market specific circumstances.[550]

Consequently, the arm's length principle is unlikely to produce a single market value. This makes it difficult to assess a deviation from the reference system, given that it is impossible to know exactly what transfer prices, or what profit margins are required by the reference system. Only a methodology is provided, as opposed to a material content that can be deducted from the sole reading of the law. Given that the arm's length principle has an abstract and partly subjective nature that is unlikely to produce a single market value, the selectivity test becomes peculiar as it no longer can consist in a straightforward test of whether or not a tax measure complies with the law. Some level of approximation of what the reference system prescribes is necessary, to test whether or not the tax measure is in line with the reference system. As a result, if at first sight the selectivity test does not require the approximation of values, I draw the conclusion that such an approximation becomes necessary when the purpose of a rule is to approximate an economic value (in this case the taxable income of a member of a multinational group), but when at the same time the reference system includes solely a methodology to determine such an economic value.

For the reasons explained above, there is a divergence between the logic of the selectivity test in State aid law, and that of the arm's length principle with respect to the approximation of values, given that while State aid law requires precision and objectivity, the arm's length principle has an approximative and subjective nature. Actually, a divergence with the logic of State aid law when it comes to the assessment of a deviation from the reference system is not exclusive to the arm's length principle. Difficulties would also arise for other rules that do not have a precise and objective material content, but rely on principles or on subjective considerations. Various types of tax rules have a subjective or abstract dimension. To name a few examples, difficulties would exist to assess a deviation from the reference system for rules implying the existence of a permanent establishment (for instance with respect to the assessment of whether a person is habitually playing the 'principal role' leading to the conclusion of contracts[551]), rules attributing profits to permanent establishments in connection to the performance of 'significant people functions',[552] rules granting tax treaty benefits for a person deemed as the 'beneficial owner' of an item of income,[553] rules denying a tax treaty benefit when obtaining that benefit was 'one of the principal

---

550. An evidence for the often diverging interpretations of the arm's length principle is the ever growing number of disputes in relation to the interpretation of Art. 9 of double taxation conventions. For an overview of court cases relating to the interpretation of the arm's length principle in several countries, see Eduardo Baistrocchi and Ian Roxan (eds), *Resolving Transfer Pricing Disputes: A Global Analysis* (Cambridge University Press 2012). In this respect, the US Supreme Court considered that 'even though most nations have adopted the "arm's length" approach in its general outlines, the precise rules under which they reallocate income among affiliated corporations often differ substantially' (US Supreme Court, Case 81-523, 463 US 159, *Container Corporation of America v. Franchise Tax Board of California* 191, 27 June 1983).
551. *See* Art. 5(5) of the 2017 OECD Model Tax Convention.
552. *See* para. 20 of the commentary on Art. 7 of the 2017 OECD Model Tax Convention.
553. *See* e.g., Arts 10(2), 11(2), and 12(1) of the 2017 OECD Model Tax Convention.

purposes of an arrangement',[554] or general anti-avoidance provisions.[555] All these examples share with the arm's length principle a subjective or abstract dimension, which precludes the possibility to perform the selectivity test by simply comparing the reference system with the tax measure. Instead, to assess whether such tax measures deviate from the reference system, the selectivity analysis must rely on a judgment consisting in deducting from the abstract reference system certain concrete implications.[556] This contrasts with situations where tax rules are objective and include, in the wording of the law, the conditions to be fulfilled so as to be applicable; in such cases, the selectivity analysis is also more objective, and does not need to be relying to a great extent on a judgment that necessarily includes some level of subjectivity.[557]

Moreover, while certain of the examples mentioned above obey to a 'yes or no logic',[558] others share with the arm's length principle a measurement of economic values with a range of possible outcomes: for example, rules on the attribution of profits to permanent establishments are similar to the arm's length principle in that they are likely to result in a range of profits; also, the effect of a general anti-avoidance rule may be to replace a given arrangement with another one that matches the reality, with a range of possible arrangements to replace the initial one. Accordingly, the selectivity test becomes necessarily subjective when it assesses rules that have a subjective dimension. This leads me to concluding that the arm's length principle is not the only rule that has a different logic than the selectivity test.

Now that is was argued that there is a divergence between the logic of the selectivity test in State aid law and that of the arm's length principle with respect to the approximation of values, how to assess whether a tax levied on the basis of a generally formulated arm's length provision deviates from the reference system? For tax rules such as the arm's length principle that include an abstract and subjective dimension, as mentioned above one cannot escape the need to assess a deviation from the reference system by also relying on abstract and subjective judgments. Despite a difference in the logic of the rules on State aid and of a generally formulated arm's length provision, this

---

554. *See* Art. 29(9) of the 2017 OECD Model Tax Convention.
555. *See* e.g., Art. 6 of the anti-avoidance directive (Council Directive (EU) 2016/1164 of 12 July 2016 laying down rules against tax avoidance practices that directly affect the functioning of the internal market [2016] OJ L 193/1).
556. For example, one would need to assess whether in a given case a person habitually plays the 'principal role' leading to the conclusion of contracts, performs 'significant people functions', or whether a conduct or arrangement can be deemed to be motivated by tax reasons.
557. For example, the duration of the depreciation of an asset is normally set in an objective manner in the reference system, which implies that the selectivity test needs solely to compare the reference system with the actual tax measure with little need for judgment (some judgment may still be necessary, for example to ensure that the qualification as an asset is correct). Another example is the interest limitation rule of the anti-avoidance directive (*see* Art. 4 of the anti-avoidance directive, Council Directive (EU) 2016/1164 of 12 July 2016 laying down rules against tax avoidance practices that directly affect the functioning of the internal market [2016] OJ L 193/1). This rule builds mostly on objective notions, as opposed to subjective notions such as whether or not a loan is motivated by tax reasons; accordingly, the selectivity test in the case of the interest limitation rule can be performed with little need for subjective judgment, although some appreciation remains necessary to ensure that the rules are applicable.
558. For example, provisions limiting tax treaty benefits either enable, or deprive a taxpayer from enjoying certain treaty benefits. There is no measurement of economic values under these tests.

difference does not prevent the application of State aid law. Indeed, the European Commission and the Union courts are used to making assessments of the effects of the market forces, in particular when assessing the existence of an aid under the market economy operator test. For the purpose of making assessments of the market value of various transactions, the way of reasoning and the methodology that are relied on by the European Commission and the Union courts are often comparable to the application of the arm's length principle by domestic courts. For example, the General Court analysed the use by the European Commission of the capital asset pricing model, to assess the compatibility with State aid law of the yield provided by a given industry.[559] The capital asset pricing model is also applied for the purpose of the enforcement of the arm's length principle, as illustrated by the *Fiat* case.[560] Another example is the quantification of an aid on the basis of the notion of 'reasonable profit';[561] this notion has a subjective and approximative dimension, and resembles the general goal under the arm's length principle of earning a profit that is in line with the relative contributions of the parties to a transaction, as evidenced by a functional analysis.[562] Accordingly, the application of the selectivity test to a tax levied under a generally formulated arm's length provision is not precluded by the need to approximate values under the arm's length principle, although this assessment necessarily contains some degree of approximation.

Moreover, in areas other than taxes, the European Commission does tolerate certain divergences from an ideal market value, something that is conceptually close to the notion of arm's length range. An example is found in the previous Communication on State aid and the sale of lands and buildings by public authorities; in this document, the Commission considered that 'If, after a reasonable effort to sell the land and buildings at the market value, it is clear that the value set by the valuer cannot be obtained, a divergence of up to 5% from that value can be deemed to be in line with market conditions'.[563] This tolerance for deviations from an ideal market value is close to the concept of range for tax measures based on the arm's length principle, and shows that it might be compatible with State aid law to approximate economic values with some degree of subjectivity, and even with some margin of error. Consequently,

---

559. *See* Joined Cases T-319/12 and T-321/12, *Kingdom of Spain, Ciudad de la Luz, SAU and Sociedad Proyectos Temáticos de la Comunidad Valenciana, SAU v. European Commission*, ECLI:EU:T:2014:604.
560. *See* Commission Decision (EU) 2016/2326 of 21 October 2015 on State aid SA.38375 (2014/C ex 2014/NN) which Luxembourg granted to Fiat [2016] OJ L 351/1, para. 57.
561. *See* e.g., the *Altmark* case where the CJEU considered that the compensation for services of general economic interest 'cannot exceed what is necessary to cover all or part of the costs incurred in the discharge of public service obligations, taking into account the relevant receipts and a *reasonable profit* for discharging those obligations' (emphasis added): Case C-280/00, *Altmark Trans and Regierungspräsidium Magdeburg*, ECLI:EU:C:2003:415, para. 92.
562. *See* paras 1.51 and following of the 2017 OECD transfer pricing guidelines, especially the second sentence of para. 1.56.
563. *See* Commission Communication on State aid elements in sales of land and buildings by public authorities [1997] OJ C 209/3, para. 2(b). This Communication was replaced by certain parts in the notice on the notion of State aid (*see* Commission Notice on the notion of State aid as referred to in Article 107(1) of the Treaty on the Functioning of the European Union [2016] OJ C 262/1, para. 229, second indent).

although the subjective dimension of the arm's length principle increases the difficulty of the assessment of a deviation from the reference system, it is not conceptually irreconcilable with the selectivity test.[564]

Given the divergence between the logic of the selectivity test in State aid law and that of the arm's length principle with respect to the approximation of values, but also considering that the two are not conceptually impossible to reconcile, it should now be wondered whether the logic of the selectivity test should exercise a particular influence on the assessment of deviations from a reference system including a generally formulated arm's length provision. In particular, the precision aimed at for State aid law purposes could influence the notion of arm's length range described in the OECD transfer pricing guidelines, especially by narrowing down the breadth of the range, or even by aiming at a particular point in the range. Although the European Commission relies on the concept of range with respect to tax settlements,[565] it does not seem to fully endorse the notion of arm's length range as it is described in the OECD transfer pricing guidelines. For example, in the *Starbucks* case, it mentioned that 'the point in the range closest to the most likely market outcome should be used for the purposes of pricing controlled transactions'.[566] Also, in the *Fiat* decision the European Commission argued that the lower quartile provided a less reliable approximation than the median.[567]

In my view this approach is questionable, as there is no objective reason to consider *a priori* that any given point in the range is the right value, unless some differences in comparability justify aiming for a particular direction in the range.[568] It is precisely because it is in most cases impossible to arrive at a singe value that the concept of range has been developed.[569] To support the idea that the median is the closest value to the market value, the Commission referred in the *Fiat* decision to

---

564. For a different view, whereby subjectivity may, as such, entail selectivity, *see* Phedon Nicolaides, 'State Aid Rules and Tax Rulings' (2016) 15 European State Aid Law Quarterly 416, 426.
565. *See* Commission Notice on the notion of State aid as referred to in Art. 107(1) of the Treaty on the Functioning of the European Union [2016] OJ C 262/1, para. 176(b), where it is referred to the concept of a 'reasonable range'.
566. *See* Commission Decision (EU) 2017/502 of 21 October 2015 on State aid SA.38374 (2014/C ex 2014/NN) implemented by the Netherlands to Starbucks [2017] OJ L 83/38, para. 396.
567. *See* Commission Decision (EU) 2016/2326 of 21 October 2015 on State aid SA.38375 (2014/C ex 2014/NN) which Luxembourg granted to Fiat [2016] OJ L 351/1, para. 135.
568. For example, if the controlled transaction that is being tested under the arm's length principle is not perfectly comparable to the transactions identified as part of a comparability analysis, the choice of the value or the range of values to set the transfer prices might account for such differences in comparability. That might be the case when the tested transaction is performed by a party in a given country, while the arm's length range compiles observations from several countries with different features.
569. Various reasons explain the need to rely on a range of values. Among others, there needs to be some room for appreciation as part of an analysis that implements the arm's length principle. Since this principle implies the approximation of a value to get the most reliable result, the values compiled in the comparability analysis should be adjusted in different manners. This may depend on various factors such as the industry, the functional analysis, or the economic situation. There is thus a need for flexibility that is acknowledged in most sources that provide interpretative guidance on the arm's length principle, such flexibility being impossible by considering that only the median is the right value.

paragraph 3.57 of the 2010 OECD transfer pricing guidelines.[570] However, I submit that this position is an overinterpretation of what the OECD transfer pricing guidelines recommend. On the one hand, this paragraph does not intend at being applied generally, but only in case a sufficiently accurate analysis cannot be performed: paragraph 3.57 relies on the assumption that 'some comparability defects remain that cannot be identified and/or quantified'. On the other hand, the paragraph does not explicitly recommend the use of the median, but rather that of 'statistical tools that take account of central tendency to narrow the range (e.g., the interquartile range or other percentiles)', something that is broader than the sole median. This criticism of the position taken by the Commission is confirmed by paragraph 3.62, which mentions the median as an example among several measures of central tendency. At the same time, although the approach of the European Commission is questionable, it must be recognised that giving preference to the median facilitates the selectivity test, and mitigates the risk of making significant errors given that the median gives a balanced approximation of the values included in the range.[571]

Not only is the interpretation of the guidelines by the Commission questionable, but also it might be in breach of the reference system. The assessment of deviations from the reference system must be done consistently with the principles applicable in a given Member State: if the reference system in force in a Member State implies that any value within the range is compatible with the arm's length principle, the selectivity test should imply that a deviation from the reference system is at hand only if tax is levied based on a value that is outside the range. Here, a parallel can be made with the case law of the CJEU in the area of the freedoms of movement, in which the CJEU found that taxpayers may structure their transactions in a tax-efficient manner, as long as the requirements set by the Court to benefit from the protection of the freedoms of movement are met.[572] The acceptance of any value within the range is supported by the

---

570. *See* Commission Decision (EU) 2016/2326 of 21 October 2015 on State aid SA.38375 (2014/C ex 2014/NN) which Luxembourg granted to Fiat [2016] OJ L 351/1, para. 295. Paragraph 3.57 of the 2010 and 2017 OECD transfer pricing guidelines reads as follows (the paragraph was not amended as part of the changes made to the guidelines in 2017): '(i)t may also be the case that, while every effort has been made to exclude points that have a lesser degree of comparability, what is arrived at is a range of figures for which it is considered, given the process used for selecting comparables and limitations in information available on comparables, that some comparability defects remain that cannot be identified and/or quantified, and are therefore not adjusted. In such cases, if the range includes a sizeable number of observations, statistical tools that take account of central tendency to narrow the range (e.g., the interquartile range or other percentiles) might help to enhance the reliability of the analysis'.
571. This may be why the median is favoured as a reference point in a report drafted by the EU Joint Transfer Pricing Forum, when the pricing of an intercompany transaction has fallen outside the range and the income of an associated enterprise has to be adjusted: *see* European Commission, 'EU Joint Transfer Pricing Forum Report on the use of Comparables in the European Union' (European Commission 2016) 12, point d).
572. It can particularly be observed that in the areas of VAT and direct taxation, the CJEU has accepted that taxpayers act in a way that mitigates their tax burden without infringing the freedoms of movement, as long as the requirements of substance are met. In other words, the Court did not find an obligation to pay the highest amount of taxes implied by the different options faced by a taxpayer when structuring its activities: *see* particularly Case C-255/02, *Halifax plc*, ECLI:EU:C:2006:121 (especially at para. 73), and Case C-196/04, *Cadbury Schweppes plc*, ECLI:EU:C:2006:544 (especially at para. 36). Transposed to the area of State aid

case law of the CJEU where the Court found the arm's length principle justified and proportionate to attain the objective of prevention of tax avoidance.[573] In my view, accepting the arm's length principle should reasonably mean to also accept its approximative nature.

The conclusions of this section are twofold. First, the arm's length principle has a different logic than the selectivity test, but this does not prevent the application of the selectivity test and the assessment of a deviation from the reference system. Second, the selectivity test should not exercise a particular influence on the approximation of values, in particular on the notion of range. The essence of the rules on State aid should be to accept what the reference system prescribes. This means that if the reference system is to be interpreted in line with the OECD transfer pricing guidelines, a tax measure should be deemed to deviate from the reference system only if tax is levied on the basis of a value that is outside the range.

Despite the conclusions of this section, the fact remains that the assessment of a deviation from the reference system is, for a generally formulated arm's length provision, a difficult matter. However, the difficulty of assessing deviations from the reference system come not from the selectivity test, but from the characteristics of the arm's length principle, in particular its abstract and approximative nature. Such difficulties are likely to increase with the complexity of the application of the arm's length principle to the reality of multinational enterprises. For example, the increased integration of multinational enterprises makes it all the more difficult to find reliable comparable independent information, and thus to assess whether a deviation from the reference system is at hand. In this respect, McLure stressed that economic interdependence may 'defy quantification'.[574] Similarly, the US Supreme Court found that the arm's length principle 'may fail to account for contributions to income resulting from functional integration, centralization of management, and economies of scale'.[575] These difficulties are not, however, those of the State aid rules; they are rather intrinsic consequences of the choice of a Member State to legislate on the basis of the arm's length principle.

5.5 CONCLUSION

The main conclusion from this chapter is that a generally formulated arm's length provision may be a prima facie selective measure, on the basis of both the de jure selectivity test and the de facto selectivity test. There are, accordingly, certain tensions

---

law and the arm's length principle, the findings of the CJEU in *Halifax* and *Cadbury Schweppes* should imply a right for the taxpayer to set the prices of intercompany transactions in the lowest or highest end of the arm's length range, so as to be subject to tax on the lowest (but still at arm's length) income.
573. *See* Case C-524/04, *Test Claimants in the Thin Cap Group Litigation*, ECLI:EU:C:2007:161, para. 83; C-311/08, *Société de Gestion Industrielle SA*, ECLI:EU:C:2010:26, para. 66.
574. *See* Charles E. McLure, 'Tax Assignment and Subnational Fiscal Autonomy' (2000) 54 Bulletin for International Taxation 626, 633.
575. *See* US Supreme Court, Case 81-523, 463 US 159, *Container Corporation of America v. Franchise Tax Board of California* 181, 27 June 1983.

Chapter 5: Prima Facie Selectivity of the ALP

between the arm's length principle, assuming it is interpreted in the light of the OECD transfer pricing guidelines, and the selectivity test.[576] This allocation method may also prove prima facie selective in its application, especially when tax is levied on the basis of a value that is below what the arm's length principle prescribes.[577] However, it is argued in this chapter that the choice of a transfer pricing method, the reliance on sources of interpretation, as well as the intrinsic need to approximate results and to rely on ranges cannot constitute parameters for which State aid law implies, as such, a general preference. Instead, I consider that the assessment of deviations from the reference system should be performed on a case-by-case basis, by considering the facts and circumstances of a given situation, together with the applicable legal framework.

After applying the selectivity test to a generally formulated arm's length provision, I now turn to transfer pricing safe harbours.

---

576. In this respect Rädler has expressed a 'hope' that 'the ECJ jurisprudence on direct taxes and the standard OECD principles (...) be brought closer together': *see* Albert J. Rädler, 'Can the developed world (= OECD) follow the EU tax principles established by the European Court of Justice?' in *Regards critiques et perspectives sur le droit et la fiscalité – Liber amicorum Cyrille David* (LGDJ 2005) 325.
577. In this respect, it can be observed that the combined effects of State aid law and free movement law might be difficult to reconcile. Indeed, on the one hand State aid law precludes the levy of tax below what the arm's length principle prescribes. On the other hand, free movement law precludes the levy of tax above what the arm's length principle requires (*see* particularly Case C-311/08, *Société de Gestion Industrielle SA v. État belge*, ECLI:EU:C:2010:26, para. 72).

CHAPTER 6
Prima Facie Selectivity of Transfer Pricing Safe Harbours

6.1 INTRODUCTION

There are different types of transfer pricing safe harbours. The 2017 OECD transfer pricing guidelines define safe harbours in the transfer pricing context as 'a provision that applies to a defined category of taxpayers or transactions and that relieves eligible taxpayers from certain obligations otherwise imposed by a country's general transfer pricing rules'.[578] What is analysed in this chapter of the book is the use of transfer pricing safe harbours for the purpose of the allocation of the corporate tax base among multinational enterprises, when the safe harbours supplement an allocation method based on a generally formulated arm's length provision.[579] Safe harbours that do not aim at the allocation of the corporate tax base, such as those related to compliance requirements, are not studied here.[580]

---

578. *See* para. 4.102 of the 2017 OECD transfer pricing guidelines.
579. If the Member States are willing to implement a transfer pricing safe harbour, it is most likely that their tax system includes a generally formulated arm's length provision that is completed by certain safe harbours, instead of only providing material rules with fixed margins alone; in this last case, the Member States would need to provide a high number of rules to cover many possible types of transactions, functional profiles, industries, circumstances, etc. This type of allocation method is outside the scope of this book. Here, it can be mentioned that a trend has been observed towards the development of transfer pricing safe harbours that relate to low-value adding services, in accordance with the recommendations of Chapter 7 of the 2017 OECD transfer pricing guidelines: *see* Sergio André Rocha, *The Future of Transfer Pricing – General Report* (IFA Cahiers Volume 102B, Sdu 2017) 42–45.
580. An example of safe harbour related to compliance issues is the requirement to file a country-by-country report only for multinational enterprises with annual consolidated group revenue of more than EUR 750 million (*see* para. 5.52 of the 2017 OECD transfer pricing guidelines; Council Directive (EU) 2016/881 of 25 May 2016 amending Directive 2011/16/EU as regards mandatory automatic exchange of information in the field of taxation [2016] OJ L 146/8, Annex III, section I, point 4).

Safe harbours raise issues of State aid law that are different from those raised by a generally formulated arm's length provision, given that while the former is an objective and pre-determined allocation method, the latter has an approximative dimension as a consequence of being an abstract principle. By providing pre-determined material criteria relating to the allocation of the corporate tax base, such as profit margins or ranges thereof, safe harbours have a more objective and foreseeable character than a generally formulated arm's length provision. There is no need for the approximation of values, although the eligibility for a safe harbour still entails a subjective assessment that creates a risk of difference in treatment or of arbitrary assessment.

This chapter focuses on differences in treatment that stem from the design (section 6.2) as well as from the effects (section 6.3) of the law, assuming that the tax systems of the Member States include a transfer pricing safe harbour. The conclusions of this chapter are presented in section 6.4.

6.2 DE JURE SELECTIVITY

To study whether a transfer pricing safe harbour implies a difference in treatment between undertakings that are in a comparable situation, one needs to determine the material content of such a safe harbour. Here, one can distinguish between two categories of transfer pricing safe harbours: those that enforce the arm's length principle, and those that deviate from it.[581] I shall consider each of these safe harbours in turn, at sections 6.2.1 and 6.2.2 below. In these sections it is assumed that the reference system is made of a corporate income tax system that includes a generally formulated arm's length provision interpreted in the light of the 2017 OECD transfer pricing guidelines, and that this provision is supplemented by a transfer pricing safe harbour.

6.2.1 Transfer Pricing Safe Harbours That Enforce the Arm's Length Principle

The OECD transfer pricing guidelines include several types of transfer pricing safe harbours. An example is the 5% profit mark-up for certain eligible low value-adding intragroup services;[582] a second example concerns the limitation of *ex post* adjustments

---

581. In this respect, the risk of divergence from the arm's length principle is acknowledged in the 2017 OECD transfer pricing guidelines, *see* paras 4.111–4.113. For that reason, the guidelines recommend the use of safe harbours only in limited cases: para. 4.129 refers to the use of safe harbours 'in cases involving smaller taxpayers or less complex transactions'. The guidelines also recommend the use of safe harbours on a bilateral or multilateral basis for low risk functions involving distribution, manufacturing, and research and development: *see* Annex I to Chapter IV of the 2017 guidelines. The 1995 guidelines were significantly more cautious towards safe harbours, as it was stated at para. 4.120 of these guidelines that 'safe harbours are generally not compatible with the enforcement of transfer prices consistent with the arm's length principle'.
582. *See* para. 7.61 of the 2017 OECD transfer pricing guidelines.

Chapter 6: Prima Facie Selectivity of Transfer Pricing Safe Harbours

of the value of intangibles to important deviations from the *ex ante* value;[583] a third example is the measurement at cost (instead of in value) of the contributions to cost contribution arrangement for intercompany services, where the difference between the value and costs is 'relatively insignificant'.[584]

In the case of transfer pricing safe harbours that aim at enforcing the arm's length principle, the selectivity criterion seems at first sight not to be fulfilled, because the material content of the safe harbour does not deviate from the generally formulated arm's length provision. However, the arguments that were discussed for a generally formulated arm's length provision are likely to be also valid in the context of a transfer pricing safe harbour, if such a safe harbour has the same scope as a generally formulated arm's length provision: the corrective effect limited to members of multinational enterprises, as well as the assumed correctness of the benchmark provided by the market forces, might imply a difference in treatment between associated enterprises and independent enterprises or domestic groups. The result would be a risk that a transfer pricing safe harbour is prima facie de jure selective (assuming that the reference system is made of the general corporate income tax system and that the comparison is between independent and associated enterprises), given that a difference in treatment between associated enterprises and independent enterprises as well as members of domestic groups would stem from the design of the law. The conclusion would be different if the reference system consisted in the allocation methods, or if the comparison were made between different associated enterprises, given that all undertakings would be subject to the same treatment.

It may also be wondered whether the fixed nature of a transfer pricing safe harbour may, as such, entail a selective treatment. Certain scholars have argued that the fixed element of a rule might imply its selectivity.[585] Indeed, at first sight the fact that a transfer pricing safe harbour is necessarily limited in its scope to certain types of undertakings (e.g., companies with revenues below a certain threshold), functional profiles (e.g., companies with less complex functions),[586] or transactions (e.g., low value-adding intercompany services), seems to imply a selective treatment because the fixed nature of the safe harbour would not be available to all undertakings. Yet this view is, in my opinion, not convincing when a transfer pricing safe harbour implements the arm's length principle generally applicable in a Member State and is available to all eligible undertakings, given that an economically similar treatment

---

583. See para. 6.193, point iii) of the 2017 OECD transfer pricing guidelines. This paragraph limits the corrections made *ex post* to transactions involving the transfer or use of so-called hard-to-value intangibles to deviations that exceed 20% of the price determined at the time of the transaction. In other words, *ex post* adjustments are not accepted when the *ex post* value is up to 20% higher or lower than the *ex ante* value. It is a safe harbour in the sense that no correction is made *ex post* up to a difference of 20% with the value *ex ante*.
584. See para. 8.28 of the 2017 OECD transfer pricing guidelines.
585. For example, it has been argued that although the idea of safe harbours, or 'average benchmarks', may seem appealing, it necessarily favours and disadvantages different undertakings: see Luca Rubini, *The Definition of Subsidy and State Aid: WTO and EC Law in Comparative Perspective* (Oxford University Press 2009) 250, with further references at footnotes 99 and 100.
586. This is what para. 4.129 of the 2017 OECD transfer pricing guidelines recommends.

would be available to other undertakings under the general, not predetermined rule. In this respect, there are examples outside the field of tax law that show that various types of safe harbours may be compatible with State aid law: for instance, the concept of *de minimis* aid functions as a material safe harbour.[587] There are also particular applications of the concept of *de minimis* aid, such as in the area of regional aids.[588] Another example is provided by the block exemption regulation.[589] Moreover, there are certain safe harbours that target particular sectors, such as the financial sector,[590] that have been found compatible with the State aid rules. For example, the General Court has found that 'the mere use by the Commission of a minimum return corresponding to the average return in the sector concerned as an analytical tool, used in the course of considering all factors relevant to the case before it, does not infringe Article [107(1) of the TFEU]'.[591] This means that the predetermined character of a safe harbour does not, as such, entail a selective treatment.

It follows from the above observations that a transfer pricing safe harbour that enforces the arm's length principle raises the same issues of de jure selectivity as a generally formulated arm's length provision, as studied above at section 5.2. In my opinion, the fixed nature of a safe harbour does not, as such, entail a selective treatment.[592]

I now turn to transfer pricing safe harbours that deviate from the arm's length principle.

6.2.2 Transfer Pricing Safe Harbours That Deviate from the Arm's Length Principle

In case a safe harbour supplements a generally formulated arm's length provision but deviates from the arm's length principle, the tax system entails a potentially selective measure as a consequence of the difference in treatment under the two allocation

---

587. *See* Commission Regulation (EU) No 1407/2013 of 18 December 2013 on the application of Arts 107 and 108 of the Treaty on the Functioning of the European Union to de minimis aid [2013] OJ L 352/1.
588. The Guidelines on regional State aid permit, for notified schemes benefiting small-and medium-sized enterprises, that certain maximum amounts of aid serve as safe harbours; the effect is that as long as the aid remains below the maximum permissible, the aid is considered to be acceptable: *see* Guidelines on regional State aid for 2014-2020 [2013] OJ C 209/1, para. 82.
589. *See* Commission Regulation (EU) No 651/2014 of 17 June 2014 declaring certain categories of aid compatible with the internal market in application of Arts 107 and 108 of the Treaty [2014] OJ L 187/1.
590. For example, certain measures computed according to pre-determined figures and percentages in favour of banks in the context of the financial crisis are deemed not to constitute State aid: *see* Communication from the Commission on the application, from 1 August 2013, of State aid rules to support measures in favour of banks in the context of the financial crisis [2013] OJ C 216/1.
591. *See* Cases T-228/99 and T-233/99, *Westdeutsche Landesbank Girozentrale v. European Commission*, ECLI:EU:T:2003:57, para. 258.
592. Luja argued, however, that the fixed nature of a safe harbour might raise State aid concerns, because of 'the absence of an objective case-by-case assessment': *see* Raymond H.C. Luja, '(Re)shaping Fiscal State Aid: Selected Recent Cases and Their Impact' (2012) 40 Intertax 120, 121.

Chapter 6: Prima Facie Selectivity of Transfer Pricing Safe Harbours

methods, as well as if one compares associated enterprises that are subject to the transfer pricing safe harbour to independent enterprises or members of domestic groups. A potential difference in treatment is recognised in the guidelines, which mention that '(s)afe harbours may raise equity and uniformity issues' given that 'one would create two distinct sets of rules'.[593] There are two ways for a transfer pricing safe harbour to deviate from the arm's length principle: the safe harbour rule may result in a lower, or a higher amount of income than what the arm's length principle prescribes. I will start by considering the case of a safe harbour that decreases the tax burden normally implied by the arm's length principle. I will then turn to the opposite situation, i.e., when the safe harbour rule exceeds what the arm's length principle prescribes.

If the safe harbour rule provides for a lower amount of income than under the arm's length principle, there is a deviation from the reference system given that the safe harbour results in a more favourable treatment than under the main rule. For example, if certain manufacturers would normally be entitled under the arm's length principle to a net margin of 10% of their costs, but that under a safe harbour the net margin is set to 5% of the same costs, the safe harbour provides a benefit in the form of a tax saving. In this case, the generally formulated arm's length provision constitutes the main rule, and the safe harbour the exception, given the broad scope of the former, and the much narrower one of the latter.

Assuming that the advantageous safe harbour is granted only to certain undertakings, for example through an agreement provided on a case-by-case basis by the tax administration, there is no doubt that the safe harbour rule is prima facie selective, as it entails a more favourable treatment that is not available to all undertakings that are in a comparable situation, not even all the eligible ones. However, the question is raised whether the advantageous safe harbour necessarily entails a prima facie selective treatment if it is available to all eligible undertakings. In the example provided above, the safe harbour implying a lower remuneration for certain manufacturers may be available to all manufacturers having a given functional profile, i.e., the manufacturers performing certain functions, assuming certain risks, and using certain assets. Eventually, the favourable safe harbour results in two sets of rules being more or less favourable, but being available in parallel. A comparison could be made with two possible depreciation mechanisms for certain assets, one being more favourable than the other, but both being available. At first sight, if the favourable safe harbour is available to all undertakings that are eligible, there seems to be no prima facie selective treatment: the reference system includes both the generally formulated arm's length provision and the favourable safe harbour, and its general availability precludes any deviation from the reference system. However, the effect of the safe harbour is a potentially favourable treatment for certain categories of undertakings, i.e., the eligible undertakings, albeit with no distinction within this category: in the example above, the manufacturers that are eligible to the safe harbour benefit from a more favourable

---

593. *See* para. 4.126 of the 2017 OECD transfer pricing guidelines.

treatment than other undertakings that are not eligible to the safe harbour, such undertakings being taxed on the basis of an arm's length amount of income.

In my view, the case law of the CJEU points to the conclusion that such transfer pricing safe harbours are prima facie selective, because they deviate from the reference system in favour of certain types of undertakings: from a State aid perspective, the question raised is comparable to the rules analysed by the Court in cases such as *Adria-Wien* and *World Duty Free Group*, where advantageous rules benefitting certain industries (*Adria-Wien*) or certain operations (*World Duty Free Group*) were found selective. Only the extent of the deviation from the reference system could possibly save such advantageous safe harbours from being prima facie selective, assuming the deviation from the arm's length principle is not material,[594] as a consequence of the approximative nature of the arm's length principle.[595] Moreover, outside the field of taxes, the European Commission has developed methodologies the objective of which is to enforce market conditions, but that rely on approximations that are tolerated and considered to give a sufficient indication of being market oriented.[596]

The second way for a transfer pricing safe harbour to deviate from the arm's length principle is the case where the safe harbour rule results in a higher amount of income than what the arm's length principle prescribes. This leads to an overtaxation in the country providing the safe harbour rule, which the taxpayer may find worthwhile, for example to avoid a dispute with the tax administration. No advantage – in terms of taxes paid – is granted to the undertakings that rely on the safe harbour. The undertakings that do not rely on the safe harbour but on the generally formulated arm's length provision would, in contrast, be allocated a lower amount of income. The two categories of undertakings would thus be subject to a difference in treatment. A difference in treatment could also be created with independent enterprises and members of domestic group.

This raises the question of whether there is a deviation from the reference system that would imply prima facie selectivity, to the benefit of the undertakings that are not eligible to the safe harbour.

---

594. *See* European Commission, 'DG Competition Working Paper on State Aid and Tax Rulings' (2016) < http://ec.europa.eu/competition/state_aid/legislation/working_paper_tax_rulings. pdf > accessed 6 February 2018, para. 23. For that reason, the Commission mentioned that the State aid control of tax rulings should focus on 'cases where there is a manifest breach of the arm's length principle'.
595. *See* Commission Notice on the notion of State aid as referred to in Art. 107(1) of the Treaty on the Functioning of the European Union [2016] OJ C 262/1, para. 171 where the European Commission emphasised 'the uncertainty inherent' to the transfer pricing methods or the statistical tools employed for the 'approximation exercise' of the arm's length principle.
596. An example concerns State guarantees, for which the Commission in a notice from 2008 describes several criteria that, if they are followed, rule out the existence of State aid, but that do rely on concrete approximations of market conditions: *see* Commission Notice on the application of Arts 87 and 88 of the EC Treaty to State aid in the form of guarantees [2008] OJ C 155/10. This notice has been relied on by the Commission to allow certain Member States to enact methods that may, on a case-by-case basis, depart from market conditions, but that on an overall level provide sufficient certainty as to the implementation of market conditions (*see* e.g., Commission decision of 29 July 2016 in case State aid 45125 (2016/N) – Greece – methodology to calculate the aid element in State guarantees to companies [2016] OJ C 425/1).

Chapter 6: Prima Facie Selectivity of Transfer Pricing Safe Harbours

The determination of the undertakings benefitting from the favourable regime is less clear than in the case of transfer pricing safe harbours that are below the arm's length principle, because there is no particular category of undertakings that benefits from the more favourable treatment. However, the breadth of the selectivity concept in the case law of the CJEU points to the conclusion that tax systems including safe harbours that allocate a higher amount of income than the arm's length principle might be prima facie selective. I reach this conclusion on the basis of two alternative ways of reasoning. Under a first way of reasoning, if the reference system is made of the less favourable rule, then the application of the general arm's length provision would imply a deviation from the reference system. Arguments against the prima facie selectivity of the arm's length principle could be the high number of undertakings relying on that principle and the lack of precision in the determination of the beneficiaries of the measure, but both arguments have been rejected by the CJEU.[597] A similar conclusion would be reached under a second way of reasoning where it is assumed that each allocation method constitutes an independent reference system, the two systems resulting in different treatments that would breach the principle of non-discrimination: the existence of two parallel sets of rules with different outcomes would be inconsistent, and thus breach the principle of non-discrimination implied by the selectivity requirement. However, if one assumes the optional character of the safe harbour, i.e., if there is a possibility for all eligible undertakings to be taxed according to the generally formulated arm's length provision, the outcome is the lack of selective treatment given that all undertakings may benefit from the most advantageous taxation. Cases where the CJEU found that an option given to the taxpayer to alleviate a discriminatory tax treatment point to the same conclusion, although such cases have not been judged on the basis of the State aid rules.[598] A decision issued by the Commission with respect to a special regime for the taxation of undertakings involved in the wholesale of diamonds supports this view, as the regime provided a form of safe harbour that implied more certainty, but also a higher tax burden for most undertakings.[599]

The conclusion from the above analysis is that the prima facie selectivity test requires that transfer pricing safe harbours abide by the arm's length principle, in case they have been implemented in a tax system that includes, as a main allocation method, a generally formulated arm's length provision. If a transfer pricing safe

---

597. Indeed, the CJEU has consistently held that the number of undertakings benefitting from a measure does not preclude its selectivity (*see* e.g., Joined Cases C-20/15 P and C-21/15 P, *European Commission v. World Duty Free Group*, ECLI:EU:C:2016:981, para. 80). The *Gibraltar* case provides an example of this position, as the measure benefited almost all undertakings (28,798 of 29,000 companies: *see* Joined Cases C-106/09 P and C-107/09 P, *European Commission v. Government of Gibraltar*, ECLI:EU:C:2011:732, para. 55). Similarly, the Court does not define selectivity as a rule that necessarily identifies with precision the beneficiaries of an advantage, it is enough that a rule derogates from the reference system (*see* e.g., Joined Cases C-20/15 P and C-21/15 P, *European Commission v. World Duty Free Group*, ECLI:EU:C:2016:981, para. 71).
598. *See* for example the cases ruled with respect to the levy of exit taxes and the possibility to give taxpayers the option to spread the levy of the tax over several years: Case C-164/12, *DMC Beteiligungsgesellschaft mbH v. Finanzamt Hamburg-Mitte*, ECLI:EU:C:2014:20, para. 62.
599. *See* Commission Decision of 29 July 2016 on State Aid SA.42007 (2015/N) – Belgium Alternative income tax regime for the wholesale diamond sector [2016] OJ C 369/1.

harbour deviates from the arm's length principle in a manner that allocates a lower amount of income to the beneficiaries of the safe harbour, the safe harbour rule is likely to be prima facie selective, even if it is available to all eligible undertakings, no matter whether the comparison is made between different associated enterprises or between independent and associated enterprises. Transfer pricing safe harbours that imply a higher tax burden are also likely to be selective, unless an option is granted to be taxed under the generally formulated arm's length provision.

After considering transfer pricing safe harbours in the light of the de jure selectivity test, attention is paid to the de facto selectivity test.

6.3 DE FACTO SELECTIVITY

Following the de jure analysis, I now turn to the study of the potential de facto selectivity of transfer pricing safe harbours. It was mentioned above that two types of safe harbours are relevant to study in this book: those that implement the arm's length principle, and those that deviate from the principle. However, as it was found that transfer pricing safe harbours that deviate from the arm's length principle are most likely to be de jure selective, the study of de facto selectivity is of little relevance for these safe harbours.[600] Accordingly, the de facto selectivity test is carried out in this section only with respect to transfer pricing safe harbours that implement the arm's length principle.

The conclusions reached with respect to the potential de facto selectivity of a generally formulated arm's length provision do not apply similarly to safe harbours. It was concluded at section 5.3 that although the arm's length principle seems at first sight not to entail any risk of de facto selectivity (given the theoretical neutrality of this principle), a closer look at the rationale for the principle reveals selective aspects with respect to the importance given to the parameters chosen in the OECD transfer pricing guidelines, as well as the approximation of results for intercompany transactions with no direct benchmark provided by the open market. The first aspect, i.e., the parameters chosen in the guidelines to allocate the corporate tax base, applies both to a generally formulated arm's length provision and to transfer pricing safe harbours: in this respect, the fixed character of safe harbours does not change the need to rely on the economic characteristics of the parties to a transaction, this time with respect to the eligibility to the safe harbour, as well as to the determination of the profit levels applicable under the safe harbour. In contrast, a different conclusion is reached with respect to the second aspect that may trigger the de facto selectivity of a generally formulated arm's length provision: transfer pricing safe harbours would raise no issue with respect to the approximation of results, given that a safe harbour would normally provide the level of profits that should be earned for a given intercompany transaction:[601] the uncertainty would be eliminated by the fixed character of the safe harbour.

---

600. Indeed, the method that should first be used as part of the selectivity test is the investigation of the possible de jure selectivity of a State measure. As evidenced in the *Gibraltar* case, it is only if a measure is not de jure selective that the de facto selectivity concept is applied.
601. *See* e.g., para. 7.61 of the 2017 OECD transfer pricing guidelines.

Accordingly, the risk for de facto selectivity of transfer pricing safe harbours that implement the arm's length principle is lower than for a generally formulated arm's length provision, although it is not removed. At the same time, the scope of a transfer pricing safe harbour is necessarily narrower than that of a generally formulated arm's length provision: for many intercompany transactions, no transfer pricing safe harbour can be provided in the law, because transfer pricing safe harbours can only be implemented for the least complex types of intercompany transactions.[602] Consequently, the selectivity issues raised by a generally formulated arm's length provision would remain.

6.4 CONCLUSION

This chapter considered two types of transfer pricing safe harbours: those that implement the arm's length principle, and those that deviate from it. The former raises mostly the same issues with respect to the selectivity test as a generally formulated arm's length provision, whether it is de jure or de facto selectivity that is considered. The fixed nature of a safe harbour does not, as such, entail a selective treatment; to the contrary, it avoids the approximative nature of a generally formulated arm's length provision, and thus decreases the chances of being de facto selective. However, transfer pricing safe harbours that implement the arm's length principle have, by definition, only a limited scope of application.[603] Therefore, even if this allocation method is generally more in harmony with the selectivity test than a generally formulated arm's length provision, it cannot replace it, except in certain limited cases. When it comes to transfer pricing safe harbours that deviate from the arm's length principle, this allocation method appears clearly selective, unless the safe harbours imply a higher tax burden than the arm's length principle, and an option is given to the taxpayers to be taxed under the generally formulated arm's length provision.

The last allocation method to which the selectivity test is applied is a system of formula apportionment with firm-specific factors. It is the subject of the next chapter of this book.

---

602. *See* para. 4.129 of the 2017 OECD transfer pricing guidelines.
603. Indeed, transfer pricing safe harbours can reliably be applied only to intercompany transactions where one party performs relatively simple functions and where comparable independent transactions can be found on the open market, to provide an accurate benchmark of the effects of the market forces for such specific transactions. Examples of such intercompany transactions are low value-adding intra-group services (*see* paras 7.43 and following of the 2017 OECD transfer pricing guidelines), low risk manufacturing services, low risk distribution services, and low risk research and development services (*see* annex I to Chapter IV of the 2017 OECD transfer pricing guidelines).

CHAPTER 7
Prima Facie Selectivity of a System of Formula Apportionment with Firm-Specific Factors

7.1 INTRODUCTION

This chapter applies the selectivity test to a system of formula apportionment with firm-specific factors. Although it is unlikely that the Member States apply unilaterally a comprehensive system of formula apportionment instead of a generally formulated arm's length provision, they may very well apply a formula-based allocation method that does share certain similarities with a system of formula apportionment, such as the profit split method or hybrid methods that combine the arm's length principle with formulary features. In addition, as argued in section 1.2, it cannot be excluded that certain aspects of a CCCTB are subject to the rules on State aid, although taxation under harmonised rules would most likely be an action attributable to the Union, thereby excluding the applicability of State aid law.

To start with, contrary to a generally formulated arm's length provision, but similarly to transfer pricing safe harbours, a system of formula apportionment with firm-specific factors does not raise major issues of principle with respect to the application of this allocation method. This is because of the pre-determined nature of as system of formula apportionment, which, as safe harbours, has a rather mechanistic application. In contrast, I analysed at section 5.4 above some of the aspects of the application of the arm's length principle that do raise difficult issues, these being due to the abstract and approximative nature of the arm's length principle. Accordingly, this chapter studies only the prima facie selectivity of a system of formula apportionment with firm-specific factors from the perspective of the design (de jure selectivity) as well as the effects (de facto selectivity) of the law. Other potential issues of State aid law relating to a system of formula apportionment are not in the scope of this chapter.[604]

Before delving into the selectivity test of a system of formula apportionment with firm-specific factors, it is important to place this test in relation to the other steps of the methodology to conduct a selectivity analysis, in particular the determination of the reference system and of the right comparator. Indeed, the selectivity test leads to clearly different outcomes, depending on which reference system is chosen, and which comparator is relied on. This is because a system of formula apportionment is fundamentally different from the taxation of independent enterprises and members of domestic groups. If, contrary to what I concluded in Chapters 2 and 4 above, the reference system is made of the sole allocation method (here, a system of formula apportionment), or if the right comparison is between members of multinational enterprises, then no comparison would be made with independent enterprises or members of domestic groups; although different systems of taxation would apply to these categories of undertakings, these differences would not be in the scope of the selectivity test. Accordingly, the selectivity test would be limited to the system of formula apportionment. Under these assumptions, prima facie selectivity could still be at hand, for example if different formulas apply to different undertakings (de jure selectivity), or as a consequence of the effects of the system of formula apportionment (de facto selectivity).[605] If in contrast, as it is suggested in Chapters 2 and 4 of this book, the reference system should consist of the whole corporate income tax system and the comparison should be between independent and associated enterprises, a clear difference in treatment would appear between these categories of undertakings as a consequence of the design of the law, and this difference would be included in the scope of the selectivity test.

In this chapter, I will take into account the different alternatives described above. This chapter is structured as follows. I will begin by studying in section 7.2 prima facie selectivity with respect to the design of the law, i.e., de jure selectivity. This question is mostly relevant if the reference system is made of the whole corporate income tax system, and assuming that the comparison is between members of multinational enterprises and independent enterprises or members of domestic groups. I will then turn in section 7.3 to the analysis of the effects of the law, i.e., de facto selectivity. This second question is mostly relevant in case the reference system is made of the sole allocation method, or if the comparison is between members of multinational enterprises. The conclusions of this chapter are presented in section 7.4.

---

604. For example, how to consolidate income is not considered in this chapter.
605. It is recalled here that other aspects of an allocation method than the sharing mechanism are excluded from the scope of this study. A system of formula apportionment may indeed have other de jure selective features, such as limitations to the eligibility to this system of taxation.

7.2 DE JURE SELECTIVITY

In this section I will analyse the de jure selectivity of a system of formula apportionment with firm-specific factors. I will start by considering, as assumptions, the findings of Chapters 2 and 4 of this book. I will then turn to the opposite assumptions.

Based on the reference system identified in Chapter 2, and assuming that the right comparator is between members of multinational enterprises and independent enterprises or domestic groups, a clear difference in treatment is created by a system of formula apportionment, as the formula applies only to members of multinational enterprises. This difference in treatment has been described by Weiner and Mintz as 'capital import non-neutrality'.[606] Independent enterprises and members of domestic groups would be taxed on the basis of the general corporate income tax system, whereas members of multinational enterprises would be taxed on the income allocated on the basis of the formula. Therefore, under these assumptions a system of formula apportionment with firm-specific factors is certainly prima facie de jure selective, as it creates a difference in treatment that stems from the design of the law.

If the reference system consists of the allocation method (here, a system of formula apportionment), or if the right comparator is between different multinational enterprises, a system of formula apportionment with firm-specific factors would not be per definition selective, as opposed to the situation discussed above. As the comparison is between different associated enterprises members of multinational groups, the de jure selectivity test will depend on the content of the system of formula apportionment. There are two main situations: either a system of formula apportionment has a single formula, or is has several. If the same formula applies to all undertakings (i.e., all associated enterprises members of multinational groups), no de jure selectivity is at hand from the perspective of the sharing mechanism, because the law implies the same treatment for all comparable undertakings.[607] If, in contrast, different formulas are used, a difference in treatment is created between the various undertakings to which the system applies. The question is particularly relevant with respect to industry-specific formulas. From an economic point of view, as well as from a general equality perspective, there may be convincing reasons for having different allocation keys:[608] as stressed by Weiner, '(a)pplying the same formula to all industries can create distortions

---

606. *See* Joann Martens Weiner and Jack Mintz, 'An Exploration of Formula Apportionment in the European Union' (2002) 42 European Taxation 346, 348.
607. Selectivity could nevertheless be at hand if the system's effects favour certain undertakings: *see* the de facto selectivity test at section 7.3 below.
608. For an overview of industry-specific formulas *see* Joann Martens-Weiner, *Company Tax Reform in the European Union: Guidance from the United States and Canada on Implementing Formulary Apportionment in the EU* (Springer 2006) 55–57. *See also* para. D193 of the 2017 UN transfer pricing manual, where it is mentioned that '(i)f a country opts for the application of different margins these may be established at different levels of specificity. In other words, such margins could be determined by economic sector (e.g., the primary sector, i.e., the extraction or production of raw materials; secondary sectors such as manufacturing; and tertiary sectors such as services). A country may differentiate further, so that the margins could be determined by line of business at different levels of specificity according to the necessity and ability of a country to determine them'.

and perceptions of unfairness'.[609] For instance, for a company that transports persons or goods across the borders, the apportionment factors may be located in the country of origin, while the value it creates is partly due to the possibility to travel through other countries where no assets, sales, or employees are located. There are examples where systems of formula apportionment have been completed by industry-specific factors limited to certain industries. An illustration is provided by the exception to the main formula for the taxation of banks in Canada: while the normal formula implies to share income based on 'gross revenue' and 'salaries and wages', the law applies a formula that allocates the income of banks based on 'salaries and wages', as well as 'loans and deposits'.[610] It can also be mentioned that industry-specific apportionment factors are suggested in the 2016 proposal for a CCCTB: exceptions to the main apportionment method are suggested for financial institutions, insurance companies, companies involved in the exploration or production of oil or gas, as well as the operation of ships or aircraft in international traffic or the operation of boats engaged in inland waterways transport.[611]

However, even if it may be economically motivated to apply different formulas to various industries, a system with industry-specific formulas would most probably be prima facie de jure selective, since a clear difference in treatment would stem from the design of the law. Industry-specific formulas could constitute a means to favour certain undertakings or industries through tax subsidies. Despite the fact that the Commission's practice has sometimes paid attention to the particularities of different sectors of the economy,[612] the case law of the Union courts has most often found tax measures in favour of a given industry to be selective.[613] For example, the *Adria-Wien* case clearly precludes the Member States from granting advantages to undertakings that are pursuing certain specific activities. I also find support for this conclusion in the *Fineco* case, where the General Court found a measure limited to specialised investment vehicles to be selective because their shareholders could benefit from more favourable investment conditions,[614] or in the *World Duty Free Group*, where an advantageous treatment given to undertakings that invest in non-resident companies was found by the CJEU in breach of the State aid rules.

---

609. *See* Joann Martens Weiner, 'The European Union and Formula Apportionment: Caveat Emptor' (2001) 41 European Taxation 381.
610. *See* e.g., section 404(1) of the Canadian Income Tax Regulations < http://www.laws-lois.justice.gc.ca/eng/regulations/C.R.C.,_c._945/page-20.html#h-69 > accessed 20 January 2018.
611. *See* European Commission, 'Proposal for a Council Directive on a Common Consolidated Corporate Tax Base (CCCTB)' COM(2016) 683 final, Arts 40–43.
612. In this respect, Lovdahl Gormsen recalls examples where the Commission in State aid cases paid attention to the particularities of the banking, agricultural, or environmental sectors: *see* Liza Lovdahl Gormsen, 'EU State Aid Law and Transfer Pricing: A Critical Introduction to a New Saga' (2016) 7 Journal of European Competition Law & Practice 369, 378 (with references to the European Commission's decisions at footnote 89).
613. *See* Conor Quigley, 'Direct Taxation and State Aid: Recent Developments Concerning the Notion of Selectivity' (2012) 40 Intertax 112, 114.
614. *See* Case T-445/05, *Associazione italiana del risparmio gestito and Fineco Asset Management SpA v. Commission of the European Communities*, ECLI:EU:T:2009:50.

To conclude, the preliminary steps of the selectivity analysis are decisive when it comes to the potential de jure selectivity of a system of formula apportionment. If the reference system consists of the whole corporate income tax system and the comparison is between independent and associated enterprises, a system of formula apportionment is most probably prima facie de jure selective. In contrast, if the reference system is made of the sole allocation method, or if the right comparison is between members of multinational enterprises, de jure selectivity will depend on the design of the formula: with a single formula, no selectivity is created by the design of the law; on the other hand, different formulas would entail a difference in treatment that stems from the law, thus making the system of formula apportionment prima facie de jure selective.

After considering the de jure selectivity test of a system of formula apportionment with firm-specific factors, attention is now paid to the de facto selectivity test.

7.3 DE FACTO SELECTIVITY

7.3.1 Introduction

As emphasised above, if the reference system is made solely of an allocation method, or if multinational enterprises are not deemed to be in a comparable situation to independent enterprises or to domestic groups, the selectivity test should be carried out between members of multinational enterprises: State aid law would then require different members of multinational enterprises to be treated alike. If a system of formula apportionment with firm-specific factors has a single formula, such an allocation method seems, at first sight, to qualify for a general measure, because there is no difference in treatment that stems from the law. The CJEU has also stated that 'in the absence of European Union rules governing the matter, it falls within the competence of the Member States (…) to designate bases of assessment and to spread the tax burden across the different factors of production and economic sectors';[615] this sentence seems to imply that the elements of a formula cannot imply a selective treatment. However, as evidenced by the *Gibraltar* case, even non-discriminatory measures may produce a selective effect if, in practice, they treat differently various undertakings that are in a comparable situation. Therefore, a system of formula apportionment with firm-specific factors may not, from the outset, escape the de facto selectivity test.

The main purpose of this section is to apply the de facto selectivity test to a system of formula apportionment that relies on an allocation key based on firm-specific factors. Other types of formulas, such as formulas based on macro-economic parameters or industry-specific data are not considered in this book; formulas of this kind have not been introduced in federal systems, and seem unlikely with no harmonised

---

615. *See* Joined Cases C-106/09 P and C-107/09 P, *European Commission v. Government of Gibraltar*, ECLI:EU:C:2011:732, para. 97, which confirmed the finding of the General Court (*see* Joined Cases T-211/04 and T-215/04, *Government of Gibraltar*, ECLI:EU:T:2008:595, para. 146).

rules, since a State would probably not be willing to unilaterally introduce an allocation method that has no connection with the source[616] of income.[617] This section may also contribute incidentally to the study of the de facto selectivity test of other allocation methods that apportion profits on the basis of a formula, such as the profit split method,[618] a combination of the arm's length principle and formula apportionment (i.e., so-called hybrid systems),[619] or the attribution of profits to permanent establishments.[620]

The first question studied in this section is whether a formula-based allocation method with firm-specific apportionment factors is likely to be a general measure, or if it may be de facto selective based on the study of the apportionment factors sales, tangible assets and labour (section 7.3.2). It is concluded that a system of formula apportionment with firm-specific factors has direct and different effects on different undertakings, mostly due to the location of the apportionment factors, and the direct or indirect use of the factors. This gives a system of formula apportionment with firm-specific factors an intrinsically, de facto selective nature. In order to better

---

616. Indeed, firm-specific factors are meant to have a connection with the source of income, although, as discussed later in this book, that connection is weaker than under the arm's length principle. In contrast, formulas that would share income based on macro-economic parameters or industry-specific data have no connection to the source of income. On the definition of the concept of source, *see* Porus F. Kaka, 'Source Taxation: Do We Really Know What We Mean?' (2017) 86 Tax Notes International 1221, with further references.
617. *See* European Commission, 'Company Taxation in the Internal Market' COM(2001)582 final 414–415, where the Commission mentions the national VAT base or the gross domestic product as possible allocation keys that apply at a macroeconomic level. As emphasised by Weiner, 'the apportionment formula does not need to follow the traditional practice of reflecting the characteristics of the company. The EU Member States may decide to distribute income using macroeconomic factors, such as per capita national income, or according to industry average factor ratios rather than according to firm-specific factors': *see* Joann Martens Weiner, *Company Tax Reform in the European Union: Guidance from the United States and Canada on Implementing Formulary Apportionment in the EU* (Springer 2006) 46. However, both the European Commission and Weiner conclude that macroeconomic formulas are not a realistic option within the European Union. Weiner emphasises that the Member States are likely to favour a formula based on firm-specific factors, as the connection such factors create with the source of income makes it more politically acceptable.
618. Although differences exist between a system of formula apportionment and the profit split method (e.g., the predetermined or flexible character of these allocation methods, or the determination of the profit that is being split), the latter allocation method may be based on apportionment factors that produce results that are comparable to those reached under the former, especially in situations where the arm's length principle is incapable of allocating profits that are in excess of the sum of the routine profits of the group members: *see* Reuven Avi-Yonah and Zachée Pouga Tinhaga, 'Unitary Taxation and International Tax Rules' (2014) 26 ICTD Working Paper < https://papers.ssrn.com/sol3/Delivery.cfm/SSRN_ID2602240_code 572410.pdf?abstractid=2351920&mirid=1 > accessed 6 February 2018, who at 7 consider that 'in the absence of comparables the result reached under [unitary taxation] is equivalent to what could be reached under [separate accounting]'. Similarly *see also* Giammarco Cottani, 'Formulary Apportionment: A Revamp in the Post-Base Erosion and Profit Shifting Era?' (2016) 44 Intertax 755, 758.
619. *See* Yariv Brauner, 'Formula Based Transfer Pricing' (2014) 42 Intertax 615, 621.
620. This concerns primarily tax treaties that do not implement the authorised OECD approach. In this respect, *see* Art. 7(4) of the OECD Model Tax Convention up to the 2008 update, as well as Art. 7(4) of the UN Model Tax Convention: profits may be apportioned to a permanent establishment if it has been a 'customary' method within an enterprise, and as long as this is done in accordance with the separate entity approach.

understand what creates a de facto selective effect, it is then analysed what parameters in the design of a formula-based allocation method may influence the de facto selectivity test (section 7.3.3). The reason for including such a section is that there is no international standard for a system of formula apportionment with firm-specific factors, as opposed to the well-developed and acknowledged OECD transfer pricing guidelines. There is, accordingly, a need for research on the consequences of the selectivity test on the apportionment factors of a formula-based allocation method. The conclusions are presented in section 7.4.

7.3.2 Is a System of Formula Apportionment with Firm-Specific Factors a General or a Selective Measure?

Assuming that a formula-based allocation method with firm-specific apportionment factors does not distinguish between different undertakings on the basis of their size, location, industry, profitability, or any other specific criteria, but applies indistinctly to all undertakings, such a method would at first sight appear general.[621] The apportionment factors could be compared to substantive rules that apply similarly to all undertakings, as opposed to rules that are the consequence of a particular choice.[622] The scope of a system of formula apportionment is, accordingly, quite broad. This seems to indicate that a formula-based allocation method with firm-specific apportionment factors that do not explicitly distinguish between different undertakings is a general measure.

However, the case law of the CJEU points to a different conclusion. Measures that are restricted to certain operations, but that are in principle available to all undertakings, have been found selective, as illustrated by the *World Duty Free Group* case. Moreover, certain tax measures that are not restricted to certain operations and that are explicitly available to all undertakings may be selective as well, if their effects are to favour certain undertakings, as illustrated by the *Gibraltar* case. In my view, it is clear that a system of formula apportionment with firm-specific factors may potentially have de facto selective effects, for the reason that the elements of the formula are directly connected to the features of certain undertakings, and thus produce different effects for different undertakings. It is true that firm-specific factors may not be related to certain types of undertakings or operations as such, (as opposed to the *World Duty Free Group*

---

621. *See* e.g., European Commission, 'Communication from the Commission to the Council, the European Parliament and the European Economic and Social Committee – Towards a more effective use of tax incentives in favour of R&D' COM(2006) 728 final, where the Commission at para. 1.2 considered that 'In most cases, R&D tax incentives that are open to all firms irrespective of size, sector or location are considered to be general measures.' Similarly, *see* Commission notice on the application of the State aid rules to measures relating to direct business taxation [1998] OJ C 384/3, para. 14.
622. This argument is, convincingly in my view, raised by Nicolaides who stressed that the CJEU in *World Duty Free Group* found the Spanish measure selective, although it applied as a consequence of the choice of a company. Nicolaides argues that different effects or consequences are the natural outcome of any general measure that is open to all companies, but is not voluntarily chosen by all companies: *see* Phedon Nicolaides, 'Excessive Widening of the Concept of Selectivity' (2017) 16 European State Aid Law Quarterly 62, 65.

case where a given category of operations – investments in non-resident companies – could be identified), if one chooses apportionment factors that most undertakings are likely to have, such as sales, labour, or tangible assets. Nevertheless, an allocation of the tax base that depends on the characteristics and the organisation of the undertakings does produce different effects that vary with such characteristics and organisation: as emphasised by McLure, when the apportionment factors are firm-specific, the system of formula apportionment results in a direct tax on the apportionment factors.[623] A system of formula apportionment could be compared to the combination of a property tax (if the formula includes the assets factor), social contributions or taxes on wages (if the formula includes the payroll factor), and a sales tax (if the formula includes the sales factor).

From a competition perspective there is not necessarily a fundamental difference between an income tax computed on the basis of a formula that includes these elements, and the levy of other taxes, not labelled as income taxes, but the amount of which is connected to the same type of elements. A system of formula apportionment with firm-specific apportionment factors may also interfere with the international allocation of resources between the Member States. In addition, empirical evidence seems to show that the choice and the weight of the apportionment factors does exercise an influence on investment decisions, something that strengthens the conclusion that a system of formula apportionment with firm-specific factors is likely to be prima facie de facto selective.[624] Finally, while it may be argued that the measure at hand in *World Duty Free Group* was the consequence of a choice that should come with certain consequences,[625] the association between companies resident of different countries is not a business operation. It is rather a choice to carry out operations within a multinational group, and this choice is more an organisational one than a business operation such as buying or selling shares; a company is not likely to regularly set up a foreign subsidiary and terminate its activities, while it is more likely to buy and sell shares as portfolio investments. Undertakings would more easily avoid being discriminated against with tax rules that relate to their business operations, than to their organisation.

Accordingly, at first glance a formula-based allocation method with firm-specific apportionment factors is a prima facie selective measure, because it is likely to produce different effects on different undertakings. This preliminary conclusion is analysed in more details below, in the light of the firm-specific apportionment factors that are most likely to be used by the Member States as part of a system of formula apportionment, namely sales (section 7.3.2.1), tangible assets (section 7.3.2.2), and labour (section

---

623. *See* Charles E. McLure, 'The State Corporate Income Tax: Lambs in Wolves Clothing' in Henry J. Aaron and Michael J. Boskin (eds), *The Economics of Taxation* (Brookings Institution 1980) 327.
624. *See* Joann Martens-Weiner, *Company Tax Reform in the European Union: Guidance from the United States and Canada on Implementing Formulary Apportionment in the EU* (Springer 2006) 95–98.
625. *See* Phedon Nicolaides, 'Excessive Widening of the Concept of Selectivity' (2017) 16 European State Aid Law Quarterly 62, 65.

7.3.2.3). I choose to study these apportionment factors as they are included in the proposal for a CCCTB,[626] and are used, partly or wholly, at the subnational level in the US and in Canada.[627]

7.3.2.1 The Sales Factor

The first apportionment factor studied is the sales factor. Here, I assume that the Member States rely on the concept of sales by destination.[628] Sales by destination shares the consolidated income of a multinational enterprise on the basis of the countries in which goods or services are sold to the end-customer. Here, two main alternatives exist to measure the sales, with varying impact on the de facto selectivity analysis. If intragroup sales are accounted for, then the multinational enterprise may influence how the total sales are shared between different countries, thus also influencing the allocation of the corporate tax base.[629] In contrast, if – as suggested in the CCCTB proposal[630] – intragroup sales are excluded from the computation of the total sales, it is only the sales made to the end-customers that will impact how the corporate tax base is allocated among the various countries. This last alternative has the advantage of being subject to the market forces, as it is eventually the final

---

626. *See* European Commission, 'Proposal for a Council Directive on a Common Consolidated Corporate Tax Base (CCCTB)' COM(2016) 683 final, Art. 28.
627. In the United States, different states have different formulas. For an overview of such formulas *see* the information compiled by the Federation of Tax Administrators < https://www.taxadmin.org/assets/docs/Research/Rates/apport.pdf > accessed 20 January 2018. Over time, a trend can be observed whereby States have been giving more weight to the sales factor, which observers find not to be motivated by the objective to increase tax revenues, but rather to promote a business-friendly corporate income tax. In Canada, a single formula applies, subject to certain exceptions: *see* section 402(3)(a) of the Canadian Income Tax Regulations (< http://www.laws-lois.justice.gc.ca/eng/regulations/C.R.C.,_c._945/page-19.html#h-66 > accessed 20 January 2018); according to this provision, the main rule for the allocation of income among the Canadian provinces consists in sharing (with equal weight) the income in proportion to the 'gross revenue' and the 'salaries and wages' in each province.
628. The concept of sales by destination is relied on in the proposal for a common consolidated corporate tax base. The main conceptual reason for using sales by destination, as opposed to sales by origin, is to spread the tax burden between origin (where capital and labour are mostly located) and destination (where the sales eventually take place thanks to the demand of final customers). In this respect, the Commission considers that '(t)he role of a sales factor in the formula is to represent the demand side in the generation of income and for that it has to be measured at destination' (European Commission, 'CCCTB: possible elements of the sharing mechanism' (2007) CCCTB/WP060\doc\en, para. 46). However, in the United States the use of sales by destination is only the main rule and there are exceptions, mainly due to the complexity of this concept. Among various issues, the location of the place of destination may be a complex matter. For a description of the concept of sales by destination in the context of formula apportionment, *see* European Commission, 'Proposal for a Council Directive on a Common Consolidated Corporate Tax Base (CCCTB)' COM(2016) 683 final, Art. 38.
629. For instance, by establishing a company in a country that owns goods and controls the most important parts of the logistics process, a share of the corporate tax base (the share that corresponds to the income earned through the functions performed by the employees of this logistics company) would be allocated to this country, depending on the levels of the transfer prices and the sales made in other countries.
630. *See* European Commission, 'Proposal for a Council Directive on a Common Consolidated Corporate Tax Base (CCCTB)' COM(2016) 683 final, Art. 37.

customers that decide the amount and location of the sales. At the same time, the sales at destination factor is not free from potential manipulations that would have an effect on the allocation of the corporate tax base, particularly through the choice between intragroup or outsourced sales activities, or the decision about where to pass the property to the customer.[631]

From a State aid perspective, it is clear that the problem with the sales by destination factor, after deduction of intragroup sales, is that only domestic sales create a tax liability, not foreign sales. This constitutes an advantage for exporting companies, as opposed to companies with domestic sales which are fully liable to tax in their State of residence on the profits from such sales.[632] To illustrate the advantage given to exporting companies, McLure and Hellerstein emphasise, taking the example of a manufacturing company with no assets or labour abroad that exports all its production, that 'under the equally weighted three-factor formula, if the corporation exported all its output, it would pay state tax on two third of its profits; under the formula that double-weights sales, it would pay state tax on half of its profits. By comparison, under sales-only apportionment, it would pay no state tax, if it exported all its output'.[633] In contrast, no matter which factors the formula includes and how they are weighted, these authors stress that 'the corporation would pay state tax on all its income, if it exported none of its output'.[634] In other words, the sales factor gives an advantageous treatment that is limited to companies that sell abroad. There are other reasons to believe that the sales factor is de facto selective: for example, exporting companies that outsource their sales to foreign related distributors would be disadvantaged in their country of origin compared to those that sell to foreign unrelated distributors or to end-customers, since the effect of sales by destination and of the exclusion of intragroup sales from the profit apportionment is the exemption from tax of the profits made on sales to unrelated distributors or to end-customers.

---

631. In this respect *see* J. Clifton Fleming Jr., Robert J. Peroni and Stephen E. Shay, 'Formulary Appointment in the U.S. International Income Tax System: Putting Lipstick on a Pig?' (2014) 36 Michigan Journal of International Law 1, 40.
632. Although trade law is not in the scope of this book, it can simply be observed that a comparable reasoning is found in the decision of the appellate body of the World Trade Organisation, according to which a US rule exempting foreign income was considered to be a prohibited export subsidy: *see* Report of the Appellate Body, 'United States – Tax Treatment for "Foreign Sales Corporations" – Recourse to Article 21.5 of the DSU by the European Communities' (2002) WT/DS108/AB/RW. For an analysis of this issue *see* Wolfgang Schön, 'Destination-Based Income Taxation and WTO Law: A Note' in Heike Jochum, Peter Essers, Michael Lang, Norbert Winkeljohann, and Bertil Wiman (eds), *Practical Problems in European and International Tax Law – Essays in Honour of Manfred Mössner* (IBFD 2016) 429; Charles E. McLure Jr. and Walter Hellerstein, 'Does Sales-Only Apportionment Of Corporate Income Violate International Trade Rules?' (2002) 96 Tax Notes International 1315. These two contributions to the doctrine reach different conclusions on the compatibility with international trade law of rules that allocate income to the country of destination.
633. *See* Charles E. McLure Jr. and Walter Hellerstein, 'Does Sales-Only Apportionment of Corporate Income Violate International Trade Rules?' (2002) 96 Tax Notes International 1315, 1318.
634. *Ibid.*

Consequently, assuming that the companies to which the sales factor applies to different extents are in a comparable situation,[635] the sales factor appears as de facto selective. One argument that speaks for the sales factor to be a general measure is the resemblance of this allocation method to a tax system based on a territorial approach, under which only domestic income is subject to tax: it has been suggested that the exemption of foreign income does not breach the State aid rules, at least when it is not introduced as an exception from a system of worldwide taxation, but constitutes the main rule.[636] However, the position taken by the CJEU in the *World Duty Free Group* case points clearly to the sales factor being selective: a rule that was generally designed but that favoured companies exporting capital through making foreign acquisitions – as opposed to domestic acquisitions – was found selective. The Court also made clear that a measure providing a tax advantage only to undertakings engaged in export activities and carrying out certain investment transactions abroad was selective.[637]

In the light of the foregoing, I conclude that sales by destination as an apportionment factor implies a prima facie de facto selective treatment. I will consider below the assets factor.

7.3.2.2 *The Assets Factor*

The second apportionment factor studied in this section is the assets factor. It is assumed that the assets factor does not include intangible, financial and current assets,[638] as observed in the proposal for a CCCTB and some of the formula apportionment systems used at subnational level in the US.[639] Here, it is assumed that the assets factor includes only tangible assets.

Similarly to the sales factor, the assets factor functions as a direct tax on an element that distinguishes between different undertakings, this time depending on their ownership of assets. In my view, there are multiple reasons for the assets factor to entail a risk of being de facto selective. One reason is that an asset factor that includes tangible assets implies a disadvantage for companies with business activities that rely on such assets, as opposed to undertakings that rely mostly on other types of assets. In view of the *Adria-Wien* case, the tax relief provided to companies that use other than tangible assets is likely to make the tax measure prima facie selective,

---

635. The CJEU seems to find exporting and non-exporting companies to be in a comparable situation, as it did not exclude their comparability in the *World Duty Free Group* case.
636. See e.g., António Carlos Dos Santos, *L'Union européenne et la régulation de la concurrence fiscale* (Bruylant 2009) 464.
637. *See* Joined Cases C-20/15 P and C-21/15 P, *European Commission v. World Duty Free Group*, ECLI:EU:C:2016:981. *See also* Joined Cases 6/69 and 11/69, *Commission of the European Communities v. French Republic*, ECLI:EU:C:1969:68, paras 20 and 21.
638. This does not mean that the profits that are generated by other than tangible assets are not subject to tax, they are just not taken into account for the purpose of sharing the profits. In this respect *see* Reuven S. Avi-Yonah, 'Between Formulary Apportionment and the OECD Guidelines: A Proposal for Reconciliation' (2010) 2 World Tax Journal 3, 11, footnote 25: 'any formula that "ignores" intangibles in fact assigns their value to the entire MNE (divided based on the other factors used in the formula)'.
639. The formula used by the Canadian provinces does not include the asset factor.

especially since the undertakings that receive different treatments do not need to be competitors for selectivity to be at hand. An example of difference in treatment is the application of the assets factor to banks and factories: while banks mostly own financial assets, factories would typically own substantial tangible assets, possibly on the top of manufacturing intangibles. The effect of the formula would be to favour banks, as the formula would not allocate income to banks as a consequence of the ownership of financial assets.

To name some other reasons for which the assets factor is likely to entail a selective treatment, there would probably be a difference in treatment between undertakings that have a different use of various assets: for example, two competitors could decide to invest differently, one in owned assets and the other in leased assets. Two competitors could also decide to perform an in-house or an outsourced activity, with different effects of the assets factor on the allocation of the corporate tax base. Similarly, companies with a domestic or foreign use of tangible assets (e.g., domestic or foreign manufacturing) would receive a different treatment, as an advantage would be given to companies with tangible assets located abroad.

To sum up, the effects of the assets factor are most likely to imply a selective treatment, similarly to the sales factor. The last apportionment factor that is considered in this section is the labour factor.

7.3.2.3 *The Labour Factor*

Labour is a firm-specific factor that, as the sales and assets factors, is closely linked to the characteristics of different undertakings. Therefore, it carries the risk, as such, of being de facto selective. I will consider the potential de facto selectivity of the labour factor in more details below.

The labour factor would typically build on the cost of the people employed by a firm, the number of employees, or a combination of the two, as suggested in the proposal for a CCCTB.[640] No matter what content is given to the labour factor, it will necessarily favour certain undertakings, to the detriment of others. If one first considers the cost of the employees, the effect of that factor is that the allocation of the corporate tax base will vary with the levels of wages and of the other compensations paid to the employees. This factor is thus likely to favour companies with lower levels of wages (e.g., because they have less educated staff), as opposed to undertakings with higher levels of wages. If one now focuses on the number of employees, that factor would clearly advantage undertakings with relatively fewer employees in one country (e.g., the more productive undertakings), than comparable undertakings with more employees, as the tax burden in that country would increase with the number of employees. Taking into account the number of employees would also treat differently undertakings depending on whether or not they outsource tasks or perform them in-house.

---

640. *See* European Commission, 'Proposal for a Council Directive on a Common Consolidated Corporate Tax Base (CCCTB)' COM(2016) 683 final, Art. 32.

Chapter 7: Prima Facie Selectivity of FA

Consequently, the labour factor entails a de facto selective treatment. It will especially, as for sales and tangible assets, create a difference in treatment to the detriment of undertakings with domestic activities, because undertakings with foreign activities would be exempt from tax on the profits generated by the apportionment factors located abroad.

After having analysed the potential de facto selectivity of the three apportionment factors, the conclusions from section 7.3.2 are presented below.

7.3.2.4 Conclusion

It was demonstrated above that a system of formula apportionment with firm-specific factors has direct and different effects on different undertakings, mostly due to the location of the apportionment factors (the factors are located domestically or abroad), and the direct or indirect use of the factors (i.e., in-house or outsourced). This gives a system of formula apportionment with firm-specific factors an intrinsically, de facto selective nature. The obvious de facto selective nature of a system of formula apportionment is also due to the national perspective of the selectivity test, since differences in treatment are considered at a domestic level, as opposed to a cross-border level.

This conclusion may, however, appear inconsistent with other areas of application of State aid law, if one is disregarding the way the tax is categorised in a given tax system: assuming a system of formula apportionment is categorised as a direct tax on the apportionment factors, as opposed to an income tax, the advantage given to undertakings with a relatively lower representation of certain apportionment factors may not necessarily entail de facto selectivity. Indeed, the existence of taxes on certain specific factors such as assets[641] or sales[642] has, in certain cases, been accepted by the CJEU or by the European Commission, despite the different and direct effects on different undertakings. It has also been argued in the doctrine that the CJEU may have ruled differently in the *Gibraltar* case, if the tax system did not intend at implementing an income tax.[643] Accordingly, these arguments point to the idea that the de facto

---

641. *See* e.g., Case C-522/13, *Ministerio de Defensa and Navantia SA v. Concello de Ferrol*, ECLI:EU:C:2014:2262.
642. *See* e.g., a decision on advertising taxes: Commission Decision (EU) 2017/329 of 4 November 2016 on the measure SA.39235 (2015/C) (ex 2015/NN) implemented by Hungary on the taxation of advertisement turnover [2017] OJ L 49/36.
643. *See* Raymond Luja, 'Material Selectivity after Gibraltar' in Dennis Weber (ed), *EU Income Tax Law – Issues for the Years Ahead* (IBFD 2013) 115. The general objective to subject all companies to a tax on income might have influenced what the CJEU considered was a normal tax, the amount of which is related to the income earned by the taxpayers, not their physical presence per se. Against this background, the fact that 99% of the companies were exempted from the tax as a consequence of the factors creating the tax liability may have played a role in finding the regime de facto selective. If the Government of Gibraltar did not intend to tax companies on their income, but to simply levy a fixed fee on the number of employees and on the surface of the business property occupied, the Court may have reasoned differently.

selectivity of firm-specific apportionment factors might be increased by the sole fact that a system of formula apportionment is formally part of a corporate income tax system.

After studying whether a formula-based allocation method with firm-specific apportionment factors is likely to be a general measure or if it may be de facto selective, I will now consider the parameters of a system of formula apportionment that may influence the de facto selectivity test.

7.3.3 The Parameters of a System of Formula Apportionment That May Influence the De Facto Selectivity Test

Given the lack of international standard for a system of formula apportionment with firm-specific factors, there is a need for research on the different parameters of a formula-based allocation method that may influence the de facto selectivity test. Moreover, a system of formula apportionment gives room for flexibility as part of the design of such an allocation method, something that motivates the investigation of different options for the determination of the elements of a formula-based allocation method. In my view, there are three aspects that may come into play in the de facto selectivity test of a system of formula apportionment with firm-specific factors: the number and the spread of the apportionment factors (section 7.3.3.1), the connection of the apportionment factors to the concept of income (section 7.3.3.2), and the connection of the apportionment factors to the market forces (section 7.3.3.3). These parameters may influence the prima facie selectivity analysis, or serve as justifications for prima facie selective measures.[644]

7.3.3.1 *Number and Spread of the Apportionment Factors*

Does the number of apportionment factors influence the likelihood of a system of formula apportionment to be de facto selective? In my view, there may be a link between the two, without however such a link being necessarily decisive on the outcome of the de facto selectivity test. I believe that choosing a single-factor formula – as for example observed at subnational level in the US – carries a higher risk of being de facto selective than a formula based on several factors, because it makes it easier to target certain undertakings (or categories of undertakings) for which the factor is more or less represented. The European Commission has expressed the same view in the preparatory works to the CCCTB.[645] For instance, a formula based solely on sales, as used at the subnational level in the US by certain states like California or Michigan, is likely to result in favouring undertakings that are exporting goods or services: whereas

---

644. The justification analysis is the subject of Chapter 8 of the book.
645. *See* European Commission, 'CCCTB: possible elements of the sharing mechanism' (2007) CCCTB/WP060\doc\en, para. 10: 'If a formula consists of three or more factors the relocation of one unit of one of these factors would shift less than one unit of the tax base'. Accordingly, the more factors are included in the formula, the lower is the risk for a selective effect on certain undertakings.

companies selling on the domestic market will have all their income subject to tax in the country of origin, companies selling abroad will be exempt from tax to the extent of their foreign sales, thus receiving an advantage that is not available to undertakings that do not export. In this respect, it can be observed that the US Supreme Court did find a distortive effect for an allocation key including only one apportionment factor (tangible property), with the result that this allocation method was struck down for producing an unfair allocation of income.[646]

On the other hand, choosing a formula with several elements in the allocation key makes it less likely to be de facto selective, as it is the combined effect of all the factors that is subject to the selectivity test.[647] The US Supreme Court reasoned in this manner when it considered that the three-factor formula previously used by California reflected 'a very large share of the activities by which value is generated', something that would 'avoid the sorts of distortions' that were present in the case where an allocation key contained only one apportionment factor.[648] Therefore, if it can be assumed that different undertakings have different characteristics, it would be reasonable to conclude that the more elements are included in the formula, the less likely it is that only certain undertakings receive a favourable treatment.

The outcome of the de facto selectivity test should also be under the influence of the spread in the apportionment factors of a formula-based allocation method: the diversity in the apportionment factors increases the chance that a formula results in the taxation of different types of business activities with no preference for certain categories of undertakings. Indeed, the more spread the elements of the allocation key, the less likely it is that a system of formula apportionment in effect favours certain undertakings, as the differences in the elements of the allocation key mitigate the margins of the Member States to manipulate the formula so as to favour certain (groups of) undertakings.

It was argued above that the number and the spread of the apportionment factors should reasonably exercise an influence on the outcome of a de facto selectivity test. Yet, this proposed way of reasoning is only an indication of what seems the most likely. This indication is not sufficient to draw any definite conclusions, something that can only be done on the basis of an analysis of the actual effects of an actual system of formula apportionment. In addition, the case law of the CJEU indicates that a system of formula apportionment with several apportionment factors that are also quite different from each other does not necessarily prevent the rules from being de facto selective. Indeed, the rules at hand in *Gibraltar* were based on three factors that were quite different from each other: the number of employees, the occupation of property for

---

646. *See* US Supreme Court, Case 334, 283 US 123, *Hans Rees' Sons, Inc. v. North Carolina ex rel. Maxwell*, 13 April 1931.
647. For a similar reasoning *see* Charles E. McLure Jr. and Walter Hellerstein, 'Does Sales-Only Apportionment of Corporate Income Violate International Trade Rules?' (2002) 96 Tax Notes International 1315, who at 1322 claim that while a sales-only apportionment formula is likely to be in breach of trade law, a formula based on a double weight for sales together with other apportionment factors would be 'acceptable'.
648. *See* US Supreme Court, Case 81-523, 463 US 159, *Container Corporation of America v. Franchise Tax Board of California* 183, 27 June 1983.

business purposes, and a registration fee. However, the number and the diversity of the factors of the formula did not prevent it from being de facto selective.

The next parameter that is studied in this section, and that may influence the de facto selectivity test, is the connection of the apportionment factors to the concept of income.

7.3.3.2 Connection of the Apportionment Factors to the Concept of Income

In this section I suggest the idea that the pursuance of the objective to tax income is, in itself, a relevant indication of whether or not an apportionment factor, or a combination of apportionment factors, favours certain undertakings. This is because the objective to tax income is intrinsically neutral,[649] and non-discriminatory. Of course, how one defines the notion of income may produce different effects on different undertakings, but at a general level the objective to tax income remains neutral. If one assumes that all commercial companies do pursue the objective of earning income, then taxing all commercial companies on their income would tend to be a general measure, since by aiming at taxing income, the Member States would not be favouring certain categories of undertakings. The Member States would, instead, apply a measure that targets equally all undertakings. Accordingly, whether or not an apportionment factor effectively captures the income of all undertakings is a parameter that, in my view, should influence the outcome of the de facto selectivity test. I also find support to this argument in the *Gibraltar* case, where the CJEU stated that '(t)he requirement to make a profit and the capping of taxation of profits are per se general measures applicable without distinction to all economic operators and are therefore not liable to confer selective advantages'.[650]

Of course, different undertakings are likely to earn income thanks to relying on different factors, so the choice of certain apportionment factors with the aim of ensuring a connection to the concept of income is necessarily a proxy, and an incorrect one. Even though the apportionment factors of a system of formula apportionment may contribute to earning income, it is possible that income be attributed to an enterprise below, or in excess of its contribution to the global profits.[651] Indeed, as emphasised by the US Supreme Court, '(t)he formula apportionment method divides [income] on the basis of a mathematical generalization'.[652] Nevertheless, by increasing the chance that the apportionment factors contribute to earning income, the likelihood of such factors to produce effects that are favourable only to certain undertakings should reasonably

---

649. Neutrality is an aspect that makes a measure general, as opposed to selective: *see* Joined Cases C-106/09 P and C-107/09 P, *European Commission v. Government of Gibraltar*, ECLI:EU:C:2011:732, para. 81.
650. *See* Joined Cases C-106/09 P and C-107/09 P, *European Commission v. Government of Gibraltar*, ECLI:EU:C:2011:732, para. 80.
651. For example, a group member that only has assets (which imply a cost through depreciation) and employees (which imply wage costs), but no sales, may be attributed a profit under a formula that includes the assets, labour, and sales factors.
652. *See* US Supreme Court, 27 June 1983, Case 81-523, 463 US 159, *Container Corporation of America v. Franchise Tax Board of California* 188.

decrease. In other words, ensuring a connection between the apportionment factors and the concept of income is likely to mitigate the risk that such apportionment factors are prima facie de facto selective.

In the view of the majority of observers, the three apportionment factors analysed in this chapter do have some connection with the concept of income, although certain empirical studies point to the contrary.[653] First, it can be observed that the US Supreme Court found that a formula based on assets, labour and sales reflects 'a very large share of the activities by which value is generated'.[654] Second, the formula suggested as part of the CCCTB proposal includes the same apportionment factors; these factors are considered by the European Commission to ensure that 'profits are taxed where they are actually earned',[655] which is close to the concept of source of income. Third, it seems difficult to argue that the apportionment factors sales, labour, and assets have no connection with the concept of income. I will consider these three factors in turn:

- Sales are necessarily contributing to earning income, because with no sales there are no profits, only costs. However, sales alone do not suffice to earn income, and the sales function does not necessarily contribute to earning income more than other functions.
- It has been argued by several scholars that the labour factor is crucial for the earning of income. For instance, Vann has argued that '(a)ll the individuals contribute to the profit and their relative salaries are the most reliable measure of contribution'.[656] Tavares and Owens also insist on the need to take into account human capital to split residual profits.[657] Thus, the labour factor, when it includes the levels of wages, is likely to capture some of the creation of value of an enterprise, and thus the income it generates.
- Assets may contribute to earning income, but this may vary with the type of asset and the circumstances. Intangible assets are most likely to contribute to earning income,[658] as illustrated by the devotion of a whole chapter of the OECD transfer pricing guidelines to this topic.[659] Yet, it is usually considered, for practical rather than theoretical reasons, that intangible assets cannot be

---

653. Certain empirical studies point to a weak connection between the apportionment factors sales, labour and capital, and the earning of income: see e.g., James R. Hines, 'Income Misattribution under Formula Apportionment' (2010) 54 European Economic Review 108, who at 117 concludes that 'the factors that enter the formulas do not accurately correspond to the determinants of business incomes'; in the study conducted by this author, variations in the apportionment factors sales, labour, and capital explain only 22% of variations in profits.
654. See US Supreme Court, Case 81-523, 463 US 159, *Container Corporation of America v. Franchise Tax Board of California* 183, 27 June 1983.
655. See European Commission, 'Proposal for a Council Directive on a Common Consolidated Corporate Tax Base (CCCTB)' COM(2016) 683 final, preamble, para. 10.
656. See Richard J. Vann, 'Taxing International Business Income: Hard-Boiled Wonderland and the End of the World' (2010) 2 World Tax Journal 291, 332.
657. See Romero J.S. Tavares and Jeffrey Owens, 'Human Capital in Value Creation and Post-BEPS Tax Policy: An Outlook' (2015) 69 Bulletin for International Taxation 590, 596.
658. See Marcel Olbert and Christoph Spengel, 'International Taxation in the Digital Economy: Challenge Accepted?' (2017) 9 World Tax Journal 3, 35-37.
659. In this respect, see Chapter 6 of the 2017 OECD transfer pricing guidelines.

used as an apportionment factor.[660] That leaves the assets factor to tangible assets, which in certain cases may have a strong connection to the concept of income (e.g., the immovable property of a company involved in the real estate business), while in other cases the connection may be weaker (e.g., in the case of obsolete inventory). However, in all cases tangible assets are likely to have some connection with the concept of income, albeit a weak one.

Consequently, I find it reasonable to conclude that each of the three factors is likely to contribute to the earning of income. Of course, other firm-specific apportionment factors may also have a connection with the concept of income. For example, according to certain authors, capital is the most important factor for the generation of income.[661] Others suggest that profits be split based on the operating expenses incurred by the members of a multinational enterprise.[662] However, if one assumes, as it is done here, that the apportionment factors of a formula-based method should preferably have a strong connection to the concept of income to decrease the risk that such a formula is de facto selective, I believe that the provision of capital and the notion of operating expenses appear less suitable than the other apportionment factors. The motivation of this statement is simple: companies do not intrinsically need to be wholly financed by capital, as they can also be financed by debt. In addition, the fact that a company has capital does not need to imply that it pursues an economic activity that generates income. Turning to the use of operating expenses as an apportionment factor, it needs to be stressed that the accounting notion of operating expenses includes several types of expenses that have a more or less direct link with the earning of income. Most operating expenses may, to some extent, contribute to earning income (otherwise a rational economic operator would not incur such expenses), but the link to the concept of income is stronger for certain expenses than for others. It is especially more likely that labour costs (which are normally included in the operating expenses) have a stronger connection to the concept of income than most of the other components of the operating expenses, as argued by Vann,[663] as well as Tavares and Owens.[664] Therefore, although the general notion of operating expenses can be assumed to contribute to earning income, the labour costs, which are a component of the operating expenses,

---

660. *See* European Commission, 'CCCTB: possible elements of the sharing mechanism' (2007) CCCTB/WP060\doc\en, paras 33–35.
661. *See* e.g., Joann Martens Weiner and Jack Mintz, 'An Exploration of Formula Apportionment in the European Union' (2002) 42 European Taxation 346, 350.
662. *See* e.g., Reuven S. Avi-Yonah, Kimberly A. Clausing and Michael C. Durst, 'Allocating Business Profits for Tax Purposes: A Proposal to Adopt a Formulary Profit Split' (2009) 9 Florida Tax Review 497; Wolfgang Schön, 'International Tax Coordination for a Second-Best World (Part III)' (2010) 3 World Tax Journal 227, 250; Marcel Olbert and Christoph Spengel, 'International Taxation in the Digital Economy: Challenge Accepted?' (2017) 9 World Tax Journal 3, 38.
663. *See* Richard J. Vann, 'Taxing International Business Income: Hard-Boiled Wonderland and the End of the World' (2010) 2 World Tax Journal 291, 332.
664. *See* Romero J.S. Tavares and Jeffrey Owens, 'Human Capital in Value Creation and Post-BEPS Tax Policy: An Outlook' (2015) 69 Bulletin for International Taxation 590, 596.

are likely to have a stronger connection to the concept of income; the risk of de facto selectivity would thus be decreased by using labour costs instead of operating expenses.

I discussed above the connection of each apportionment factor to the concept of income. This discussion should be completed by the consideration of the combined effect of several apportionment factors. In my view, if one takes into account the general effect of a formula on all undertakings, the combination of several apportionment factors will better capture the income generated by different types of undertakings than a formula relying on fewer factors, or a single one. This point is also made by the European Commission, which observed, as part of the preparatory works on the proposal for a CCCTB, that '(a) mix of factors is (...) more likely to capture all the key profit-generating factors'.[665]

A closer look at the effects of the apportionment factors confirms the general statement made above, as the combination of the three apportionment factors sales, labour, and assets reaches some form of equilibrium between different types of undertakings. In particular, the combination of the three apportionment factors reaches a balance between manufacturing companies and countries (represented mostly by the assets and labour factors), on the one hand, and distribution companies and countries (represented mostly by the sales), on the other hand. These two categories of undertakings can also be distinguished as reflecting the place of origin and the place of destination of goods or services. A balanced system of formula apportionment would thus also imply some form of equilibrium in the international allocation of resources.

In this respect, it can be observed that the formula used in Canada, which shares with equal weight the income in proportion to the sales and the labour costs in each province, achieves a well-balanced allocation of the taxing rights between the place of origin (labour) and the place of destination (sales). A lesser importance is given to the place of destination in the proposal for a CCCTB and the so-called Massachusetts formula, which assign one third to the place of destination (sales), and two-third to labour and assets, which are more likely to be located at the place of origin. However, given the argument developed above as to the number and the diversity of the apportionment factors, a formula that includes three factors is less likely to entail de facto selectivity than a two-factor formula such as the Canadian one. It is also possible to weight the apportionment factors in different fashions, to achieve certain results. Consequently, the Canadian formula is not likely to be the most suitable model in the search for a formula-based allocation method that reduces the risks of being de facto selective.

It can also be observed that there is an interesting conceptual difference between sales, assets, and labour. While the former apportionment factor is not tangible, the two latters are tangible. Sales do not, as such, create an income tax liability under traditional tax principles, whether one considers the rules on residence or the rules on permanent establishments. On the other hand, the presence of tangible assets may lead

---

665. *See* European Commission, 'CCCTB: possible elements of the sharing mechanism' (2007) CCCTB/WP060\doc\en, para. 10.

to a fixed place of business, and the presence of labour may lead to a fixed place of business or a dependent agent. This difference becomes particularly relevant when considering the digital economy, which may create value in certain countries with little or no physical presence. Accordingly, a combination of apportionment factors that includes the sales factor and tangible factors such as labour and tangible assets would be likely to reach a balance between undertakings that are more or less concerned by the digitalisation of the economy, since companies active in the digital economy may have little or no physical presence in the countries of sales, while they may have assets and employees in their country of origin.[666] Therefore, the conceptual difference between sales, assets, and labour comes as an additional argument in favour of including in a formula all the three apportionment factors so as to reach a well-balanced outcome that is less likely to be de facto selective.

As a conclusion, it is argued in this section that ensuring a connection between the firm-specific apportionment factors and the concept of income is likely to reduce the risk of a system of formula apportionment being de facto selective. The combination of sales, labour, and tangible assets seems to be an appropriate proxy to capture the notion of income, although it is by definition imperfect. This combination seems also to ensure a well-balanced allocation of the taxing rights between the places of origin and destination, as well as between different types of undertakings, which may explain why these factors are frequently applied at subnational level in the US, and are included in the proposal for a CCCTB. By weighting the apportionment factors, an even more accurate connection to the concept of income could be reached, something that would decrease the chances of the system of formula apportionment to be de facto selective.

The next parameter of a formula-based allocation method that may influence the de facto selectivity test is the connection of the apportionment factors to the effects of the market forces.

7.3.3.3 *Connection of the Apportionment Factors to the Market Forces*

In the 2016 notice, the European Commission describes the need to achieve 'market-based outcomes' as part of a transfer pricing analysis, to avoid the risk that such an analysis deviates from the reference system and proves selective.[667] Earlier in this book I have argued against the existence of an obligation to implement the arm's length principle that would result from Article 107(1) of the TFEU.[668] However, one has to recognise that the market forces are a relevant criterion for the purpose of the de facto selectivity test. This is because of the inherent neutrality of the effects of the market forces, both towards the Member States and towards undertakings. By relying on the

---

666. On the challenges of the digital economy on international tax principles, *see* Frans Vanistendael, 'Digital Disruption in International Taxation' (2018) 89 Tax Notes International 175; Marcel Olbert and Christoph Spengel, 'International Taxation in the Digital Economy: Challenge Accepted?' (2017) 9 World Tax Journal 3.
667. *See* Commission Notice on the notion of State aid as referred to in Art. 107(1) of the Treaty on the Functioning of the European Union [2016] OJ C 262/1, paras 171–174.
668. *See* Chapter 2 of this book.

effects of the market forces when designing the sharing mechanism of an allocation method, a Member State can hardly be willing to favour certain undertakings, because it is not the Member State or an undertaking that can decide over the effects of the market, but the meeting between demand and supply. Therefore, by choosing apportionment factors that are under the influence of the market forces, a Member State would, in my view, reduce the risk of a system of formula apportionment being de facto selective.

As I see it, the three apportionment factors studied in this chapter are, to some extent, subject to the market forces:

- Obviously a multinational enterprise decides what to sell, where to sell it, and for what price. However, if one assumes that undertakings pursue the objective of maximising their profits, sales by destination should be an apportionment factor that a multinational enterprise is not likely to be willing to manipulate through refusing to sell to certain customers or in certain countries.[669] The sales factor is subject to the market forces, both with respect to the place where the sales are incurred, and the amount of such sales. However, the sales factor is subject to the market forces only to the extent of the sales that are made to third parties. Intragroup sales are, in most cases, not subject to the market forces. However, as it is assumed in this chapter that the sales factor disregards intragroup sales, this apportionment factor is fully subject to the market forces.
- The labour factor is also subject to the effects of the market forces, especially when it comes to the levels of the wages of the employees, which are the result of a negotiation between the employer and the employee. This negotiation is subject to the market forces. The location of an employee is a decision that can be made by a multinational enterprise with little influence of the market forces, for example by deciding to locate a given function in a given country; however, the existence of qualified work force and the general levels of wages, are parameters that are not controlled by the employer. The number of employees is partly subject to the market forces: on the one hand, the employer decides how many persons to employ, while on the other hand it is the labour market that provides the work force. Therefore, if income is shared on the basis of the labour costs or the number of employees, this apportionment factor would be subject to the effects of the market forces, but to a lower extent than the sales factor.
- The assets factor is also subject to the market forces, but to a lower extent than the sales factor. The purchase price of an asset would normally reflect the market forces, if it has been purchased from a third party. The value of an asset on a balance sheet is also subject to various rules, such as depreciation, over which a multinational enterprise has little control, unless the choice is given

---

669. *See* Reuven S. Avi-Yonah, Kimberly A. Clausing and Michael C. Durst, 'Allocating Business Profits for Tax Purposes: A Proposal to Adopt a Formulary Profit Split' (2009) 9 Florida Tax Review 497, 509.

between different depreciation methods. On the other hand, the location of an asset is largely decided by an undertaking. Accordingly, assets may be subject to the market forces, but to a lower extent than the sales factor.

Consequently, the three apportionment factors discussed above reflect more or less the effects of the market forces, with the sales factor having, in my view, the strongest connection with the market forces. If one agrees with the idea that a connection with the market forces tends to make a measure general, then including the sales, labour, and assets factors would mitigate the selective nature of a formula-based allocation method with firm-specific apportionment factors, especially if the sales factor is assigned more weight in the formula than the other apportionment factors.

7.4 CONCLUSION

I started this chapter by stressing that the selectivity test of a system of formula apportionment with firm-specific factors applies differently depending on which answers are brought to two questions: the choice of the reference system, and the determination of the right comparator. I will present the conclusions of this chapter by referring to these two questions. First, if the reference system is made of the whole corporate income tax system, and assuming that the comparison should be between independent and associated enterprises (as is suggested in Chapters 2 and 4 of this book), the application of a system of formula apportionment to members of multinational enterprises creates a clear difference in treatment between these categories of undertakings. That would be a consequence of the design of the law, which is why it was concluded at section 7.2 that a system of formula apportionment with firm-specific factors is certainly prima facie de jure selective. This makes it unnecessary to consider the de facto selectivity test.

Second, assuming that the reference system consists of the system of formula apportionment, or if the right comparator is between different multinational enterprises, the selectivity test applies in a fundamentally different manner. No comparison would be made with the treatment of independent enterprises or members of domestic groups, something that would mitigate the risk that a system of formula apportionment with firm-specific factors is selective. The system of formula apportionment could only be de jure selective if different formulas apply to different undertakings; in contrast, if the same formula applies to all undertakings, I concluded that no de jure selectivity would be at hand. Instead, it is the de facto selectivity test that would become relevant. In this respect, I concluded in this chapter, on the basis of the case law of the CJEU, that a system of formula apportionment with firm-specific factors would be likely to be de facto selective, because it would effectively correspond to a direct tax on the apportionment factors. The system would favour or disadvantage different undertakings, depending on the representation of the apportionment factors in their organisation. At the same time, I argued that there are several parameters that may influence the de facto selectivity test: the risk of selectivity decreases with both the number of apportionment factors and their diversity. It was also suggested that the fact that apportionment factors are connected to the concept of income and to the effects of the market forces should mitigate (but not necessarily eliminate) the risk of de facto selectivity. Moreover, these parameters may also be relied on as part of the justification analysis.

At this stage, it is interesting to ask what formula carries the lowest risk of being de facto selective. Is there a formula that entails no risk of de facto selectivity? The answer is, in my view, negative. The choice of the apportionment factors, and the weight given to them, contains an arbitrary dimension since there cannot be a clearly superior manner to spread the tax burden across the apportionment factors. The differences between the formulas observed in the US, Canada, and in the proposal for a CCCTB, illustrate the lack of consensus about this issue.[670] Nevertheless, by having several factors and a sufficient spread between them, the risk for de facto selectivity is decreased. Both sales, labour, and tangible assets have some connection to the market forces and to the concept of income. Combining these factors achieves some balance between different undertakings, and between places of origin and destination. A preference has been evidenced in this chapter for the sales factor, which I submit should be given a heavier weight than the other factors. This is because the sales factor combines a strong connection to the concept of income, as well as an obvious link to the effects of the market forces. Sales is also likely to favour the place of destination, whereas labour and assets favour the place of origin; having those three factors, and giving more weight to sales makes it unlikely to clearly favour certain undertakings.

Based on these considerations, an option to decrease the risk of de facto selectivity could be the so-called double-weighted sales formula,[671] whereby sales are assigned half of the apportionment, while assets and labour receive a quarter each. This formula could achieve a balanced spread between manufacturing and distribution companies, manufacturing and sales countries, undertakings that are more or less active in the digital economy, as well as between capital and labour as value adding factors. Furthermore, it has been argued by some economists that sales as an apportionment factor may trigger less distortions than labour and capital, something that could influence the trade conditions and the allocation of resources across the internal market.[672] Putting a stronger emphasis on the sales factor may also be consistent with the interpretation of the arm's length principle that is done by the European Commission in certain of its decisions relating to transfer pricing rulings granted by the Member States; it has indeed been argued that this interpretation of the arm's length principle 'is also about where income should be sourced, taxed, and attributed';[673] the outcome might be a reinforcement of the taxing rights of the source

---

670. *See* Peggy B. Musgrave, 'Interjurisdictional Equity in Company Taxation: Principles and Applications to the European Union' in Sijbren Cnossen (ed), *Taxing Capital Income in the European Union: Issues and Options for Reform* (Oxford University Press 2000) 46.
671. In this respect *see* e.g., Joann M. Weiner, 'Using the Experience in the U.S. States to Evaluate Issues in Implementing Formula Apportionment at the International Level' (1996) 13 Tax Notes International 2113, 2124.
672. *See* James R. Hines, 'Income Misattribution under Formula Apportionment' (2010) 54 European Economic Review 108, 110 with further references at footnote 2.
673. *See* Porus F. Kaka, 'Source Taxation: Do We Really Know What We Mean?' (2017) 86 Tax Notes International 1221, 1233.

jurisdictions.[674] Finally, a parallel can be made to international trade law, where it has been observed, with respect to systems of formula apportionment, that '(a)n assignment of no more than half the weight to sales would appear not to violate international trade rules'.[675]

This chapter concludes the selectivity test of a generally formulated arm's length provision (Chapter 5), transfer pricing safe harbours (Chapter 6), and a system of formula apportionment with firm-specific factors (Chapter 7). After having emphasised a number of situations where the allocation methods might be prima facie selective, the next step is to consider the justification and proportionality tests. This is the purpose of Chapter 8 of this book.

---

674. *See* Reuven S. Avi-Yonah and Gianluca Mazzoni, 'The Apple State Aid Decision: A Wrong Way to Enforce the Benefits Principle?' (2016) 84 Tax Notes International 837, 844.
675. *See* Charles E. McLure, 'Replacing Separate Entity Accounting and the Arm's Length Principle with Formulary Apportionment' (2002) 56 Bulletin for International Taxation 586, 594.

CHAPTER 8
The Justification and Proportionality Tests

8.1 INTRODUCTION

Tax measures that are prima facie selective, whether as a consequence of the design, the effects, or the application of the law, may be justified by the nature or the general scheme of the reference system.[676] This form of rule of reason, illustrated e.g. by the reasoning of the Court in the *Adria Wien* case,[677] has been found to resemble the justification analysis of measures that are in breach of the freedoms of movement.[678] The justification analysis gained importance as the CJEU seems to have evolved towards making the selectivity test a mere discrimination test,[679] given that the existence of a difference in treatment between comparable undertakings is sufficient to create prima facie selectivity. The only way for such a difference in treatment to be compatible with the selectivity test, and thus with State aid law, is the successful justification of that difference by the nature or the general scheme of the reference system.

---

676. *See* Case 173/73, *Italian Republic v. Commission of the European Communities*, ECLI:EU:C:1974:71, para. 33; Case C-143/99, *Adria-Wien Pipeline GmbH, Wietersdorfer & Peggauer Zementwerke GmbH*, ECLI:EU:C:2001:598, para. 42; Case C-452/10 P, *BNP Paribas and Banca Nazionale del Lavoro SpA (BNL) v. European Commission*, ECLI:EU:C:2012:366, para. 101.
677. Case C-143/99, *Adria-Wien Pipeline GmbH*, ECLI:EU:C:2001:598, paras 49–53.
678. *See* Rita Szudoczky, 'Convergence of the Analysis of National Tax Measures under the EU State Aid Rules and the Fundamental Freedoms' (2016) 15 European State Aid Law Quarterly 357, 372.
679. *See* e.g., Case C-487/06 P, *British Aggregates Association v. Commission of the European Communities and United Kingdom*, ECLI:EU:C:2008:757, para. 82. *See also* Case T-620/11, *GFKL Financial Services AG v. European Commission*, ECLI:EU:T:2016:59, para. 100.

The extent of the justifications that have been admitted by the Union courts is limited to the inner logic,[680] or the 'basic and guiding principles' of a tax system.[681] The Court has also referred to the 'technique of taxation'[682] to potentially justify a derogation from the reference system. Indeed, the justification analysis has been described as a way to examine 'whether a measure entails an advantage by way of deviance from a general tax principle'.[683] In contrast, a measure that conforms to general tax principles or the logic of the tax system would be 'cleared from State aid suspicion'.[684] Given that the justification test supposes a deep understanding of the logic of a tax system, while such a logic in most cases is not likely to be explicitly described in the law, this test is necessarily subjective and complex.[685] Indeed, as emphasised by Advocate General Darmon, the justification test needs to identify a derogation from what is normal,[686] something that he considers 'unquestionably related to political and philosophical conceptions regarding the role of the State and the limits of its intervention in the economic sphere'.[687] Therefore, the application of the justification test in the case law of the Union courts is hardly foreseeable, and has been criticised for its lack of clarity.[688]

---

680. *See* Case C-222/04, *Ministero dell'Economia e delle Finanze v. Cassa di Risparmio di Firenze SpA, Fondazione Cassa di Risparmio di San Miniato and Cassa di Risparmio di San Miniato SpA*, ECLI:EU:C:2006:8, para. 137.
681. The CJEU emphasises that '(a) measure which creates an exception to the application of the general tax system may be justified by the nature and overall structure of the tax system if the Member State concerned can show that that measure results directly from the basic or guiding principles of its tax system. In that connection, a distinction must be made between, on the one hand, the objectives attributed to a particular tax scheme which are extrinsic to it and, on the other, the mechanisms inherent in the tax system itself which are necessary for the achievement of such objectives': *see* Case C-88/03, *Portuguese Republic v. Commission of the European Communities*, ECLI:EU:C:2006:511, para. 81. *See also* Joined Cases C-78/08 to C-80/08, *Paint Graphos*, ECLI:EU:C:2011:550, where at para. 65 the CJEU refers to 'the basic or guiding principles' of the tax system.
682. *See* Case C-222/04, *Ministero dell'Economia e delle Finanze v. Cassa di Risparmio di Firenze SpA, Fondazione Cassa di Risparmio di San Miniato and Cassa di Risparmio di San Miniato SpA*, ECLI:EU:C:2006:8, para. 137.
683. *See* Thomas Jaeger, 'From Santander to LuxLeaks – and Back' (2015) 24 European State Aid Law Quarterly 345, 350.
684. *See* Thomas Jaeger, 'Tax Incentives Under State Aid Law: A Competition Law Perspective' in Isabelle Richelle, Wolfgang Schön, and Edoardo Traversa (eds), *State Aid Law and Business Taxation* (Springer 2016) 45.
685. *See* Richard Plender, 'Definition of Aid' in Andrea Biondi, Piet Eeckhout, and James Flynn (eds), *The Law of State Aid in the European Union* (Oxford University Press 2004), who at 27 argues that the justification test 'postpones the difficulty, but does not resolve it'. In a similar vein, Lyal summarised the justification test through asking a question: 'does this rule make sense in terms of this tax or of the tax system as a whole?': *see* Richard Lyal, 'Transfer Pricing Rules and State Aid' (2015) 38 Fordham International Law Journal 1017, 1036.
686. *See* Joined Cases C-72/91 and C-73/91, *Firma Sloman Neptun Schiffahrts AG v. Seebetriebsrat Bodo Ziesemer der Sloman Neptun Schiffahrts AG*, ECLI:EU:C:1992:130, Opinion of AG Darmon, para. 53.
687. *See* Joined Cases C-72/91 and C-73/91, *Firma Sloman Neptun Schiffahrts AG v. Seebetriebsrat Bodo Ziesemer der Sloman Neptun Schiffahrts AG*, ECLI:EU:C:1992:130, Opinion of AG Darmon, para. 55.
688. *See* Case C-83/98 P, *French Republic v. Ladbroke Racing Ltd and Commission of the European Communities*, ECLI:EU:C:1999:577, Opinion of AG Cosmas, who at para. 19 considered that the CJEU had not defined precisely 'what is or may be included within the concept of the "nature

Chapter 8: The Justification and Proportionality Tests

The limitation of the scope of the justification analysis to the inner logic of a tax system implies that the justification test be interpreted restrictively.[689] Similarly to free movement law,[690] the reliance on the inner logic of a tax system takes into account the objective of a measure,[691] or the 'main objective' in case a measure pursues several objectives.[692] Objectives that are extrinsic to a tax system cannot, in principle, justify a measure that is prima facie selective,[693] although certain inconsistencies in the case law have been emphasised.[694]

Moreover, a measure that is justified by the nature or the general scheme of the reference system must also pass the proportionality test. Indeed, the principle of proportionality is a central characteristic of EU primary law.[695] This is also true for State aid law, when it applies to tax law. As a result, a tax measure that is justified by the nature or the general scheme of the tax system should not go beyond what is necessary to attain the objective it pursues.[696] Contrary to the prima facie selectivity assessment,

---

and general scheme of a system"'. *See also* Denis Waelbroeck, 'La compatibilité de systèmes fiscaux généraux avec les règles en matière d'aides d'État dans le traité CE' in *Mélanges John Kirkpatrick* (Bruylant 2004) 1021, 1034–1035; Marilyne Sadowsky, *Droit de l'OMC, droit de l'Union européenne et fiscalité directe* (Larcier 2013) 468–469, with further references.

689. *See e.g.*, the *British Aggregates* case, where the CJEU interpreted restrictively the possibility for a Member State to justify a prima facie selective measure: Case C-487/06 P, *British Aggregates Association v. Commission of the European Communities and United Kingdom*, ECLI:EU:C:2008:757, paras 86–88. *See also* Case T-251/11, *Republic of Austria v. European Commission*, ECLI:EU:T:2014:1060, para. 117. *See also* Denis Waelbroeck, 'La compatibilité de systèmes fiscaux généraux avec les règles en matière d'aides d'État dans le traité CE' in *Mélanges John Kirkpatrick* (Bruylant 2004) 1021, who at 1038 emphasises that the justification of a measure should be '*suffisamment directe et incontestable*'; Humbert Drabbe, 'The Test of Selectivity in State Aid Litigation: The Relevance of Drawing Internal and External Comparisons to Identify the Reference Framework' in Alexander Rust and Claire Micheau (eds), *State aid and Tax Law* (Kluwer Law International 2013) 101.
690. *See e.g.*, the *Centros* case in which the CJEU stressed the need to deny the benefit of EU law by assessing the conduct of a person 'in the light of the objectives pursued' by the national provisions: Case C-212/97, *Centros Ltd v. Erhvervs- og Selskabsstyrelsen*, ECLI:EU:C:1999:126, para. 25. Generally, on the topic of the justification of restrictions to the freedom of movement, *see* Peter Oliver, 'When, If Ever, Can Restrictions on Free Movement Be Justified on Economic Grounds?' (2016) 41 European Law Review 147; this author concludes at 175 that the CJEU's reluctance to admit economic objectives is 'clearly understandable, considering that this strikes at the heart of the internal market'.
691. *See* Case C-308/01, *GIL Insurance Ltd and Others v. Commissioners of Customs & Excise*, ECLI:EU:C:2004:252, paras 74–76.
692. *See e.g.*, Case T-287/11, *Heitkamp BauHolding GmbH v. European Commission*, ECLI:EU:T:2016:60, para. 165.
693. It is settled case law that extrinsic objectives cannot justify a State measure that is prima facie selective: *see e.g.*, Case C-487/06 P, *British Aggregates Association v. Commission of the European Communities and United Kingdom*, ECLI:EU:C:2008:757, para. 92, with respect to environmental objectives. *See also* Case C-6/12, *P Oy*, ECLI:EU:C:2013:525, with respect to objectives related to employment.
694. *See* Rita Szudoczky, 'Convergence of the Analysis of National Tax Measures under the EU State Aid Rules and the Fundamental Freedoms' (2016) 15 European State Aid Law Quarterly 357, 373–374.
695. On the use of analogies by the CJEU, *see* Jörgen Hettne and Ida Otken Eriksson, *EU-Rättslig Metod: Teori Och Genomslag i Svensk Rättstillämpning* (2nd edn, Norstedts Juridik 2011) 260–269.
696. *See* Joined Cases C-78/08 to C-80/08, *Paint Graphos*, ECLI:EU:C:2011:550, para. 75. The principle of proportionality is also found at Art. 5(4) of the TEU with respect to 'Union action'.

Jérôme Monsenego

where the burden of proof lies on the Commission,[697] it is the Member States that have the burden of providing evidence that a prima facie selective measure is able to be justified, and is in line with the principle of proportionality.[698]

How to identify what constitutes the nature or general scheme of the tax system, i.e., what Jaeger describes as general tax principles? It has been argued in the doctrine that there may be an international benchmark of what constitutes the logic of a tax system. For example, Rossi-Maccanico, referring to Avi-Yonah,[699] argues that 'all the tax systems of developed countries abide to common principles of customary international law including the prohibition of abuse of taxation, the single-tax and the benefit principles'.[700] The result would be that such common principles would make it possible to 'probe Member States' tax regimes against their own internal logic', so as to investigate whether certain tax measures 'are contradicting the tax nature of systems of reference'.[701] Although it may be argued that tax systems are converging,[702] it is in my opinion incorrect to generally state that all or most countries are bound by certain common principles of customary international law. First, I have argued elsewhere on the basis of the case law of the International Court of Justice, that there is no customary international law that would have a binding effect on the fiscal sovereignty of countries.[703] There is no reason to believe that different conclusions should be reached as part of the justification analysis of prima facie selective measures for State aid purposes. Second, it would be impossible to precisely identify the scope of common principles, were they to be part of binding customary international law. Third, there are examples of taxes, in various countries, that contradict the principles described above as common.[704] Instead of trying to identify certain common tax principles, I carry out the justification and proportionality tests in this chapter on the basis of the objective

---

On the function of the principle of proportionality, see Tor-Inge Harbo, *The Function of Proportionality Analysis in European Law* (Brill Nijhoff 2015).
697. See Case C-279/08 P, *European Commission v. Kingdom of the Netherlands*, ECLI:EU:C:2011:551, para. 62.
698. See e.g., Joined Cases C-106/09 P and C-107/09 P, *European Commission v. Government of Gibraltar*, ECLI:EU:C:2011:732, para. 146.
699. See Reuven S. Avi-Yonah, *International Tax as International Law – An Analysis of the International Tax Regime* (Cambridge University Press 2007).
700. See Pierpaolo Rossi-Maccanico, 'Fiscal State Aids, Tax Base Erosion and Profit Shifting' (2015) 24 EC Tax Review 63, 66.
701. See Pierpaolo Rossi-Maccanico, 'Fiscal State Aids, Tax Base Erosion and Profit Shifting' (2015) 24 EC Tax Review 63, 66.
702. See Reuven S. Avi-Yonah and Gianluca Mazzoni, 'Are Taxes Converging? Review of Eduardo Baistrocchi (ed), A Global Analysis of Tax Treaty Disputes (Cambridge University Press 2017)' (2017) 573 Public Law and Legal Theory Research Paper Series.
703. See Jérôme Monsenego, *Taxation of Foreign Business Income Within the European Internal Market* (IBFD 2012), Chapter 2.
704. For example, the US Supreme Court found that there is no obligation imposed on the US States to apply the arm's length principle, although most countries do apply it as an allocation method: see US Supreme Court, Case 81-523, 463 US 159, *Container Corporation of America v. Franchise Tax Board of California*, 161, 27 June 1983. Moreover, the 'single tax principle' might be contradicted by various types of provisions, such as tax systems that apply the exemption method with no subject-to-tax clause. The prohibition of abuse is not either a principle that is always applied (e.g., certain hybrids are tolerated, CFC taxation is not always levied), and for the countries that do apply a principle of abuse, the application of the principle may greatly differ from one country to another.

Chapter 8: The Justification and Proportionality Tests

pursued by a corporate income tax system, which is assumed in this book to be the taxation of the net income of all corporations. This objective, in its turn, has several implications for the design and the needs of a corporate income tax system, such as the prevention of tax avoidance.

From a methodological perspective, this chapter is not written as an individual chapter, but as a complement to some of the earlier parts of the book. Chapters 2, 3, and 4 dealt with the analysis of the elements of the selectivity test that are common to the three allocation methods: the determination of the reference system, the potential relevance of the market economy operator test, and the comparability analysis. Chapters 5-7 identified certain circumstances under which an allocation method may be prima facie selective. The measures that were identified as being potentially prima facie selective would need to be tested in the light of the justification and proportionality tests, for the selectivity analysis to be complete. Yet it is not possible to carry out a comprehensive justification and proportionality analysis for all the measures that were found potentially prima facie selective throughout the book. On the one hand, the justification and proportionality tests are to a great extent linked to the earlier steps of a selectivity analysis, in particular the choice of the reference system and the determination of its objective, the choice of the comparators, the outcome of the comparability analysis, and the nature of the deviation from the reference system. This opens for a myriad of different alternatives of prima facie selective measures. On the other hand, the justification and proportionality tests are specific to certain national circumstances, such as the relation between the rule under examination and the remaining system of which it forms part, as well as the precise wording of a rule. Moreover, the Union courts have not developed considerable guidance on the application of the justification and proportionality tests to tax measures, which means that important assumptions need to be made to carry out these tests in the context of the methods for the allocation of the corporate tax base.

Therefore, in this chapter it is chosen to focus on a selection of hypothetical cases made of a combination of assumptions, that are likely to be prima facie selective in the light of the objective to tax corporations on their net income. The cases that are studied in this chapter are only cases of prima facie selectivity where the selectivity results from the design or the effects or the law, which makes it possible, under certain assumptions, to suggest certain ways of reasoning as part of the justification and proportionality tests. These cases have all been identified in the previous chapters as being potentially prima facie selective. By so doing, this chapter contributes to the selectivity analysis of several allocation methods, under various assumptions. However, this chapter cannot reach final answers as to the selectivity of the allocation methods, something that could only be done on a case-by-case basis by taking into account the national context of an allocation method.

The first question studied in this chapter concerns the justification of an allocation method that is limited to members of multinational enterprises, given that all three allocation methods have been found to imply some form of prima facie de jure selective treatment as a consequence of their limited scope of application, assuming the reference system is made of the whole corporate income tax system, and the right comparator is between independent and associated enterprises (section 8.2). Next, the justification and proportionality tests are applied to certain cases of prima facie selectivity relating to the arm's length principle (section 8.3), transfer pricing safe harbours that deviate from the arm's length principle (section 8.4), and systems of formula apportionment with firm-specific factors (section 8.5). The conclusions of this chapter are presented in section 8.6.

8.2 THE JUSTIFICATION OF AN ALLOCATION METHOD LIMITED TO MEMBERS OF MULTINATIONAL ENTERPRISES

I argued in Chapter 2 that the corporate tax rules of the Member States, assuming they pursue the objective of taxing the net income of all corporations, need allocation methods to ensure that this objective is achieved for all types of companies. The differences between independent enterprises and domestic groups, on the one hand, and multinational groups, on the other hand, require to supplement the corporate income tax system with an allocation method. Indeed, in a cross-border context, the transfer prices of controlled transactions influence directly the taxable income of the parties to the transactions, and thus the taxes paid in their respective countries of residence.[705] Associated enterprises resident of different countries enjoy potential tax planning opportunities because of the combination of the diverging corporate income tax rates in different countries, and the possibility to control the terms of intercompany transactions.

In a domestic context, the prices of transactions between associated enterprises members of a domestic group do influence the taxable income and the taxes paid by the group members, but it is the same country that will tax the profits of all companies, contrary to a cross-border situation. Moreover, when a group taxation regime applies, the levels of the transfer prices would usually not matter, as the domestic group would be taxed on its net income. In other words, the tax avoidance concerns that are fully relevant in a cross-border context are less preoccupying in the context of domestic groups. The transfer prices of transactions between independent enterprises raise even lower concerns, given that such prices are under the influence of the market forces and are assumed, in most cases, to produce fiscally acceptable results.

I draw the conclusion, from the points made above, that the inner logic of a corporate income tax system implies a need for an allocation method, to – when necessary – adjust the income of associated enterprises and prevent the risks of tax avoidance described in the previous paragraphs. It would threaten the inner logic and the objective of a corporate income tax system not to control, and if necessary adjust, the income of members of multinational enterprises as a consequence of the tax planning opportunities made available through group membership.

More specifically, there are two fiscal reasons for applying allocation methods only to adjust the income of multinational enterprises: the prevention of tax avoidance, and the need to share the income of multinational enterprises among their members.

---

705. *See* Jérôme Monsenego, *Introduction to Transfer Pricing* (Kluwer Law International 2015) 3–7.

Chapter 8: The Justification and Proportionality Tests

An allocation method has this dual function:[706] first, as argued above the anti-avoidance function of an allocation method belongs to the inner logic of a corporate income tax system. The anti-avoidance function is purely national, it contributes to the achievement of the objective of a corporate income tax system. The prevention of tax avoidance has been found 'consubstantial' to the objective of collecting revenue,[707] which I find convincing: there is a legitimate need to ensure that the purpose of a given rule is enforced, i.e., that the avoidance of the normal effect of a tax rule is prevented. This is obviously a need from a fiscal perspective, to levy the tax revenues that are necessary to support public expenditure; it is also needed from a constitutional perspective, to respect the fundamental principle of equality before the law.[708] Therefore, if an allocation method effectively pursues the objective of prevention of tax avoidance, its objective would be consistent with that of the corporate income tax system.

Second, the sharing function of an allocation method has, in contrast to the anti-avoidance function, a cross-border perspective, that of sharing profits between countries on a basis that is acceptable to them. This function reminds the justification, accepted in the area of free movement law together with other justifications, of the need to safeguard a balanced allocation between the Member States of the power to impose taxes.[709] However, justifications in State aid law are acceptable only if they are needed by the nature or the general scheme of the reference system, i.e., by the inner logic of a corporate income tax system. In this respect, the sharing function of an allocation method may – but does not necessarily – contribute to the achievement of the domestic objective of a corporate income tax system. To the extent an allocation method approximates the notion of income as it is defined in the domestic law of a given State, the objective of the allocation method would be consistent with that of the actual corporate income tax system. On the other hand, there are allocation methods that do not so clearly pursue the objective of approximating the notion of income of a country, such as advantageous safe harbours that deviate from the arm's length principle. These latter allocation methods may pursue other objectives, for instance that of attracting foreign direct investments. In such cases, the sharing function of an allocation method is not consistent with the nature or the general scheme of the reference system, and thus cannot justify a measure that is prima facie selective.

At this point, I do not state that all allocation methods are justified by the nature or the general scheme of a corporate income tax system. I only conclude that the inner

---

706. Similarly, *see* Case C-382/16, *Hornbach-Baumarkt AG v. Finanzamt Landau*, ECLI:EU:C:2017:974, Opinion of AG Bobek, para. 24.
707. *See* Edoardo Traversa and Pierre M. Sabbadini, 'Anti-avoidance Measures and State Aid in a Post-BEPS-Context: An Attempt at Reconciliation' in Isabelle Richelle, Wolfgang Schön, and Edoardo Traversa (eds), *State Aid Law and Business Taxation* (Springer 2016) 104, with reference to the Commission notice of 1998 on the application of the State aid rules to measures relating to direct business taxation.
708. Concurring, *see* Saturnina Moreno González, 'Les aides d'État à caractère fiscal: le critère de sélectivité de la mesure' in Gilbert Orsoni (ed), *Mélanges en l'honneur de Pierre Beltrame* (Presses Universitaires d'Aix-Marseille 2010) 392.
709. *See* e.g. Case C-172/13, *European Commission v. United Kingdom of Great Britain and Northern Ireland*, ECLI:EU:C:2015:50, para. 24.

logic of a corporate income tax system needs an allocation method in the presence of intercompany transactions between members of multinational enterprises. It is consistent with the logic of a corporate income tax system to limit the application of an allocation method to members of multinational enterprises, if the allocation method effectively pursues the objective of prevention of tax avoidance. This view is supported by the cases where the CJEU recognised the right of the Member States to prevent the abuse of tax rules. The Court has come to this conclusion when applying the rules on State aid,[710] but also – although other areas do differ from State aid law[711] – in other fields such as free movement law[712] and secondary law.[713] In such cases, the prevention of tax avoidance was found to be a legitimate objective that may be pursued by the Member States, even at the cost of differences in treatment between various categories of taxpayers,[714] or when the principle of prohibition of abuse had not yet been firmly established in the case law.[715] Moreover, the potential justification of a prima facie selective measure is, as I see it, reinforced in case the allocation method also approximates the notion of income as it is defined in the domestic law of a given

---

710. *See* in particular Case C-6/12, *P Oy*, ECLI:EU:C:2013:525, para. 26, where the CJEU found that 'the objective of avoiding trade in losses' could justify a tax measure that was prima facie selective. *See also* Case C-308/01, *GIL Insurance Ltd and Others v. Commissioners of Customs & Excise*, ECLI:EU:C:2004:252, para. 78.
711. *See* Timothy Lyons, 'State Aid, Taxation and Abuse of Law' in Rita de la Feria and Stefan Vogenauer (eds), *Prohibition of Abuse of Law – A New General Principle of EU Law?* (Hart Publishing 2011) 507.
712. *See* Case C-446/03, *Marks & Spencer plc v. David Halsey (Her Majesty's Inspector of Taxes)*, ECLI:EU:C:2005:763, para. 50; Case C-196/04, *Cadbury Schweppes plc and Cadbury Schweppes Overseas Ltd v. Commissioners of Inland Revenue*, ECLI:EU:C:2006:544, para. 59; Joined Cases C-504/16 and C-613/16, *Deister Holding AG and Juhler Holding A/S v. Bundeszentralamt für Steuern*, ECLI:EU:C:2017:1009, para. 96.
713. *See* Case C-255/02, *Halifax plc, Leeds Permanent Development Services Ltd and County Wide Property Investments Ltd v. Commissioners of Customs & Excise*, ECLI:EU:C:2006:121, para. 70; Case C-251/16, *Edward Cussens and Others v. T. G. Brosman*, ECLI:EU:C:2017:881, paras 27–33.
714. It is emphasised, however, that it is debated whether the notion of abuse of law may vary between different cases, and more generally between differences sources of law. In this respect, *see* Frans Vanistendael, 'Dispositions anti-abus et droit communautaire en matière fiscale' in Edoardo Traversa and Vincent Deckers (eds), *Liber Amicorum Jacques Autenne – Promenades sous les portiques de la fiscalité* (Bruylant 2010) 84–88; *see also* Case C-6/16, *Eqiom SAS, formerly Holcim France SAS and Enka SA v. Ministre des Finances et des Comptes publics*, ECLI:EU:C:2017:641, para. 64, where the Court found that 'the objective of combating fraud and tax evasion, whether it is relied on under Article 1(2) of the Parent-Subsidiary Directive or as justification for an exception to primary law, has the same scope'.
715. For example, in the field of VAT, the CJEU ruled that the principle of prohibition of abusive practices is applicable to periods before the *Halifax* case was delivered. The Court found that the principles of legal certainty and of the protection of legitimate expectations do not preclude the application of the principle of prohibition of abusive practices: *see* Case C-251/16, *Edward Cussens and Others v. T. G. Brosman*, ECLI:EU:C:2017:881, paras 39–44. This raises the question of the scope of the principle of prohibition of abusive practices; in this respect, it has been argued that '(i)n substantive terms, the prohibition of abuse, if allowed to develop too strongly, could undermine the foundations of the Internal Market': *see* Anthony Arnull, 'What is a General Principle of EU Law?' in Rita de la Feria and Stefan Vogenauer (eds), *Prohibition of Abuse of Law – A New General Principle of EU Law?* (Hart Publishing 2011) 22; concurring, *see* Karsten Engsig Sørensen, 'What Is a General Principle of EU Law? A Response' in Rita de la Feria and Stefan Vogenauer (eds), *Prohibition of Abuse of Law – A New General Principle of EU Law?* (Hart Publishing 2011) 29.

Chapter 8: The Justification and Proportionality Tests

State, because the corrective effect of the allocation method would eventually be consistent with the nature of the tax system.

Accordingly, at this stage it is concluded – with no consideration for a particular allocation method – that the anti-avoidance and income sharing effects of an allocation method might justify a selective treatment, assuming that such an allocation method effectively pursues objectives that are consistent with the inner logic of a corporate income tax system.

The next step of the justification analysis is the consideration of the specific case of each allocation method. It is the purpose of the three following sections.

8.3 THE JUSTIFICATION AND PROPORTIONALITY TESTS APPLIED TO THE SELECTIVE ASPECTS OF A GENERALLY FORMULATED ARM'S LENGTH PROVISION

It was emphasised in Chapter 5 of this book that a generally formulated arm's length provision is, in several respects, likely to be prima facie selective. This concerns especially the limited corrective effect of this allocation method (section 8.3.1), and the approximation of results for intercompany transactions with no direct benchmark provided by the open market (section 8.3.2).

8.3.1 The Limited Corrective Effect of a Generally Formulated Arm's Length Provision

I found in Chapter 5 that the arm's length principle has, in most cases, a corrective effect only towards associated enterprises, something that may favour independent enterprises and members of domestic groups. This is a consequence of the scope of application of an arm's length provision, which in most domestic laws is limited to cross-border intercompany transactions.

The limited corrective effect of the arm's length principle entails the prima facie de jure selectivity of this allocation method. The question is now whether the difference in treatment with other undertakings that are not subject to this rule is able to be justified by the nature or the general scheme of a corporate income tax system. In my view, the answer is likely to be positive. It was mentioned earlier in this book that multinational enterprises enjoy potential tax planning opportunities that are not available to independent enterprises or to domestic groups, which creates a need for an allocation method as a complement to the rules of a corporate income tax system that have a purely domestic scope of application. A generally formulated arm's length provision interpreted in the light of the 2017 OECD transfer pricing guidelines fulfils a function that is consistent with the objective of a corporate income tax system to tax the net income of corporations, because of the anti-avoidance effect of an arm's length provision, as well as its strong connection to the concept of income. This does not mean that intercompany transactions entered at non-arm's length terms are necessarily and generally abusive as such: the use by associated enterprises of the freedom to contract at terms that deviate from market terms may be legitimate from the perspective of civil law. However, from a fiscal perspective, the tax systems of the Member States need to be able to counter the abusive use of the freedom to contract by associated enterprises, when the exercise of such a freedom entails consequences that render impossible the attainment of the objective of a corporate income tax system.[716]

The same freedom to contract is enjoyed by independent enterprises as well as members of domestic groups. However, these two categories of undertakings are, in most cases, not subject to the corrective effect of the arm's length principle. This grants the arm's length principle an anti-avoidance character that is limited to members of multinational enterprises. The fact that independent transactions are not reassessed in the light of a requirement to implement market terms is an inherent consequence of the difference between independent and associated enterprises, only the former being subject to the market forces. Differences with the treatment of domestic groups may also be explained by the implementation of the principle of neutrality at a domestic level, and the fact that domestic companies are all eventually taxed in the same country: if a group taxation regime applies in a country, the net income of the group would be subject to tax no matter which group member formally reports the income. Therefore, in my view the limited corrective effect of the arm's length principle is able to be justified by the need to prevent tax avoidance: the combined effect of the arm's length principle used as an allocation method towards multinational enterprises, and of the lack of such a rule in other situations, results in all categories of undertakings being taxed consistently with the objective of a corporate income tax system, i.e., the objective to tax all undertakings on their net income.

Moreover, it can be observed that in the context of the fundamental freedoms, the arm's length principle has been considered as a justified method to prevent tax avoidance and preserve the balanced allocation of the power to impose taxes between the Member States.[717] It is the same reason that justifies a breach of the freedom of establishment, and a breach of equality between members of multinational enterprises as well as independent enterprises or domestic groups: the need to let the Member States tax the revenues generated in their territory, despite the potential effects of group membership.

I suggested above that the limited corrective effect of the arm's length principle should be justified by the nature or the general scheme of a corporate income tax system. The next step of the analysis is the proportionality test. Here, the guidance of the CJEU in the area of free movement law is relevant to consider. This guidance lies on two criteria to meet the proportionality test. First, I recall that the CJEU, in its case law on the application of the freedoms of movement, has found that the principle of proportionality requires that the corrective effect of the arm's length principle be limited to the right interpretation of the principle, to re-establish the situation that

---

716. For an analysis of the differences between civil law and tax law, see Jérôme Monsenego, 'La correction des prix de transfert entre sociétés apparentées au regard du concept civiliste de liberté contractuelle – Vers un renforcement de la théorie de l'autonomie du droit fiscal?' (2012) 9 Revue de Droit Fiscal 30.
717. See Case C-311/08, Société de Gestion Industrielle SA, ECLI:EU:C:2010:26, para. 66.

Chapter 8: The Justification and Proportionality Tests

would have existed with no tax avoidance.[718] In other words, only a reassessment up to what the arm's length principle prescribes can justify an infringement of the freedom of movement.[719] This requirement of the principle of proportionality in free movement law is also valid, in my opinion, in the context of the rules on State aid, given the emphasis put by the CJEU on the need to limit infringements to these two areas of European law to measures that are necessary to attain the objective of the prevention of tax avoidance.[720] The definition of the 'right interpretation' of the arm's length principle should be assessed, in my view, in the light of the analyses made in this book with regard to the material content of the reference system,[721] as interpreted by the sources of interpretation that were discussed at section 5.4.2 above.

Second, the CJEU found in the context of the freedoms of movement that the principle of proportionality was enforced when the burden of proof of the breach of the arm's length principle lied on the tax administration.[722] I see no reason for deviating from this finding in the area of State aid law: the principle of proportionality is a general principle related to the rule of law,[723] according to which a measure should not go beyond what is necessary to attain the objective it pursues. If the achievement of the objective to prevent tax avoidance in the area of free movement law does not tolerate that the burden of proof of the justification of transfer prices rests on the taxpayer, the principle of proportionality should reasonably have the same content in the area of the rules on State aid.

At this stage, I find it necessary to raise a point with respect to the principle of legal certainty. The CJEU has found that a rule which does not meet the requirements of the principle of legal certainty cannot be considered to be proportionate to the objectives it pursues.[724] For that reason, the Court ruled that a Belgian anti-abuse provision was incompatible with the freedom to provide services, as it was framed in such terms that it was not possible, at the outset, 'to determine its scope with sufficient precision'; the applicability of the rule was found to remain 'a matter of uncertainty'.[725]

---

718. See Case C-524/04, *Test Claimants in the Thin Cap Group Litigation v. Commissioners of Inland Revenue*, ECLI:EU:C:2007:161, para. 83; Case C-311/08, *Société de Gestion Industrielle SA*, ECLI:EU:C:2010:26, para. 72.
719. See the clear statement of the Court in the *SIAT* case: 'where the transaction in question goes beyond what the companies concerned would have agreed under fully competitive conditions, the corrective tax measure must, in order not to be considered disproportionate, be confined to the part which exceeds what would have been agreed under such conditions' (see Case C-318/10, *Société d'investissement pour l'agriculture tropicale SA (SIAT) v. État belge*, ECLI: EU:C:2012:415, para. 52).
720. Concurring, see Mario Tenore, 'APAs and State Aid: A New Era of European Tax Law?' in Dennis Weber (ed), *EU Law and the Building of Global Supranational Tax Law: EU BEPS and State Aid* (IBFD 2017) 201.
721. See section 2.3.
722. See e.g., Case C-311/08, *Société de Gestion Industrielle SA v. État belge*, ECLI:EU:C:2010:26, para. 75.
723. On the principle of proportionality in tax law see Christina Moëll, *Proportionalitetsprincipen i Skatterätten* (Juristförlaget i Lund 2003); in the area of EU law, see Ulf Bernitz and Anders Kjellgren, *Europarättens Grunder* (7th edn, Norstedts Juridik 2018) 164–168.
724. See Case C-318/10, *Société d'investissement pour l'agriculture tropicale SA (SIAT) v. État belge*, ECLI:EU:C:2012:415, para. 59.
725. See Case C-318/10, *Société d'investissement pour l'agriculture tropicale SA (SIAT) v. État belge*, ECLI:EU:C:2012:415, para. 57.

Contrary to the Belgian rule at hand in *SIAT*, the CJEU has not found the arm's length principle to be intrinsically at odds with the principle of legal certainty, given that it found the arm's length principle in line with the principle of proportionality. The *SGI* case provides a good illustration of the compatibility of the arm's length principle with the principle of proportionality. I consider that *in theory*, a generally formulated arm's length provision is precise because it relies on an objective (although subjectively determined) benchmark, the one provided by the open market.

However, I have mentioned in this book that the arm's length principle, being only an abstract principle, is intrinsically approximative, and necessarily includes a subjective dimension. I emphasised that the functioning of the arm's length principle, in particular through the choice of a transfer pricing method and the use of ranges of values, implied an inherent imprecision. That imprecision is, to me, hard to reconcile with the need for precision expressed by the Court as part of the proportionality test. The fact that the arm's length principle implies a high level of imprecision and a lack of legal certainty is clearly illustrated by the number of disputes about its application, and the complexity of such disputes. It is also illustrated by the diverging interpretations of the arm's length principle observed in different countries, although the rationale of the principle is the same. Consequently, while the CJEU did not find the arm's length principle in breach of the principle of legal certainty, I see convincing reasons for reconsidering this position. The *theoretical* precision of the arm's length principle does not, in my mind, suffice to make its *actual* imprecision fully proportionate to the objectives pursued by a corporate income tax system. This is especially true in the area of State aid law, where so much emphasis is put on the effects of State measures. Consequently, in my view, a generally formulated arm's length provision is, in practice (i.e., as opposed to in theory), at odds with the principle of legal certainty.

The second feature of a generally formulated arm's length provision that needs to be justified, as well as tested in the light of the principle of proportionality, concerns situations that lack a direct benchmark provided by the open market.

8.3.2 Prima Facie Selectivity for Situations That Lack a Direct Benchmark Provided by the Open Market

I concluded in section 5.3.2 that an interpretation of the arm's length principle as an obligation to tax group members in a strictly identical manner to independent enterprises may imply a selective treatment, as soon as independent and associated enterprises are not in a fully comparable situation.[726] Such an interpretation of the

---

726. For example, when multinational enterprises earn profits that are in excess of those earned by independent enterprises, attributing to the formers the profits observed from the latters would leave the excess profits untaxed, as no benchmark supporting their taxation could be deduced from the observation of independent enterprises. *See* Richard Collier and Joseph L Andrus, *Transfer Pricing and the Arm's Length Principle After BEPS* (Oxford University Press 2017) 125.

arm's length principle is not recommended by the OECD transfer pricing guidelines, but it cannot be excluded that the arm's length principle is interpreted in this manner.[727]

In my view, this case of prima facie selectivity cannot be justified by the nature or the general scheme of a corporate income tax system. The objective of such a system is the taxation of the net income of corporations. This means that the nature or the general scheme of a corporate income tax system should be to design rules that support the achievement of the objective of the system. Income is earned by the profit-generating activities of undertakings, whether they are independent or members of a group. If group members have a different functional profile than independent enterprises, the achievement of the objective of the corporate income tax system commands to deviate from the observations of the market so as to eventually levy tax on their actual income. An opposite approach, i.e., strictly relying on the conditions observed between independent enterprises without adjusting the terms of transactions observed on the open market, carries the risk of levying tax in breach of the reference system applicable in a Member State.

Consequently, when the characteristics of an intercompany transaction are so particular that no direct benchmark is provided by the open market, the inner logic of the reference system implies to apply the arm's length principle as correctly as possible, but, if necessary, by relying only indirectly on observations from the open market. Therefore, deviations from observations observed on the open market, as long as they correctly approximate the income earned by the tested parties, are consistent with the logic of the corporate income tax system. By so doing, associated enterprises can be taxed on an approximation of their own income, not on the basis of the income that is observed from an independent enterprise that is not in a comparable situation: the inner objective of the corporate income tax system is preserved, although this might imply deviations from observations on the open market.

Finally, similarly to what I suggested at section 8.3.1, the principle of proportionality would command that the arm's length principle be applied properly, to achieve the objective of the reference system through correctly accounting for the differences in comparability between independent and associated enterprises. The observations made at section 8.3.1 with respect to the principle of legal certainty are equally relevant here.

In the following section I will apply the justification and proportionality tests to the selective features of transfer pricing safe harbours.

---

727. In particular, some decisions taken by the European Commission, together with the 2016 notice, seem to imply that the arm's length principle as it would result from Art. 107(1) of the TFEU does not have the exact same content as what is recommended in the OECD transfer pricing guidelines; the European Commission seems to favour the use of the most direct transfer pricing methods, in particular the CUP method, something that may result in the strict application to associated enterprises of the conditions existing between independent enterprises.

8.4 THE JUSTIFICATION AND PROPORTIONALITY TESTS APPLIED TO THE SELECTIVE FEATURES OF TRANSFER PRICING SAFE HARBOURS

This section considers transfer pricing safe harbours that apply in parallel to a generally formulated arm's length provision, i.e., an additional allocation method the scope of which is limited to certain types of intercompany transactions. I argued in section 6.2.1 that transfer pricing safe harbours that are implemented in parallel to a generally formulated arm's length provision, and that enforce the arm's length principle, may be prima facie selective, as they share the selective features of a generally formulated arm's length provision. The next step is to investigate whether this case of prima facie selectivity can be justified by the nature or the general scheme of a corporate income tax system. In this respect, the justification and proportionality tests of a generally formulated arm's length provision are also relevant for transfer pricing safe harbours that implement the arm's length principle, given that I found these two allocation methods prima facie selective for the same reasons. Therefore, it is referred to the previous section of this book for the justification of the selective features of transfer pricing safe harbours that implement the arm's length principle. The only difference between the two allocation methods concerns the predetermined nature of a transfer pricing safe harbour: while I argued above that the approximative and subjective nature of the arm's length principle is at odds with the principle of legal certainty, transfer pricing safe harbours remove the imprecision that is inherent to a generally formulated arm's length provision. Therefore, the selective features of transfer pricing safe harbours are, in my opinion, more likely to be in line with the principle of legal certainty than a generally formulated arm's length provision, thanks to the fixed element of a safe harbour.

I now turn to the justification and proportionality tests of a transfer pricing safe harbour that deviates from the arm's length principle. I concluded in Chapter 6 of this book that safe harbours that deviate from the arm's length principle, whether upwards or downwards, are likely to entail a prima facie selective treatment, unless the safe harbours imply a higher tax burden than the arm's length principle, and an option is given to the taxpayers to be taxed under the generally formulated arm's length provision. Prima facie selectivity is obvious no matter if the comparison is between independent and associated enterprises,[728] between associated enterprises and domestic groups,[729] or between different multinational enterprises.[730] I shall consider below whether such a situation of prima facie selectivity may be justified by the inner logic of a corporate income tax system. I will answer this question by considering the purpose and the scope of transfer pricing safe harbours, in the light of the objective of a corporate income tax system.

---

728. This is because independent enterprises are, by definition, subject to the market forces, while only certain associated enterprises are eligible to the safe harbour.
729. This is because the sum of the income of the members of a domestic group is under the influence of the market forces, contrary to the undertakings that are eligible to the transfer pricing safe harbour.
730. This is because a safe harbour would typically apply only to certain types of intercompany transactions, the others being subject to the normal application of the arm's length principle.

Chapter 8: The Justification and Proportionality Tests

Transfer pricing safe harbours that affect the determination of the taxable income of associated enterprises (as opposed to safe harbours limited to compliance issues) have a general purpose of providing foreseeability and simplicity, to the benefit of multinational enterprises and tax administrations. According to the 2017 OECD transfer pricing guidelines, the basic benefits of safe harbours are compliance relief, certainty, and administrative simplicity.[731] Given that transfer pricing safe harbours normally imply the use of predetermined prices or margins (or ranges thereof), it can reasonably be assumed that the scope of transfer pricing safe harbours will be limited to intercompany transactions with a low degree of complexity, as recommended in the guidelines.[732] The opposite solution, such as applying a transfer pricing safe harbour to a company owning intangible property or an entrepreneur, would imply too high a risk of arriving at a level of profits that does not match the functional profile of the actual undertaking; a risk of double taxation or double non-taxation would also exist, given that other countries would not be likely to recognise the application of the same safe harbour.

The general purpose of transfer pricing safe harbours does not fundamentally contradict the State aid rules. I even argued in Chapter 6 that the predetermined character of safe harbours matches the need for precision that is inherent to State aid law, and mentioned in the beginning of this section that this predetermined character is also consistent with the principle of legal certainty. However, this does not justify the departure from the reference system that is implied by a safe harbour that deviates from the arm's length principle, especially not in the light of the inner logic of the corporate income tax system. There is no reason that directly flows from a corporate income tax system to apply, for certain intercompany transactions only, safe harbours that deviate from the arm's length principle. In my view, no justification accepted by the Union courts applies to the case of transfer pricing safe harbours that deviate from the arm's length principle. Such safe harbours actually run against some of the justifications that were accepted by the Union courts and that were confirmed at paragraph 139 of the Commission's notice on the notion of State aid, in particular the need to prevent tax avoidance,[733] and the principle of neutrality.[734] The justifications described by the European Commission in the 2016 notice in relation to '(f)ixed basis tax regime for specific activities' would, in my opinion, lead to the same conclusion.[735]

Moreover, it is clear that the deviation from the reference system implied by safe harbours that do not implement the arm's length principle would be in breach of the principle of proportionality. This is because the objective of the corporate income tax system, and the need for simplicity as well as foreseeability, could be achieved by less

---

731. *See* paras 4.105 and following of the 2017 OECD transfer pricing guidelines.
732. *See* para. 4.129 of the 2017 OECD transfer pricing guidelines.
733. This is because transfer pricing safe harbours that deviate from the arm's length principle might increase the risk of double non-taxation, or at least the tax planning opportunities: *see* paras 4.114 and 4.122 and following of the 2017 OECD transfer pricing guidelines.
734. This is because transfer pricing safe harbours that deviate from the arm's length principle imply a differential treatment between the undertakings that are eligible to the safe harbour rule, and those which are not.
735. *See* Commission Notice on the notion of State aid as referred to in Art. 107(1) of the Treaty on the Functioning of the European Union [2016] OJ C 262/1, paras 181 and 182.

far reaching measures, in particular transfer pricing safe harbours that do enforce the arm's length principle.[736] Indeed, safe harbours that enforce the arm's length principle would have a twofold benefit: first, that of achieving the objective of the corporate income tax system (the taxation of the net income of all undertakings); second, that of correcting some of the drawbacks of a generally formulated arm's length provision, in particular the need to approximate values. There is simply no reason that is intrinsic to a corporate income tax system to implement transfer pricing safe harbours that deviate from the arm's length principle, when the same Member State has implemented a generally formulated arm's length provision. The reasons for choosing such safe harbours are rather extrinsic to the reference system, such as an effort to enhance the attractiveness of a country,[737] or the willingness to maximise fiscal revenues;[738] however, as explained by the European Commission, 'it is not possible to rely on external policy objectives which are not inherent to the system'.[739]

To sum up, in my opinion a transfer pricing safe harbour that deviates from the arm's length principle is prima facie selective, and cannot be justified by the nature or the general scheme of a corporate income tax system. I will consider below the possible justification of the prima facie selective aspects of a system of formula apportionment with firm-specific factors.

8.5 THE JUSTIFICATION AND PROPORTIONALITY TESTS APPLIED TO THE SELECTIVE ASPECTS OF A SYSTEM OF FORMULA APPORTIONMENT WITH FIRM-SPECIFIC FACTORS

I explained in Chapter 7 of this book that the selectivity analysis of a system of formula apportionment with firm-specific factors is highly dependent on two issues: the choice of the reference system, and the determination of the right comparator. I identified two different assumptions to apply the selectivity test, which led to two different cases of prima facie selectivity. I will now apply the justification and proportionality tests to these two cases of prima facie selectivity. To that end, I will first study the case where the reference system is made of the whole corporate income tax system, and the comparison is between independent and associated enterprises. Here, a system of formula apportionment raises the question of de jure selectivity (section 8.5.1). Second, the justification analysis is applied to the case where the reference system is made of the sole allocation method, or the comparison is between different associated enterprises. This time, it is de facto selectivity that is relevant (section 8.5.2).

---

736. A risk of deviation from the reference system nevertheless still exists with transfer pricing safe harbours that do enforce the arm's length principle, as evidenced in chapter 6 of this book.
737. In case the safe harbour provides for a taxable income that is below what the arm's length principle would prescribe.
738. In case the safe harbour provides for a taxable income that is above what the arm's length principle would prescribe.
739. *See* Commission Notice on the notion of State aid as referred to in Art. 107(1) of the Treaty on the Functioning of the European Union [2016] OJ C 262/1, para. 138, with references to case law at footnote 213.

8.5.1 De Jure Selectivity

If it is considered that the reference system is made of an allocation method, and assuming that members of multinational enterprises are in a comparable situation to independent enterprises, a clear difference in treatment appears between the two categories of undertakings: independent enterprises would be taxed on their income, as it is determined by the corporate income tax system and subject to the market forces, while associated enterprises would eventually be taxed on the income that is attributed by the formula. It was concluded in Chapter 7 that, under these assumptions, a system of formula apportionment is prima facie de jure selective, because the difference in treatment between the two categories of undertakings stems from the design of the law.

Can such a difference in treatment be justified by the nature or the general scheme of the corporate income tax system? Although it was concluded at section 8.2 above that the limited corrective effect of an allocation method to members of multinational enterprises might be consistent with the objective of a corporate income tax system (and thus with its inner logic), these preliminary conclusions need to be confirmed by the analysis of the particular case of each allocation method. There are various fiscal arguments that speak in favour of applying a system of formula apportionment to allocate the profits of multinational enterprises to different jurisdictions. The main argument relates to the difficulty, or even the impossibility of applying the arm's length principle in certain cases. I emphasised some of these difficulties in Chapter 5, especially in relation to situations where the open market provides no reliable benchmark. Generally, it can be observed that with the digitalisation of the economy, the globalisation of trade, or the integration between the members of multinational enterprises,[740] the arm's length principle is difficult to apply, because of the lack of comparability between independent and associated enterprises. A system of formula apportionment with firm-specific factors would share profits on the basis of a predetermined, fixed formula, that is applicable even in the most complex or unique situations. Other arguments support a system of formula apportionment, such as the administrative ease to apply it thanks to its mechanistic character, and the flexibility offered to the Member States by the possibility to choose the allocation key.

Although these arguments might be convincing from a fiscal point of view, they are not necessarily valid from a State aid perspective. A prima facie selective measure may only be justified in the light of the inner logic of the tax system: there should be a superior need to deviate from the reference system, for such a measure to be in line with the nature or the general scheme of the reference system. The proportionality test needs also to be met. My interpretation of the justifications that have been admitted by the Union courts and in the Commission's practice is that the deviation should be necessary to ensure that the logic of the tax system is preserved, which seems close to ensuring that the objective(s) pursued by the tax system – if necessary in interaction

---

740. *See* paras 9.6 and 9.35 of the 2017 OECD transfer pricing guidelines.

with other taxes[741] – can be met. It is true that, as argued above at section 8.2, the use of an allocation method exclusively with respect to members of multinational enterprises may be justified by the inner logic of a corporate income tax system, in particular the need to prevent tax avoidance. However, this does not mean that any allocation method is justified by the nature or the general scheme of a corporate income tax system.

Here, the issue is, in my opinion, that a system of formula apportionment would imply a general and unconditional deviation from the reference system implying diverging tax outcomes, with no connection to the actual need for such a deviation. A generally applying system of formula apportionment would eventually result in two alternative tax systems being applied in parallel: the taxation of independent enterprises on their income computed according to the domestic tax system and subject to the market forces, and the taxation of associated enterprises on the income allocated by a formula. Depending on the circumstances and on the allocation key, one system may be more favourable than the other, but in any case the existence of two systems that apply in parallel with different outcomes results in a clear difference in treatment.

This general and unconditional deviation from the reference system cannot be systematically justified by the nature or the logic of the corporate income tax system, because there is no general need to deviate from the normal application of the tax system for all multinational enterprises, and all intercompany transactions. The inner logic of the tax system does not require a system of formula apportionment by the sole effect of cross-border group membership. There are several arguments that support this statement. For example, in the case of a multinational enterprise where the members do not transact with each other but with third parties, there is no need to apply a system of formula apportionment and deviate significantly from the normal effect of the corporate income tax system: the application of the normal rules would suffice to levy tax in accordance with the objective of the system. A general acceptance for a system of formula apportionment would also open tax planning opportunities: for example, an independent enterprise subject to the general corporate income tax system could simply set up a subsidiary in a foreign country for the members of the newly created group to be qualified as associated enterprises, and thus become eligible to the system of formula apportionment; this simple operation would result in the parent company being taxed differently by the sole effect of group membership. Therefore, in my view, the inner logic of a corporate income tax system cannot provide a general and unconditional right to apply a system of formula apportionment that is limited to the members of a multinational enterprise. In addition, no matter which apportionment factors are chosen, the connection with the concept of income will necessarily be weaker than under the normal corporate income tax system, i.e., the objective of the tax system would not be fully achieved. Therefore, the inner logic of a corporate income tax system cannot require the general application of a set of rules that does not

---

741. *See* Richard Lyal, 'Transfer Pricing Rules and State Aid' (2015) 38 Fordham International Law Journal 1017, who at 1036 stresses that 'it may at times be necessary to have regard to a wider context'. *See also* Case C-308/01, *GIL Insurance Ltd and Others v. Commissioners of Customs & Excise*, ECLI:EU:C:2004:252.

ensure the attainment of the objectives of this system. It must be concluded, therefore, that a system of formula apportionment with firm-specific factors cannot be justified by the nature or the general scheme of a corporate income tax system, assuming the reference system is made of the whole corporate income tax system, and the right comparator is between independent and associated enterprises. This conclusion is strengthened if one considers the proportionality test: the arm's length principle would be a less far-reaching allocation method to attain the objective of the corporate income tax system, given that it would not entail as strong a deviation from the concept of income, thereby being closer to the objective of the corporate income tax system. The conclusion is that the existence of cross-border intercompany transactions does not, per se, justify the general and unconditional use of a system of formula apportionment with firm-specific factors. In my view, that conclusion is not dependent on which firm-specific factors are chosen.

The above conclusion might need to be nuanced when the arm's length principle cannot be applied in a reliable manner, for example because of a lack of comparables due to the uniqueness or the complexity of the intercompany transactions that take place within a multinational enterprise. In such cases, the use of a formula-based allocation method may be the only solution to attribute income to associated enterprises, given that the open market would not provide a reliable benchmark. Therefore, on a case-by-case basis and as a solution of last resort, a formula-based allocation method might be the best solution to respect the inner logic of a corporate income tax system, and eventually levy tax on the basis of a proxy that provides a relevant estimate of the income of an associated enterprise, if the reliable application of the arm's length principle is made impossible by the specific features of the transaction at hand.

However, when applying a formula-based allocation method in such cases of last resort, the principle of proportionality would command, in my view, that such a method keeps, as far as possible, a connection with the remaining tax system, and thus with the concept of income as well as the effects of the market forces, so as to minimise deviations from the normal rules. If the inner logic of a tax system requires the use of a formula-based allocation method as well as a connection with both the concept of income and the effects of the market forces, this combination would be best achieved through relying on the profit split method, rather than a system of formula apportionment with a predetermined allocation formula. This is, on the one hand, because this method is meant to implement or approximate the arm's length principle, which implies a connection with the concept of income as well as with the effects of the market forces. On the other hand, the profit split method can rely only indirectly on information provided by the open market, which helps solve the cases where no reliable benchmark is provided by transactions between independent enterprises.[742] Moreover, the allocation key of a profit split arrangement is chosen on a case-by-case basis, something that enables the choice of a methodology that, in each situation, has the closest possible connection to the concept of income, as opposed to the general and

---

742. *See* para. 2.118 of the 2017 OECD transfer pricing guidelines.

unconditional deviation from the reference system implied by a unique and predetermined formula under a system of formula apportionment.

Consequently, even in the cases where the arm's length principle is difficult to apply, the inner logic of a corporate income tax system would not require a general deviation from this principle with no attempt at keeping some connection to the concept of income: the proportionality test indicates that it is less far-reaching to apply the profit split method, although the open market provides only an indirect (or even non-existent) indication about how to allocate income. I realise that, in these cases, the actual difference between the profit split method and a system of formula apportionment may be thin, if no comparables are provided by the open market;[743] however, a difference does exist, through the flexibility given by the profit split method to choose, on a case-by-case basis, an allocation key that has some connection to the concept of income,[744] and to the effects of the market forces.[745]

At this point, it is important to mention a decision of the European Commission that supports the idea suggested in this section, i.e., the justification of the use of a formula-based allocation method in situations where the open market provides no direct benchmark for the allocation of profits. It is a decision where the Commission found that undertakings involved in the wholesale of diamonds could be taxed under a regime that clearly deviated from the general corporate income tax regime. According to the alternative tax system, the costs of goods sold were approximated as a percentage of the revenues, instead of corresponding to the actual costs. This system was justified by the nature or the general scheme of the reference system, given the difficulty to value diamonds. That difficulty justified a derogation from the normal regime, which was limited to a minimal extent.[746] Similarly, when the arm's length principle cannot be reliably applied, especially through the use of the more direct transfer pricing methods, this decision indicates that it might be justified to rely on a formula-based allocation method; however, since the arm's length principle is more consistent with the objective of a corporate income tax system than a formula-based allocation method, the principle of proportionality points to keeping a connection to the concept of income and to the effects of the market forces to limit the derogation from the reference system to a minimal extent, something that is achieved by relying on the profit split method.

I now turn to the justification and proportionality tests of the de facto selective features of a system of formula apportionment with firm-specific factors.

---

743. Similarly, see Reuven S. Avi-Yonah, 'Between Formulary Apportionment and the OECD Guidelines: A Proposal for Reconciliation' (2010) 2 World Tax Journal 3, 16; Giammarco Cottani, 'Formulary Apportionment: A Revamp in the Post-Base Erosion and Profit Shifting Era?' (2016) 44 Intertax 755, 758.
744. For example, by relying on the value drivers that are relevant in the situation at hand to choose the elements of the allocation key. See section 7.3.3.2 for an analysis of the connection of apportionment factors to the concept of income.
745. For example, by relying on elements on which the taxpayer has no or little control, such as the sales to third parties. See section 7.3.3.3 for an analysis of the connection of apportionment factors to the market forces.
746. See Commission Decision of 29 July 2016 on State Aid SA.42007 (2015/N) – Belgium Alternative income tax regime for the wholesale diamond sector [2016] OJ C 369/1.

8.5.2 De Facto Selectivity

After considering the case of a comparison between independent and associated enterprises, it is now assumed that the reference system consists of the sole allocation method, or that the comparison for State aid purposes is between different associated enterprises. Under these assumptions, the Member States would not be prevented by the rules on State aid to tax multinational enterprises on the basis of a system that deviates from the normal corporate income tax regime. However, a system of formula apportionment with firm-specific factors would not be immune against the State aid rules: it was argued in Chapter 7 that such a system may be de facto selective because it effectively results in a direct tax on such factors, thereby favouring or disadvantaging certain undertakings depending on the existence, and the location of the apportionment factors. It was found that the highest risk of de facto selectivity concerns allocation methods with one, or few apportionment factors. Indeed, with a single or a low number of apportionment factors comes a higher likelihood that the effects of the formula target certain undertakings that are identified, or identifiable, which would make the formula prima facie de facto selective. It was also argued that the risk of selectivity decreases with the number of apportionment factors, their diversity, their connection to the concept of income, and their link to the effects of the market forces. Therefore, not every system of formula apportionment with firm-specific factors is likely to be de facto selective.

If the system is prima facie de facto selective, the next step of a selectivity analysis is the justification and proportionality tests. Here, there are no different tax systems that exist in parallel: it is assumed that the same system of formula apportionment is applied to all members of multinational enterprises. Since different formulas have different effects, the outcome of the justification analysis is dependent on the choice of the apportionment factors, and on their relative weight. This makes it impossible to provide in this section a comprehensive and definite justification analysis, given that different formulas are likely to lead to different outcomes.[747] Rather, it is suggested a way of reasoning to conduct the justification and proportionality tests.

In my view, two elements, which are closely related to each other, are particularly important when considering the justification analysis: the prevention of tax avoidance, and a connection with the concept of income. The more a formula would be connected to the concept of income and help prevent tax avoidance, the more likely it is to be justified by the nature or the general scheme of a corporate income tax system. On the one hand, the prevention of tax avoidance belongs to the inner logic of a corporate income tax system, because with no prevention of tax avoidance, the very existence of the tax base is threatened.[748] On the other hand, there is a strong link between the connection of a formula to the concept of income, and the possibility to

---

747. For a study of different alternatives for systems of formula apportionment, *see* Estefanía López Llopis, 'Formulary Apportionment in the European Union' (2017) 45 Intertax 631.
748. Concurring, *see* Edoardo Traversa and Pierre M. Sabbadini, 'Anti-avoidance Measures and State Aid in a Post-BEPS-Context: An Attempt at Reconciliation' in Isabelle Richelle, Wolfgang Schön, and Edoardo Traversa (eds), *State Aid Law and Business Taxation* (Springer 2016) 104.

justify the selective effects of a system of formula apportionment with firm-specific factors. Indeed, since it is assumed in this book that a corporate income tax system builds on the objective to tax the net income of all corporations, a set of tax rules that tends to achieve this objective, tends also to be consistent with the inner logic of the reference system. Moreover, the concept of income is intrinsically neutral and non-discriminatory, since it can reasonably be assumed that most commercial companies do pursue the objective of earning profits; that would make a system of formula apportionment with a strong connection to the concept of income an appropriate means of achieving the objective of the corporate income tax system. Accordingly, the selectivity and the justification analyses coincide in this respect, given that the connection of a formula to the concept of income should have consequences both on the prima facie selectivity of a formula, and on the possibility to justify a prima facie selective formula by the nature or the general scheme of the system.

The arguments suggested above should preclude the justification of a formula with a single apportionment factor. This is for the reason that various firm-specific apportionment factors have a directly selective effect on different undertakings, but with no direct connection to the inner logic of a corporate income tax system: firm-specific apportionment factors, taken separately, resemble more a direct tax on various elements such as property or labour costs, than an income tax, which applies to the difference between revenues and all the expenses that contribute to earning the revenues. One firm-specific apportionment factor cannot correctly mirror the concept of income, especially not when it is applied to all multinational enterprises, given that different undertakings are likely to earn income thanks to relying on different elements.[749] Moreover, no apportionment factor can, alone, prevent tax avoidance.[750] It is actually more likely that the use of a single apportionment factor enhances the risks of tax avoidance, given that undertakings could organise their operations to minimise the presence of this factor in a given country. Consequently, a system of formula apportionment with a single firm-specific factor is de facto selective, and cannot be justified by the nature or the general scheme of the corporate income tax system.

As the number and the diversity of the apportionment factors grows, the risk of de facto selectivity is decreasing, and the chances of justifying a prima facie selective

---

749. For example, it has been observed from a US perspective, and in the light of WTO law that a sales-only apportionment would not be justified by 'common sense, economic analysis, judicial precedent, standard practice, the legislative history of sales-only apportionment, and federal law': *see* Charles E. McLure Jr. and Walter Hellerstein, 'Does Sales-Only Apportionment Of Corporate Income Violate International Trade Rules?' (2002) 96 Tax Notes International 1315, 1320.
750. It could be argued that apportionment factors that have a connection to the market forces are suitable to prevent tax avoidance, as the taxpayer has no control on the effects of the market forces. For example, the sales-by-destination factor could be seen as a suitable means to prevent tax avoidance, as the end-clients of a multinational enterprise are normally not movable. However, the suitability of this apportionment factor, alone, as a means to prevent tax avoidance has been criticised by Schön, in view of the fact that the traditional levy of corporate taxes in two steps (one at the corporate level, one at the shareholder level) would be jeopardised by a sales-based corporate income tax: *see* Wolfgang Schön, 'International Tax Coordination for a Second-Best World (Part III)' (2010) 3 World Tax Journal 227, 257. This speaks for combining the sales factor with other, origin-based apportionment factors.

measure increase. This is because a higher number of apportionment factors, especially if such factors are diverse and connected to the notion of income, increases the chances to correctly capture the value drivers of an undertaking, and thus the income generated by the apportionment factors in a given country. The prevention of tax avoidance is also improved by increasing the number and the diversity of the apportionment factors. However, the number and the diversity of the apportionment factors do not, as such, have a necessary connection to the concept of income, or to the prevention of tax avoidance: it is just more likely that these effects get stronger as the number and the diversity of the factors increase. Therefore, more than the number and the diversity as such, it is mainly the connection between the apportionment factors and the concept of income as well as the prevention of tax avoidance that may justify the selectivity of a formula-based allocation method.[751]

As already mentioned in Chapter 7, no direct connection can exist between the concept of income and a formula-based allocation method with firm-specific factors, given that a formula is a proxy that can only incorrectly approximate the contribution to income of certain apportionment factors. However, this approximation can be improved by choosing the apportionment factors, and weighting them. In this respect, it was argued in section 7.3.3.2 that the factors sales, labour, and tangible assets are likely to have some connection to the concept of income. Each factor has advantages and drawbacks in view of establishing a connection with the earning of income, as well as the need to prevent tax avoidance in a given country.[752] It was also emphasised that various arguments indicate that a heavier weight should be given to the sales factor than to the other factors, which resulted in the proposal to assign sales half of the apportionment, while assets and payroll receive a quarter each, i.e., the so-called double-weighted sales formula.

To conclude, by combining the three apportionment factors sales, labour, and tangible assets, with possibly assigning a heavier weight to the sales factor, a system of formula apportionment with firm-specific factors that is prima facie selective would have some consistency with the objective of a corporate income tax system. Such a combination of apportionment factors might also prevent certain tax planning opportunities, although it cannot be said that these factors will necessarily prevent all forms of tax avoidance.

8.6 CONCLUSION

The conclusions of this chapter can be very short, as the general conclusions on the selectivity of the three allocation methods are presented in Chapter 9 of this book.

---

751. On the suitability of a system of formula apportionment to prevent tax avoidance *see* Michael C. Durst, 'Beyond BEPS: A Tax Policy Agenda for Developing Countries' (2014) 18 ICTD Working Paper < https://assets.publishing.service.gov.uk/media/57a089c1ed915d622c0003ab/WP18-FINAL.pdf> accessed 11 February 2018, 12.
752. *See* Yariv Brauner, 'Formula Based Transfer Pricing' (2014) 42 Intertax 615, especially at 618–622 for a review of arguments and references to the doctrine.

As mentioned in the introductory section to this chapter, no final answers can be provided here as to the justification of the selective features of the allocation methods. That can only be done on a case-by-case basis, by taking into account the national context of an allocation method. The prima facie selective features of a generally formulated arm's length provision, and of a transfer pricing safe harbour that implements the arm's length principle, can in most respects be justified by the nature or the general scheme of a corporate income tax system. However, in practice it may be difficult to bring the evidence that the principle of proportionality has been enforced, which is a question that can only be answered on a case-by-case basis. Transfer pricing safe harbours that deviate from the arm's length principle are, in contrast, most likely to be unable of justification. The selectivity test of a system of formula apportionment with firm-specific factors is highly dependent on the previous steps of this test. However, no matter which assumptions are made, such an allocation method would be at tension with the selectivity criterion. I suggested different ways of reasoning to decrease the risk that a system of formula apportionment with firm-specific factors is selective.

The general conclusions from this study are presented in the following chapter.

CHAPTER 9
Conclusion

9.1 INTRODUCTION

In this chapter, I will present the conclusions from the research conducted in this book. I will first summarise the main learnings from this study (section 9.2). Based on these findings, I will suggest a classification of the allocation methods in the light of the selectivity test, from the least to the most selective one, to contribute to the search for an allocation method that best meets the requirements of the selectivity criterion (section 9.3.)

9.2 MAIN LEARNINGS FROM THE STUDY

The outcome of the selectivity test of the three allocation methods studied in this book depends on several parameters, which can be divided in two main categories: issues that are common to the three allocation methods, and issues that are particular to each allocation method. These two categories correspond to the two parts of the book.

The questions analysed in the first part of the book emphasised three elements of the selectivity test that are common to all the allocation methods. These elements are the determination of the reference system, the potential relevance of the market economy operator test, and the comparability analysis. How one analyses these elements has fundamental consequences on the application of the State aid rules to the allocation methods, because the direction taken by the selectivity analysis is dependent on the answers brought to these common issues.

I concluded in Chapter 2 that the reference system should be made of the binding elements of the corporate income tax system of a given Member State, which includes both the basic principles of the tax system and the allocation method. I argued that Article 107(1) of the TFEU cannot intrinsically imply an obligation to apply the arm's length principle or any other allocation method, although this article does imply an obligation to provide equal treatment. In Chapter 3, I found that the market economy operator test can have no binding effect on the design of the allocation methods, or on the assessment of a possible deviation from the reference system, whether or not such methods are relying on the arm's length principle. When it comes to the comparability analysis, I emphasised in Chapter 4 the differences between members of multinational enterprises, and two other categories of undertakings, namely independent enterprises and members of domestic groups. Despite the factual and legal differences existing between these categories of undertakings, I found that when the comparison is made in the light of the objective of a corporate income tax system – which is assumed to be the taxation of the net income of all corporations – these three categories of undertakings are in a comparable situation, assuming they all have a commercial objective.

Before moving to a summary of the second part of the book, it is worth emphasising how central the notion of comparability is to the topic of this book.[753] The outcome of the selectivity analysis is utterly dependent on the comparability test: if the notion of comparability is defined in a narrow manner, the comparison is between members of multinational enterprises, and the room of manoeuvre for the tax policies of the Member States is quite broad. The Member States could decide, for example, to tax multinational enterprises based on rules that deviate from the taxation of independent undertakings. By contrast, if comparability is defined broadly, the comparison is between all types of undertakings, something that reduces the tax policy choices of the Member States.

The second part of the book analyses the selectivity of each allocation method, both based on the findings of part one, and assuming that different conclusions are reached on the common issues to the allocation methods. In this part, I found that the three allocation methods are likely, at some point, to favour certain undertakings over others, and thus be prima facie selective. However, I also emphasised that the different allocation methods are prima facie selective for different reasons, given that they have different rationales and ways of functioning: on the one hand, the arm's length principle is an abstract principle, and with that comes a subjective and approximative dimension in its application and interpretation. On the other hand, the two other allocation methods rely on a pre-determined and more mechanistic functioning, although transfer pricing safe harbours contain a subjective dimension with respect to the eligibility to such safe harbours.

I concluded in Chapter 5 that a generally formulated arm's length provision may be a prima facie selective measure, on the basis of both the de jure selectivity test and the de facto selectivity test. However, I argued in Chapter 8 that the prima facie selective features of a generally formulated arm's length provision should be able to be justified by the nature or the general scheme of a corporate income tax system, if such a tax system pursues the objective of taxing all undertakings on their net income, and if the arm's length principle is correctly applied. I also emphasised that the imprecision

---

753. In this respect, Advocate General Wahl emphasised that 'the crux of the assessment of selectivity lies in the comparison of undertakings': see Case C-203/16 P, *Dirk Andres (administrator of Heitkamp BauHolding GmbH), previously Heitkamp BauHolding GmbH v. European Commission*, ECLI:EU:C:2017:1017, Opinion of AG Wahl, para. 93.

of the application of a generally formulated arm's length provision is at odds with the principle of legal certainty, although the arm's length principle is, in theory, an objective measure.

When it comes to transfer pricing safe harbours, I suggested in Chapters 6 and 8 that only safe harbours that implement the arm's length principle do not entail a selective treatment. Safe harbours that deviate from the arm's length principle do entail a selective treatment, unless they provide for a higher level of profits than what the arm's length principle prescribes, and are optional. Here, it can be observed that the OECD transfer pricing guidelines recommend concluding bilateral or multilateral safe harbours to mitigate the risk that transfer pricing safe harbours are in breach of the arm's length principle.[754]

With respect to a system of formula apportionment with firm-specific factors, I pointed to the need to distinguish between two series of assumptions: under the first series of assumptions, the reference system is made of the whole corporate income tax system, and the comparison is between independent and associated enterprises. Under the second series of assumptions, the reference system is made of an allocation method, or the comparison is between associated enterprises. In the former case, I found in Chapter 7 that the application of a system of formula apportionment to members of multinational enterprises makes the allocation method prima facie de jure selective. I argued in Chapter 8 that no justification is likely to be valid, unless the arm's length principle cannot be reliably applied; the principle of proportionality would then imply that the use of a formula-based allocation method be as closely as possible connected to the concept of income and to the effects of the market forces, so as to limit the derogation from the reference system to a minimal extent. That would be best achieved by relying on the profit split method.

Under the second series of assumptions, the Member States have greater leeway to implement a system of formula apportionment, because it is not precluded by a comparison with the taxation of independent enterprises. However, even in this case, a system of formula apportionment with firm-specific factors is likely to be prima facie de facto selective, because it effectively corresponds to a direct tax on the apportionment factors. However, I argued in Chapters 7 and 8 that there are several parameters that make a formula less discriminatory and more consistent with the objective of a corporate income tax system. A formula that is reasonably balanced, and that should have a higher chance to pass the justification and proportionality tests, is the 'double-weighted sales formula', whereby sales are assigned half of the apportionment, while assets and labour receive a quarter each. However, this formula is only more consistent with the objective of a corporate income tax system. It cannot be asserted with all certainty that this formula is justified by the nature or the general scheme of a corporate income tax system, and that it is proportionate to the objectives pursued by such a system. In this respect, a legal dogmatic analysis can hardly provide an objective answer to the delimitation of the scope of the selectivity criterion. This is due to the subjectivity that characterises the application of the State aid rules, and more

---

754. *See* para. 4.119 of the 2017 OECD transfer pricing guidelines.

generally the primary law of the EU, to domestic provisions. As emphasised by Komárek, 'there is no consensus as regards the ultimate goals of European integration (its *finalité*)'.[755] However, the lack of consensus with respect to the *finalité* of European integration does not prevent the CJEU from choosing where and how to draw a line between general and selective measures,[756] and thus to distinguish between general and selective apportionment formulas.

After having summarised the main learnings from this study, I now turn to the suggestion of a classification of the allocation methods in the light of the selectivity test, from the least to the most selective method.

9.3 CLASSIFICATION OF THE ALLOCATION METHODS FROM THE LEAST TO THE MOST SELECTIVE ONE

A conclusion from this study is that the three allocation methods have certain potentially selective features. This speaks for combining different allocation methods, so that members of multinational enterprises are taxed in the least selective manner. From a tax policy perspective, this solution has been analysed in the academic literature. Already in 1933, Carroll observed that for most countries, 'it may be necessary to resort to fractional apportionment in respect of certain items of income',[757] while the arm's length principle is the main rule. Certain scholars have suggested combining the arm's length principle with formula apportionment,[758] and it has been argued that these two allocation methods are not incompatible with each other.[759] It has also been observed that no allocation method is clearly superior to the others, given that all methods have advantages and drawbacks;[760] in this respect, the US Supreme

---

755. *See* Jan Komárek, 'Legal Reasoning in EU Law' in Anthony Arnull and Damian Chalmers (eds), *The Oxford Handbook of European Union Law* (Oxford University Press 2015) 40, emphasis not added.
756. In this vein, although mostly with respect to the application of the freedoms of movement to direct taxation, *see* Daniel Gutmann, 'Some Theoretical Thoughts on Judicial Power and Taw Law, with a Particular Focus on the ECJ' in Luc Hinnekens and Philippe Hinnekens (eds), *A Vision of Taxes Within and Outside European Borders – Festschrift in Honor of Prof. Dr. Frans Vanistendael* (Kluwer Law International 2008) 485.
757. *See* Mitchell. B. Carroll, *Taxation of National and Foreign Enterprises: Volume 4 Methods of Allocating Taxable Income* (League of Nations 1933) 96, para. 332. However, it should be emphasised that the correctness of the views of Carroll has been nuanced in the study conducted by Langbein: *see* Stanley I. Langbein, 'The Unitary Method and the Myth of Arm's Length' (1986) 30 Tax Notes 625.
758. *See* e.g., Yariv Brauner, 'Formula Based Transfer Pricing' (2014) 42 Intertax 615; J. Clifton Fleming Jr., Robert J. Peroni and Stephen E. Shay, 'Formulary Appointment in the U.S. International Income Tax System: Putting Lipstick on a Pig?' (2014) 36 Michigan Journal of International Law 1, 54.
759. *See* e.g., Michael C. Durst, 'Beyond BEPS: A Tax Policy Agenda for Developing Countries' (2014) 18 ICTD Working Paper < https://assets.publishing.service.gov.uk/media/57a089c1ed 915d622c0003ab/WP18-FINAL.pdf > accessed 11 February 2018, who at 6 argues that 'the BEPS analysis can help to dispel what has been, historically, an erroneous perception – that the arm's length and formulary approaches to taxation are in principle incompatible'.
760. Even at the time the arm's length principle was being developed, scholars were aware of the limits of this principle. *See* e.g., the analysis of Carroll on the notion of 'residuum': Mitchell. B. Carroll, *Taxation of National and Foreign Enterprises: Volume 4 Methods of Allocating Taxable*

Court found that both the arm's length principle and formula apportionment 'are imperfect proxies for an ideal which is not only difficult to achieve in practice but also difficult to describe in theory'.[761]

The study conducted in this book makes it possible to suggest a classification of the allocation methods in the light of the selectivity test, from the least to the most selective one. This classification is only suggested at a theoretical level, with no consideration for domestic law or tax treaty law. The allocation method that has the lowest risk of being selective is a transfer pricing safe harbour that implements the arm's length principle: it lies on a strong connection to the concept of income as well as on the effects of the market forces,[762] while decreasing the approximation that is intrinsic to a generally formulated arm's length provision. In other words, a transfer pricing safe harbour that implements the arm's length principle is more in line with the principle of legal certainty, than a generally formulated arm's length provision. Yet transfer pricing safe harbours that implement the arm's length principle have necessarily a limited scope of application, given that this method can only apply to intercompany transactions with a low level of complexity.[763]

A generally formulated arm's length provision would come as the second least selective method, as it builds on a strong connection to the concept of income as well as on the effects of the market forces, while in theory providing for a high degree of neutrality between all categories of undertakings. This allocation method, which in principle is applicable to any type of intercompany transaction, is nevertheless difficult to apply when the degree of comparability with independent transactions decreases. The more difficult it is to apply the arm's length principle, the higher chance that it is imprecise and unforeseeable, and thus at odds with the principle of legal certainty.

Income (League of Nations 1933) 192, para. 677. According to Wilkie, '(g)oing back in time with Carroll's comments seems like encountering a discussion in the present': *see* J. Scott Wilkie, 'Reflecting on the "Arm's Length Principle": What is the "Principle"? Where Next?' in Wolfgang Schön and Kai A. Konrad (eds), *Fundamentals of International Transfer Pricing in Law and Economics* (Springer 2012) 139, footnote 4. One of the major criticisms made to the arm's length principle is the non-relevance of the fiction it tries to achieve, given the difference between multinational enterprises and independent enterprises: *see* e.g., Ulf Andresen, 'Comments on Professor Schoueri's Lecture "Arm's Length: Beyond the Guidelines of the OECD"' (2015) 69 Bulletin for International Taxation 717, 719. *See also* Yariv Brauner, 'Value in the Eye of the Beholder: The Valuation of Intangibles for Transfer Pricing Purposes' (2008) 28 Virginia Tax Review 79, who at 159 considers that 'the theoretical advantage of the arm's length standard, based on a classical market approach to valuation, is lost in practice'. Formula apportionment has also been criticised in the doctrine, for example because of the possibility to locate the apportionment factors abroad, and thus be subject to tax domestically on only a portion of the corporate tax base: *see* J. Clifton Fleming Jr., Robert J. Peroni and Stephen E. Shay, 'Formulary Appointment in the U.S. International Income Tax System: Putting Lipstick on a Pig?' (2014) 36 Michigan Journal of International Law 1, who at 36 stress that formula apportionment 'adversely affects the ability of [companies that operate domestically] to compete against MNEs'.

761. *See* US Supreme Court, Case 81-523, 463 US 159, *Container Corporation of America v. Franchise Tax Board of California* 182, 27 June 1983.
762. *See* para. 1.14 of the 2017 OECD transfer pricing guidelines, where it is argued that the arm's length principle 'provides the closest approximation of the workings of the open market'.
763. *See* para. 4.129 of the 2017 OECD transfer pricing guidelines.

Accordingly, the arm's length principle has an intrinsic weakness[764] when multinational enterprises and independent enterprises are in a different situation, and yet need to be compared to each other.[765] In these situations, the position advocated in the OECD transfer pricing guidelines, which I argued is justified, is to accept some departure from observations made on the open market,[766] for example by relying on the profit split method.[767] Therefore, I argued that it would be incorrect if the selectivity criterion required to be strictly relying on the CUP method, or on information provided directly by the open market.

Last, a general system of formula apportionment with firm-specific factors is most likely prima facie selective and impossible to justify by the logic of a corporate income tax system, if the reference system is not limited to the allocation method and the comparability analysis is between independent and associated enterprises. This does not preclude the application of formula-based methods through profit split, when more direct transfer pricing methods are not reliable. A general system of formula apportionment with firm-specific factors could only be implemented by the Member States if the reference system is made of the sole allocation method or if the comparison is between associated enterprises, and assuming that the formula is not de facto selective. In this respect, it was argued that the 'double-weighted sales formula' seems as the least de facto selective formula.

In this section, I have evidenced the superiority of the arm's length principle to a system of formula apportionment with firm-specific factors, when these methods are considered in the context of State aid law. This might appear paradoxical in the light of the logic of the rules on State aid, and calls for a few reflections. Indeed, the logic of State aid law should imply a preference for clear and foreseeable rules, to avoid differences in treatment due to approximations, as well as risks of arbitrary treatments. The arm's length principle is also at odds, in my view, with the principle of legal certainty, which is a requirement to meet the principle of proportionality. In its functioning, formula apportionment is more objective than the arm's length principle.[768] But because of the effects of the apportionment factors, formula apportionment is intrinsically more likely to be selective: no matter how an allocation key is designed, one cannot escape the fact that the elements of the allocation key will have a direct and different influence on different undertakings. If formula apportionment is based on firm-specific factors, the outcome is a tax on the apportionment factors with

---

764. Concurring, *see* Reuven S. Avi-Yonah, 'Between Formulary Apportionment and the OECD Guidelines: A Proposal for Reconciliation' (2010) 2 World Tax Journal 3, 4–5.
765. For an illustration of this paradox, *see* the guidance with respect to intangibles that have 'unique characteristics'. While the 2017 guidelines recognise at para. 6.116 the existence for certain intangibles of 'unique characteristics', the guidelines nevertheless stress that it is 'critical to assess whether potential comparables in fact exhibit similar profit potential' (para. 6.116, *in fine*). Similarly, *see* para. 6.138 of the 2017 OECD transfer pricing guidelines.
766. *See* e.g., para. 6.127 of the 2017 OECD transfer pricing guidelines, where it is recognised that the lack of reliable comparables makes it difficult to support 'a comparables-based transfer pricing analysis'.
767. *See* e.g., para. 6.148 of the 2017 OECD transfer pricing guidelines with respect to the use of the profit split method for intercompany transactions that concern intangible property.
768. The objectivity of formula apportionment is in the reliance on a fixed formula, not in the choice and the weight of the factors of the formula.

Chapter 9: Conclusion

the unavoidable effect of an influence on behaviours, thus creating distortions in the allocation of resources, and eventually on trade and competition.[769]

The fact that the arm's length principle is more in line with the selectivity criterion than a system of formula apportionment with firm-specific factors is supported by the stronger link that the notion and the source of income have with the arm's length principle, than with a system of formula apportionment.[770] A system of formula apportionment 'does not attempt to determine precisely where income originates',[771] although a connection to the source of income may be approximated through relying on factors that contribute to earning income. If one accepts the assumption that all undertakings aim at maximising their income, the allocation method with the strongest connection to the concept of income appears as also being the most neutral one in a system that aims at taxing income. In contrast, a formula with firm-specific factors cannot be fully neutral, no matter which factors are chosen, and how they are weighted against each other. Consequently, the conclusions reached in this study are confirmed by the inner logic of the two allocation methods.

---

769. *See* e.g., Roger Gordon and John D. Wilson, 'An Examination of Multijurisdictional Corporate Income Taxation under Formula Apportionment' (1986) 54 Econometrica 1357, who argue that a system of formula apportionment creates distortions that do not exist under separate accounting and the arm's length principle, or even with direct taxes on the apportionment factors.
770. *See* e.g., Charles E. McLure, 'Replacing Separate Entity Accounting and the Arm's Length Principle with Formulary Apportionment' (2002) 56 Bulletin for International Taxation 586, 587; *see also* at 592: '(i)t seems prima facie clear as a conceptual matter that the *base* of an income tax should be taxed where income originates' (emphasis not added). *See also* Charles E. McLure and Joann M. Weiner, 'Deciding Whether the European Union Should Adopt Formulary Apportionment of Company Income' in Sijbren Cnossen (ed), *Taxing Capital Income in the European Union: Issues and Options for Reform* (Oxford University Press 2000) 258.
771. *See* Charles E. McLure, 'Replacing Separate Entity Accounting and the Arm's Length Principle with Formulary Apportionment' (2002) 56 Bulletin for International Taxation 586, 587.

Bibliography

Books and Articles

Agell A, 'Rättsdogmatik eller konstruktiv rättsvetenskap' in Åke Frändberg, Ulf Göransson, and Torgny Håstad (eds), *Festskrift till Stig Strömholm* (Iustus Förlag 1997).

Ahlborn A, and Berg C, 'Can State Aid Control Learn from Antitrust? The Need for a Greater Role for Competition Analysis under the State Aid Rules' in Andrea Biondi, Piet Eeckhout, and James Flynn (eds), *The Law of State Aid in the European Union* (Oxford University Press 2004).

Akkermans B, and Ramaekers E, 'Article 345 TFEU (ex Article 295 EC), Its Meanings and Interpretations' (2009) 15 European Law Journal 292.

Aldestam M, 'Skatteåtgärder som statligt stöd enligt artikel 87 i unionsfördraget' (2001) Skattenytt 87.

Aldestam M, *EC State Aid Rules Applied to Taxes* (Uppsala 2005).

Andresen U, 'Comments on Professor Schoueri's Lecture "Arm's Length: Beyond the Guidelines of the OECD"' (2015) 69 Bulletin for International Taxation 717.

Anestis P, and Mavroghenis S, 'The Market Investor Test' in Michael Sánchez Rydelski (ed), *The EC State Aid Regime: Distortive Effects of State Aid on Competition and Trade* (Cameron May 2006).

Arnull A, 'What Is a General Principle of EU Law?' in Rita de la Feria and Stefan Vogenauer (eds), *Prohibition of Abuse of Law – A New General Principle of EU Law?* (Hart Publishing 2011).

Avi-Yonah R S, 'The Rise and Fall of Arm's Length: A Study in the Evolution of U.S. International Taxation' (1995) 15 Virginia Tax Review 89.

Avi-Yonah R S, *International Tax as International Law – An Analysis of the International Tax Regime* (Cambridge University Press 2007).

Avi-Yonah R S, Clausing K A, and Durst M C, 'Allocating Business Profits for Tax Purposes: A Proposal to Adopt a Formulary Profit Split' (2009) 9 Florida Tax Review 497.

Avi-Yonah R S, 'Between Formulary Apportionment and the OECD Guidelines: A Proposal for Reconciliation' (2010) 2 World Tax Journal 3.

Avi-Yonah R S, and Benshalom I, 'Formulary Apportionment – Myths and Prospects' (2011) 3 World Tax Journal 371.

Bibliography

Avi-Yonah R S, 'Splitting the Unsplittable: Toward a Formulary Approach to Allocating Residuals Under Profit Split' (2013) 12 University of Michigan Public Law Research Paper 378 < https://papers.ssrn.com/sol3/papers.cfm?abstract_id = 2369944 > accessed 18 January 2018.

Avi-Yonah R S, and Pouga Tinhaga Z, 'Unitary Taxation and International Tax Rules' (2014) 26 ICTD Working Paper < https://papers.ssrn.com/sol3/Delivery.cfm/SSRN_ID2602240_code572410.pdf?abstractid = 2351920&mirid = 1 > accessed 6 February 2018.

Avi-Yonah R S, and Mazzoni G, 'The Apple State Aid Decision: A Wrong Way to Enforce the Benefits Principle?' (2016) 84 Tax Notes International 837.

Avi-Yonah R S, and Mazzoni G, 'Are Taxes Converging? Review of Eduardo Baistrocchi (ed), A Global Analysis of Tax Treaty Disputes (Cambridge University Press, 2017)' (2017) 573 Public Law and Legal Theory Research Paper Series.

Backer K D, and Miroudot S, *Mapping Global Value Chains* (OECD Trade Policy Papers 159, OECD 2013).

Baistrocchi E, and Roxan I (eds), *Resolving Transfer Pricing Disputes: A Global Analysis* (Cambridge University Press 2012).

Bernitz U, and Kjellgren A, *Europarättens Grunder* (7th edn, Norstedts Juridik 2018).

Blessing P H, 'Divergence of Third Party Pricing from Arm's Length Results' in Philip Baker and Catherine Bobbett (eds), *Tax Polymath: A Life in International Taxation – Essays in honour of John F. Avery Jones* (IBFD 2011).

Brauner Y, 'Value in the Eye of the Beholder: The Valuation of Intangibles for Transfer Pricing Purposes' (2008) 28 Virginia Tax Review 79.

Brauner Y, 'Formula Based Transfer Pricing' (2014) 42 Intertax 615.

Brokelind C, 'The Evolution of International Income Tax Law Applied to Global Trade' (2006) 34 Intertax 126.

Brokelind C, 'Intellectual Property, Taxation and State Aid Law' in Isabelle Richelle, Wolfgang Schön and Edoardo Traversa (eds), *State Aid Law and Business Taxation* (Springer 2016).

Buus T, and Brada J, 'Economics of Transfer Pricing Reviewed' (2008) < https://ssrn.com/abstract = 954333 > accessed 18 January 2018.

Calderón J, 'The OECD Transfer Pricing Guidelines as a Source of Tax Law' (2007) 37 Intertax 4.

Carlos Dos Santos A, *L'Union européenne et la régulation de la concurrence fiscale* (Bruylant 2009).

Carroll M B, *Taxation of National and Foreign Enterprises: Volume 4 Methods of Allocating Taxable Income* (League of Nations 1933).

Chérot J-Y, *Les aides d'État dans les Communautés européennes* (Economica 1998).

Collier R, and Andrus J L, *Transfer Pricing and the Arm's Length Principle After BEPS* (Oxford University Press 2017).

Cornella S, 'The "Market Economy Investor Principle" to Evaluate State Aid: Latest Development and New Perspectives' (2015) 22 Maastricht Journal of European and Comparative Law 553.

Cottani G, 'Formulary Apportionment: A Revamp in the Post-Base Erosion and Profit Shifting Era?' (2016) 44 Intertax 755.

Bibliography

Cyndecka M, 'The Applicability and Application of the Market Economy Investor Principle' (2016) 15 European State Aid Law Quarterly 381.

Dahlberg M, and Wiman B, *The Taxation of Foreign Passive Income for Groups of Companies – General Report* (IFA Cahiers Volume 98A, Sdu 2013).

Danon R J, 'Treaty Abuse in the Post-BEPS World: Analysis of the Policy Shift and Impact of the Principal Purpose Test for MNE Groups' (2018) 72 Bulletin for International Taxation 31.

De Broe L, 'Can Tax Treaties Confer State Aid?' (2017) 5 EC Tax Review 228.

De Cecco F, *State Aid and the European Economic Constitution* (Hart 2013).

De La Feria R, and Fuest C, 'The Economic Effects of EU Tax Jurisprudence' (2016) 41 European Law Review 44.

Di Bucci V, and Stobiecka-Kuik A, 'The Temporal Application of the State Aid Rules' in *EC State Aid Law – Le Droit des Aides d'Etat dans la CE – Liber Amicorum Francisco Santaolalla Gadea* (Kluwer Law International 2008).

Douénias S, 'Défense et illustration ... de la fiscalité internationale' in Sami Douénias (ed), *Mélanges Pascal Minne – Fiscalité internationale et patrimoniale* (Bruylant 2017).

Dourado A P, 'The Interest Limitation Rule in the Anti-Tax Avoidance Directive (ATAD) and the Net Taxation Principle' (2017) 26 EC Tax Review 112.

Drabbe H, 'The Test of Selectivity in State Aid Litigation: The Relevance of Drawing Internal and External Comparisons to Identify the Reference Framework' in Alexander Rust and Claire Micheau (eds), *State aid and Tax Law* (Kluwer Law International 2013).

Dubout E, and Maitrot de la Motte A, 'Normalité, sélectivité et légitimité des régimes fiscaux dans l'Union européenne: les paradis fiscaux au purgatoire des aides d'État?' (2012) 5 Revue de Droit Fiscal 44.

Durst M C, 'Beyond BEPS: A Tax Policy Agenda for Developing Countries' (2014) 18 ICTD Working Paper < https://assets.publishing.service.gov.uk/media/57a089c1ed915d622c0003ab/WP18-FINAL.pdf > accessed 11 February 2018.

Engelen F, and Gunn A, 'State Aid: Towards a Theoretical Assessment Framework' in Alexander Rust and Claire Micheau (eds), *State aid and Tax Law* (Kluwer Law International 2013).

Englisch J, 'EU State Aid Rules Applied to Indirect Tax Measures' (2013) 22 EC Tax Review 9.

Engsig Sørensen K, 'What Is a General Principle of EU Law? A Response' in Rita de la Feria and Stefan Vogenauer (eds), *Prohibition of Abuse of Law – A New General Principle of EU Law?* (Hart Publishing 2011).

Fleming Jr. J C, Peroni R J, and Shay S E, 'Formulary Appointment in the U.S. International Income Tax System: Putting Lipstick on a Pig?' (2014) 36 Michigan Journal of International Law 1.

Forrester E, 'Is the State Aid Regime a Suitable Instrument to Be Used in the Fight Against Harmful Tax Competition?' (2018) 27 EC Tax Review 19.

Friederiszick H W, Röller L-H, and Verouden V, 'European State Aid Control: an Economic Framework' in Paolo Buccirossi (ed), *Handbook of Antitrust Economics* (MIT Press 2008).

Giraud A, and Petit S, 'Tax Rulings and State Aid Qualification: Should Reality Matter?' (2017) 16 European State Aid Law Quarterly 233.

Glenn D L, 'Formula Apportionment no Solution to BEPS, OECD Rep Says' (2014) 73 Tax Notes International 692.

Gordon R, and Wilson J D, 'An Examination of Multijurisdictional Corporate Income Taxation under Formula Apportionment' (1986) 54 Econometrica 1357.

Greil G, 'The Dealing at Arm's Length Fallacy: A Way Forward to a Formula-Based Transactional Profit Split?' (2017) 45 Intertax 624.

Grespan D, and Santamato S, 'Favouring Certain Undertakings or the Production of Certain Goods': Advantage' in Wolfgang Mederer, Nicola Pesaresi, and Marc Van Hoof (eds), *4 EU Competition Law: State Aid* (Claeys & Casteels 2008).

Grubert H, 'Destination-Based Income Taxes: A Mismatch Made in Heaven?' (2015) 69 Tax Law Review 43.

Gutmann D, 'Some Theoretical Thoughts on Judicial Power and Tax Law, with a Particular Focus on the ECJ' in Luc Hinnekens and Philippe Hinnekens (eds), *A Vision of Taxes Within and Outside European Borders – Festschrift in Honor of Prof. Dr. Frans Vanistendael* (Kluwer Law International 2008).

Hamaekers H, 'Arm's Length – How Long?' (2001) 8 International Transfer Pricing Journal 30.

Hancher L, 'EU State Aid Law – Déjà Vu All Over Again?' in Leigh Hancher, Tom Ottervanger, and Piet Jan Slot (eds), *EU State Aids* (5th edn, Sweet & Maxwell 2016).

Hancher L, 'The General Framework' in Leigh Hancher, Tom Ottervanger, and Piet Jan Slot (eds), *EU State Aids* (5th edn, Sweet & Maxwell 2016).

Harbo T-I, *The Function of Proportionality Analysis in European Law* (Brill Nijhoff 2015).

Haslehner W, 'Double Taxation Relief, Transfer Pricing Adjustments and State Aid Law' in Isabelle Richelle, Wolfgang Schön and Edoardo Traversa (eds), *State Aid Law and Business Taxation* (Springer 2016).

Hellerstein W, 'The Case for Formulary Apportionment' (2005) 12 International Transfer Pricing Journal 103.

Hellner J, *Metodproblem i rättsvetenskapen: studier i förmögenhetsrätt* (Jure 2001).

Hernández Guerrero V, 'Defining the Balance Between Free Competition and Tax Sovereignty in EC and WTO Law: The "Due Respect" to the General Tax System' (2004) 5 German Law Journal 87.

Hettne J, and Otken Eriksson I, *EU-Rättslig Metod: Teori Och Genomslag i Svensk Rättstillämpning* (2nd edn, Norstedts Juridik 2011).

Hickman A, 'The Application of Revised Transfer Pricing Rules to Aspects of Business Models' (2016) 44 Intertax 730.

Hines J R, 'Income Misattribution under Formula Apportionment' (2010) 54 European Economic Review 108.

Hirshleifer J, 'On the Economics of Transfer Pricing' (1956) 29 The Journal of Business 172.

Hofmann H, 'Activity in a Multi-level System: Motivations for Aid, Why Control It, Evolution of Aid in the EU' in Herwig C. H. Hofmann and Claire Micheau (eds), *State Aid Law of the European Union* (Oxford University Press 2016).
Holmes K, *The Concept of Income* (IBFD 2001).
Holmström B, and Tirole J, 'Transfer Pricing and Organizational Form' (1991) 7 The Journal of Law, Economics, and Organization 201.
Honoré M, 'State Aid and Taxation – All Clear?' (2015) 24 European State Aid Law Quarterly 306.
Hougardy Y, 'La capacité contributive' in Edoardo Traversa and Vincent Deckers (eds), *Liber Amicorum Jacques Autenne – Promenades sous les portiques de la fiscalité* (Bruylant 2010).
Hultqvist A, *Legalitetsprincipen vid inkomstbeskattningen* (Juristförlaget 1995).
Idot L, 'Notion d'aide et critère de l'investisseur privé en économie de marché' (2012) 8-9 Europe 335.
Ismer R, and Piotrowski S, 'The Selectivity of Tax Measures: A Tale of Two Consistencies' (2015) 43 Intertax 559.
Jaeger T, 'From Santander to LuxLeaks – and Back' (2015) 24 European State Aid Law Quarterly 345.
Jaeger T, 'Tax Incentives Under State Aid Law: A Competition Law Perspective' in Isabelle Richelle, Wolfgang Schön and Edoardo Traversa (eds), *State Aid Law and Business Taxation* (Springer 2016).
Jaeger T, 'Tax Concessions for Multinationals: In or Out of the Reach of State Aid Law?' (2017) 8 Journal of European Competition Law & Practice 221.
Jansen N, 'Making Doctrine for European Law' in Rob van Gestel, Hans-W. Micklitz, and Edward L. Rubin (eds), *Rethinking Legal Scholarship – A Transatlantic Dialogue* (Cambridge University Press 2017).
Jareborg N, Rättsdogmatik som vetenskap, (2004) Svensk Juristtidning 1.
Joris T, and De Cock W, 'Is Belgium and Forum 187 v. Commission a Suitable Legal Source for an EU "At Arm's Length Principle"?' (2017) 16 European State Aid Law Quarterly 607.
Kahn P W, 'Freedom and Method' in Rob van Gestel, Hans-W. Micklitz, and Edward L. Rubin (eds), *Rethinking Legal Scholarship – A Transatlantic Dialogue* (Cambridge University Press 2017).
Kaka P F, 'Source Taxation: Do We Really Know What We Mean?' (2017) 86 Tax Notes International 1221.
Kane M A, 'Transfer Pricing, Integration and Synergy Intangibles: A Consensus Approach to the Arm's Length Standard' (2014) 6 World Tax Journal 282.
Kardachaki A, and van Hulten M, 'Report on the EUCOTAX Conference "State Aid, Intangibles and Rulings"' (2017) 26 EC Tax Review 284.
Karpenschif M, *Droit européen des aides d'État* (Bruylant 2015).
Karpenschif M, 'Le critère de l'opérateur en économie de marché et la crise financière' in Valérie Giacobbo-Peyronnel and Christophe Verdure (eds), *Contentieux du droit de la concurrence et de l'Union européenne – questions d'actualité et perspectives* (Bruylant 2017).

Kavanagh J, and Robins N, 'Corporate Tax Arrangements Under EU State Aid Scrutiny – The Application of the Market Economy Operator Principle' (2015) 14 European State Aid Law Quarterly 358.

Khan N, and Borchardt K-D, 'The Private Market Investor Principle: Reality Check or Distorting Mirror?' in *EC State Aid Law: Liber Amicorum in Honour Francisco Santaolalla* (Kluwer Law International 2008).

Kleineman J, 'Rättsdogmatisk Metod' in Fredric Korling and Mauro Zamboni (eds), *Juridisk Metodlära* (Studentlitteratur 2013).

Kobetsky M, 'The Case for Unitary Taxation of International Enterprises' (2008) 62 Bulletin for International Taxation 201.

Komárek J, 'Legal Reasoning in EU Law' in Anthony Arnull and Damian Chalmers (eds), *The Oxford Handbook of European Union Law* (Oxford University Press 2015).

Kyriazis D A, 'From Soft Law to Soft Law Through Hard Law: The Commission's Approach to the State Aid Assessment of Tax Rulings' (2016) 15 European State Aid Law Quarterly 428.

Lang M, 'Tax Rulings and State Aid Law' (2015) 3 British Tax Review 391.

Lang M, 'State Aid and Taxation: Selectivity and Comparability Analysis' in Isabelle Richelle, Wolfgang Schön and Edoardo Traversa (eds), *State Aid Law and Business Taxation* (Springer 2016).

Langbein S I, 'The Unitary Method and the Myth of Arm's Length' (1986) 30 Tax Notes 625.

Lion P, 'Comprendre la planification fiscale internationale et le cadre dans lequel elle s'opère' in Sami Douénias (ed), *Mélanges Pascal Minne – Fiscalité internationale et patrimoniale* (Bruylant 2017).

Lipinsky J, and Wolters J, 'Time will Tell – A Brief Contemplation on the Temporal Application of Substantive State Aid Rules in the Light of the Recent Andersen-Judgment of the CJEU' (2016) 15 European State Aid Law Quarterly 193.

López Llopis E, 'Formulary Apportionment in the European Union' (2017) 45 Intertax 631.

López López H, 'General Thought on Selectivity and Consequences of a Broad Concept of State Aid in Tax Matters' (2010) 9 European State Aid Law Quarterly 807.

Lovdahl Gormsen L, 'EU State Aid Law and Transfer Pricing: A Critical Introduction to a New Saga' (2016) 7 Journal of European Competition Law & Practice 369.

Lovdahl Gormsen L, and Mifsud-Bonnici C, 'Legitimate Expectation of Consistent Interpretation of EU State Aid Law: Recovery in State Aid Cases Involving Advanced Pricing Agreements on Tax' (2017) 8 Journal of European Competition Law & Practice 423.

Luja R, 'Tax Treaties and State Aid: Some Thoughts' (2004) 44 European Taxation 234.

Luja R, '(Re)shaping Fiscal State Aid: Selected Recent Cases and Their Impact' (2012) 40 Intertax 120.

Luja R, 'Material Selectivity after Gibraltar' in Dennis Weber (ed), *EU Income Tax Law – Issues for the Years Ahead* (IBFD 2013).

Luja R, 'The Attribution of State Aid to Member States in the Exercising of Options in Directives' (2013) 12 European State Aid Law Quarterly 119.

Bibliography

Luja R, 'The Selectivity Test: The Concept of Sectoral Aid' in Alexander Rust and Claire Micheau (eds), *State aid and Tax Law* (Kluwer Law International 2013).

Luja R, 'State Aid Benchmarking and Tax Rulings: Can We Keep It Simple?' in Isabelle Richelle, Wolfgang Schön and Edoardo Traversa (eds), *State Aid Law and Business Taxation* (Springer 2016).

Luja R, 'Do State Aid Rules Still Allow European Union Member States to Claim Fiscal Sovereignty?' (2016) 25 EC Tax Review 323.

Lyal R, 'Transfer Pricing Rules and State Aid' (2015) 38 Fordham International Law Journal 1017.

Lyons T, 'State Aid, Taxation and Abuse of Law' in Rita de la Feria and Stefan Vogenauer (eds), *Prohibition of Abuse of Law – A New General Principle of EU Law?* (Hart Publishing 2011).

Maitrot de la Motte A, *Droit fiscal de l'Union européenne* (2nd edn, Bruylant 2016).

Maitrot de la Motte A, 'L'identification des "paramètres pertinents pour établir la sélectivité" des avantages fiscaux' (2017) 26 Revue de Droit Fiscal 37.

Malherbe J, Les États-Unis au secours de leurs multinationales (2016) 37 Revue de Droit Fiscal 3.

Matsos G, 'Systematic Misconceptions of State Aid Law in the Area of Taxation' (2014) 13 European State Aid Law Quarterly 491.

McLure C E, 'The State Corporate Income Tax: Lambs in Wolves Clothing' in Henry J. Aaron and Michael J. Boskin (eds), *The Economics of Taxation* (Brookings Institution 1980).

McLure C E, and Weiner J M, 'Deciding Whether the European Union Should Adopt Formulary Apportionment of Company Income' in Sijbren Cnossen (ed), *Taxing Capital Income in the European Union: Issues and Options for Reform* (Oxford University Press 2000).

McLure C E, 'Tax Assignment and Subnational Fiscal Autonomy' (2000) 54 Bulletin for International Taxation 626.

McLure C E, and Hellerstein W, 'Does Sales-Only Apportionment of Corporate Income Violate International Trade Rules?' (2002) 96 Tax Notes International 1315.

McLure C E, 'Replacing Separate Entity Accounting and the Arm's Length Principle with Formulary Apportionment' (2002) 56 Bulletin for International Taxation 586.

Melz P, 'General Legal Report: Legal Aspects of Taxation for Non-fiscal Purposes' in Jane Bolander (ed), *Yearbook for Nordic Tax Research 2009: The Non-fiscal Purposes of Taxation* (DJØF 2009).

Merola M, 'The Rebus of Selectivity in Fiscal Aid: A Nonconformist View on and Beyond Case Law' (2016) 39 World Competition 533.

Micheau C, *Droit des Aides d'État et des Subventions en Fiscalité – Droit de l'Union Européenne et de l'OMC* (Larcier 2013).

Micheau C, 'Tax Selectivity in European Law of State Aid: Legal Assessment and Alternative Approaches' (2015) 40 European Law Review 323.

Micheau C, 'Evolution of State Aid Rules: Conceptions, Challenges, and Outcomes' in Herwig C. H. Hofmann and Claire Micheau (eds), *State Aid Law of the European Union* (Oxford University Press 2016).

Moëll C, *Proportionalitetsprincipen i Skatterätten* (Juristförlaget i Lund 2003).

Monsenego J, 'La correction des prix de transfert entre sociétés apparentées au regard du concept civiliste de liberté contractuelle – Vers un renforcement de la théorie de l'autonomie du droit fiscal?' (2012) 9 Revue de Droit Fiscal 30.

Monsenego J, *Taxation of Foreign Business Income within the European Internal Market* (IBFD 2012).

Monsenego J, 'The Substance Requirement in the OECD Transfer Pricing Guidelines: What Is the Substance of the Substance Requirement?' (2014) 21 International Transfer Pricing Journal 9.

Monsenego J, *Introduction to Transfer Pricing* (Kluwer Law International 2015).

Moreno González S, 'Les aides d'État à caractère fiscal: le critère de sélectivité de la mesure' in Gilbert Orsoni (ed), *Mélanges en l'honneur de Pierre Beltrame* (Presses Universitaires d'Aix-Marseille 2010).

Moreno González S, 'State Aid and Tax Competition: Comments on the European Commission's Decisions on Transfer Pricing Rulings' (2016) 15 European State Aid Law Quarterly 556.

Musgrave P B, 'Interjurisdictional Equity in Company Taxation: Principles and Applications to the European Union' in Sijbren Cnossen (ed), *Taxing Capital Income in the European Union: Issues and Options for Reform* (Oxford University Press 2000).

Nicolaides P, 'Fiscal State Aid in the EU: The Limits of Tax Autonomy' (2004) 27 World Competition 365.

Nicolaides P, 'State Aid Rules and Tax Rulings' (2016) 15 European State Aid Law Quarterly 416.

Nicolaides P, 'Excessive Widening of the Concept of Selectivity' (2017) 16 European State Aid Law Quarterly 62.

Nicolaides P, 'What Is Normal?' (2017) 16 European State Aid Law Quarterly 146.

Nicolaides P, 'Selectivity Requires Comparison' (2018) < http://stateaidhub.eu/blogs/stateaiduncovered/post/9125 > accessed 24 January 2018.

Olbert M, and Spengel C, 'International Taxation in the Digital Economy: Challenge Accepted?' (2017) 9 World Tax Journal 3.

Oliver P, 'When, If Ever, Can Restrictions on Free Movement Be Justified on Economic Grounds?' (2016) 41 European Law Review 147.

Panayi C, 'Limitation on Benefits and State Aid' (2004) 44 European Taxation 83.

Parish M, 'On the Private Investor Principle' (2003) 28 European Law Review 70.

Persson Österman R, *Kontinuitetsprincipen i den svenska inkomstbeskattningen* (Juristförlaget 1997).

Plender R, 'Definition of Aid' in Andrea Biondi, Piet Eeckhout, and James Flynn (eds), The Law of State Aid in the European Union (Oxford University Press 2004).

Poiares Maduro M, 'Interpreting European Law: Judicial Adjudication in a Context of Constitutional Pluralism' (2007) 1 European Journal of Legal Studies 137.

Porter M, *Competitive Advantage* (Free Press 1985).

Porter M, 'The Five Competitive Forces that Shape Competitive Theory' (2008) 86 Harvard Business Review 78.

Quigley C, 'Direct Taxation and State Aid: Recent Developments Concerning the Notion of Selectivity' (2012) 40 Intertax 112.

Quigley C, *European State Aid Law and Policy* (3rd edn, Hart Publishing 2015).

Rabe G, 'Statliga stöd' (2017) Skattenytt 386.

Rädler A J, 'Can the Developed World (=OECD) Follow the EU Tax Principles Established by the European Court of Justice?' in *Regards critiques et perspectives sur le droit et la fiscalité – Liber amicorum Cyrille David* (LGDJ 2005).

Rasch M, and Wroblewski P, 'European Commission Decision on Fiat: State Aid Case Explained' (2016) 23 International Transfer Pricing Journal 440.

Reichel J, 'EU-Rättslig Metod' in Fredric Korling and Mauro Zamboni (eds), *Juridisk Metodlära* (Studentlitteratur 2013).

Robillard R, 'Profit-Split Methods and the OECD: Leaning Toward Formulary Apportionment?' (2017) 87 Tax Notes International 1005.

Rocha S A, *The Future of Transfer Pricing – General Report* (IFA Cahiers Volume 102B, Sdu 2017).

Rose V, and Bailey D, 'State Aids' in Vivien Rose and David Bailey (eds) *Bellamy and Child: European Union Law of Competition* (7th edn, Oxford University Press 2013).

Ross M, 'State Aids and National Courts: Definitions and Other Problems – a Case of Premature Emancipation?' (2000) 37 Common Market Law Review 401.

Rossi-Maccanico P, 'Fiscal State Aids, Tax Base Erosion and Profit Shifting' (2015) 24 EC Tax Review 63.

Rubini L, *The Definition of Subsidy and State Aid: WTO and EC Law in Comparative Perspective* (Oxford University Press 2009).

Rust A, and Micheau C (eds), *State Aid and Tax Law* (Kluwer Law International 2013).

Sabbadini P M, *Les aides d'État – Aspects juridiques et économiques* (Larcier 2015).

Sadowsky M, *Droit de l'OMC, droit de l'Union européenne et fiscalité directe* (Larcier 2013).

Sadowsky M, 'Vers un système fiscal standard?' (2013) 25 Revue de Droit Fiscal 57.

Schippers M L, and Verhaeren C E, 'Taxation in a Digitizing World: Solutions for Corporate Income Tax and Value Added Tax' (2018) 27 EC Tax Review 61.

Schön W, 'Taxation and State Aid Law in the European Union' (1999) 36 Common Market Law Review 911.

Schön W, 'International Tax Coordination for a Second-Best World (Part I)' (2009) 1 World Tax Journal 67.

Schön W, 'International Tax Coordination for a Second-Best World (Part III)' (2010) 3 World Tax Journal 227.

Schön W, 'Transfer Pricing, the Arm's Length Standard and European Union Law' in Isabelle Richelle, Wolfgang Schön and Edoardo Traversa (eds), *Allocating Taxing Powers Within the European Union* (Springer 2013).

Schön W, 'Destination-Based Income Taxation and WTO Law: a Note' in Heike Jochum, Peter Essers, Michael Lang, Norbert Winkeljohann and Bertil Wiman (eds), *Practical Problems in European and International Tax Law – Essays in Honour of Manfred Mössner* (IBFD 2016).

Schön W, 'State Aid in the Area of Taxation' in Leigh Hancher, Tom Ottervanger, and Piet Jan Slot (eds), *EU State Aids* (5th edn, Sweet & Maxwell 2016).

Schön W, and Traversa E (eds), *State Aid Law and Business Taxation* (Springer 2016).

Schön W, 'Tax Legislation and the Notion of Fiscal Aid: A Review of 5 Years of European Jurisprudence' in Isabelle Richelle, Wolfgang Schön and Edoardo Traversa (eds), *State Aid Law and Business Taxation* (Springer 2016).

Schoueri L E, 'Arm's Length: Beyond the Guidelines of the OECD' (2015) 69 Bulletin for International Taxation 690.

Schreiber U, and Fell L M, 'International Profit Allocation, Intangibles and Sales-Based Transactional Profit Split' (2017) 9 World Tax Journal 1.

Sheppard L A, 'EU Amazon Case: Is Transfer Pricing Really the Issue?' (2015) 77 Tax Notes International 291.

Silberztein C, and Granel B, 'La dépendance de fait en matière de prix de transfert' (2016) 51-52 Revue de Droit Fiscal 47.

Strömholm S, *Rätt, rättskällor och rättstillämpning – En lärobok i allmän rättslära* (5th edn, Norstedts Juridisk 1996).

Szudoczky R, *The Sources of EU Law and Their Relationships: Lessons for the Field of Taxation* (IBFD 2014).

Szudoczky R, 'Convergence of the Analysis of National Tax Measures under the EU State Aid Rules and the Fundamental Freedoms' (2016) 15 European State Aid Law Quarterly 357.

Taferner A, and Wouda Kuipers J, 'Tax Rulings: In Line with OECD Transfer Pricing Guidelines, but Contrary to EU State Aid Rules?' (2016) 56 European Taxation 134.

Tavares R J S, and Owens J, 'Human Capital in Value Creation and Post-BEPS Tax Policy: An Outlook' (2015) 69 Bulletin for International Taxation 590.

Tavares R J S, 'Multinational Firm Theory and International Tax Law: Seeking Coherence' (2016) 8 World Tax Journal 243.

Tavares R J S, Bogenschneider B N, and Pankiv M, 'The Intersection of EU State Aid and U.S. Tax Deferral: A Spectacle of Fireworks, Smoke, and Mirrors' (2016) 19 Florida Tax Review 121.

Temple Lang J, 'The Gibraltar State Aid and Taxation Judgment – A "Methodological Revolution"?' (2012) 11 European State Aid Law Quarterly 805.

Temple Lang J, 'Autogrill España and Banco Santander: The Concept of "General" Tax Measures Clarified for State Aid' (2015) 5 European Law Review 763.

Tenore M, 'APAs and State Aid: A New Era of European Tax Law?' in Dennis Weber (ed), *EU Law and the Building of Global Supranational Tax Law: EU BEPS and State Aid* (IBFD 2017).

Terra B, 'Value Added Tax and State Aid Law in the European Union' (2012) 40 Intertax 101.

Traversa E, and Sabbadini P M, 'Anti-avoidance Measures and State Aid in a Post-BEPS-Context: An Attempt at Reconciliation' in Isabelle Richelle, Wolfgang Schön and Edoardo Traversa (eds), *State Aid Law and Business Taxation* (Springer 2016).

Traversa E, and Sabbadini P M, 'State-Aid Policy and the Fight Against Harmful Tax Competition in the Internal Market: Tax Policy in Disguise?' in Werner Haslehner, Georg Kofler, and Alexander Rust (eds), *EU Tax Law and Policy in the 21st Century* (Kluwer Law International 2017).

Treidler O, and Jung S, 'Economic Valuation Techniques for Transfer Pricing' (2017) 85 Tax Notes International 561.

Vanistendael F, 'Legal Framework for Taxation' in Victor Thuronyi (ed), 1 *Tax Law Design and Drafting* (International Monetary Fund 1996).

Vanistendael F, 'Dispositions anti-abus et droit communautaire en matière fiscale' in Edoardo Traversa and Vincent Deckers (eds), *Liber Amicorum Jacques Autenne – Promenades sous les portiques de la fiscalité* (Bruylant 2010).

Vanistendael F, 'Are the EU and U.S. Headed for a Tax War?' (2016) 83 Tax Notes International 1057.

Vanistendael F, 'Digital Disruption in International Taxation' (2018) 89 Tax Notes International 175.

Vann R J, 'Taxing International Business Income: Hard-Boiled Wonderland and the End of the World' (2010) 2 World Tax Journal 291.

Verlinden I, and Markey B, 'From Compliance to the C-Suite: Value Creation Analysed Through the Transfer Pricing Lens' (2016) 44 Intertax 774.

Villar Ezcurra M, 'The Concept of "Environmental Tax" in a State Aid Context When a Fiscal Energy Measure Is Concerned' (2017) 16 European State Aid Law Quarterly 11.

Vogel L, European State Aid Law (Bruylant 2017).

Waelbroeck D, 'La compatibilité de systèmes fiscaux généraux avec les règles en matière d'aides d'État dans le traité CE' in *Mélanges John Kirkpatrick* (Bruylant 2004).

Ward D, et al., *The Interpretation of Income Tax Treaties with Particular Reference to the Commentaries on the OECD Model* (IFA/IBFD 2005).

Wathelet M, and Bonhomme N, 'La Commission et la jurisprudence de la Cour en matière fiscale' in Edoardo Traversa and Vincent Deckers (eds), *Liber Amicorum Jacques Autenne – Promenades sous les portiques de la fiscalité* (Bruylant 2010).

Wattel P J, 'Some Fringe Areas of EU State Aid Law in Direct Tax Matters' in Dennis Weber (ed), *EU Income Tax Law – Issues for the Years Ahead* (IBFD 2013).

Weatherill S, *The Internal Market as a Legal Concept* (Oxford University Press 2017).

Weiner J M, 'Using the Experience in the U.S. States to Evaluate Issues in Implementing Formula Apportionment at the International Level' (1996) 13 Tax Notes International 2113.

Weiner J M, 'The European Union and Formula Apportionment: Caveat Emptor' (2001) 41 European Taxation 381.

Weiner J M, and Mintz J, 'An Exploration of Formula Apportionment in the European Union' (2002) 42 European Taxation 346.

Weiner J M, Company Tax Reform in the European Union: Guidance from the United States and Canada on Implementing Formulary Apportionment in the EU (Springer 2006).

Bibliography

Wilkie J S, 'Reflecting on the "Arm's Length Principle": What is the "Principle"? Where Next?' in Wolfgang Schön and Kai A. Konrad (eds), *Fundamentals of International Transfer Pricing in Law and Economics* (Springer 2012).

Williamson O, 'The Theory of the Firm as Governance Structure: From Choice to Contract' (2002) 16 Journal of Economic Perspectives 171.

Wittendorff J, 'The Arm's-Length Principle and Fair Value: Identical Twins or Just Close Relatives?' (2011) 62 Tax Notes International 223.

Material Published by the OECD

OECD, *Transfer Pricing and Multinational Enterprises* (OECD 1979)

OECD, *Transfer Pricing Guidelines for Multinational Enterprises and Tax Administrations* (OECD 1995)

OECD, *2010 Report on the Attribution of Profits to Permanent Establishments* (OECD 2010)

OECD, *Transfer Pricing Guidelines for Multinational Enterprises and Tax Administrations* (OECD 2010)

OECD, *Action Plan on Base Erosion and Profit Shifting* (OECD 2013)

OECD, *Addressing the Tax Challenges of the Digital Economy, Action 1 – 2015 Final Report* (OECD 2015)

OECD, *Aligning Transfer Pricing Outcomes with Value Creation, Actions 8-10 – 2015 Final Reports* (OECD 2015)

OECD, *Revenue Statistics 2016 – Tax revenue trends in the OECD* (OECD 2016)

OECD, *Tax Policy Reforms 2017* (OECD 2017)

OECD, *Transfer Pricing Guidelines for Multinational Enterprises and Tax Administrations* (OECD 2017)

OECD, *BEPS Action 10 – Revised Guidance on Profit Splits* (OECD 2017)

OECD, *Model Tax Convention on Income and on Capital* (OECD 2017)

Material Published by the United Nations

United Nations, *Practical Manual on Transfer Pricing for Developing Countries* (United Nations 2017)

Other Documents

Vienna Convention on the Law of Treaties (1969)

US General Accounting Office, 'IRS Could Better Protect U.S. Tax Interests In Determining The Income Of Multinational Corporations' (1981)

Report of the Appellate Body, 'United States – Tax Treatment for "Foreign Sales Corporations" – Recourse to Article 21.5 of the DSU by the European Communities' (2002) WT/DS108/AB/RW

Council Resolution of 8 June 2010 on coordination of the Controlled Foreign Corporation (CFC) and thin capitalisation rules within the European Union [2010] OJ C 156/1

U.S. Department of the Treasury White Paper, The European Commission's recent Investigations of Transfer Pricing Rulings (2016)

Federation of Tax Administrators https://www.taxadmin.org/assets/docs/Research/Rates/apport.pdf, accessed 20 January 2018

Table of Cases

Court of Justice

30/59, *De Gezamenlijke Steenkolenmijnen in Limburg v. High Authority of the European Coal and Steel Community*, ECLI:EU:C:1961:2, **2**

6/69 and 11/69, *Commission of the European Communities v. French Republic*, ECLI:EU:C:1969:68, **105, 167**

173/73, *Italian Republic v. Commission of the European Communities*, ECLI:EU:C:1974:71, **1, 37, 94, 105, 181**

283/81, *Srl CILFIT and Lanificio di Gavardo SpA v. Ministry of Health*, ECLI:EU:C:1982:335, **16**

270/83, *Commission of the European Communities v. French Republic*, ECLI:EU:C:1986:37, **85**

234/84, *Kingdom of Belgium v. Commission of the European Communities*, ECLI:EU:C:1986:302, **58**

248/84, *Federal Republic of Germany v. Commission of the European Communities*, ECLI:EU:C:1987:437, **107**

303/88, *Italian Republic v. Commission of the European Communities*, ECLI:EU:C:1991:136, **66**

C-261/89, *Italian Republic v. Commission of the European Communities*, ECLI:EU:C:1991:367, **65**

C-305/89, *Italian Republic v. Commission of the European Communities*, ECLI:EU:C:1991:142, **66**

C-225/91, *Matra SA v. Commission of the European Communities*, ECLI:EU:C:1993:239, **2**

C-279/93, *Finanzamt Köln-Altstadt v. Roland Schumacker*, ECLI:EU:C:1995:31, **80, 84, 85**

C-39/94, *Syndicat français de l'Express international and others v. La Poste and others*, ECLI:EU:C:1996:285, **59, 60**

C-241/94, *French Republic v. Commission of the European Communities*, ECLI:EU:C:1996:353, **128**

C-353/95 P, *Tiercé Ladbroke SA v. Commission of the European Communities*, ECLI:EU:C:1997:596, **77, 82, 98**

Table of Cases

C-75/97, *Kingdom of Belgium v. Commission of the European Communities*, ECLI:EU:C:1999:311, **107**

C-212/97, *Centros Ltd v. Erhvervs- og Selskabsstyrelsen*, ECLI:EU:C:1999:126, **183**

C-256/97, *Déménagements-Manutention Transport SA (DMT)*, ECLI:EU:C:1999:332, **128**

C-390/98, *H.J. Banks & Co. Ltd v. The Coal Authority*, ECLI:EU:C:2001:456, **71**

C-143/99, *Adria-Wien Pipeline GmbH*, ECLI:EU:C:2001:598, **3, 46, 76, 86, 95, 181**

C-328/99 and C-399/00, *Italian Republic and SIM 2 Multimedia SpA v. Commission of the European Communities*, ECLI:EU:C:2003:252, **68**

C-482/99, *French Republic v. Commission of the European Communities*, ECLI:EU:C:2002:294, **68**

C-280/00, *Altmark Trans and Regierungspräsidium Magdeburg*, ECLI:EU:C:2003:415, **59, 141**

C-324/00, *Lankhorst-Hohorst GmbH and Finanzamt Steinfurt*, ECLI:EU:C:2002:749, **43**

C-83/01 P, C-93/01 P and C-94/01 P, *Chronopost SA, La Poste and French Republic v. Union française de l'express (Ufex), DHL International, Federal express international (France) SNC and CRI.E. SA*, ECLI:EU:C:2003:388, **67**

C-126/01, *Ministre de l'économie, des finances et de l'industrie v. GEMO SA*, ECLI:EU:C:2003:622, **106**

C-308/01, *GIL Insurance Ltd and Others v. Commissioners of Customs & Excise*, ECLI:EU:C:2004:252, **46, 183, 188, 198**

C-255/02, *Halifax plc, Leeds Permanent Development Services Ltd and County Wide Property Investments Ltd v. Commissioners of Customs & Excise*, ECLI:EU:C:2006:121, **143, 188**

C-319/02, *Petri Manninen*, ECLI:EU:C:2004:484, **77, 84**

C-88/03, *Portuguese Republic v. Commission of the European Communities*, ECLI:EU:C:2006:511, **23, 35, 49, 182**

C-182/03 and C-217/03, *Kingdom of Belgium and Forum 187 ASBL v. Commission of the European Communities*, ECLI:EU:C:2006:416, **15, 31, 46, 49, 63, 80**

C-446/03, *Marks & Spencer plc v. David Halsey* (Her Majesty's Inspector of Taxes), ECLI:EU:C:2005:763, **84, 188**

C-196/04, *Cadbury Schweppes plc and Cadbury Schweppes Overseas Ltd v. Commissioners of Inland Revenue*, ECLI:EU:C:2006:544, **143, 188**

C-222/04, *Ministero dell'Economia e delle Finanze v. Cassa di Risparmio di Firenze SpA, Fondazione Cassa di Risparmio di San Miniato and Cassa di Risparmio di San Miniato SpA*, ECLI:EU:C:2006:8, **182**

C-408/04 P, *Commission of the European Communities v. Salzgitter AG*, ECLI:EU:C:2008:236, **108**

C-524/04, *Test Claimants in the Thin Cap Group Litigation*, ECLI:EU:C:2007:161, **44, 144, 191**

C-487/06 P, *British Aggregates Association v. Commission of the European Communities and United Kingdom*, ECLI:EU:C:2008:757, **48, 78, 181, 183**

C-418/07, *Société Papillon v. Ministère du Budget, des Comptes publics et de la Fonction publique*, ECLI:EU:C:2008:659, **77, 85**

Table of Cases

C-460/07, *Sandra Puffer v. Unabhängiger Finanzsenat, Außenstelle Linz*, ECLI:EU:C:2009:254, **9**

C-78/08 to C-80/08, *Paint Graphos*, ECLI:EU:C:2011:550, **19, 46, 49, 82, 182, 183**

C-279/08 P, *European Commission v. Kingdom of the Netherlands*, ECLI:EU:C:2011:551, **184**

C-311/08, *Société de Gestion Industrielle (SGI) v. Belgian State*, ECLI:EU:C:2010:26, **33, 50, 84, 144, 145, 190, 191**

C-103/09, *The Commissioners for Her Majesty's Revenue and Customs v. Weald Leasing Ltd*, ECLI:EU:C:2010:804, **4**

C-106/09 P and C-107/09 P, *European Commission v. Government of Gibraltar*, ECLI:EU:C:2011:732, **2, 20, 48, 77, 78, 104–106, 153, 161, 172, 184**

C-239/09, *Seydaland Vereinigte Agrarbetriebe GmbH & Co. KG v. BVVG Bodenverwertungs-und -verwaltungs GmbH*, ECLI:EU:C:2010:778, **127**

C-81/10 P, *France Télécom SA*, ECLI:EU:C:2011:811, **137**

C-124/10 P, *Commission v. Électricité de France (EDF)*, ECLI:EU:C:2012:318, **58, 61, 68**

C-318/10, *Société d'investissement pour l'agriculture tropicale SA (SIAT) v. État belge*, ECLI:EU:C:2012:415, **33, 191**

C-403/10 P, *Mediaset SpA v. European Commission*, ECLI:EU:C:2011:533, **137**

C-417/10, *Ministero dell'Economia e delle Finanze, Agenzia delle Entrate v. 3M Italia SpA*, ECLI:EU:C:2012:184, **3, 55, 83**

C-452/10 P, *BNP Paribas and Banca Nazionale del Lavoro SpA (BNL) v. European Commission*, ECLI:EU:C:2012:366, **181**

C-18/11, *The Commissioners for Her Majesty's Revenue & Customs contre Philips Electronics UK Ltd*, ECLI:EU:C:2012:532, **85**

C-6/12, *P Oy*, ECLI:EU:C:2013:525, **94, 128, 183, 188**

C-164/12, *DMC Beteiligungsgesellschaft mbH v. Finanzamt Hamburg-Mitte*, ECLI:EU:C:2014:20, **153**

C-214/12 P, C-215/12 P and C-223/12 P, *Land Burgenland v. European Commission*, ECLI:EU:C:2013:682, **71**

C-172/13, *European Commission v. United Kingdom of Great Britain and Northern Ireland*, ECLI:EU:C:2015:50, **187**

C-518/13, *Eventech Ltd v. The Parking Adjudicator*, ECLI:EU:C:2015:9, **55, 71**

C-522/13, *Ministerio de Defensa and Navantia SA v. Concello de Ferrol*, ECLI:EU:C:2014:2262, **11, 100, 169**

C-5/14, *Kernkraftwerke Lippe-Ems GmbH v. Hauptzollamt Osnabrück*, ECLI:EU:C:2015:354, **79, 95**

C-15/14 P, *European Commission v. MOL Magyar Olaj- és Gázipari Nyrt.*, ECLI:EU:C:2015:362, **11**

C-252/14, *Pensioenfonds Metaal en Techniek v. Skatteverket*, ECLI:EU:C:2016:402, **77, 98**

C-449/14 P, *DTS Distribuidora de Televisión Digital, SA v. European Commission*, ECLI:EU:C:2016:848, **1**

C-524/14 P, *European Commission v. Hansestadt Lübeck*, ECLI:EU:C:2016:971, **3, 10, 37, 46, 48, 75, 79, 82, 87**

C-526/14, *Kotnik and others*, ECLI:EU:C:2016:570, **14**

Table of Cases

C-20/15 P and C-21/15 P, *European Commission v. World Duty Free Group*, ECLI:EU:C:2016:981, **3, 7, 10, 35, 75, 77, 79, 82, 85, 88, 90, 103, 105, 106, 153, 167**

C-100/15 P, *Netherlands Maritime Technology Association, formerly Scheepsbouw Nederland v. European Commission*, ECLI:EU:C:2016:254, **24**

C-131/15 P, *Club Hotel Loutraki AE and Others v. European Commission*, ECLI:EU:C:2016:989, **59, 63**

C-164/15 P and C-165/15 P, *European Commission v. Aer Lingus Ltd*, ECLI:EU:C:2016:990, **46, 48, 76, 137**

C-648/15, *Republic of Austria v. Federal Republic of Germany*, ECLI:EU:C:2017:664, **16**

C-6/16, *Eqiom SAS, formerly Holcim France SAS and Enka SA v. Ministre des Finances et des Comptes publics*, ECLI:EU:C:2017:641, **188**

C-70/16 P, *Comunidad Autónoma de Galicia and Redes de Telecomunicación Galegas Retegal, SA (Retegal) v. European Commission*, ECLI:EU:C:2017:1002, **3, 75**

C-74/16, *Congregación de Escuelas Pías Provincia Betania v. Ayuntamiento de Getafe*, ECLI:EU:C:2017:496, **2, 10, 100**

C-251/16, *Edward Cussens and Others v. T. G. Brosman*, ECLI:EU:C:2017:881, **188**

C-300/16 P, *European Commission v. Frucona Košice a.s.*, ECLI:EU:C:2017:706, **65**

C-504/16 and C-613/16, *Deister Holding AG and Juhler Holding A/S v. Bundeszentralamt für Steuern*, ECLI:EU:C:2017:1009, **188**

C-529/16, *Hamamatsu Photonics Deutschland GmbH v. Hauptzollamt München*, ECLI:EU:C:2017:984, **126**

General Court

T-459/93, *Siemens SA v. Commission of the European Communities*, ECLI:EU:T:1995:100, **137**

T-16/96, *Express Ltd v. Commission of the European Communities*, ECLI:EU:T:1998:78, **69**

T-296/97, *Alitalia – Linee aeree italiane SpA v. Commission of the European Communities*, ECLI:EU:T:2000:289, **65, 67, 130**

T-55/99, *Confederación Española de Transporte de Mercancías (CETM) v. Commission of the European Communities*, ECLI:EU:T:2000:223, **106**

T-228/99 and T-233/99, *Westdeutsche Landesbank Girozentrale v. European Commission*, ECLI:EU:T:2003:57, **61, 66–68, 70, 150**

T-92/00 and T-103/00, *Territorio Histórico de Álava – Diputación Foral de Álava v. Commission of the European Communities*, ECLI:EU:T:2002:61, **106**

T-308/00, *Salzgitter AG v. European Commission*, ECLI:EU:T:2013:30, **108**

T-196/04, *Ryanair Ltd v. Commission of the European Communities*, ECLI:EU:T:2008:585, **61**

T-211/04 and T-215/04, *Government of Gibraltar*, ECLI:EU:T:2008:595, **161**

T-163/05, *Bundesverband deutscher Banken v. Commission*, ECLI:EU:T:2010:59, **67**

T-445/05, *Associazione italiana del risparmio gestito and Fineco Asset Management SpA v. Commission of the European Communities*, ECLI:EU:T:2009:50, **160**

T-1/08, *Buczek Automotive sp. z o.o. v. European Commission*, ECLI:EU:T:2011:216, **2**

T-468/08, *Tisza Erőmű kft v. European Commission*, ECLI:EU:T:2014:235, **106**
T-303/10, *Wam Industriale SpA v. European Commission*, ECLI:EU:T:2012:505, **68**
T-251/11, *Republic of Austria v. European Commission*, ECLI:EU:T:2014:1060, **183**
T-287/11, *Heitkamp BauHolding GmbH v. European Commission*, ECLI:EU:T:2016:60, **183**
T-479/11 and T-157/12, *French Republic and IFP Énergies nouvelles v. European Commission*, ECLI:EU:T:2016:320, **92**
T-620/11, *GFKL Financial Services AG v. European Commission*, ECLI:EU:T:2016:59, **181**
T-500/12, *Ryanair Ltd*, ECLI:EU:T:2015:73, **46**
T-319/12 and T-321/12, *Kingdom of Spain, Ciudad de la Luz, SAU and Sociedad Proyectos Temáticos de la Comunidad Valenciana, SAU v. European Commission*, ECLI:EU:T:2014:604, **141**
T-375/15, *Germanwings GmbH v. European Commission*, ECLI:EU:T:2017:289, **66**

Opinions of the Advocates General at the Court of Justice

C-30/59, *De Gezamenlijke Steenkolenmijnen in Limburg v. High Authority of the European Coal and Steel Community*, ECLI:EU:C:1960:41, Opinion of AG Lagrange, **105**
C-234/84, *Kingdom of Belgium v. Commission of the European Communities*, ECLI:EU:C:1986:151, Opinion of AG Lenz, **68**
C-72/91 and C-73/91, *Firma Sloman Neptun Schiffahrts AG v. Seebetriebsrat Bodo Ziesemer der Sloman Neptun Schiffahrts AG*, ECLI:EU:C:1992:130, Opinion of AG Darmon, **182**
C-83/98 P, *French Republic v. Ladbroke Racing Ltd and Commission of the European Communities*, ECLI:EU:C:1999:577, Opinion of AG Cosmas, **182**
C-280/00, *Altmark Trans and Regierungspräsidium Magdeburg*, ECLI:EU:C:2002:188, Opinion of AG Léger, **60**
C-308/01, *GIL Insurance Ltd*, ECLI:EU:C:2003:481, Opinion of AG Geelhoed, **77**
C-237/04, *Enirisorse SpA v. Sotacarbo SpA*, ECLI:EU:C:2006:21, Opinion of AG Poiares Maduro, **77**
C-106/09 P and C-107/09 P, *European Commission v. Government of Gibraltar*, ECLI:EU:C:2011:215, Opinion of AG Jääskinen, **107**
C-303/13 P, *European Commission v. Jørgen Andersen*, ECLI:EU:C:2015:340, Opinion of AG Wathelet, **54**
C-66/14, *Finanzamt Linz v. Bundesfinanzgericht, Außenstelle Linz*, ECLI:EU:C:2015:242, Opinion of AG Kokott, **2**
C-20/15 P and C-21/15 P, *European Commission v. World Duty Free Group*, ECLI:EU:C:2016:624, Opinion of AG Wathelet, **3, 18, 87**
C-203/16 P, *Dirk Andres (administrator of Heitkamp BauHolding GmbH), previously Heitkamp BauHolding GmbH v. European Commission*, ECLI:EU:C:2017:1017, Opinion of AG Wahl, **25, 45–47, 78, 80, 137, 206**

Table of Cases

C-236/16, *Asociación Nacional de Grandes Empresas de Distribución (ANGED) v. Generalitat de Catalunya*, ECLI:EU:C:2017:852, Opinion of AG Kokott, **7**, **23**, **24**, **51**, **79**

C-382/16, *Hornbach-Baumarkt AG v. Finanzamt Landau*, ECLI:EU:C:2017:974, Opinion of AG Bobek, **27**, **84**, **187**

National Court Cases

US Supreme Court, Case 334, 283 US 123, *Hans Rees' Sons, Inc. v. North Carolina ex rel. Maxwell*, 13 April 1931, **171**

US Supreme Court, Case 81-523, 463 US 159, *Container Corporation of America v. Franchise Tax Board of California* 183, 27 June 1983, **171**, **173**, **184**

US Court of Appeals for the Second Circuit, Case 933 F.2d 1084, *Bausch & Lomb Incorporated and Consolidated Subsidiaries*, 14 May 1991, **138**

French Conseil d'État, Case 372097, *Société LifeStand Vivre Debout*, 15 April 2016, **90**

Table of Legislation

Treaty and Secondary Legislation Within the European Union

Council Directive 2006/112/EC of 28 November 2006 on the common system of value added tax [2006] OJ L 347/1, **4**

Consolidated version of the Treaty on the Functioning of the European Union [2016] OJ C 262/1, **3, 14, 20, 23, 26, 27, 29, 31, 34, 37, 44, 47, 49, 50, 58–60, 63, 74, 75, 79, 100, 103, 107, 126, 133, 138, 141, 142, 152, 176, 195, 196**

Consolidated version of the Treaty on European Union [2016] OJ C 202/1, **19, 183**

Council Directive (EU) 2016/881 of 25 May 2016 amending Directive 2011/16/EU as regards mandatory automatic exchange of information in the field of taxation [2016] OJ L 146/8, **147**

Council Directive (EU) 2016/1164 of 12 July 2016 laying down rules against tax avoidance practices that directly affect the functioning of the internal market [2016] OJ L 193/1, **70, 140**

National Legislation

Section 22(7) of the Swedish income tax act *Inkomstskattelag* (1999:1229), **4**

Section 404(1) of the Canadian Income Tax Regulations, **160**

Section 402(3)(a) of the Canadian Income Tax Regulations, **165**

European Commission

European Commission Decisions

Commission Decision 2000/392/EC of 8 July 1999 on a measure implemented by the Federal Republic of Germany for Westdeutsche Landesbank – Girozentrale [2000] OJ L 150/1, **92**

Commission Decision 2003/81/EC of 22 August 2002 on the aid scheme implemented by Spain in favour of coordination centres in Vizcaya C 48/2001 (ex NN 43/2000) [2003] OJ L 031/26, **126**

Commission Decision 2003/601/EC of 17 February 2003 on aid scheme C54/2001 (ex NN55/2000) Ireland – Foreign Income [2003] OJ L 204/51, **47**

Commission Decision 2004/76/EC of 13 May 2003 on the aid scheme implemented by France for headquarters and logistics centres [2004] OJ L 23/1, **26**

Commission Decision of 18 July 2007 State aid NN 34/2007 (ex CP 189/2004) — Germany Capital contributions NORD/LB [2008] OJ C 4/1, **67**

Commission Decision 2008/711/EC of 11 March 2008 on State aid C 15/07 (ex NN 20/07) implemented by Italy on the tax incentives in favour of certain restructured banks [2008] OJ L 237/70, **49**

Commission Decision 2009/809/EC of 8 July 2009 on the groepsrentebox scheme which the Netherlands is planning to implement [2009] OJ L 288/26, **47, 102**

Commission Decision of 28 October 2009 on State aid C 10/07 (ex NN 13/07) implemented by Hungary for tax deductions for intra-group interest [2010] OJ L 42/3, **102**

Commission Decision of 7 July 2015 in State Aid SA.36574 (2015/NN, ex 2013/CP) – France – Alleged aid to Altrad [2015] OJ C 369/1, **67, 130**

Commission Decision (EU) 2017/502 of 21 October 2015 on State aid SA.38374 (2014/C ex 2014/NN) implemented by the Netherlands to Starbucks [2017] OJ L 83/38, **6, 15, 26, 29, 31, 34, 47, 104, 142**

Commission Decision (EU) 2016/2326 of 21 October 2015 on State aid SA.38375 (2014/C ex 2014/NN) which Luxembourg granted to Fiat [2016] OJ L 351/1, **6–7, 15, 35, 47, 101, 104, 124, 126, 129, 141–143**

Commission Decision (EU) 2016/1699 of 11 January 2016 on the excess profit exemption State aid scheme SA.37667 (2015/C) (ex 2015/NN) implemented by Belgium [2016] OJ L 260/61, **7, 15, 34, 47, 101**

European Commission

Commission Decision 2016/634 of 21 January 2016 on aid measure SA.25338 (2014/C) (ex E 3/2008 and ex CP 115/2004) implemented by the Netherlands – Corporate tax exemption for public undertakings [2016] OJ L 113/148, **24**

Commission Decision of 18 February 2016 State Aid SA.42225 (2015/N) – Lithuania, Regional aid scheme for the promotion of the development of strategic information and communication technology (ICT) projects on strategic ICT sites [2016] OJ C 142/1, **69**

Commission Decision (EU) 2016/1846 of 4 July 2016 on the measure SA.41187 (2015/C) (ex 2015/NN) implemented by Hungary on the health contribution of tobacco industry businesses [2016] OJ L 282/43, **81**

Commission Decision of 29 July 2016 in case State aid 45125 (2016/N) – Greece – methodology to calculate the aid element in State guarantees to companies [2016] OJ C 425/1, **152**

Commission Decision of 29 July 2016 on State Aid SA.42007 (2015/N) – Belgium Alternative income tax regime for the wholesale diamond sector [2016] OJ C 369/1, **153, 200**

Commission Decision (EU) 2017/1283 of 30 August 2016 on State aid SA.38373 (2014/C) (ex 2014/NN) (ex 2014/CP) implemented by Ireland to Apple [2017] OJ L 187/1, **7, 10, 15, 26–29, 79**

Commission Decision (EU) 2017/329 of 4 November 2016 on the measure SA.39235 (2015/C) (ex 2015/NN) implemented by Hungary on the taxation of advertisement turnover [2017] OJ L 49/36, **81, 169**

Commission Decision (EU) 2018/160 of 30 June 2017 on the State aid SA.44351 (2016/C) (ex 2016/NN) implemented by Poland for the tax on the retail sector [2018] OJ L 29/38, **26, 81**

Commission Decision (EU) 2017/2116 of 27 July 2017 on aid scheme SA.38398 (2016/C, ex 2015/E) implemented by France – Taxation of ports in France [2017] OJ L 332/24, **102**

Commission Decision of 19 December 2017 on State aid SA.33829 (2012/C) Maltese tonnage tax scheme and other State measures in favour of shipping companies and their shareholders, **1**

European Commission Regulations

Commission Regulation (EU) No 1407/2013 of 18 December 2013 on the application of Articles 107 and 108 of the Treaty on the Functioning of the European Union to de minimis aid [2013] OJ L 352/1, **137, 150**

Commission Regulation (EU) No 651/2014 of 17 June 2014 declaring certain categories of aid compatible with the internal market in application of Articles 107 and 108 of the Treaty [2014] OJ L 187/1, **69, 150**

European Commission

European Commission Communications and Notices

Commission Communication to the Member States – Application of Articles 92 and 93 of the EEC Treaty and of Article 5 of Commission Directive 80/723/EEC to public undertakings in the manufacturing sector [1993] OJ C 307/3, **64**

Commission Communication on State aid elements in sales of land and buildings by public authorities [1997] OJ C 209/3, **141**

Commission notice on the application of the State aid rules to measures relating to direct business taxation [1998] OJ C 384/3, **46, 107, 163**

European Commission, 'Company Taxation in the Internal Market' COM(2001)582 final, **162**

European Commission, 'Communication from the Commission to the Council, the European Parliament and the European Economic and Social Committee – Towards a more effective use of tax incentives in favour of R&D' COM(2006) 728 final, **163**

Commission Notice on the application of Articles 87 and 88 of the EC Treaty to State aid in the form of guarantees [2008] OJ C 155/10, **152**

Communication from the Commission to the Member States on the application of Articles 107 and 108 of the Treaty on the Functioning of the European Union to short-term export-credit insurance [2012] OJ C 392/1, **59**

European Commission, 'Communication from the Commission to the European Parliament, the Council, the European Economic and Social Committee and the Committee of the Regions – EU State Aid Modernisation' COM(2012) 209 final, **69**

Communication from the Commission – European Union framework for State aid in the form of public service compensation [2012] OJ C 8/15, **66**

Communication from the Commission on the application, from 1 August 2013, of State aid rules to support measures in favour of banks in the context of the financial crisis [2013] OJ C 216/1, **14, 150**

Commission Notice on the notion of State aid as referred to in Article 107(1) of the Treaty on the Functioning of the European Union [2016] OJ C 262/1, **3, 14, 20, 23, 26, 27, 29, 31, 34, 37, 44, 47, 49, 50, 58–60, 63, 74, 75, 79, 100, 103, 107, 126, 133, 138, 141, 142, 152, 176, 195, 196**

Other Documents Issued by the European Commission

European Commission, 'CCCTB: possible elements of the sharing mechanism' (2007) CCCTB/WP060\doc\en, **165, 170, 174, 175**

Guidelines on regional State aid for 2014-2020 [2013] OJ C 209/1, **69, 150**

European Commission, 'Draft Commission Notice on the notion of State aid pursuant to Article 107(1) TFEU' (2014), **58, 60**

State aid – Ireland – State aid SA.38373 (2014/C) (ex 2014/NN) – Alleged aid to Apple – Invitation to submit comments pursuant to Article 108(2) of the Treaty on the Functioning of the European Union [2014] OJ C 369/22, **59, 63**

European Commission

State aid – Luxembourg – State aid SA.38944 (2014/C) (2014/NN) – Alleged aid to Amazon – Invitation to submit comments pursuant to Article 108(2) of the Treaty on the Functioning of the European Union [2015] OJ C 44/13, **59, 63, 128**

European Commission, 'DG Competition Working Paper on State Aid and Tax Rulings' (2016) < http://ec.europa.eu/competition/state_aid/legislation/working_paper _tax_rulings.pdf > accessed 6 February 2018, **29, 126, 152**

European Commission/Deloitte, 'Study on the Application of Economic Valuation Techniques for Determining Transfer Prices of Cross Border Transactions between Members of Multinational Enterprise Groups in the European Union' (European Commission 2016), **68, 128**

European Commission, 'EU Joint Transfer Pricing Forum Report on the use of Comparables in the European Union' (European Commission 2016), **71, 136, 138, 143**

European Commission, 'Proposal for a Council Directive on a Common Consolidated Corporate Tax Base (CCCTB)' COM(2016) 683 final, **5, 10, 17, 160, 165, 168, 173**

State aid SA.44896 (2017/C) (ex 2017/NN) – Potential State aid scheme regarding UK Group Financing Exemption – Invitation to submit comments pursuant to Article 108(2) of the Treaty on the Functioning of the European Union [2017] OJ C 400/10, **24, 45**

State aid SA.44888 (2016/NN) (ex 2016/EO) – Luxembourg – Possible State aid in favour of GDF Suez – Invitation to submit comments pursuant to Article 108(2) of the Treaty on the Functioning of the European Union [2017] OJ C 36/13, **43, 47, 80**

European Commission, 'State Aid Scoreboard 2017: Results, trends and observations regarding EU28 State Aid expenditure reports for 2016' (European Commission 2017), **3**

OECD Council Recommendations

OECD, Recommendation of the Council on the Determination of Transfer Pricing between Associated Enterprises [C(95)126/Final, as amended], **136**

OECD, Recommendation of the Council concerning the Model Tax Convention on Income and on Capital [C(97)195/FINAL], **136**

Index

A

Ability-to-pay, 80, 82, 89-90, 118
Abuse, 96, 113, 184, 188
Advantage, 10-11, 31, 35, 46-47, 49, 57, 59-62, 87, 115, 116, 119, 152, 160, 165-169, 171, 172, 182, 203, 208
Allocation method, 1, 3-10, 12-15, 17, 19-21, 25-37, 41-45, 49-53, 55, 56, 58-63, 72-74, 76, 82, 85-87, 89, 94, 97-99, 102-105, 111, 112, 114-116, 119, 124-125, 132-134, 145, 147-151, 153, 155, 157-159, 161-164, 167, 170, 171, 175-178, 180, 185-189, 194, 196-201, 203-211
Apple, 28
Application of the law, 53, 54, 104, 107, 124-144, 181
Apportionment factors, 5, 32-33, 160, 162-165, 167-179, 201-203, 207, 210-211
Arm's length principle, 1, 4-6, 8, 12, 13, 17-20, 26, 28-44, 50, 54, 55, 58, 60, 62-74, 86, 93, 104, 111-116, 118-125, 127-129, 132-145, 148-155, 157, 162, 176, 179, 186, 187, 189-197, 199, 200, 204-211
Arm's length range, 71, 128, 141, 142

Asset, 5, 33, 66, 67, 76, 80, 96, 99, 116, 117, 123, 131, 134, 137, 141, 151, 160, 162, 164, 166-169, 173-179, 203, 207

B

Benchmark, 23, 26-28, 30, 31, 37-41, 46, 54, 63, 64, 67, 68, 70, 72, 86, 93, 107-109, 112, 114-117, 119-124, 130-131, 149, 154, 184, 189, 192-193, 197, 199, 200
Business restructuring, 50

C

Capital, 48, 50, 141, 159, 167, 173, 174, 179
CFC. *See* Controlled Foreign Corporation (CFC)
Common consolidated corporate tax base (CCCTB), 5, 6, 9, 17, 157, 160, 165, 167, 168, 170, 173, 175, 176, 179
Comparability, 20, 21, 25, 36-38, 40, 65, 67, 71, 74-102, 105, 115-120, 124, 138, 142, 143, 185, 193, 197, 205, 206, 209, 210
Comparable Uncontrolled Price (CUP) method, 129, 210

Index

Competition, 2, 28, 31–34, 48, 50, 59, 60, 63, 85–88, 106, 108–109, 137, 164, 211
Control, 10–11, 25, 28, 31, 46, 48, 54, 61, 63, 72, 81, 88, 90–93, 98, 101, 112, 117, 134, 177–178, 186
Controlled Foreign Corporation (CFC), 81
Cost contribution arrangement, 6, 134, 149
Cost plus method, 31
Court of Justice, 184
Credit, 97
CUP method. *See* Comparable Uncontrolled Price (CUP) method

D

De facto selectivity, 7, 20, 56, 74, 105–107, 109, 111, 116–124, 131, 144, 154–155, 158, 161–179, 196, 200–203, 206, 207, 210
De jure selectivity, 20, 104, 105, 111–116, 144, 148–154, 157–161, 178, 185, 189, 196–200, 206, 207
Design of the law, 103, 104, 107, 115, 149, 158–161, 178, 197
Difference in treatment, 3, 19, 20, 24, 27, 28, 51, 55, 75, 84, 103–105, 111, 113, 118, 119, 121, 125, 148–152, 158–161, 168, 169, 178, 181, 189, 197, 198
Digital economy, 130, 176, 179
Digitalisation, 8, 176, 197
Discrimination, 3, 77, 83–84, 137, 181
Dispute, 97, 152, 192

Dividend, 98
Dogmatic method, 14, 15

E

Effects of the law, 105, 124, 158
Equality, 37, 38, 41–43, 53, 116, 159, 187, 190
European Commission (EC), 1, 6, 7, 10, 11, 14, 15, 19, 20, 25, 26, 28, 30, 34, 35, 46, 57–59, 62, 63, 68, 74, 80, 99, 101–102, 111, 125, 126, 129–130, 132, 138, 141–143, 152, 169, 170, 173, 175, 176, 179, 195, 196, 200
European Union (EU), 1, 2, 5, 10, 13, 14, 16–18, 30, 35, 44, 83, 132, 136, 161

F

Factual comparability, 20, 30, 35, 75, 76, 82, 83, 85–95, 103
Fiat, 104, 141, 142
Financial asset, 168
Firm, 91–93, 96, 168
Firm-specific factors, 3, 5, 6, 8, 10, 12, 20, 32, 41, 103, 109, 123, 155, 157–180, 186, 196–204, 207, 210, 211
Fixed margin, 41
Formula apportionment, 1, 3, 5, 6, 8, 10, 12, 13, 17, 20, 32, 33, 41, 42, 51, 74, 103, 109, 122, 123, 155, 157–180, 186, 196–204, 207–211
Formula-based allocation method, 6, 10, 157, 162–164, 170, 171, 175, 176, 178, 199, 200, 203, 207
Freedom of movement, 84, 191
Fundamental freedoms, 43, 190

G

General Court (GC), 61, 141, 150, 160
Generally formulated arm's length provision, 3-5, 10, 17, 20, 41, 42, 50, 51, 72, 103, 104, 109, 111-145, 147-155, 157, 180, 189-194, 196, 204, 206, 207, 209
Globalisation, 8, 130, 197
Group taxation, 84, 96, 98, 99, 113, 186, 190

H

Harmful tax competition, 2, 55
Hybrid, 5, 6, 60, 97, 157, 162

I

Income, 1, 4, 5, 8-10, 26-28, 32-34, 38-42, 44-55, 58, 74-82, 88-90, 94-102, 105, 107, 112-114, 116-118, 120, 121, 124, 128, 133, 139, 144, 148, 149, 151-154, 158-162, 164-179, 184-190, 192-211
Intangible asset, 173-174
Intangible property, 112, 121, 130, 195
Integration, 39, 92, 94, 122, 130, 144, 197, 208
Interest expense, 4, 48, 50, 51

J

Judge, 8, 153
Justification, 20, 27, 31, 37, 44, 48, 99, 100, 109, 113, 170, 179-204, 207

L

Labour, 5, 33, 162, 164, 166, 168-169, 173-179, 202, 203, 207
Legal comparability, 85, 89, 96, 99
Legal source, 14, 28, 45, 52-54, 73, 132

M

Market economy operator test, 19, 20, 56-74, 130, 141, 185, 205
Market forces, 4, 19, 30, 33, 37, 57-60, 62-74, 93, 112-116, 118, 119, 122, 127-129, 131, 138, 141, 149, 165, 170, 176-179, 186, 190, 197-201, 207, 209
Multinational enterprise, 1, 3, 5-8, 25-28, 30, 33, 35, 38, 40-43, 45, 49, 51, 58, 70, 74, 82, 84-86, 88-91, 93-95, 97-102, 112-114, 116, 118-121, 131, 144, 147, 149, 158, 159, 161, 165, 174, 177, 178, 185-190, 194, 195, 197-199, 201, 202, 206-208, 210

N

Neutrality, 40, 44, 64, 78, 96, 99, 113, 120, 154, 159, 176, 190, 195, 209
Non-discrimination, 3, 24, 30, 82, 153
Normal taxation, 46, 49, 109

O

OECD model tax convention, 6, 53, 74, 91, 111, 116, 132, 134
OECD transfer pricing guidelines, 5, 6, 17, 29, 31, 36, 38, 39, 43, 54, 58, 64-73, 85, 86, 93, 112, 114-121, 123, 125, 127-130, 132-135, 138, 142-145, 147, 148, 154, 163, 173, 189, 193, 195, 207, 210
Open market, 4, 6, 33, 38, 40, 65, 73, 112, 114, 115, 117-125, 131, 154, 189, 192-193, 197, 199, 200, 210

P

Payroll, 164, 203

Index

Permanent establishment, 4, 89, 97, 139, 140, 162, 175
Prevention of tax avoidance, 96, 144, 185–188, 190, 191, 195, 198, 201–203
Prima facie selectivity, 3, 19, 20, 23, 103, 109, 111–145, 147–155, 157–181, 183–189, 192–194, 196, 197, 201–204, 206, 207, 210
Principle of legality, 25, 55
Principle of non-discrimination, 3, 24, 30, 153
Profit split method, 6, 38, 39, 122–124, 130, 131, 157, 199, 200, 207, 210
Proportionality, 19, 20, 103, 109, 180–204, 207, 210

R

Recovery, 137
Reference system, 19, 20, 23–56, 72–79, 85, 88, 103–105, 107, 108, 125–145, 148, 149, 151–153, 158, 159, 161, 176, 178, 181–183, 185, 187, 191, 193, 195–202, 205–207, 210
Residence, 97, 100, 166, 175, 186
Retroactivity, 54

S

Safe harbours, 1, 3, 5, 8, 10, 12, 17, 20, 32, 41, 42, 51, 74, 103, 109, 125, 145, 147–155, 157, 180, 186, 187, 193–196, 204, 206, 207, 209
Sales, 5, 33, 123, 134, 141, 160, 162, 164–169, 171, 173, 175–180, 203, 207, 210
Selective, 1, 3, 7, 8, 10, 17, 19, 20, 31, 51, 52, 56, 73, 81, 87, 103–107, 109, 112, 114–120, 124, 125, 128, 131, 137, 144, 145, 149–155, 159–181, 183–185, 187–211
Selectivity, 1–3, 6–15, 17–20, 22–27, 31, 35, 44, 45, 49, 55–63, 72–76, 78, 82, 83, 86, 87, 94, 102–107, 109, 111–145, 147–181, 183, 185, 186, 189, 192–194, 196–211
Source, 4, 15, 17, 28, 38, 45, 52–54, 63, 73, 92, 125, 132–136, 145, 173, 179, 191, 211
Sovereignty, 26, 35, 108, 184
Starbucks, 104, 142
State aid control, 11, 25, 28, 31, 46, 48, 54, 61, 63, 72, 98
State resources, 1, 60
Subsidy, 49, 59, 84, 160, 164, 198

T

Tangible asset, 5, 33, 162, 164, 167–169, 173–176, 179, 203
Tax avoidance, 96, 144, 185–188, 190, 191, 195, 198, 201–203
Tax competition, 2, 50
Taxing rights, 50, 97, 175, 176, 179
Tax planning, 86, 186, 189, 198, 203
Tax policy, 8, 10, 13, 206, 208
Tax treaty, 1, 9, 14, 17, 18, 53, 97, 139, 153, 209
Tested party, 116, 193
Thin capitalisation, 4
TNMM. *See* Transactional net margin method (TNMM)
Trade, 8, 28, 48, 85, 106, 179, 180, 197, 211
Transactional net margin method (TNMM), 32, 129

U

United Nations (UN), 132

EUCOTAX Series on European Taxation

(1) Peter HJ Essers, Guido JME de Bont & Eric CCM Kemmeren (eds), *The Compatibility of Anti-Abuse Provisions in Tax Treaties with EC Law*, 1998 (ISBN 90-411-9678-1).
(2) Gerard TK Meussen (ed.), *The Principle of Equality in European Taxation*, 1999 (ISBN 90-411-9693-5).
(3) Michael Lang (ed.), *Tax Treaty Interpretation*, 2001 (ISBN 90-411-9857-1).
(4) Pasquale Pistone, *The Impact of Community Law on Tax Treaties: Issues and Solutions*, 2002 (ISBN 90-411-9860-1).
(5) René Offermanns, *The Entrepreneurship Concept in a European Comparative Tax Law Perspective*, 2002 (ISBN 90-411-9887-3).
(6) Michael Lang & Mario Züger, *Settlement of Disputes in Tax Treaty Law*, 2002 (ISBN 90-411-9904-7).
(7) Carlo Pinto, *Tax Competition and EU Law*, 2003 (ISBN 90-411-9913-6).
(8) Michael Lang, Hans-Jörgen Aigner, Ulrich Scheuerle & Markus Stefaner, *CFC Legislation, Tax Treaties and EC Law*, 2004 (ISBN 90-411-2284-2).
(9) Mattias Dahlberg, *Direct Taxation in Relation to the Freedom of Establishment and the Free Movement of Capital*, 2005 (ISBN 90-411-2363-6).
(10) Michael Lang, Judith Herdin & Ines Hofbauer, *WTO and Direct Taxation*, 2005 (ISBN 90-411-2371-7).
(11) Dennis Weber, *Tax Avoidance and the EC Tray Freedoms: A Study of the Limitations under European Law for the Prevention of Tax Avoidance*, 2005 (ISBN 90-411-2402-0).
(12) Félix Alberto Vega Borrego, *Limitations on Benefits Clauses on Double Taxation Conventions*, 2005 (ISBN 90-411-2370-9).
(13) Michael Lang, Josef Schuch & Claus Staringer, *ECJ-Recent Developments in Direct Taxation*, 2006 (ISBN 90-411-2509-4).
(14) Reuven S. Avi-Yonah, James R. Hines Jr. & Michael Lang, *Comparative Fiscal Federalism. Comparing the European Court of Justice and the US Supreme Court's Tax Jurisprudence*, 2007 (ISBN 978-90-411-2552-1).
(15) Christiana HJI Panayi, *Double Taxation, Tax Treaties, Treaty-Shopping and the European Community*, 2007 (ISBN 978-90-411-2658-0).
(16) Dennis Weber, *The Influence of European Law on Direct Taxation: Recent and Future Developments*, 2007 (ISBN 978-90-411-2667-2).
(17) Michael Lang & Pasquale Pistone, *The EU and Third Countries: Direct Taxation*, 2007 (ISBN 978-90-411-2665-8).
(18) Oskar Henkow, *Financial Activities in European VAT: A Theoretical and Legal Research of the European VAT System and Preferred Treatment of Financial Activities*, 2007 (ISBN 978-90-411-2703-7).
(19) Michael Lang (ed.), *Tax Compliance Costs for Companies in an Enlarged European Community*, 2008 (ISBN 978-90-411-2666-5).

(20) Michael Lang (ed.), *Source versus Residence. Problems Arising from the Allocation of Taxing Rights in Tax Treaty Law and Possible Alternatives*, 2008 (ISBN 978-90-411-2763-1).
(21) Ioanna Mitroyanni, *Integration Approaches to Group Taxation in the European Internal Market*, 2008 (ISBN 978-90-411-2779-2).
(22) Rolf Eicke, *Tax Planning with Holding Companies. Repatriation of US Profits from Europe:Concepts, Strategies, Structures*, 2008 (ISBN978-90-411-2794-5).
(23) Peter Essers et al. (ed.), *The Influence of IAS/IFRS on the CCCTB, Tax Accounting, Disclosure and Corporate Law Accounting Concepts: 'A Clash of Cultures'*, 2008 (ISBN 978-90-411-2819-5).
(24) Tonny Schenk-Geers, *International Exchange of Information and the Protection of Taxpayers*, 2009 (ISBN 978-90-411-3142-3).
(25) Raymond Adema, *UCITS and Taxation: Towards Harmonization of the Taxation of UCITS*, 2009 (ISBN 978-90-411-2839-3).
(26) Michael Lang, Jianwen Liu & Gongliang Tang (eds), *Europe–China Tax Treaties*, 2010 (ISBN 978-90-411-3216-1).
(27) Michael Lang, Pasquale Pistone, Josef Schuch & Claus Staringer (eds), *Procedural Rules in Tax Law in the Context of European Union and Domestic Law*, 2010 (ISBN 978-90-411-3376-2).
(28) Sjaak J.J.M. Jansen, *Fiscal Sovereignty of the Member States in an Internal Market: Past and Future*, 2011 (ISBN 978-90-411-3403-5).
(29) Dennis Weber & Bruno da Silva, *From Marks & Spencer to X Holding: The Future of Cross-Border Group Taxation*, 2011 (ISBN 978-90-411-3399-1).
(30) Claus Bohn Jespersen, *Intermediation of Insurance and Financial Services in European VAT*, 2011 (ISBN 978-90-411-3732-6).
(31) Sabine Heidenbauer, *Charity Crossing Borders: The Fundamental Freedoms' Influence on Charity and Donor Taxation in Europe*, 2011 (ISBN 978-90-411-3813-2).
(32) Michael Lang, et al., *The Future of Indirect Taxation: Recent Trends in VAT and GST Systems around the World*, 2012 (ISBN 978-90-411-3797-5).
(33) Harm van den Broek, *Cross-Border Mergers within the EU: Proposals to Remove the Remaining Tax Obstacles*, 2012 (ISBN 978-90-411-3824-8).
(34) Michael Lang, et al. (eds), *Tax Treaty Case Law around the Globe – 2011*, 2012 (ISBN 978-90-411-3876-7).
(35) Dennis Weber (ed.), *CCCTB: Selected Issues*, 2012 (ISBN 978-90-411-3872-9).
(36) Daniël Smit, *EU Freedoms, Non-EU Countries and Company Taxation*, 2012 (ISBN 978-90-411-4041-8).
(37) Rita de la Feria, *VAT Exemptions: Consequences and Design Alternatives*, 2013 (ISBN 978-90-411-3276-5).
(38) Karin Simader, *Withholding Taxes and the Fundamental Freedoms*, 2013 (ISBN 978-90-411-4842-1).
(39) Madeleine Merkx, *Establishments in European VAT*, 2013 (ISBN 978-90-411-4554-3).
(40) Carla De Pietro, *Tax Treaty Override*, 2014 (ISBN 978-90-411-5406-4).

(41) G.K. Fibbe & A.J.A. Stevens (eds), *Hybrid Entities and the EU Direct Tax Directives*, 2015 (ISBN 978-90-411-5942-7).
(42) Gerard Staats, *Personal Pensions in the EU*, 2015 (ISBN 978-90-411-5953-3).
(43) Michael Lang & Ine Lejeune (eds), *VAT/GST in a Global Digital Economy*, 2015 (ISBN 978-90-411-5952-6).
(44) Massimo Basilavecchia, Lorenzo del Federico & Pietro Mastellone (eds), *Tax Implications of Environmental Disasters and Pollution*, 2015 (ISBN 978-90-411-5611-2).
(45) Cristina Trenta, *Rethinking EU VAT for P2P Distribution*, 2015 (ISBN 978-90-411-6137-6).
(46) Marie Lamensch, Edoardo Traversa & Servaas van Thiel (eds), *Value Added Tax and the Digital Economy: The 2015 EU Rules and Broader Issues*, 2016 (ISBN 978-90-411-6612-8).
(47) Raffaele Petruzzi, *Transfer Pricing Aspects of Intra-Group Financing*, 2016 (ISBN 978-90-411-6732-3).
(48) Mario Grandinetti (ed.), *Corporate Tax Base in the Light of the IAS/IFRS and EU Directive 2013/34: A Comparative Approach*, 2016 (ISBN 978-90-411-6745-3).
(49) Bruno da Silva, *The Impact of Tax Treaties and EU Law on Group Taxation Regimes*, 2016 (ISBN 978-90-411-6905-1).
(50) Michael Lang, Alfred Storck & Raffaele Petruzzi (eds), *Transfer Pricing in a Post-BEPS World*, 2016 (ISBN 978-90-411-6710-1).
(51) Marta Papis-Almansa, *Insurance in European VAT: Current and Preferred Treatment in the Light of the New Zealand and Australian GST Systems*, 2017 (ISBN 978-90-411-8360-6).
(52) Wolfgang Speckhahn, *Real Estate Investment Trusts In Europe: Europeanising Tax Regimes*, 2017 (ISBN 978-90-411-8360-6).
(53) Frank J.G. Nellen, *Information Asymmetries in EU VAT*, 2017 (ISBN 978-90-411-8837-3).
(54) Erik Ros, *EU Citizenship and Direct Taxation*, 2017 (ISBN 978-90-411-8584-6).
(55) Werner Haslehner, Georg Kofler & Alexander Rust (eds), *EU Tax Law and Policy in the 21st Century*, 2017 (ISBN 978-90-411-8815-1).
(56) Claudia Sanò, *National Legal Presumptions and European Tax Law*, 2018 (ISBN 978-90-411-6613-5).
(57) Christoph Marchgraber, *Double (Non-)Taxation and EU Law*, 2018 (ISBN 978-90-411-9410-7).
(58) Dennis Weber & Jan van de Streek (eds), *The EU Common Consolidated Corporate Tax Base: Critical Analysis*, 2018 (ISBN 978-90-411-9233-2).
(59) Werner Haslehner (ed.), *Investment Fund Taxation: Domestic Law, EU Law, and Double Taxation Treaties*, 2018 (ISBN 978-90-411-9669-9).
(60) Jérôme Monsenego, *Selectivity in State Aid Law and the Methods for the Allocation of the Corporate Tax Base*, 2018 (ISBN 978-90-411-9413-8).